YOUR ATARI®
COMPUTER

A Guide to ATARI® 400/800™ Computers

By Lon Poole
with Martin McNiff
and Steven Cook

OSBORNE/McGraw-Hill
Berkeley, California

The following are trademarks of Atari, Inc. *Your ATARI® Computer* is not sponsored or approved by or connected with Atari, Inc. All references to the following trademarks (registered trademarks noted with ®) in the text of this book are to the trademarks of Atari, Inc.

ATARI® ⋏®
ATARI® 400™ Computer
ATARI® 410™ Program Recorder
ATARI® 800™ Computer
ATARI® 810™ Disk Drive
ATARI® 820™ 40-Column Printer
ATARI® 822™ Thermal Printer
ATARI® 825™ 80-Column Printer
ATARI® 830™ Acoustic Modem
ATARI® 850™ Interface Module
Star Raiders™
Music Composer™
Memory Module™

Published by OSBORNE/McGraw-Hill
630 Bancroft Way
Berkeley, California 94710
U.S.A.

For information on translations and book distributors outside the U.S.A., please write OSBORNE/McGraw-Hill at the above address.

YOUR ATARI® COMPUTER
A GUIDE TO ATARI® 400/800™ COMPUTERS

1234567890 HCHC 8765432

ISBN 0-931988-65-9

Cover design by Mary Borchers

Cover illustration by J.V. Benes

Book composition by K.L.T. van Genderen

Photos by Harvey Schwartz unless otherwise credited

CONTENTS

ACKNOWLEDGMENTS

This book would not exist without the assistance of the people at Atari, Inc. We wish to especially thank J. Peter Nelson and Sandy Bertino, who graciously arranged equipment loans for our first-hand forays into the dark, half-charted regions of ATARI BASIC. We used the same equipment for the photographs in the book. Thanks also to Go Sugiura of AMDEK Corporation for the use of one of their color monitors. Yes, a color monitor does display a considerably sharper image than a television set.

Cynthia Greever tested most of the programs listed in the book and researched facts for the appendixes. Finally, we wish to thank John Crane and his colleagues at John Crane Consulting. They reviewed the manuscript and made many excellent suggestions for improvements. We, of course, bear the responsibility for any errors, misconceptions, and misinterpretations that remain.

INTRODUCTION

This book is your guide to the ATARI home computers. It describes the ATARI 400 and ATARI 800 computers themselves and covers the common external devices and accessories, including disk drive and printers. We assume you have access to an ATARI home computer system that is completely hooked up according to the instructions in the appropriate operator's manual provided with each system component. We do not explain how to install your system, but rather how to use it once it is installed.

The book is divided into three parts. Each part focuses on one kind of ATARI computer user. The first part addresses the person who plans to use commercially prepared programs but has little or no desire to program the computer. The second part teaches the programmer or prospective programmer how to use BASIC* on the ATARI computer. The third part organizes information about the ATARI computer in the style of a reference manual for the user who understands the generalities but needs to look up the specifics. These three parts are not mutually exclusive. Users of the first part may venture into the second part just to see what BASIC programming is all about. Users of the second and third parts are likely to find themselves referring to the first part from time to time.

---

* This book covers only standard ATARI BASIC, sometimes called Sheperdson BASIC. Another version of BASIC, Microsoft BASIC, is available as an accessory from Atari, Inc. A third version, called BASIC A+, is available from Optimized Systems Software, of Cupertino, California. Neither Microsoft BASIC nor BASIC A+ is covered in this book.

The first two chapters answer two questions: "What is an ATARI computer?" and "How do you make it work?" You have probably noticed that an ATARI computer system consists of several pieces of equipment all strung together with wires and cables. The first chapter tells you what all the pieces are and what they do. The second chapter tells you how to operate each component part. With this knowledge you are ready to use any of the ready-to-run programs that are widely available for word processing, financial analysis, bookkeeping, computer-aided instruction, and entertainment.

Chapters 3 through 10 teach you how to write your own BASIC programs. Chapter 3 starts things off with a tutorial approach to the fundamentals of standard ATARI BASIC. Chapter 4 continues with coverage of advanced programming topics and BASIC features.

Several advanced topics are important enough to warrant their own chapters. Chapter 5 covers using the program recorder to record and read back data in BASIC. Chapter 6 explains how to use the ATARI printers, with emphasis on the ATARI 825 80-column printer. Chapter 7 explains how to use the disk drive to store programs and data files. Chapters 8 and 9 tell you how to program graphics on the display screen. These two chapters also explore ways to bypass BASIC to achieve some special graphics effects. Chapter 10 sounds out the ATARI computer's audio abilities.

Chapter 11 begins the reference section of the book. Here you will find detailed coverage of each statement and function available in standard ATARI BASIC, including disk statements. The Appendixes conclude the reference section.

1
PRESENTING THE ATARI PERSONAL COMPUTERS

A complete ATARI personal computer system includes several separate pieces of equipment. Figure 1-1 shows a typical system, centered around an ATARI 800 computer. Your system may not look exactly like the one pictured. System components come from a long list of optional equipment, but every system has three components in common: the ATARI 400 or 800 computer itself, the built-in keyboard, and a television. Let's take a closer look at each of these and at some of the more common pieces of optional equipment. This chapter will not describe how to hook up any of these components to the ATARI computer. For complete installation instructions, refer to the operator's manual supplied with your ATARI 400/800 computer, or with the individual piece of equipment.

THE COMPUTER COMPONENTS

There are two models of the ATARI personal computer. The ATARI 400 (Figure 1-2) and ATARI 800 (Figure 1-3) computers are identical underneath the packaging. There is no electronic difference between them. Their performance is identical, and they obey the same instructions.

Anything you can do on the ATARI 400 computer, you can do on the ATARI 800 computer. The reverse is generally true, but not always. The ATARI 800 computer has some features that make it more versatile than the ATARI 400 computer. You can personally change the memory capacity of the ATARI 800 computer, but the memory capacity of the ATARI 400 computer is relatively fixed at the time you buy it. You have the choice of using a television monitor with the ATARI 800 computer for a sharper display, but the ATARI 400 computer can only use a regular television set. The keyboard on the ATARI 800 computer is larger and more like a

1

FIGURE 1-1. A typical ATARI personal computer system

FIGURE 1-2. The ATARI 400 personal computer

FIGURE 1-3. The ATARI 800 personal computer

typewriter keyboard, while the ATARI 400 computer has a flat panel. You can plug in two accessory cartridges on the ATARI 800 computer, versus one on the ATARI 400 computer.

The ATARI 400 computer does have a raison d'être. It has a sealed keyboard which protects the interior from dust, lint, and spilled liquids. It is more compact, weighs less, and costs less than the ATARI 800 computer.

From this point on, we will refer to both models collectively as the ATARI computer. Where photographs and illustrations show one model, you can assume they apply to the other model as well. We will note anything to the contrary.

The Keyboard and Television

The keyboard and television screen make communications with the ATARI computer possible. The keyboard transfers instructions from your fingertips into the computer. To facilitate touch-typing, the keys are arranged in the same order as on a standard typewriter. But the ATARI 400 computer is not well suited to touch-typing because of the compact size and different feel of its keyboard. Both keyboards have some keys you won't find on a typewriter. These special keys are discussed in Chapter 2.

The *display screen* is usually an ordinary color television set. The ATARI 800 computer also accepts a color television monitor. A black-and-white television set will also work, but colors will show up in shades of gray. The screen not only

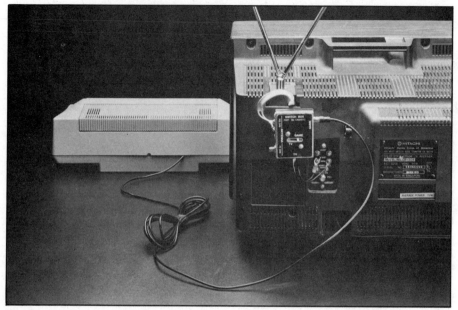

FIGURE 1-4. Typical television set hookup

displays everything you type so you can visually verify its accuracy, it also displays the reactions of the computer to your instructions.

The standard display screen has several different modes of operation. One is for monochromic text (for example, black-and-white or blue-and-white) only. Two other modes produce text in as many as four different colors. There are also modes designed especially for graphics. In the monochromic text mode, the standard screen is divided into 24 lines of 40 characters each. The other modes subdivide the screen differently. Graphics are discussed further in Chapters 8 and 9.

Most ATARI computer owners use a television set for their display screen either because they have one or because it provides a good excuse to get one. The television monitor produces a sharper picture than a television set in the computer environment, but you can't use it to watch your favorite show.

The television set connects directly to the ATARI computer through a switch box which attaches to the television antenna terminal (Figure 1-4). With the switch in one position, the television functions as a television, but with the switch in the other position, the television takes its orders from the ATARI computer.

A television monitor requires no switch box; it attaches directly to the five-pin socket on the side of the ATARI 800 computer (Figure 1-5).

Inside the Console

The ATARI 400/800 computer console houses the part of the computer that controls, with your guidance, the rest of the system. Lurking beneath the keyboard

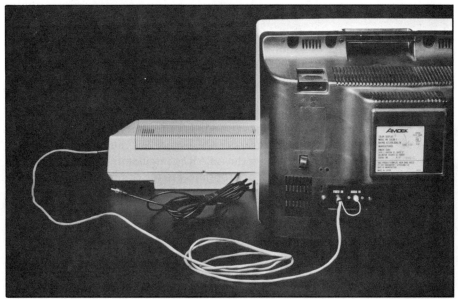

FIGURE 1-5. Typical television monitor hookup

FIGURE 1-6. Hatch for plug-in cartridges

are all the electronics that give the ATARI computer its personality. Fortunately, you need never concern yourself with these undercover items.

The ATARI 400 has a hatch on top which opens to accept a plug-in cartridge. The ATARI 800 computer will accept two cartridges (Figure 1-6). In fact, the entire top comes off the ATARI 800 computer, allowing access to the main memory banks (Figure 1-7).

Memory

Computer memory is typically measured in units called *bytes*. Each byte of memory can hold one character or a similar amount of data. Depending on the number of chips, your ATARI computer has anywhere from 18,432 to 61,440 bytes of memory. This is usually stated 18K to 60K, where K represents 1024 bytes. The amount of memory available determines how much the computer can do, as you will see later.

The ATARI computer actually has two kinds of memory. One is called *ROM* (read-only memory). Its contents never change, even when you turn off the power. ROM contains the programs that give the ATARI computer its unique identity and enable it to understand and respond appropriately to the commands you type in at the keyboard. The other kind of memory is called *RAM* (random-access memory, also called read/write memory). The contents of RAM can be changed. In fact, the program in RAM determines what task the ATARI computer will currently perform. RAM works only as long as the power remains on. As soon as you turn off the ATARI computer, everything disappears from RAM.

On the ATARI 800 computer, RAM comes in separate 8K or 16K plug-in modules (Figure 1-8). You plug in the RAM modules underneath the top cover (Figure 1-7) in some combination to provide as much RAM as you need.

Changing the RAM capacity of an ATARI 400 computer is not a task for the average user. Some ATARI computer dealers do have the facilities to do it.

FIGURE 1-7. ATARI 800 computer memory banks

The 410 Program Recorder

Fortunately, you can use a cassette tape recorder to transfer programs to and from RAM, thereby storing a whole library of programs on cassettes. The 410 Program Recorder (Figure 1-9) is designed specifically to work with an ATARI computer. A single 30-minute cassette can hold as many as 51,200 characters.

FIGURE 1-8. ATARI 800 computer plug-in RAM memory modules

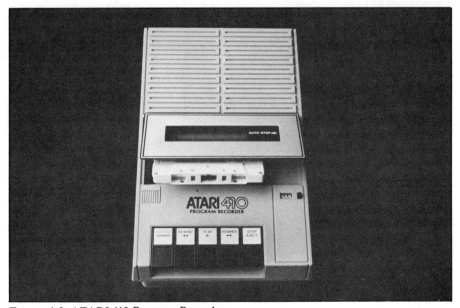

FIGURE 1-9. ATARI 410 Program Recorder

The 810 Disk Drive

A disk drive far surpasses the program recorder as a program storage device. It is more reliable, stores more, and operates faster. The disk drive easily and quickly stores data such as names and addresses for a mailing list, or correspondence for a word processor. The 810 Disk Drive (Figure 1-10) stores as many as 92,160 characters on each removable diskette.

Programs

The programs you use with your system are as much a part of the system as any of the physical devices. Several different classes of programs must coexist in order for the ATARI computer to perform any specific chore. Programs that do things like game playing, word processing, accounting, and financial analysis are called *application programs*. You often transfer them to RAM from a cassette or diskette. When you want your ATARI computer to be a word processor, for instance, you use the diskette with the word processing application program on it and transfer the program into RAM. Chapter 2 explains how to do this. Application programs also come on ROM cartridges (Figure 1-11) that you plug in underneath the hatch of either ATARI personal computer (Figure 1-6). If you want to play a game, you plug in the appropriate cartridge.

More often than not, programmers write application programs in a programming language that is easy for them to use but too advanced for the ATARI computer to

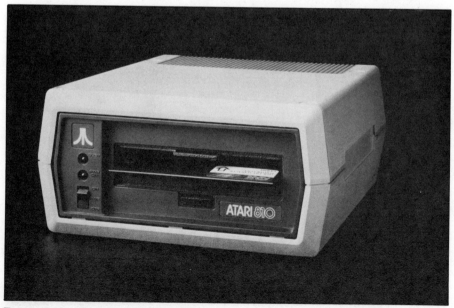

FIGURE 1-10. ATARI 810 Disk Drive

FIGURE 1-11. Some plug-in ROM cartridges

understand without some help. A special program called an *interpreter* does just what its name implies. It translates the application program from the language in which it is written to a language the computer can understand. The interpreter for standard ATARI BASIC comes on a ROM cartridge which plugs in under the hatch of either ATARI personal computer.

The interpreter in turn relies on another program to coordinate the system components. This program, called the *operating system* program, performs fundamental system operations like transferring programs from cassette or disk to memory, and echoing keystrokes on the display screen. The ATARI operating system program always resides in ROM. On the ATARI 800 computer, the operating system is in a plug-in module under the top cover (Figure 1-7).

Game Controls

There are three kinds of game controls that attach to the front of the ATARI computer (Figure 1-12). Joysticks, paddles, and keyboard controllers are commonly used with games, and are showing up increasingly often in other programs. However, many applications do not require these game controls, so your system may not have them.

Printers

Many applications, especially in business and finance, need a printer to produce reports on paper. There are three ATARI printers. The 820 Printer and 822 Thermal Printer (Figure 1-13) connect directly to the ATARI communications line. The 825 Wide-Carriage Printer connects to the ATARI computer through the 850 Interface Module (Figure 1-14). Printers other than ATARI printers can be

FIGURE 1-12. Game controls

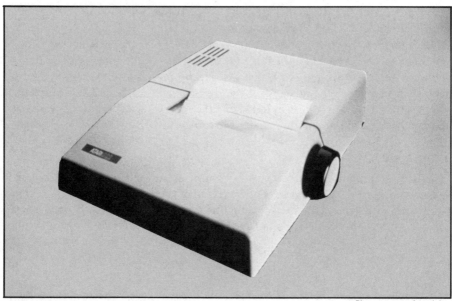

FIGURE 1-13. ATARI 822 Thermal Printer

Photo courtesy of Atari, Inc.

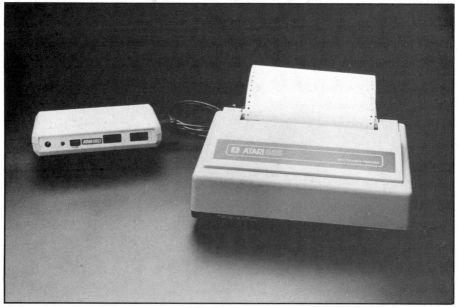

FIGURE 1-14. ATARI 825 Printer and ATARI 850 Interface Module

attached to the 850 Interface Module too. There are printers of every size, price, and description. Some will print correspondence that looks just as good as anything a typewriter can produce. Others will reproduce your graphics displays (in color, in some cases). There are also printers that are a compromise between the two.

2
HOW TO OPERATE THE ATARI COMPUTER

Any computer system can be a bit intimidating when you first sit down in front of it. This chapter will make you more comfortable around the ATARI computer by explaining how to use it. Before you read any further, make sure your system is set up properly. The operator's manuals that come with each piece of equipment have complete instructions to help you with the installation procedure. If you need more assistance to be sure you've done it right, check with someone else who uses an ATARI computer like yours, or with your computer dealer.

INSTALLING ROM CARTRIDGES

The ROM cartridge installed in your ATARI computer can make quite a difference in the way it behaves. The cartridge is under the hatch cover on top of the console (Figure 2-1). The ATARI 400 computer has one cartridge socket. The ATARI 800 computer has two; almost all cartridges go in the left socket. If there is another cartridge in the socket, grasp it firmly and pull it straight up and out. Hold the cartridge you plan to use so the label is facing you. Plug it into the socket. Press firmly on top of the cartridge to make sure it is all the way in. Close the hatch, and you're done.

If no cartridge is installed, the ATARI computer operates in *memo pad mode*. The computer isn't very useful in this mode; it merely displays whatever you type, as if you were typing a memo.

This book assumes that the cartridge labeled "BASIC Computing Language" is installed.

FIGURE 2-1. Installing a ROM cartridge in the ATARI 800 computer
(ATARI 400 computer similar)

TURNING ON THE POWER

Before you turn on any power switches, make sure all the system components are connected together correctly. Figure 2-2 diagrams one way to connect the pieces of a full-feature system.

You must turn on the pieces of your ATARI system in a certain order, as shown below.

1. Turn on the television. Tune it and the ATARI computer to the same channel. Set the antenna switch to "computer."
2. If you plan to use diskettes during this session, turn on Disk Drive 1. Insert a diskette which has the disk operating system on it. Close the drive door.
3. If you plan to use a component attached to one of the serial interface jacks of the 850 Interface Module, turn on the 850 Interface Module now. Otherwise, leave it off.
4. Turn on the ATARI 400/800 console.
5. Turn on the printer when you are ready to use it. The 825 Printer also requires that the 850 Interface Module be on.

If you don't follow this procedure, the ATARI computer may be unable to communicate properly with some of the system components. The steps outlined above will now be described in detail.

Step 1: The Television

First, turn on the television set or television monitor, whichever your system uses for a display screen. Let it warm up while you turn on the rest of the system. Turn

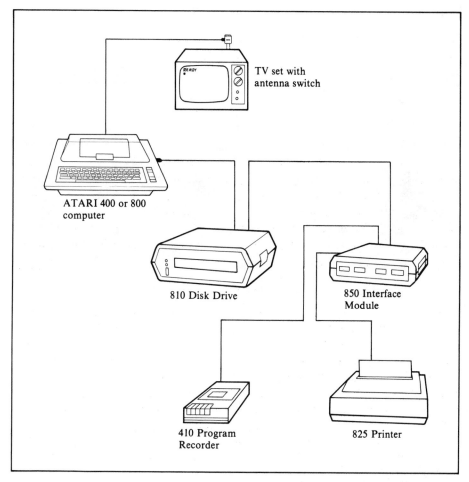

TV set with
antenna switch

ATARI 400 or 800
computer

810 Disk Drive

850 Interface
Module

410 Program
Recorder

825 Printer

FIGURE 2-2. Typical connections between ATARI system components

down the volume for now (some monitors have no volume control). The rest of this section pertains only to the television set. If your system uses a television monitor, go on to the next section.

Locate the slide switch hanging from the television antenna terminals and set it on the "computer" or "game" setting (Figure 2-3). With the switch in this position, the television set becomes the ATARI computer's display screen. Tune the television set to channel 2 or 3, whichever is weaker in your neighborhood. If you're not sure which channel to use, try channel 2. You can switch to channel 3 later if reception on channel 2 is poor.

The ATARI computer must be set to broadcast on the same channel the television is tuned to. There is a slide switch on the side of the keyboard console (Figure 2-4). Set it to match the television channel (2 or 3).

FIGURE 2-3. Setting the TV antenna slide switch

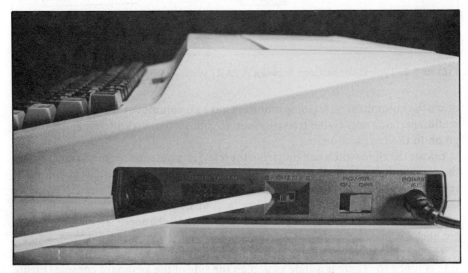

FIGURE 2-4. Selecting the ATARI computer's TV output channel

Step 2: The Disk Drive

If your system has no disk drive, or if you won't be using the one it has, skip this section. Otherwise, turn on the drive now. The drive will whirr and click for a few seconds, and its front panel lamps will light. This is normal. After a few seconds, the noises will stop and all lamps but the power indicator lamp will go off.

If you have more than one drive, you must turn on Drive 1 now; the other drives are optional. To determine which is Drive 1, look through the access hole in the back of each drive (Figure 2-5). You can see one or two switch levers. The position of these levers determines the drive number. Drive 1 has both levers all the way over to the left. You may only be able to see the black lever in front; it may be hiding the white lever behind it.

Take one of the diskettes labeled "Disk File Manager Master Copy," "Disk File Manager II Master Copy," or a duplicate copy of one of these diskettes. You can also substitute any other diskette recommended by a reliable source for use at power-on time. Carefully insert the diskette in Drive 1, label side up. Slide it all the way in and gently close the drive door. For more information on diskette handling, see the section later in this chapter on using the disk drive.

Step 3: The 850 Interface Module

Turn on the 850 Interface Module only if you plan to use a component attached to one of its serial interface jacks (Figure 2-6). Otherwise, leave it switched off for now.

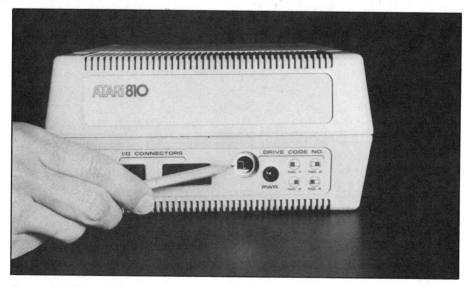

FIGURE 2-5. Determining the disk drive number

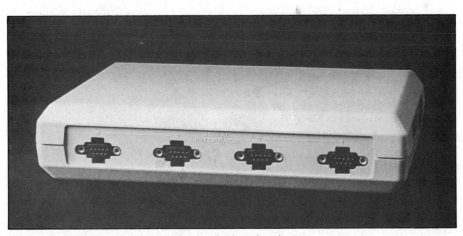

FIGURE 2-6. The 850 Interface Module serial interface jacks

Step 4: The ATARI 400/800 Console

For the fourth step, lift the hatch cover and make sure the proper ROM cartridge is installed (Figure 2-1), then close the cover securely. Double-check that all system components are correctly interconnected (Figure 2-2). Locate the power switch on the side of the console, next to where the power cord plugs into the computer (Figure 2-7). Turn the switch to "on" and turn up the television volume a bit. Things start to happen. The power lamp on the keyboard comes on. The television displays a blue field with a black border and starts to make clicking noises (if the volume is turned up enough). If the disk drive is on, it starts to whirr. Soon the message **READY** appears in white letters on the screen (Figure 2-8). The disk drive stops.

If the **READY** message does not appear after 30 seconds, something is wrong. Turn everything off, recheck all connections, and try again. If you are using the disk drive, be sure that you are using a proper diskette, that it is inserted label-side up, and that the drive door is closed. Otherwise the drive simply whirrs and makes rasping sounds. The message **BOOT ERROR** appears on the display screen.

If the ATARI computer still won't start, turn the power off. Unplug the computer and get help from someone with more experience (your dealer).

Step 5: The Printer

Once you have completed the steps described above, you can turn the printer on and off whenever you like. It must be on to print, of course, but can remain off otherwise. With the 825 Printer, the 850 Interface Module must also be on to print.

Turning Components On and Off

During a session with the computer, the ATARI 400/800 console must remain on. You can turn many other components on and off as you need them, once the initial

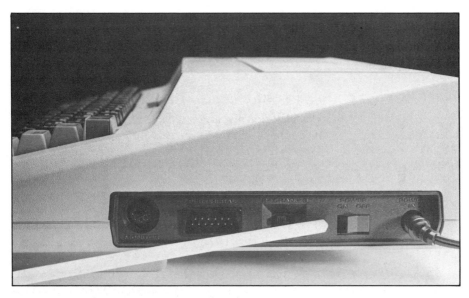

FIGURE 2-7. The console power switch on the ATARI 800 computer
(ATARI 400 computer similar)

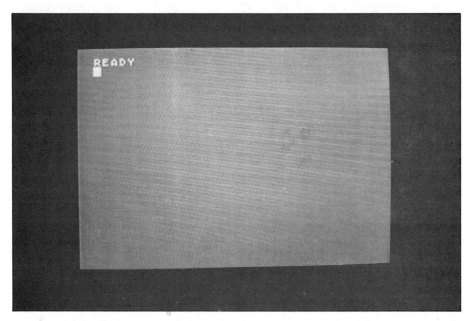

FIGURE 2-8. The display screen after a successful power-on sequence

power-on sequence is complete. The television, disk drive, and printer can all be turned off and on at will. However, the 850 Interface Module must remain on unless the only thing connected to it is the 825 Printer. In that case, you can turn it off until you need to print.

What You See on the Screen

The **READY** message on the television display screen means the ATARI computer is now ready to accept your commands via the keyboard (Figure 2-8). Just below the **READY** message you will see a white square. This white square is called the *cursor*. It marks the location where the next character you type will appear on the screen.

THE KEYBOARD

The ATARI 400 and 800 keyboards are shown in Figure 2-9. The two keyboards are similar, but the ATARI 800 keyboard is larger than the sealed ATARI 400 keyboard.

The ATARI keyboard looks much like the keyboard of an ordinary typewriter, but it has some extra keys you won't find on most typewriters. Two are on the left side, marked ESC and CTRL. Three others are on the right, marked BREAK, CAPS/LOWR, and ⋏. Several of the standard keys have extra words or symbols on them, and on the far right is a column of four yellow *special function keys*.

FIGURE 2-9. The keyboards

Take a few minutes and experiment with the keyboard. Go ahead and type on it. Nothing you type will do any harm to the computer that can't be cured by turning the power off and on again.

Automatic Repeat Feature

Hold one of the letter keys down, say the G key. A single G appears. After a few seconds, G's start streaming across the display. This automatic repeat feature of the keyboard works with every key except SHIFT, BREAK, and the yellow special function keys, including SYSTEM RESET.

Line Length

Display lines on the ATARI computer are 40 characters wide. Margins are set such that 38 of the 40 positions are usable. The two leftmost columns are outside the standard left margin.

The SYSTEM RESET Key

SYSTEM RESET is one of the yellow special function keys on the far right side of the keyboard. When you press SYSTEM RESET, everything stops. No matter what the computer is doing when SYSTEM RESET is pressed, control of the computer returns to the keyboard.

Sometimes SYSTEM RESET causes a lot of problems, especially if a disk drive is active when this key is pressed. Therefore, you must exercise extreme caution *not* to press the SYSTEM RESET key accidentally.

The RETURN Key

As you type along, the characters you type show up on the display screen. In addition, the ATARI computer saves everything you type in its memory but does not try to interpret what you type until you press the RETURN key. The RETURN key signals the computer that you have finished the line you have been typing. When you press RETURN, the computer examines everything on the line that you just typed in. If those characters are not legitimate, an error message appears.

The BREAK Key

BREAK interrupts whatever is going on and brings it to a halt. Press BREAK while entering a command, for example, and the computer disregards everything you've typed on the current display line.

When running a program, do not use the BREAK key unless specifically instructed to do so. Some programs are careful to disable it, but others will stop if BREAK is pressed. You can usually continue a program by typing the command CONT and pressing the RETURN key, but the display screen will be ruined at the very least.

The Sнιϝτ Key

When you first turn on the ATARI computer, letters are always upper-case. It doesn't matter whether or not you use the SHIFT key. The SHIFT key does affect some keys in this mode, though. You get one character by pressing a key with the SHIFT key held down and another by pressing the same key without holding the SHIFT key down. The character you get when using the SHIFT key is printed on the top edge of the key. Table 2-1 lists some SHIFT key combinations; Appendix D provides a complete list.

We use the notation SHIFT- to describe a compound keystroke involving the SHIFT key. For example, SHIFT-3 (press the SHIFT and 3 keys simultaneously) produces the # character.

The Cτʀʟ Key

CTRL is a contraction of the word "control." The CTRL key is always used together with another key in the same manner as the SHIFT key. You hold the CTRL key down while you press and release another key. We designate the use of the CTRL key in conjunction with another key by prefixing the name of the other key with CTRL-. For example, CTRL-B means press the CTRL and B keys simultaneously.

The CTRL key, like the SHIFT key, allows some keys to have an additional function. Some of the functions you get with CTRL key combinations are printed on the top edge of the keys, in reverse notation. For example, CTRL-TAB clears a tab stop. CTRL combined with any of the letter keys produces a graphics character. Table 2-2 lists some of the CTRL combinations; Appendix D provides a complete list.

The Cᴀᴘs/Lᴏᴡʀ Key

When you first turn on the ATARI computer, all the letters you type are displayed on the screen as capital letters, regardless of whether the SHIFT key was pressed when you typed them. Press the CAPS/LOWR key to get upper- and lower-case capability. Now you get lower-case letters without the SHIFT key, upper-case with it. To get back to upper-case mode, press the SHIFT and CAPS/LOWR keys at the same

TABLE 2-1. Selected Sнιϝτ Key Effects (Upper-case mode)

Keystroke	Character or Action
SHIFT-TAB	Set tab stop
SHIFT-<	Clear display screen
SHIFT->	Insert blank line
SHIFT-BACK S	Delete current line
SHIFT-CAPS/LOWR	Switch keyboard to upper-case mode

TABLE 2-2. Selected CTRL Key Combinations

Keystroke	Character or Action
CTRL-TAB	Clear tab stop
CTRL--	Move cursor up one line
CTRL- =	Move cursor down one line
CTRL- +	Move cursor left one space
CTRL-*	Move cursor right one space
CTRL-1	Freeze/restart screen display
CTRL-3	Usually results in an error
CTRL- <	Clear display screen
CTRL- >	Insert a space
CTRL-BACK S	Delete next character
CTRL-CAPS/LOWR	Switch keyboard to graphics mode

time. Press the CTRL and CAPS/LOWR keys simultaneously to switch the keyboard to graphics character mode.

The ⅄ Key

The ⅄ key switches the keyboard back and forth between normal and inverse video modes. Inverse video characters come out reversed, blue letters on a white background.

The Arrow Keys

The four arrow keys are called *up-arrow, down-arrow, left-arrow,* and *right-arrow.* They are all CTRL key combinations: CTRL-- (↑), CTRL-= (↓), CTRL-+ (←), and CTRL- ^ (→).

You will find the arrow keys very useful because they allow you to correct any typing mistakes you might make, enabling you to change information you have already entered.

The ← key works like the backspace key on a typewriter. Each time you press it, the cursor backs up one space. Try it now. Type in any word (try PRINT). Press the ← key several times and watch the cursor back up along the word you just typed in. Notice that the characters you back over do not disappear from the display screen. Try backing the cursor all the way to the left edge of the screen. When you get to the edge and press the ← key again, the cursor jumps to the right edge of the screen.

As you might suspect, the → key moves the cursor to the right along the display line. It does not erase characters it passes over. When the cursor reaches the right margin, it reappears at the left margin on the same line.

In a similar fashion, the ↑ and ↓ keys move the cursor up or down one line. With the cursor at the top of the screen, the ↑ key puts it at the bottom of the screen. With the cursor at the bottom of the screen, the ↓ key puts it at the top.

The BACK S Key

Each time you press the BACK S key, the character at the location of the cursor is erased and the cursor backs up one space. Try backing all the way to the left edge of the screen. The cursor bumps into the left margin; press BACK S again and the cursor doesn't move.

The CLEAR Key

Press CTRL-< or SHIFT-< and the display screen clears. The cursor moves to the upper left-hand corner of the screen. This corner is called the *home* position.

The INSERT and DELETE Keys

Activating the INSERT or DELETE keys requires a combination keystroke using either the CTRL key or the SHIFT key. CTRL-> inserts a blank space to the right of the cursor. CTRL-BACK S deletes the character to the right of the cursor. In either case, the cursor does not move.

SHIFT-> inserts a blank line above the line the cursor is on; the entire display from the cursor line down shifts down one line. SHIFT-BACK S deletes the whole line the cursor is on; lines below that move up on the screen.

The TAB Key

When you press the TAB key alone, the cursor advances to the next tab stop. Standard tab stops, present when you turn on the ATARI computer, are set eight columns apart. Because the standard left margin is indented two columns from the edge of the screen, the first tab stop is only six columns to the right of the left margin. SHIFT-TAB sets a new tab stop at the location of the cursor. CTRL-TAB clears the tab stop at the location of the cursor.

The ESC Key

ESC stands for "escape," which is a term left over from the days when teletypes were common computer terminals. Somehow the name has stuck. Unlike the SHIFT and CTRL keys, the ESC key is never used by holding it down while pressing another key. ESC is always pressed and released before the next key is pressed and released. This two-key operation is called an *escape sequence*.

The ESC key lets you suspend the immediate effect of keystrokes like CLEAR (SHIFT-<) in order to enter them as values. Escape sequences are mainly used in programming; they are covered more fully in Chapter 4.

The Other Keys

The other keys on the ATARI keyboard are no doubt familiar to you. There are the letters of the alphabet, the digits 0 through 9, and a standard set of symbols.

Many typists do not distinguish between the number zero and the letter "O" or the number one and the lower-case letter "l." The ATARI computer can't cope with this ambiguity. You must be very careful to type a numeral when you mean a numeral. To help you remember, the ATARI keyboard shows the zero with a slash through it, and zeros are displayed on the screen with that slash.

USING THE 410 PROGRAM RECORDER

If your ATARI system includes a program recorder, you can load programs from cassette tapes. There are many program tapes you can buy, and you can make your own as well (we'll tell you how in Chapter 3).

Handling Cassettes

Be careful with cassettes. They are easily damaged and not easily replaced. Avoid touching the surface of the tape itself. No matter how clean your skin is, natural oils will contaminate the tape. Make sure you put tapes back in their cases when they are not being used. Never store them in hot areas, direct sunlight, or near magnetic fields (like those found near electric motors).

Selecting Blank Cassettes

The 410 Program Recorder uses only audio cassettes — never digital cassettes. You can't go wrong with the best quality normal-bias tape. Good quality tapes will work too, but avoid cheap bargain cassettes. They tend to jam up after a while, rendering your valuable programs inaccessible.

Most programs take up very little tape. Therefore, short tapes tend to be just as useful as long ones.

Labeling Cassettes

You should label every cassette with information about the programs it contains. This prevents the headache of searching through cassette after cassette for the program you need.

Write-Protecting Cassettes

Each cassette has two notches in the rear edge (Figure 2-10). When the notches are uncovered, the 410 Program Recorder can sense the holes and will not record on the cassette. New blank cassettes have tabs covering the holes so the tape can be recorded on. You can protect important programs by knocking out the correct tab and exposing the hole. Later, if you want to record over a protected tape, simply cover the hole with tape.

Each cassette has two sides to it. One notch protects one side, while the other notch protects the other side. To determine which notch is correct, hold the cassette so that the exposed tape is toward you and the side you wish to protect is facing up. Remove the tab on the left side to prevent recording over the side facing up.

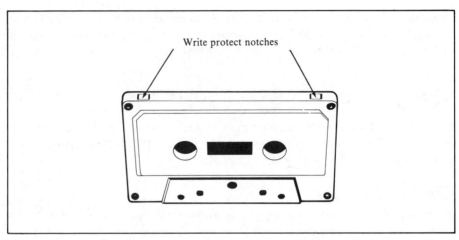

FIGURE 2-10. Cassette write-protect notches

USING THE 810 DISK DRIVE

If you have one or more disk drives connected to your ATARI computer, you can get programs on diskettes instead of cassettes.

What Kind of Diskettes to Buy

From time to time you may need extra blank diskettes. The ATARI 810 Disk Drive uses standard 5¼-inch diskettes. It can use either soft-sectored or hard-sectored diskettes, although soft-sectored are preferred. Any well-known brand of diskette will work.

Handling Diskettes

You must be very careful when you handle a diskette. Diskettes are much more delicate than cassette tapes. *Never* bend a diskette. *Never* touch the surface of the diskette (the part inside the holes), and *never* force a diskette into the drive. Always replace diskettes in their envelopes when you remove them from the drive, and protect them from heat, direct sunlight, and magnetic fields (like those found near electric motors). Be especially careful with the "Disk File Manager Master Copy" or "Disk File Manager II Master Copy" that came with the disk drive.

Write-Protecting Diskettes

Most diskettes have a square notch cut out of the right side. The 810 Disk Drive will write on a diskette only if it senses the presence of the notch. To prevent accidentally writing on a diskette, cover its notch with an adhesive label or a piece of tape (Figure 2-11).

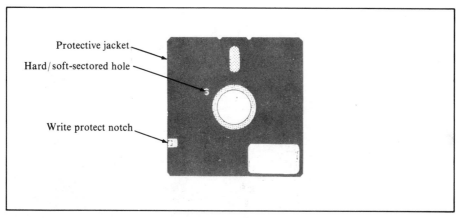

FIGURE 2-11. Write-protecting a diskette

Diskette Insertion

The proper way to insert a diskette into the disk drive is shown in Figure 2-12. Hold the diskette between your thumb and forefinger. Open the door on the disk drive and gently slide the diskette all the way into the drive. There should be almost no resistance. If the diskette will not go in easily, remove it and try again. Make sure you are holding the diskette as level as possible. Once the diskette is inside the drive, gently close the drive door. The door should close very easily. If there is any resistance, release the door and push the diskette completely into the drive, then try again. If you force the door shut you will destroy the diskette. Sometimes it helps center the diskette if you wait until after the disk starts spinning to close the door.

The Disk Operating System

Before you can use any disk drive, a special program called the *disk operating system* must be in memory. The disk operating system, or *DOS*, is a special program that controls all disk-related activities. The process of placing a copy of DOS in memory is called *booting*. In computer jargon you can say "boot the disk" or "boot the DOS," or just "boot DOS."

Turning off the ATARI 400/800 console erases DOS from memory. If you need to use a disk drive the next time you turn on the system, you must reboot DOS. You do not have to reboot DOS when you just turn a disk drive off or on.

Booting DOS

There is only one way to boot DOS. The procedure is as follows:

1. Turn on Drive 1. To determine which is Drive 1 on a multiple-drive system, look in the access hole at the back of each drive. Find the drive with both the black and white switches all the way to the left (Figure 2-5); that's Drive 1.

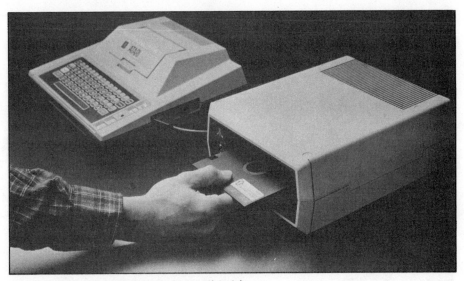

FIGURE 2-12. Inserting a diskette into a disk drive

2. Place a diskette with a copy of the disk operating system on it into Drive 1. The diskettes labeled "Disk File Manager Master Copy" and "Disk File Manager II Master Copy" have a copy of DOS on them.
3. Turn the console power off and on. The disk drive whirrs as it transfers DOS from the diskette to the computer's memory. The **READY** message appears on the display screen when the boot finishes.

You probably noticed that the standard power-on procedure described earlier in this chapter includes these steps. Thus, if you follow that procedure, you will boot DOS as a matter of course.

If any problem occurs during the boot, the message **BOOT ERROR** appears on the display screen. The disk drive may also make disconcerting rasping sounds. Boot errors occur when there is no diskette in the drive, the drive door is open, the diskette is in upside down, there is no copy of DOS on the diskette, the diskette is damaged or defective, or the disk drive malfunctions.

The DOS Menu

Part of the disk operating system is a set of utility programs. Many are strictly for programmers, but almost every disk user has occasion to use one or two of them. To use them, first boot DOS. With the same diskette still in the disk drive, type the following command on the ATARI keyboard:

    DOS

Press the RETURN key. The display screen changes to look like Figure 2-13. This is called the *DOS menu*. Your menu may look a bit different.

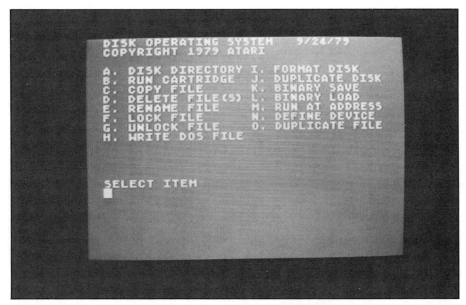

FIGURE 2-13. Typical DOS menu

There are two different versions of the disk operating system, and each has a slightly different menu. Unless you plan to program the ATARI computer, you need to use only menu items A, D, E, I, J, L, and O. Those seven are the same in both versions. With one version of the disk operating system the menu appears immediately. The other version has to access the disk drive first; it may take as long as 30 seconds for the DOS menu to appear.

> **WARNING:** The DOS command may erase the program you were last using from the ATARI computer's memory. Do not use the DOS command unless you are willing to restart the program you were last using.

The Diskette Directory

If you have successfully booted a diskette, you may be interested in knowing what programs it contains. Use the DOS command, as described above, to get the DOS menu. Select item A by typing the letter A (followed by pressing the RETURN key). This message appears at the bottom of the display screen:

```
DIRECTORY--SEARCH SPEC,LIST FILE?
```

Press the RETURN key to list all the program names on the diskette in Drive 1. If the directory flashes by too fast, try again. This time, press CTRL-1 whenever you want to freeze the display. Press CTRL-1 again to restart the display.

To list the directory on your printer, select menu item A. Then type a comma, the letter P, a colon, and press RETURN.

```
,P:
```

If your system has more than one disk drive, you may want to list the directory of a drive other than Drive 1. Once again, choose menu item A. To specify the drive you want, type the drive number, then a colon.

D1:

Then press RETURN.

There are other ways to respond to menu choice A that let you specify what kinds of program names you want to see, and more. Chapter 7 has more information.

Preparing Blank Diskettes

From time to time you may need extra diskettes for the programs you run on your ATARI computer. Before you can use a diskette for the first time, you must *format* it. The formatting process gets a diskette ready for subsequent use. If the application program you are using includes specific instructions for formatting diskettes, by all means use them. In their absence, you can use the following general instructions for preparing extra diskettes.

To format a diskette, start by getting the DOS menu on the screen. Place the diskette you want to format in a disk drive. Select DOS menu item I. The following message appears at the bottom of the display screen:

WHICH DRIVE TO FORMAT?

Type the drive number: D1, D2, D3, etc., then press RETURN.

Next you are asked to verify the disk number by entering a Y. Any other entry cancels the format operation. Enter Y and the format operation begins. It takes about one minute. When the disk drive stops making noises, the format is complete.

Now prepare a label for the new diskette. Remove the diskette from the drive and apply the label.

WARNING: The format operation erases anything that was on the diskette beforehand. Do not format a diskette that has your only copy of a program on it!

Duplicating Diskettes

You will certainly want to make backup copies of your diskettes. DOS menu item J does this, even if you have only one drive. Select item J and this message appears:

DUP DISK-SOURCE,DEST DRIVES?

Before going any further, place a write-protect label over the notch on the original diskette. This simple precaution may save you considerable grief if you make a mistake in the rest of the procedure.

Type the drive number where you plan to put the original diskette (the source), a comma, and the drive number where you plan to put the backup diskette (the destination).

D1,D1

If you specify the same source and destination drives, this message may appear:

TYPE "Y" IF OK TO USE PROGRAM AREA?

WARNING: If you type a Y in response, the duplication operation may erase the program you were last using from the computer's memory. Do not answer Y here unless you are willing to restart the program you were last using.

Type the letter Y and the duplication begins. Any other response to this question terminates the duplication process.

Messages appear on the display screen, asking you to insert first one diskette, then the other. If the source and destination drives are the same, the ATARI computer may tell you to swap diskettes several times. You insert the source diskette, the computer reads part of it into its memory, you insert the destination diskette, the computer writes that piece out, and so on until the whole diskette is duplicated. Each time you insert a diskette, you must press RETURN to signal that drive door is closed and everything is ready.

You might accidentally reverse the source and destination diskettes. If you put a write-protect label on the source, an error message will appear on the display screen. You must start the duplication process over again. If you did not write-protect the source, it may be ruined.

Under some conditions, you will not be able to boot DOS from a duplicate copy of a diskette. To rectify this situation, first boot DOS from some other diskette. Get the DOS menu on the screen, and select menu item H. This message appears:

```
DRIVE TO WRITE DOS FILES TO?
```

Place the diskette you cannot boot from in the disk drive. Type the number of that drive (D1, D2, etc.) and press RETURN. A message like this appears:

```
TYPE "Y" TO WRITE DOS TO DRIVE 1?
```

Type the letter Y, and a copy of the disk operating system is written on the diskette.

Duplicating a Program

DOS menu item O copies a program from one diskette to another. It works with one or more drives. This message appears:

```
NAME OF FILE TO MOVE?
```

Type the name of the program you wish to duplicate:

```
BLASTOFF
```

Press RETURN. Do not prefix the name with a drive number. This message appears:

```
TYPE "Y" IF OK TO USE PROGRAM AREA?
   CAUTION: A "Y" INVLIDATES MEM.SAV
```

WARNING: If you type a Y in response, the duplication operation may erase the program you were last using from the computer's memory. Do not answer Y here unless you are willing to restart the program you were last using.

Messages appear on the display screen, asking you to insert first one diskette, then the other. You may be prompted to swap diskettes several times. You insert the source diskette, the ATARI computer reads part of the program into its memory, you insert the destination diskette, the computer writes that piece out, and so on until the whole program is duplicated. If the program is not too long, it will take only one pass to duplicate it. Each time you insert a diskette, you must press RETURN to signal that the drive door is closed and everything is ready.

DOS menu item C will copy a program from one drive to another; it will also make a second copy of a program on the same diskette. See Chapter 7 for more information.

Deleting a Program

The time may come when you want to remove a program from a diskette. Choose DOS menu item D. This message appears:

```
DELETE FILE SPEC
```

Type the drive number, a colon, and the program name, like this:

```
D2:HANGMAN
```

Press RETURN. You may omit the drive number and colon if Drive 1 is used.

Renaming a Program

A program can have any name you want to give it. There are, however, a few restrictions. First, no two programs on the same diskette can have the same name. Next, the name may be no more than eight characters long. The characters you can use are the upper-case letters A through Z and the digits 0 through 9. The first character must be an upper-case letter. You can add a period followed by as many as three characters to the end of the name. This is called a file name *extension*. The extension .SYS is reserved; read Chapter 7 if you need to use it.

To rename a file, select DOS menu item E. The following message appears:

```
RENAME - GIVE OLD NAME, NEW
```

Type the name the program has now, a comma, and the name you want the program to have, like this:

```
GAME10,BOMBS
```

Press RETURN. Do not include the drive number, just the program name.

LOADING AND RUNNING A PROGRAM

There are many programs already written for the ATARI computer. Some come on cassette, some on diskette, and some on either. Before you can use a program, you must transfer it to the computer's memory from cassette or diskette. This is called *loading*. Once it is loaded, you can start the program running.

Loading a Program from Cassette

The ATARI computer has three commands for loading programs from the program recorder. They are not interchangeable. The appropriate one to use is determined when the program is recorded. If you must, you can determine the right one by trial and error. The commands are CLOAD, ENTER "C:", and LOAD "C:".

The steps for loading a program from cassette are as follows:

1. Position the tape to the start of the program. First, rewind the tape completely. Reset the tape counter to zero. If the program you want is the first one on the cassette, go on to the next step. If not, try to learn the tape counter reading where the program starts. That way you can advance the tape with the program recorder's FAST FORWARD lever. Otherwise, you must load each program in turn until you reach the one you want. Repeat the following steps for each extra program you must load.

2. On the ATARI keyboard type the CLOAD, ENTER "C:", or LOAD "C:" command. Use the one that's right for your program. Press RETURN. The ATARI console beeps once.

3. Depress the PLAY lever on the program recorder. The ATARI computer cannot tell whether you do this. If you do not, it will try to load your program and fail.

4. Press the RETURN key on the keyboard. The tape starts moving. If the volume on the television set is turned up, you will hear several seconds of silence followed by one or more short bursts of sound from the television speaker. These sounds indicate that the program is loading. The sound bursts cease when the loading finishes.

The program is now loaded. If you get any error messages during the loading process, you're probably using the wrong loading command. Try one of the others. If none works, the cassette is blank, damaged, defective, or upside down.

Loading a Program from Diskette

Some programs are loaded and run automatically when you boot DOS. In that case, all you have to do is use the correct program diskette during the power-on procedure (page 14).

You must boot DOS before you can load most programs from diskette. Once DOS is booted, you can load a program from a disk with one of two commands: ENTER "*program*" or LOAD "*program*". In use, you replace the term *program* with the drive number, a colon, and the program name, as follows:

```
LOAD "D1:LEDGER.BAS"
```

You can leave off the drive number and colon if Drive 1 is used.

Starting a Program Running

When the program you want is loaded, type RUN and press RETURN to get it started. The program takes over control of the computer, including the keyboard and display screen. To regain control, you can press BREAK in many programs. If this does not work, check the specific operating instructions for the program you are using. In a dire emergency, you can press the SYSTEM RESET key or turn the computer's power off and back on again, but in either case you will have to restart the program.

There is a single command that both loads and runs a program from cassette. It is RUN "C:". You can use it in place of the LOAD "C:" command. It will not work with programs that must be loaded with either the CLOAD or ENTER "C:" commands.

A similar command both loads and runs a program from diskette. It is RUN "*program*". You can use it in place of the LOAD "*program*" command. It will not work with programs that must be loaded with the ENTER "*program*" command.

SETTING TELEVISION COLOR

The ATARI computer features full color graphics. If any of the programs you plan to use or write will use this feature, you should adjust the color settings on your television set or TV monitor for the correct balance. The colors will be about right if you leave them unchanged from your normal television viewing. If you wish, you may adjust the contrast, brightness, color, and tint controls of your television until you get an acceptable picture.

USING GAME CONTROLLERS

The game controllers plug into the front of the ATARI 400/800 console (Figure 2-14). Instructions for your program should tell you which socket to use. If not, try each socket in turn, starting with socket number 1 on the left.

FIGURE 2-14. Game controller jacks

Knobs on the paddles rotate nearly full-circle. Some of the available rotation is unused. Starting with the knob fully clockwise, only the first two-thirds or so of rotation means anything. The last third produces no change.

The joysticks are fairly sturdy but can be damaged by overzealously leaning into them over a period of time. They respond just as fast to gentle pressure as to hard pressure. You will prolong their life appreciably by treating them with consideration.

USING THE 850 INTERFACE MODULE

If your system uses an 850 Interface Module, it also uses an 825 Printer or something connected to one of the serial interface jacks. If you use the 850 Interface Module just with the 825 Printer, you can turn it off when you are not printing. In order to use equipment attached to a serial interface jack, the 850 Interface Module must remain on all the time.

USING A PRINTER

Any of the printers need only be on when you actually print. Be careful, though. If the printer is off at the wrong time, the program trying to use it may fail.

The 825 Printer has a switch labeled ONLINE/LOCAL. It must be in the "Online" position to print. In the "Local" position you can use the REV/FWD switch to manually move the paper up or down.

ADDING RAM TO THE ATARI 800 COMPUTER

Someday you may acquire a program that won't run on your system because you don't have enough RAM. You can add more RAM to an ATARI 800 computer, up to a point. RAM comes in modules of different denominations. Atari has 8K and 16K modules; other sources have different sizes. As many as three modules plug in under the top cover.

To remove the cover, first lift the hatch. Release the two latches (Figure 2-15), then lift the whole cover up and forward (Figure 2-16).

To remove a RAM module, grasp it firmly at each end and pull straight up (Figure 2-17). It may help to wiggle the module slightly as you pull.

To install a RAM module, place it in the empty socket nearest the front. Place your thumbs on top of the module at each end. Press down with firm, even pressure. You must fill the sockets from front to back. Do not leave empty sockets in the middle or front positions. If you are using both 8K and 16K modules, put the 16K modules in front.

To replace the cover, you must fit the two metal tabs at the back of the cover into the matching holes in the ATARI 800 chassis. Slide the cover back and down until it is even with the ATARI 800 cabinet. Fasten the two latches (Figure 2-18) and close the hatch.

FIGURE 2-15. Releasing the ATARI 800 computer top cover latches

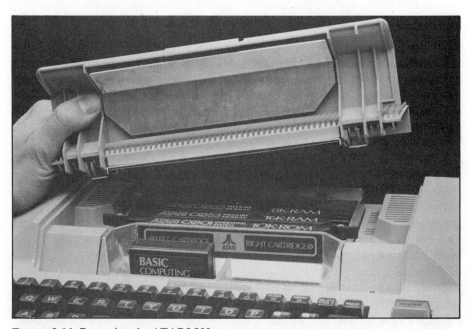

FIGURE 2-16. Removing the ATARI 800 computer top cover

FIGURE 2-17. Removing a RAM memory module (ATARI 800 computer only)

FIGURE 2-18. Fastening the ATARI 800 computer top cover latches

COPING WITH ERRORS

The ATARI computer is a marvelous piece of equipment, but it shares a problem common to all computer systems. It lacks imagination. Every instruction you give it must be exactly right or it will not work as you expected. The results of a mistake can run the gamut from annoying to aggravating to devastating.

Error Messages

When you type something incorrectly and press RETURN, the ATARI computer usually responds with a cryptic *error message*. Often the message gives you a clue as to what you did wrong; sometimes, however, it does not. The general remedy is the same in either case: retype the line. Often the message consists only of the word **ERROR** and a number. You must look up the number to get an explanation of the error. Appendix A contains a complete list of error numbers and explanations.

If the error message occurs while you are running a program, consult the program instructions.

Correcting Typing Mistakes

As you type commands on the ATARI keyboard you are bound to make mistakes. Some of the keys we described earlier make it easy to correct errors you notice on a line before you press RETURN to end the line. They are the BACK S, ← (CTRL-+), → (CTRL-^), TAB, BREAK, and CLEAR (SHIFT-<) keys and key sequences.

- The BACK S key backspaces the cursor and erases characters it passes over. Characters are replaced by blank spaces.
- The ← key moves the cursor one space to the left on the current display line without erasing the character it passes over.
- The → key moves the cursor one space to the right on the current display line without erasing the character it passes over.
- The TAB key moves the cursor right to the next tab stop, without erasing any characters it passes over.
- The BREAK key cancels the line you are currently typing.
- The CLEAR key clears the display screen and leaves the cursor in the upper left corner.

Let's see how you might use these editing features. Suppose you want to type the following command,

```
LOAD "D1:MUSIC"
```

but just before you press RETURN you notice you've made a mistake.

```
LOAS "D1:MUSIC"
```

You have several choices. You can press BREAK to cancel the line and start all over again. You can use the ← key or the BACK S key to back up and correct the mistake.

Try correcting this error with the ← key. Press and hold the CTRL and + keys. The cursor races back to the start of the line. Take your finger off the + key when the cursor gets to the error. If you back up too far, use the → key to line up the cursor over the offending S. Press the D key and presto! The line is correct. You can press RETURN with the cursor where it is; there is no need to move the cursor to the end of the line first.

Accidental BREAK

Sooner or later you will hit the BREAK key when you did not intend to. Some programs are set up to ignore the BREAK key entirely. Those that are not should have specific instructions about what to do if you accidentally press the BREAK key while running that program. Be sure you know what to do before you start your program. If you press BREAK while running a BASIC program you *will* be able to restart the program from the beginning. This is small consolation during some phases of accounting applications and the like, since running the program a second time may not work.

When BREAK takes effect, the ATARI computer stops everything it was doing. Control returns to the keyboard; you will see a message similar to the following:

```
STOPPED AT LINE 1005
```

What should you do? You can probably continue the program by typing the CONT command. If that does not work, you are out of luck. You will have to restart the program from the beginning. Before you blithely type RUN, make sure you won't ruin anything by running the program again. Check the program instructions. Ask someone else who also uses the program. Call your dealer if you have to. The solution may be complicated. Get specific instructions for your program.

3
PROGRAMMING
IN BASIC

BASIC is a computer programming language. It consists of a set of statements and commands. Each statement or command tells the computer to do something specific and fairly simple. You command the computer to perform a complex task by giving it instructions in terms of several BASIC statements. A program is simply a collection of statements. The process of selecting and arranging the statements is what programming is all about.

This chapter teaches you how to write your own BASIC programs on the ATARI computer. We could have you first memorize all the facts about each BASIC statement, one by one. But you would probably give up.

Individual statements don't mean much; it's the way you combine them. A study of individual BASIC statements quickly degenerates into learning a bunch of seemingly arbitrary rules. That tells you nothing about programming or good programming practice.

The rigorous statement definitions appear in Chapter 11. This chapter presents BASIC statements in a logical sequence. You see each new statement in a working environment, not an academic one. Look up the complete details and subtleties of individual statements in Chapter 11 when you need to, but do not try to learn programming there.

STARTING UP BASIC

There are at least three different versions of BASIC available on the ATARI computer. This book covers only the standard version shipped with the ATARI 400 and ATARI 800 computers. It resides in the ROM cartridge labeled "BASIC

Computing Language," part number CXL4002. Other versions of BASIC will be similar to standard ATARI BASIC but will differ in details.

Installing the BASIC ROM Cartridge

The ATARI computer is quite versatile. Besides knowing BASIC, it can play games, compose music, tutor, and more. If you wish to program it in standard ATARI BASIC, the "BASIC Computing Language" ROM cartridge must be installed. You will find complete instructions for installing the cartridge in Chapter 2 (Figure 2-1).

Turning On the Power

Chapter 2 also tells you the proper order in which to turn on the various system components. The ATARI computer is definitely particular about that. The console may not be able to communicate properly with the external components if you turn them on in the wrong sequence. BASIC is ready to go when you see the message **READY** displayed on the TV screen.

LEAVING BASIC

To get the ATARI computer out of BASIC, just remove the BASIC ROM cartridge. During the process, the computer turns itself off. This erases any BASIC program you might have been using.

Another way to leave BASIC is to type the command BYE and press RETURN. The computer goes into memo pad mode. It isn't very useful in this mode; it merely displays whatever you type. Press the SYSTEM RESET key to get back into BASIC.

PRINTING CHARACTERS

When you first start BASIC, it is in *immediate mode,* also called direct or calculator mode. In this mode, the computer responds immediately to any instruction you issue it. Try typing in this example:

```
PRINT "LET SLEEPING DOGS LIE"
```

Don't forget to press the RETURN key after the last quotation mark. The computer immediately displays this:

```
LET SLEEPING DOGS LIE

READY
▓
```

The computer may instead display the message **ERROR-** followed by what you typed in. This means it cannot understand your command. You probably misspelled the word PRINT. If the computer displays the number 0 instead of any message, it means you left out the first quotation mark. In either case, you can simply type the instruction again, being more careful this time. Computers are extremely particular about spelling and punctuation. Even the slightest error can cause the computer to balk, or even worse, to do the wrong thing.

A command like the one above instructs the computer to print everything between the quotation marks onto the display screen.

There is a limit to the length of the message you can put between quotation marks. The longest message can be wider than the display screen. This means a command can occupy more than one display line. Long commands automatically *wrap around* to the next lower line on the display screen. Type this, and press RETURN:

```
PRINT "UNDER NORMAL CIRCUMSTANCES, THE
 MAN WOULD BE CONSIDERED CRAZY"
```

The computer responds with this:

```
UNDER NORMAL CIRCUMSTANCES, THE MAN WO
ULD BE CONSIDERED CRAZY

READY
▓
```

ATARI BASIC allows 114 characters on a single command line. This is exactly three display lines. As you approach the limit, the computer beeps. The limit includes the PRINT command and punctuation. Anything you type past the limit is ignored when you press the RETURN key to end the line.

PRINTING CALCULATIONS

You can use the ATARI computer in immediate mode as you would a calculator; it responds directly with the answers to arithmetic calculations. Try the following examples:

```
PRINT 4+6            Addition
10

READY                Subtraction
PRINT 500-437
63

READY                Multiplication
PRINT 100*23
2300

READY                Division
PRINT 96/12
8

READY                Exponentiation
PRINT 3^2
8.99999988           Atari, Inc. is revising BASIC so that errors such as this will not occur
```

```
READY                   Combination
PRINT 3*4*10-800
-680

READY
※
```

The correct answers are on the line immediately following each of the commands. Notice that you do not use quotation marks in these examples. Enclose a calculation in quotation marks and watch what happens.

Numeric values can have a total of nine *significant digits.* Values with more than nine digits are *truncated* (chopped off) to nine or fewer nonzero digits. The limit applies to the total number of digits before and after the decimal point. The following examples illustrate how the truncation works:

```
PRINT 12.34567896
12.3456789

READY
PRINT 12.34567894
12.3456789

READY
PRINT 1234567895
1234567890

READY
※
```

If you try some of your own arithmetic calculations in immediate mode, you will notice that the result is sometimes displayed using scientific notation.

```
PRINT 123456789123
1.23456789E+11

READY
※
```

If you do not understand scientific notation, stick to simple calculations for now. We will talk more about scientific notation and numeric values later in this chapter.

Abbreviated PRINT Statement

ATARI BASIC allows you to abbreviate the PRINT statement with a question mark (?). Here are some examples you can try:

```
?"TIME MARCHES ON"
TIME MARCHES ON

READY
?13-46*6
-263

READY
※
```

ERROR MESSAGES

One message the ATARI computer will issue when it detects a situation it cannot cope with was mentioned earlier in this chapter. It displays **ERROR-** followed by the offending instruction. There is also a slightly different form of error message. When the ATARI computer thinks it knows what kind of error occurred, it displays a diagnostic error number. Consider division by 0:

```
?1/0

ERROR-     11
※
```

The official translation of error number 11 is "Floating point overflow/underflow error." In other words, dividing by 0 yields a value too large for the computer to handle.

Getting an error number helps. You still have to look up the number in Appendix A for an interpretation, but at least you have some clue as to what went wrong. Unfortunately, the computer's diagnostic abilities are limited. One error number can apply to several different situations, so do not expect a definitive analysis of your error. The ATARI computer uses fewer than 60 error numbers to diagnose the myriad of possible errors and combinations of errors.

EXTRA SPACES

Are you struggling with the question of where to put spaces in a line and where not to? ATARI BASIC is somewhat sensitive on the subject. Your best bet is to mimic the style we use in our examples. ATARI BASIC requires blank spaces in some places. Generally, you should put a blank space wherever it tends to make the line more readable. Use only one space, though. In a few instances, multiple blanks trip up BASIC. There is one place where the use of blank spaces is entirely your choice: inside PRINT statement quotation marks. If you come across a situation in which you are not sure where to put spaces, go ahead and type the line. The worst that will happen is that you will get an error message and will have to retype the line.

STATEMENTS, LINES, AND PROGRAMS

A program consists of one or more statements which provide the computer with an exact and complete definition of the task it is to perform. If the task is short and simple, the program can be short and simple as well. The immediate mode instructions we have experimented with so far are each small, simple programs. Each one has just one statement — one instruction to the computer. These are trivial cases. Most programs have 10, 100, 1000, or even more statements. Consider the following statements:

```
PRINT "COWS MOO"
COWS MOO
```

```
READY
PRINT "FOR FANCY BLUE"
FOR FANCY BLUE

READY
PRINT "HOOF-B-NU"
HOOF-B-NU

READY
※
```

Each of these immediate mode programs prints a line of text on the display screen. Each program has exactly one statement and exactly one line.

ATARI BASIC allows you to put more than one statement on a line. You separate multiple statements on the same line with a colon. Compare the following immediate mode program with the example above:

```
PRINT "COWS MOO":PRINT "FOR FANCY BLUE
":PRINT "HOOF-B-NU"
COWS MOO
FOR FANCY BLUE
HOOF-B-NU

READY
※
```

This three-statement, one-line program prints the same three lines of text as the previous three single-statement programs.

Program, Logical, and Physical Lines

There is no specific limit to the number of statements on one program line. Remember that a line cannot be longer than 114 characters, though. If you are typing a long line, the computer will beep when you type the 107th character. You are approaching the limit. Anything you type past the limit is ignored; errors are likely. So there is a limit to how much you can do with a one-line immediate mode program.

The ATARI computer treats every program line as a single line, even if it occupies more than one display line. A program line is one example of a *logical line*. The shortest logical line has one character. Normally, the longest line has 114 characters (Chapter 4 explains how to extend this to 120 characters). Thus, each logical line is made up of one, two, or three *physical lines*. Pressing the RETURN key marks the end of the logical line.

A One-Line Program

You can put quite a lot of program on one line in immediate mode. For example, consider the following statements:

```
FOR I=1 TO 722:?"A";:NEXT I:?"PHEW!"
```

At this point, don't worry what these new instructions do. Type in the line exactly as shown, ending with a RETURN. If you type it in successfully, you will see the letter **A** displayed across the next 19 lines of the display screen, followed by the message **PHEW!** on the 20th line.

```
FOR I=1 TO 722:?"A";:NEXT I:?"PHEW!"
AAAAAAAAAAAAAAAAAAAAAAAAAAAAAAAAAAAAAAAA
AAAAAAAAAAAAAAAAAAAAAAAAAAAAAAAAAAAAAAAA
AAAAAAAAAAAAAAAAAAAAAAAAAAAAAAAAAAAAAAAA
AAAAAAAAAAAAAAAAAAAAAAAAAAAAAAAAAAAAAAAA
AAAAAAAAAAAAAAAAAAAAAAAAAAAAAAAAAAAAAAAA
AAAAAAAAAAAAAAAAAAAAAAAAAAAAAAAAAAAAAAAA
AAAAAAAAAAAAAAAAAAAAAAAAAAAAAAAAAAAAAAAA
AAAAAAAAAAAAAAAAAAAAAAAAAAAAAAAAAAAAAAAA
AAAAAAAAAAAAAAAAAAAAAAAAAAAAAAAAAAAAAAAA
AAAAAAAAAAAAAAAAAAAAAAAAAAAAAAAAAAAAAAAA
AAAAAAAAAAAAAAAAAAAAAAAAAAAAAAAAAAAAAAAA
AAAAAAAAAAAAAAAAAAAAAAAAAAAAAAAAAAAAAAAA
AAAAAAAAAAAAAAAAAAAAAAAAAAAAAAAAAAAAAAAA
AAAAAAAAAAAAAAAAAAAAAAAAAAAAAAAAAAAAAAAA
AAAAAAAAAAAAAAAAAAAAAAAAAAAAAAAAAAAAAAAA
AAAAAAAAAAAAAAAAAAAAAAAAAAAAAAAAAAAAAAAA
AAAAAAAAAAAAAAAAAAAAAAAAAAAAAAAAAAAAAAAA
AAAAAAAAAAAAAAAAAAAAAAAAAAAAAAAAAAAAAAAA
PHEW!

READY
※
```

The program line is still conveniently displayed at the top of the screen. This is because the program displays just enough characters to scroll the program line to the top of the 38-column screen, but not off the screen.

When the one-line program described above is finished, the **READY** message and cursor are displayed at the bottom of the screen.

PROGRAMMED MODE

The programming we have done so far is educational and somewhat interesting, but there is only so much you can do in immediate mode. Another problem with immediate mode programs is that you have to retype the program each time you want to use it. There are some advanced editing techniques which will be discussed shortly that will allow you to reuse the program as long as it still appears on the display screen, but this is still a limitation.

What you need is a way to enter several program lines and to hold off using those lines. That way you can write programs to do tasks that are too complex for one-line programs.

There is a way to get around the problems of immediate mode: you can write programs in *programmed mode,* also called deferred or indirect mode. In programmed mode, the computer accepts and stores the program in its memory, but does not perform any of the operations specified by the program until you tell it to do so. You can enter as many program lines as you wish. Then, when you enter the appropriate command, the computer performs the operations specified by the programmed mode program.

Program Execution

The computer *executes,* or *runs,* a program when it performs the operations that the program specifies. In immediate mode each program line is executed as soon as you press the RETURN key. In programmed mode you must issue the RUN command to execute a program. Each time you do so, the program runs again.

Clearing Out Old Programs

Because the ATARI computer stores programmed mode programs in its memory, you must specifically instruct it to erase an old program before you type in a new program. Do this by typing the command NEW. If you forget to type NEW, your new program will be mixed in with your old program.

Ending Programs Properly

The end of an immediate mode program is obvious. This is not the case with programmed mode, as you will soon see. The END statement tells BASIC to stop executing your program and return to immediate mode. Therefore, an END statement should be the last statement your program executes. ATARI BASIC does not require an END statement. It will end a program automatically when it runs out of instructions. Nevertheless, careful programmers always end their programs with an END statement.

Line Numbers

Line numbers make programmed mode possible. A line number is simply a one-, two-, three-, four-, or five-digit number entered at the beginning of a program line. The line number is the only difference between a programmed mode program line and an immediate mode program line.

Try the following programmed mode program:

```
NEW

READY
10 PRINT "RUBBER BABY BUGGY BUMPERS"
20 END
RUN
RUBBER BABY BUGGY BUMPERS

READY
▓
```

Each line number must be unique. No two program lines can have the same number. If you use the same line number more than once, the computer remembers only the

most recently entered program line with that line number. To see how this works,
type in the following program lines:

```
NEW

READY
10 PRINT "FIRST LINE 10"
10 PRINT "SECOND LINE 10"
20 END
RUN
SECOND LINE 10

READY
▓
```

Line numbers determine the sequence of program lines in a BASIC program. The
first line must have the smallest line number, while the last line must have the largest
line number. Even if you type in the lines out of order, the ATARI computer will
rearrange them in the proper sequence by line number. Consider the following
program, with line numbers out of order:

```
NEW

READY
30 PRINT "CUT"
10 PRINT "FISH"
20 PRINT "OR"
40 PRINT "BAIT"
50 END
RUN
FISH
OR
CUT
BAIT

READY
▓
```

To prove that the ATARI computer does not forget programmed mode programs, clear the display screen with the CLEAR key (CTRL-<) and then rerun the
program.

```
RUN
FISH
OR
CUT
BAIT

READY
▓
```

It is a simple matter to add program lines to a program that is currently in the
computer's memory. You can add a line to the beginning, the end, or anywhere in
the middle of a program by typing the line with a line number that will position it

where you want it. Suppose you want to add a line to the beginning of the last
example program. As long as you have not typed the command NEW, the program
will still be in the computer's memory. Since the lowest line number currently in that
program is 10, any program line you type in now with a line number less than 10 will
be placed at the beginning of the program. Add the following line:

```
5 PRINT "EITHER"
RUN
EITHER
FISH
OR
CUT
BAIT

READY
▓
```

It's a good thing the original program started with line 10 rather than line 0. It's
always a good idea when assigning line numbers to start your program with a fairly
high line number and leave plenty of room between line numbers so you can add
program lines later.

Multiple-Statement Program Lines

You can put more than one statement on a single program line. The first statement
follows the line number. The second statement follows the first, with a colon
between the two statements. Keep in mind that a single program line cannot exceed
114 characters.

Listing Program Lines

You can see what program lines the computer has stored in its memory by typing the
command LIST. Try it right now. If you have not typed NEW or turned off the
machine since you tried the last example, you should see the following program
lines displayed on the screen:

```
LIST

5 PRINT "EITHER
10 PRINT "FISH"
20 PRINT "OR"
30 PRINT "CUT"
40 PRINT "BAIT"
50 END

READY
▓
```

This is called a program listing. There are variations of the LIST command which
allow you to list one line at a time or a group of lines. The latter option is especially
handy when you have a long program that will not fit on the display screen all at

once. With the last example program still in the computer's memory, typing the
command LIST 10 causes program line 10 to appear on the display screen:

```
LIST 10

10 PRINT "FISH"

READY
※
```

To list several sequential program lines, you must specify both the starting and
ending line number, as in this example:

```
LIST 20,40

20 PRINT "OR"
30 PRINT "CUT"
40 PRINT "BAIT"

READY
※
```

In ATARI BASIC, you can list all program lines up to and including a specific
program line. You can also list all program lines from a specific program line up to
the end of the program. Here are examples of those two versions of the LIST
command:

```
LIST 0,10

5 PRINT "EITHER"
10 PRINT "FISH"

READY
LIST 30,32767

30 PRINT "CUT"
40 PRINT "BAIT"
50 END

READY
※
```

Interrupting a Listing

You can halt a listing before it reaches the end by pressing the BREAK key. This is
especially useful for aborting the interminable listing of a long program.

You can temporarily freeze the listing of a program by typing CTRL-1. The listing
will resume when you type CTRL-1 again. CTRL-1 allows you to review the listing of a
long program at your own pace.

LOADING AND SAVING PROGRAMS

The ATARI 410 Program Recorder enables you to save a programmed mode
program outside the main computer and later load that program back into memory.

Suppose you have the following program in memory:

```
10 ? "FILLET OF FENNY SNAKE,"
20 ? "IN THE CAULDRON BOIL AND BAKE"
30 ? "EYE OF NEWT AND TOE OF FROG,"
40 ? "WOOL OF BAT AND TONGUE OF DOG,"
50 ? "ADDER'S FORK AND BLIND-WORM'S ST
ING"
60 ? "LIZARD'S LEG AND HOWLET'S WING,"

70 ? "FOR A CHARM OF POW'RFUL TROUBLE,
"
80 ? "LIKE A HELL-BROTH BOIL AND BUBBL
E."
90 ? "DOUBLE, DOUBLE, TOIL AND TROUBLE
;"
100 ? "FIRE BURN AND CAULDRON BUBBLE."

110 END
```

To save this program, put a tape in the program recorder. Enter the following command at the keyboard:

```
CSAVE
```

The computer beeps twice. Rewind the tape to the beginning, then simultaneously press the RECORD and PLAY levers on the program recorder. Press any key on the keyboard, except the BREAK key. The tape starts to move. If the volume on the television set is turned up, you will hear 20 seconds of a continuous high-pitched tone. This will be followed by one or more short bursts of sound from the television speaker. The sound bursts cease when the recording finishes. The tape stops.

At this point type NEW to erase the program from the computer's memory. Then type LIST to verify that it is gone.

To load the program into the computer from the tape, enter the following command at the keyboard:

```
CLOAD
```

The computer beeps once. Rewind the tape to the beginning. Depress the PLAY lever on the program recorder. Then press any key on the keyboard, except the BREAK key. The tape starts moving. If the volume on the television set is turned up, you will hear several seconds of silence followed by one or more short bursts of sound from the television speaker. These sounds indicate the program is loading. The sound bursts cease when the loading finishes. The tape stops. Use the LIST command to verify that the program is in memory.

Chapter 5 explores other ways to save and load programs on cassette. Chapter 7 explains how to save programs on diskette, which is even more convenient than cassette tape.

Saving Multiple Programs on One Tape

You may have noticed that it did not take very much tape to save the example program. A longer program would require more tape, but there is usually enough tape on one cassette to hold several BASIC programs. You can save programs sequentially on the tape: the second follows the first, the third follows the second, and so on.

Loading the second, third, and subsequent programs on a cassette is not as straightforward as loading the first. After you rewind the tape to the beginning, you must get past the first program in order to load the second, past the second to load the third, and so on. You can do this by typing the CLOAD command repeatedly until the program you want is in memory. This is a slow process, but it works.

You can speed things up considerably by using the program recorder's tape counter. Reset the tape counter to 0 when you rewind the tape to the beginning before saving a program. After saving the first program, jot down the tape counter reading. This is the starting tape counter reading for the second program. Save the second program and note the tape counter reading at the end of it (for the start of the third program).

To load the second program, rewind the tape to the beginning and reset the tape counter to 0. Then use the FAST FORWARD lever on the program recorder to position the tape counter to the reading for the start of the second program. You can use the REWIND lever on the program recorder to back the tape up if you overshoot with the FAST FORWARD lever. Now use the CLOAD command to get the second program.

ADVANCED EDITING TECHNIQUES

Chapter 2 examined ways to correct typing mistakes before pressing the RETURN key. Here is a quick summary of those simple editing techniques:

- The BACK S key backspaces the cursor and erases characters it passes over. Characters are replaced by blank spaces.
- The ← key moves the cursor one space to the left on the current display line without erasing the character it passes over.
- The → key moves the cursor one space to the right on the current display line without erasing the character it passes over.
- The TAB key moves the cursor right to the next tab stop, without erasing any characters it passes over.
- The BREAK key cancels the line you're currently typing.
- The CLEAR key clears the display screen and leaves the cursor in the upper left corner.

These simple editing techniques are useful in both immediate mode and programmed mode. Let's take a look at some other editing techniques. These new methods are particularly useful when you want to make changes to programmed mode lines.

DELETING PROGRAM LINES

To delete an entire line, type its line number and then press the RETURN key. When you list the program, you will see that the line and line number are no longer part of the program. Here is an example:

```
NEW

READY
100 PRINT "VIRTUE IS ITS OWN REWARD"
110 PRINT "IF THE SHOE FITS, WEAR IT"
120 PRINT "WHERE THERE'S SMOKE, THERE'
S FIRE"
130 PRINT "LOOK BEFORE YOU LEAP"
140 PRINT "BREVITY IS THE SOUL OF WIT"

150 END
110
130
LIST

100 PRINT "VIRTUE IS ITS OWN REWARD"
120 PRINT "WHERE THERE'S SMOKE, THERE'
S FIRE"
140 PRINT "BREVITY IS THE SOUL OF WIT"

150 END

READY
▓
```

ADDING PROGRAM LINES

You can type in new program lines in any order, at any time, in immediate mode. Their line numbers will determine their position in the program. The ATARI computer will merge them automatically with any other program lines currently in memory. Try adding line 110 back into the example above.

```
110 PRINT "IF THE SHOE FITS, WEAR IT"
LIST

100 PRINT "VIRTUE IS ITS OWN REWARD"
110 PRINT "IF THE SHOE FITS, WEAR IT"
120 PRINT "WHERE THERE'S SMOKE, THERE'
S FIRE"
140 PRINT "BREVITY IS THE SOUL OF WIT"

150 END

READY
▓
```

CHANGING PROGRAM LINES

The simplest way to change a program line is to retype it. This is unsatisfactory for several reasons. Retyping is a time-consuming chore and the chances of typographical errors are high. Fortunately, there is a way to modify program lines you have already entered into the computer's memory. This is possible because anything displayed on the screen is *live.* You can edit anything on the screen. By using the CTRL key in conjunction with several other keys, you can move the cursor around on the screen at will. This allows you to position the cursor at any point on any line that is displayed on the screen. Then you can replace, insert, or delete characters as you like.

Listing the Line to Edit

In order to edit anything, whether it is an immediate or programmed mode program line, or the response to a question asked by the computer, it must be visible on the display screen. In the case of an immediate mode line, if it's not visible, you're out of luck. You'll have to retype it. But you can redisplay programmed mode lines with the LIST statement. Simply specify starting and ending line numbers for a screen-sized section of the program. If you list too much, stop the listing with the BREAK key while the line you want to change is still on the screen. It doesn't matter how a line gets on the screen; once it's there, you can change it.

Moving the Cursor

There are seven keys that move the cursor. The BACK S, →, ←, and TAB keys have already been discussed. The space bar is another. It acts just like the → key, except it replaces every character the cursor passes over with a blank space. The ↑ and ↓ keys were mentioned in Chapter 2. The ↑ key moves the cursor up one display line at a time. When the cursor reaches the top of the screen, the ↑ key circles it around to the bottom line. Conversely, the ↓ key moves the cursor down one display line at a time. When the cursor reaches the bottom of the screen, the ↓ key circles it around to the top line.

Making Changes Permanent

You must press RETURN to effect the changes you make to a program line. The changes do not remain in effect if you simply move the cursor to another program line with the arrow keys. In that case the changes only affect the picture on the display screen. The cursor can be anywhere on the program line when you press the RETURN key. Even if the program line uses more than one display line, you can press RETURN with the cursor anywhere on the line.

Canceling Changes

There are three ways to cancel changes you've made. These only cancel changes you've made since you last pressed RETURN. They are

- · Press the BREAK key until the cursor is out of the program line
- · Use the arrow keys to move the cursor out of the program line
- · Press the CLEAR key (CTRL- <) to clear the screen display.

Replacing Characters

Replacing one character with another is simplicity itself. Merely position the cursor on the character you wish to replace, and type the replacement right over it. For example, with the cursor like this

```
100 ? "ESTIMATED TIME OF ARRIVAL."
```

you can type the characters DEPARTURE" and get this:

```
100 ? "ESTIMATED TIME OF DEPARTURE" ▓
```

Press RETURN to effect the change.

Deleting Characters

There are three ways to delete characters one at a time. You can position the cursor over the character you want to remove and press the DELETE key (CTRL-BACK S). The entire program line shifts one space left to fill the void. The character disappears. For example, with the cursor like this

```
10 PRINT "OUT, DAMNED SPOT! OUT, I STR
AY!"
```

press the DELETE key (CTRL-BACK S) twice and you will get the following:

```
10 PRINT "OUT, DAMNED SPOT! OUT, I SAY
!"
```

The BACK S key and space bar also delete characters. They both replace the old character with a blank space. BACK S moves the cursor left as it erases; the space bar moves it right.

Inserting Characters

To insert characters, you must first insert blank spaces. Then you can type other characters over the inserted spaces. Use the INSERT key (CTRL->) to insert blank spaces. Each space you insert moves the rest of the entire program line one space to the right. If this pushes the last character of the program line past the end of the display line, a new display line is appended to the program line. Consider this situation:

```
10 PRINT "PRICE PER POUND▮
20 PRINT "NUMBER OF POUNDS"
30 PRINT "TOTAL PRICE"
```

To add some text to the end of line 10, first press INSERT (CTRL->) 21 times:

```
10 PRINT "PRICE PER POUND ▓
        "
20 PRINT "NUMBER OF POUNDS"
30 PRINT "TOTAL PRICE"
```

Notice that a new display line opens up between program lines 10 and 20. Now type in the new text:

```
10 PRINT "PRICE PER POUND, WEST OF THE
   ROCKIES▓
20 PRINT "NUMBER OF POUNDS"
30 PRINT "TOTAL PRICE"
```

Press RETURN to finalize the change.

Automatic Repeat

Hold almost any key down for a few seconds and it automatically repeats. Use this feature to speed up your editing work.

REEXECUTING IN IMMEDIATE MODE

The fact that anything on the display screen is live allows you to reexecute any immediate mode statements that are still visible on the display screen. You can reexecute an immediate mode statement just as it is, or you can edit it first.

In either case, the first thing to do is position the cursor somewhere on the immediate mode line. Use the arrow keys (CTRL--, CTRL-=, CTRL-+, and CTRL-*). You can now make changes to the line using the techniques just described for replacing, deleting, and inserting characters on a line. Then, with the cursor still on the immediate mode line, press RETURN. The line executes.

To see how this works, look at the following immediate mode program which calculates the cubic feet of storage space in a $10 \times 25 \times 8$ foot room:

```
PRINT "CU. FT. OF SPACE = ";10*25*8
CU. FT. OF SPACE = 2000

READY
▓
```

You can easily change this immediate mode program to calculate the storage space in rooms of different sizes. To change the dimensions to $10 \times 25 \times 14$, for example, first position the cursor at the beginning of the immediate mode line (press CTRL-- four times). Now press and hold the → key (CTRL-*). The cursor will fast-forward along the immediate mode line. Release both keys in time to stop the cursor when it gets to the digit 8. If you overshoot or undershoot by not releasing the keys at the proper time, you can move the cursor back and forth one character at a time with the ← and → keys. For that matter, you could move the cursor from the start of the line to the 8 by pressing the → key 34 times, instead of using the automatic repeat feature. Still another alternative is to press the TAB key four times and the ← key three times. Get the cursor there any way you like.

With the cursor positioned over the 8, type in the new room dimension of 14 and press RETURN.

```
PRINT "CU. FT. OF SPACE = ";10*25*14
CU. FT. OF SPACE = 3500

READY
▓
```

PROGRAMMING LANGUAGES

A programming language is the means of communication between you and the computer. There are many different programming languages. Some, like BASIC, are general purpose languages, while others are designed to make it easy to write programs in specific areas such as business, science, graphics, text manipulation, and so forth. Programming languages are as varied as spoken languages. In addition to BASIC, other common programming languages include FORTRAN, Pascal, C, COBOL, APL, PL/M, PL-1, and FORTH.

ATARI computers can use several programming languages, BASIC and FORTH among them. This book concentrates on describing how to program the ATARI computers in BASIC.

No matter what the programming language, every program statement must be written following a well-defined set of rules. These rules taken together are referred to as *syntax*. Each programming language has its own syntax.

Programming languages, like spoken languages, have *dialects*. Dialects manifest themselves as minor variations in syntax. The ATARI computer has several such dialects of BASIC. Standard ATARI BASIC (shipped with the ATARI 400/800 computer) and Microsoft BASIC are available from Atari. BASIC A+ is available from Optimized Systems Software. Very often, programs written in one dialect will not work correctly when the ATARI computer is expecting instructions in another dialect; this is especially true of Microsoft BASIC. Furthermore, a BASIC program written for the ATARI computer may not run on another computer, even if the other computer also claims to be programmable in BASIC. However, having learned how to program your ATARI computer in any of its BASIC dialects, you will have little trouble learning any other dialect of BASIC.

Some programming language syntax rules are obvious. The addition and subtraction examples at the beginning of this chapter use syntax that is familiar to everyone. You do not have to be a programmer to understand them. But most syntax rules seem completely arbitrary and meaningless until you have learned the syntax. You should not try to seek a rationale for syntax rules; usually there is none. For example, why use an asterisk (*) to represent multiplication? Normally, you would use a cross (×) for multiplication. But the computer would have no way of differentiating between the use of "×" to represent multiplication or to represent the letter "X." Therefore, nearly all computer languages have opted for * to represent multiplication. Division is universally represented by the / sign. There is no special reason for this selection; the division sign (÷) is not present on computer keyboards, so some other character had to be selected.

ELEMENTS OF BASIC

Most of the syntax rules for BASIC concern individual statements. BASIC statement syntax deals separately with its three major elements: line numbers, data, and instructions to the computer. We will describe each in turn. There are also a few rules that pertain to the program as a whole, such as statement order. These rules will be covered in appropriate places throughout the chapter.

LINE NUMBERS REVISITED

We have already talked about line numbers to some extent. After a brief review, we will go into more detail. In programmed mode, every line of a BASIC program must have a unique line number. Line numbers determine the sequence of instructions in a program; the statement with the lowest line number is first and the statement with the highest line number is last.

Standard ATARI BASIC allows one- to five-digit line numbers with integer values between 0 and 32767.

Line Numbers as Addresses

In essence, line numbers are a way of addressing program lines. This is an important concept, since every program will contain two types of statements:

· Statements that create or modify data, and
· Statements that control the order in which operations are performed.

Clearly, the things a program does must happen in a specific, reliable order. What good would it do if the computer executed instructions at random? Normally, program execution begins with the first statement in the program and continues sequentially (Figure 3-1). Most programs, however, have some non-sequential execution sequences. That is when line numbers become important. You can instruct the computer not to execute the next line, but instead to go to a different line number and continue execution there (Figure 3-2).

DATA

The main business of computer programs is to input, manipulate, and output data. Therefore, the way a programming language handles data, whether it be numbers or text, is very important. Will will now explore the types of data you may encounter in an ATARI BASIC program.

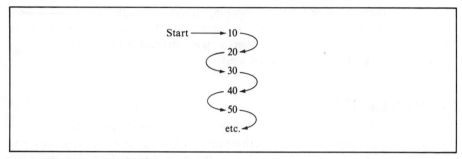

FIGURE 3-1. Sequential program execution

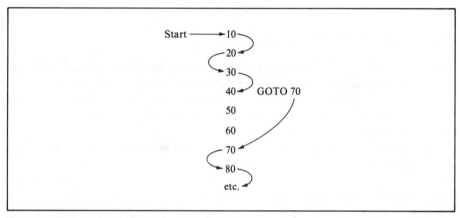

FIGURE 3-2. Non-sequential program execution

Strings

A *string* is any character or sequence of characters enclosed in quotation marks. We have already used strings with the PRINT statement as messages to be displayed on the screen. Here are some more examples of strings:

"IGNORANCE IS BLISS"

"ACCOUNT 4019-181-324-837"

"NICK CHARLES"

"SAM & ELLA CAFE"

"MARCH 18, 1956"

There is no specific limit to string length. In immediate mode, strings must fit on one program line. In Chapter 4 a way to combine strings in programmed mode will be presented. In this mode the only length restriction is imposed by the amount of memory available. A string with no characters in it is called the *null string* or *empty string*.

Most string characters are produced by typing at the keyboard. To get some characters, you just press the right key. If you want a 3, press the 3 key. Other characters may require the SHIFT, CTRL, CAPS/LOWR, or ⅄ keys, as described in Chapter 2. Appendix D lists all the ATARI BASIC string characters and tells you which key or combination of keys produces each one.

Non-Keyboard Characters

Press some keys, and characters appear on the display screen. Generally, the characters you see are the characters the string gets. This is not the case with some exotic characters, though. For example, the arrow keys (CTRL--, CTRL-= , CTRL-+ and CTRL-*) move the cursor around. These cursor movement "characters" are not part of the string. Chapter 4 describes a way to make them a part of a string value.

Non-Character Keys

Some keys cannot produce string characters under any circumstances. For example, RETURN always ends the line you're typing. Other such keys are BREAK, SYSTEM RESET, SHIFT, CTRL, and CAPS/LOWR.

Numbers

BASIC stores all numbers in the ATARI computer's memory with a decimal point. The decimal point is not fixed; there can be any number of digits on either side of it. If the number has no fractional part, the decimal point is assumed after the last digit. Numbers expressed in this way are called *floating point numbers*. The name refers to the decimal point's ability to float, accommodating fractions with different numbers of digits.

You must express all numbers without commas. For example, you must use 32000, not 32,000.

Integers

An *integer* is a number that has no fractional portion or decimal point. The number can be negative (-) or positive (+). An unsigned number is assumed to be positive. ATARI BASIC treats integers the same as it treats any other floating point numbers; there is no separate class of integers. The following numbers are integers:

        0
        1
       44
    32699
      -15

Floating Point Numbers

A floating point number can be an integer, a number with a decimal fraction, or just a decimal fraction. The number can be negative (-) or positive (+). If the number has no sign it is assumed to be positive.

Here are some examples of floating point numbers:

```
    5
  -15
65000
  161
    0
    0.5
    0.0165432
   -0.0000009
    1.6
   24.0055
  -64.2
```

Scientific Notation

Very large and very small floating point numbers are represented in ATARI BASIC using *scientific notation*. Any number that has more than ten digits in front of the decimal point will be expressed in scientific notation. Any fractional number closer to 0 than ±0.01 will be expressed in scientific notation.

A number in scientific notation has the following format:

± *number* E ± *ee*

where

±	is an optional plus sign or minus sign.
number	is an integer, fraction, or combination. The *number* portion contains the number's significant digits; it is called the *coefficient* or *mantissa*. If no decimal point appears, it is assumed to be to the right of the coefficient.
E	is always the letter E. It stands for exponent.
±	is an optional plus sign or minus sign.
ee	is a one- or two-digit exponent. The exponent specifies the magnitude of the number, that is, the number of places to the right (positive exponent) or to the left (negative exponent) that the decimal point must be moved to give the true decimal point location.

Here are some examples of scientific notation compared to the same value in standard notation:

Standard Notation	Scientific Notation
1000000000	1E+09
0.000000001	1E-09
200	2E+02
- 12345678900	-1.23456789E+10
-0.00000123456789	-1.23456789E-06

As you can see, scientific notation is a convenient way of expressing very large and very small numbers.

Number Ranges

The smallest (most negative) floating point number is -9.99999999E+97. The largest floating point number is 9.99999999E+97. When a fractional number gets closer to zero than ±9.99999999E-98 it will be converted to 0.

Roundoff

It was mentioned earlier in this chapter that floating point numbers can have nine significant digits, but no more. For a number greater than 1 or less than -1, this means only the leftmost nine digits can be nonzero. The ATARI computer replaces any digits in excess of 9 with zeros. Here are some examples (note that large numbers print in scientific notation):

```
PRINT 12345678989
1.23456789E+10

READY
?-123456789123456789
-1.23456789E+17

READY
?-150000475.75
-150000475

READY
?90000000.7558
90000000.7

READY
※
```

Fractional numbers between 1 and -1 are subject to the same limitation. In this case, though, the nine significant digits start with the first nonzero digit to the right of the decimal point. Here are some examples:

```
PRINT .1234567899
0.123456789

READY
?-.123456789123456789
-0.123456789

READY
?-123456789.123456789
-123456789

READY
?.000000000900000007558
9.00000007E-10

READY
※
```

VARIABLES

Our discussions of data thus far have only considered constant values. It is often more convenient to refer to data items by name rather than value. *Variables* are used for this purpose.

If you have studied elementary algebra, you will have no trouble understanding the concept of variables and variable names. If you have never studied algebra, then think of a variable name as a name which is assigned to a letter box (Figure 3-3). Anything which is placed in the letter box becomes the value associated with the letter box name, until something new is placed in the letter box. In computer jargon, we say a value is *stored* in a variable.

A variable does not always have to refer to the same value. This is the real power of variables — they can represent any legal value. You can change a variable's value during the course of a program. BASIC has a number of statements that do this; they will be described later.

Variable Names

Variable names can have from as many characters as will fit on a program line. The first character must be a capital letter. The rest of the characters in the variable name can be any digit or capital letter. You must end string variable names with a dollar sign, but not numeric variable names. Figure 3-4 illustrates these rules.

String Variables

Before you use a string variable, you must specify the maximum length it can have. You do this with the DIM statement, which we will describe later. If you fail to do so, an error occurs when the variable is referenced.

String variables can refer to strings of any length. The only limit is the amount of memory available when the variable is used. Blank spaces in a string count toward its total length. Blank spaces at the end of a string, called *trailing blanks,* count too.

Here are some string variable names, legal and illegal:

Legal	Illegal
A$	$
CUSTNAME$	9$
PART1$	BRAND.NAME$
RESPONSE$	a$
X8$	Name$

Numeric Variables

Numeric variables can have integer values or floating point values. Numeric values are restricted to the range -10^{97} to $+10^{97}$. If you attempt to store a value that is too large in magnitude in a numeric variable, an error occurs. When the value of a floating point variable gets closer to 0 than $\pm 9.99999999 \times 10^{-98}$ ATARI BASIC converts it to 0.

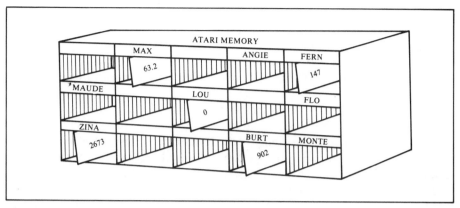

FIGURE 3-3. Variables

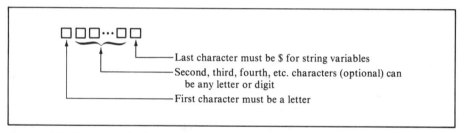

FIGURE 3-4. Naming variables

Here are some numeric variable names in ATARI BASIC, both legal and illegal:

Legal	Illegal
A	APPLICANT'SAGE
CUSTZIPCODE	3X4Z
X0	$TOTAL
PARTNO	Score

Arrays

Arrays are really nothing more than a systematic way of naming a large number of variables. They are used frequently in many types of computer programs. If you do not understand what arrays are, or how to use them, then read on. The information that follows will be very important to your programming efforts.

Conceptually, arrays are very simple things. When you have two or more data items, instead of giving each data item a separate variable name, you give the collection of data items a single variable name. The collection is called an *array;* its name is an *array name.* Individual data items are often called *array elements.* The elements in an array are numbered. You select an individual item using its position number, which is referred to as its *index.*

Arrays in standard ATARI BASIC can represent only numeric values. Chapter 4 explains a way to simulate string arrays.

Arrays are a useful shorthand means of describing a large number of related variables. Consider, for example, a table of 200 numbers. How would you like to assign a unique variable name to each of the 200 numbers? It would be far simpler to give the entire table one name, and identify individual numbers in the table by their location within the table. That is precisely what an array does for you.

As an example of array usage, consider how you might keep track of individual scores in a bowling tournament. There could be a separate variable name for each bowler (Figure 3-5). This has one advantage: the variable names can be similar to the bowlers' names. But what happens at the next tournament, where the bowlers have different names?

How about keeping the scores in an array (Figure 3-6)? Now your program doesn't care which variable name refers to which bowler. We can use BOWLER as the array name. Each element is one bowler's score. An index (enclosed in parentheses) follows the array name. Thus a specific data item (that is, one bowler's score) is identified by an array name and an index. For example, BOWLER(3) has the score for bowler number three.

Although Figure 3-6 does not show it, every array has an element with an index of 0. Therefore, there is a BOWLER(0) in addition to BOWLER(1) through BOWLER(10).

Array Dimension(s)

You must specify the number of elements in an array before you use it. You do this with a DIM statement, which will be described later.

ATARI BASIC arrays can have one or two indexes. One-dimension arrays have one index; two-dimension arrays have two indexes. A one-dimension array is like a table with just one row of numbers (Figure 3-6). The index identifies a number within the single row. An array with two dimensions is like an ordinary table of numbers with rows and columns: one index identifies the row, the other index identifies the column.

Let's extend the bowling tournament example to two dimensions. Suppose there are five teams, each with ten bowlers. There are four options for keeping track of the 50 bowlers' scores. First, each bowler could have his own variable. Second, the entire tournament could have a a single 50-element array. Third, each team could have a separate ten-element array. Fourth, the tournament could have one two-dimension array (Figure 3-7). This last choice is the best. The first index of the two-dimension array is the team number and the second index is the bowler number on that team. So BOWLER(3,2) would be the score of bowler 2 on team 3.

158	215	268	135	170	147	195	231	172	171
RAY	LEO	IDA	JAN	SUE	TED	JIM	LOU	ART	DEE

FIGURE 3-5. Using separate variable names

158	215	268	135	170	147	195	231	172	171
BOWLER(1)	BOWLER(2)	BOWLER(3)	BOWLER(4)	BOWLER(5)	BOWLER(6)	BOWLER(7)	BOWLER(8)	BOWLER(9)	BOWLER(10)

FIGURE 3-6. Using an array

165	215	207	223	137	181	157	223	148	156
BOWLER(4,0)	BOWLER(4,1)	BOWLER(4,2)	BOWLER(4,3)	BOWLER(4,4)	BOWLER(4,5)	BOWLER(4,6)	BOWLER(4,7)	BOWLER(4,8)	BOWLER(4,9)
158	193	184	152	207	210	223	176	207	229
BOWLER(3,0)	BOWLER(3,1)	BOWLER(3,2)	BOWLER(3,3)	BOWLER(3,4)	BOWLER(3,5)	BOWLER(3,6)	BOWLER(3,7)	BOWLER(3,8)	BOWLER(3,9)
197	159	202	201	202	170	162	176	137	174
BOWLER(2,0)	BOWLER(2,1)	BOWLER(2,2)	BOWLER(2,3)	BOWLER(2,4)	BOWLER(2,5)	BOWLER(2,6)	BOWLER(2,7)	BOWLER(2,8)	BOWLER(2,9)
214	136	137	166	170	211	156	218	203	205
BOWLER(1,0)	BOWLER(1,1)	BOWLER(1,2)	BOWLER(1,3)	BOWLER(1,4)	BOWLER(1,5)	BOWLER(1,6)	BOWLER(1,7)	BOWLER(1,8)	BOWLER(1,9)
153	183	133	168	206	218	211	148	169	164
BOWLER(0,0)	BOWLER(0,1)	BOWLER(0,2)	BOWLER(0,3)	BOWLER(0,4)	BOWLER(0,5)	BOWLER(0,6)	BOWLER(0,7)	BOWLER(0,8)	BOWLER(0,9)

FIGURE 3-7. Using a two-dimension array

EXPRESSIONS

How do you combine the values of variables and constants to get new values? You use *expressions*. Remember how we calculated the values of simple arithmetic problems in immediate mode? The following statement tells the ATARI computer to add 4 and 6 and display the sum:

```
PRINT 4+6
10

READY
```

This statement is almost identical:

```
PRINT A+B
0

READY
▓
```

It tells the computer to add the values of numeric variables A and B, and then display the sum.

The plus sign specifies addition. Standard computer jargon refers to the plus sign as an *operator*. Variables A and B are *operands*. The plus sign is an *arithmetic operator* because it specifies addition, which is an arithmetic operation.

Arithmetic operators are easy enough to understand; everyone learns to add, subtract, multiply, and divide in early childhood. But there are other types of operators: *relational operators* and *Boolean operators*. These are also easy to understand, but they take a little more explanation since they involve more abstract notions.

Each category of operators defines a type of expression. There are numeric expressions, relational expressions, and Boolean expressions.

Compound Expressions

The simplest expression consists of one or two operands and an operator. You can combine simple expressions to form more complex ones. You can use one or two simple expressions as the operands of a larger expression. It in turn can be an operand in another expression, and so on. We will call these built-up expressions *compound expressions*. Most expressions are compound expressions.

Precedence of Operators

Compound expressions call for more than one operation to occur. For example, this statement calls for both addition and division in the same expression:

```
PRINT A+B/10
```

There is a standard scheme for determining in what order to evaluate an expression. These rules of *precedence* will be outlined for numeric, relational, Boolean, and mixed-type expressions, in that order. First, let's look at a way to override the standard order of evaluation.

Overriding Standard Precedence

You can change the order in which the ATARI computer evaluates expressions by using parentheses. Any operation within parentheses is performed first. When more than one set of parentheses is present, the ATARI computer evaluates them from left to right.

One set of parentheses can enclose another set. This is called *nesting*. The ATARI computer evaluates the innermost set first, then the next innermost, and so forth.

Parentheses can be nested to any level. You may use them freely to clarify the order of operations being performed in an expression.

Here are some immediate mode arithmetic calculations which use parentheses:

```
PRINT (2+10)*3
36

READY
PRINT (((2+10)*3)+31)*10'
670

READY
PRINT -(2^(3+(8/4)))
-31.99993444

READY
※
```

Numeric Expressions

Numeric expressions operate on numeric variables and constants. They use arithmetic operators: addition (+), subtraction (-), multiplication (*), division (/), and exponentiation (^). They also use the unary minus (-) operator to indicate a negative numeric value. Operations are performed in this order: unary minus first, followed by exponentiation, then multiplication and division, and finally addition and subtraction. Operations of equal precedence are performed in order from left to right.

Here are some numeric expressions:

87.5 - 4.25	results in	79
1.5^(3/2/2)	results in	1.35540299
AL * (PL - 3.1 * CB)	results in	the value of AL times the result of subtracting the product of 3.1 times the value of CB from the value of PL
7.5 * 2/5	results in	3

Relational Expressions

Relational operators allow you to compare two values to see what relationship one bears to the other. You can compare whether the first is greater than, less than, equal, not equal, greater than or equal, or less than or equal to the second value. The values you compare can be constants, variables, or any kind of expressions. If the value on one side of a relational operator is a string, the value on the other side must also be a string. Other than that, you can compare one type of value to another using relational operators.

TABLE 3-1. Relational Operators

Operation	Operator
Less than	<
Greater than	>
Equal to	=
Not equal to	< >
Greater than or equal to	> =
Less than or equal to	< =

If the relationship is true, the relational expression has a numeric value of 1. If the relationship is false, the relational expression has a numeric value of 0.

Table 3-1 lists relational operators. They all have the same precedence. When more than one is present in a single expression, they are evaluated from left to right.

Here are some examples of relational expressions:

1 = 5 - 4	results in	1 (true)
14 > 66	results in	0 (false)
15 >= 15	results in	1 (true)
"AA" > "AA"	results in	0 (false)
"DUDE" < "DUKE"	results in	1 (true)
(A = B) = (A$ > B$)		depends on the values of the variables. If the value of A is equal to the value of B and the value of A$ is greater than the value of B$, then this expression results in 1 (true).

Relational expressions are easy enough to understand. One way they can be used is a bit more difficult: relational expressions can be part of a numeric expression. Relational expression values 0 (false) and 1 (true) are legitimate numeric values. This can be confusing. For example, what meaning does the expression (9 = 9) * 4 have? None, outside of a BASIC program. But in BASIC, (9 = 9) is true. True equates to 1. Therefore (9 = 9) * 4 is the same as 1 * 4, which results in 4. Here are some examples:

25 + (14 > 66)	equals	25 + 0
A + (1 = B - 4)	equals	A + 1 if B = 5, or A + 0 otherwise.

String Comparisons

You may be wondering what rules the ATARI computer uses when it compares strings. There are two considerations. First is string length. Strings of unequal lengths are not equal. (Remember that blanks count toward string length.) If a shorter string is identical to the first part of a longer string, the longer string is greater than the shorter string.

The second consideration is whether the strings contain the same characters, in the same order. Strings are compared one character at a time, starting with the leftmost character — the first character of one string with the first character of the other, the second character with the second character, and so on until one of the strings is exhausted or a character mismatch occurs. For comparison purposes, the letters of the alphabet have the order A < B, B < C, C < D, etc. Numbers that appear in strings have conventional ordering, namely 0 < 1, 1 < 2, 2 < 3, etc. Other characters that appear in strings, like +, -, $, and so on, are arbitrarily ranked in the order shown in Appendix D.

Boolean Expressions

Boolean operators give programs the ability to perform logic operations. Hence they are often called *logic operators*. There are four standard Boolean operators: AND, OR, Exclusive OR, and NOT. BASIC on the ATARI computer supports three of these operators: AND, OR, and NOT.

If you do not understand Boolean operators, then a simple supermarket shopping analogy will serve to illustrate Boolean logic. Suppose you are shopping for breakfast cereals with two children, Spike and Iola. The AND Boolean operator says you will buy a cereal if both children select that cereal. The OR Boolean operator says that you will buy a cereal if either child selects it. The NOT Boolean operator generates an opposite. If Spike insists on disagreeing with Iola, then Spike's decision is always the NOT of Iola's decision.

Computers do not work with analogies; they work with numbers. Therefore Boolean logic reduces the values it operates on to 1 or 0 (true or false). Since Boolean operators work on the values 0 and 1, they are most often used with relational expressions. Remember that relational expressions also result in a value of 0 or 1. Boolean operators can work on other types of operands, as we will see in the next section.

Table 3-2 summarizes the way in which Boolean expressions are evaluated. This table is called a *truth table*. Boolean operators have equal precedence. If several Boolean operators are present in the same expression, they are evaluated from left to right.

Here are some examples of Boolean expressions:

NOT ((3 + 4) > = 6)	results in	0 (false)
("AA" = "AB") OR ((8 * 2) = 4 ^ 2)	results in	1 (true)
NOT ("APPLE" = "ORANGE")		
AND (A$ = B$)	results in	1 (true) if A$ and B$ are equal;
		0 (false) if not.

TABLE 3-2. Boolean Truth Table

The AND operation results in a 1 only if both values are 1.

  1 AND 1 = 1   1 AND 0 = 0
  0 AND 1 = 0   0 AND 0 = 0

The OR operation results in a 1 if either value is 1.

  1 OR 1 = 1   1 OR 0 = 1
  0 OR 1 = 1   0 OR 0 = 0

The NOT operation logically complements each value.

  NOT 1 = 0
  NOT 0 = 1

Mixed-Type Expressions

What if the operands of an expression don't match the operator? That depends. You can't use string operands with numeric or Boolean operators, only with relational operators. And you can compare one string only to another string. Other than that, you can mix types freely. The result is a *mixed-type expression.*

The ATARI computer must resolve several questions when it evaluates a mixed-type expression. Which operation does it perform first? How does it convert a value from one type to another? Table 3-3 lists the operators of all types, from highest precedence to lowest. This table shows that anything in parentheses is evaluated first. If there is more than one level of parentheses present, the ATARI computer evaluates the innermost set first, then the next innermost, and so on. (Recall that we covered this concept of *nesting* earlier.) Next, numeric expressions are evaluated. After that, relational expressions are evaluated. Finally, Boolean expressions are evaluated.

ATARI BASIC converts relational and Boolean expressions to 0 if false, 1 if true. Conversely, it converts a numeric 0 to false; any other numeric value is true. Strings don't convert. However, the result of a string comparison is a numeric value (0 or 1), so you can use it in a numeric expression.

Here are some examples of mixed-type expressions:

Legal	Illegal
43 AND 137	1600 + "PENNSYLVANIA AVENUE"
(A$ = B$) AND -6.25	ST$ < = A
(K = M) = (Z$ = Y$)	NOT (A$) = B$

TABLE 3-3. Operators

	Precedence	Operator	Meaning
	High 9	( )	Parentheses denote order of evaluation
Arithmetic **Operators**	8	^	Exponentiation
	7	-	Unary Minus
	6	*	Multiplication
	6	/	Division
	5	+	Addition
	5	-	Subtraction
Relational **Operators**	4	=	Equal
	4	< >	Not equal
	4	<	Less than
	4	>	Greater than
	4	< =	Less than or Equal
	4	> =	Greater than or Equal
Boolean **Operators**	3	NOT	Logical complement
	2	AND	Logical AND
	1	OR	Logical OR
	Low		

KEYWORDS

All of the words that define a BASIC statement's operations are called *keywords*. Appendix E lists all standard ATARI BASIC keywords. You will encounter many of these keywords in this chapter; others are described elsewhere in this book.

When executing BASIC programs, the ATARI computer scans every BASIC statement, seeking out keywords. It can generally tell a variable from a keyword, but not always. Therefore, you should keep keywords out of your variable names. At least avoid using keywords at the beginning of variable names.

Abbreviating Keywords

You learned early in this book that you can abbreviate the PRINT statement with a question mark. Many other ATARI BASIC keywords can be abbreviated. You can often abbreviate a keyword by typing its first letter. For example, the letter L means LIST. How does the computer know your abbreviation is a keyword, and not a variable name? Simple: you put a period at the end of it. L. is the full abbreviation for LIST.

In some cases one letter is ambiguous. The letter L could mean LIST or LOAD. The single-letter abbreviation is arbitrarily assigned to one of the keywords, generally the one used most often. For other keywords that start with the same letter, you have to use the first two, three, or even four letters of the keyword. LO. is the abbreviation for LOAD. Appendix E lists the shortest abbreviations for each keyword. You can always use more letters than the minimum, but you must use enough letters to positively identify the keyword. Thus you can abbreviate PRINT with PRIN., PRI., or just PR..

BASIC STATEMENTS

Now consider the third major element of BASIC syntax: statements. Each statement instructs the ATARI computer to perform some kind of operation or take some action. It is common practice to use the terms *statement* and *command* interchangeably and somewhat ambiguously. Strictly speaking, a command is an instruction issued in immediate mode. The same instruction in programmed mode is a statement.

This chapter introduces you to programming concepts, stressing the way statements are used. The details you need for the most common situations are discussed in this chapter. You should also read the definitive statement descriptions in Chapter 11. These descriptions tell you all the things a statement does for you (and against you).

One last caveat before beginning. Although this chapter introduces you to programming concepts, it cannot possibly cover programming in depth. If you need more instruction in programming, consult one of the BASIC primers listed in Appendix I.

Remarks

An appropriate way to begin the discussion of BASIC statements is with the one BASIC statement the computer ignores: the remark statement. If the first three characters of a BASIC statement are REM, then the computer ignores the statement entirely. So why include such a statement? Because remarks make your program easier to read.

If you write a short program with five or ten statements, you will probably have little trouble remembering what the program does — unless you put it aside for six months and then try to use it again. If you write a longer program with 100 or 200 statements, then you are quite likely to forget something very important about the program the very next time you use it. After you have written dozens of programs, you will stand no chance of remembering each program in detail. The solution to this problem is to document your program by including remarks that describe what is going on.

Good programmers use remarks in all of their programs. All of the program examples in this chapter will include remarks, to try to get you into the habit of doing the same thing yourself.

Remark statements have line numbers, like any other statement. A remark statement's line number can be used like any other statement's line number.

Assignment Statements

Assignment statements let you assign values to variables. You will encounter assignment statements frequently in every type of BASIC program. Here is an example of an assignment statement:

```
90 REM Initialize variable X
100 LET X=3
```

In statement 100, variable X is assigned the value 3. This same statement could be rewritten like this:

```
100 X=3
```

The word LET is optional; it is usually omitted.

Here is a string variable assignment statement:

```
215 A$="ALSO RAN"
```

The string variable A$ is assigned the characters ALSO RAN. Notice that the characters are enclosed in quotation marks. The quotation marks do not become part of the string value.

Here are three assignment statements that assign values to array variable BOWLER( ), which we encountered earlier when describing arrays:

```
200 REM BOWLER() has bowler's scores
210 BOWLER(1)=150
220 BOWLER(2)=210
230 BOWLER(3)=268
```

Remember, more than one statement can be placed on a single line; therefore the three BOWLER( ) assignments could be placed on a single line, as follows:

```
200 REM BOWLER() has bowler's scores
210 BOWLER(1)=150:BOWLER(2)=210:BOWLER
(3)=268
```

Recall that a colon must separate adjacent statements appearing on the same line.

Assignment statements can include any of the arithmetic or logical operators described earlier in this chapter. Here is an example of such an assignment statement:

```
100 V=33+7/9
```

The statement above assigns the value 33.77777777 to numeric variable V; it is equivalent to the following three statements:

```
90 REM X and Y need to be initialized
separately for later use
100 X=7
110 Y=9
120 V=33+X/Y
```

which could be written on one line like this:

```
100  X=7:Y=9:V=33+X/Y
```

The following are assignment statements that perform the Boolean operations given earlier in this chapter:

```
90 REM These examples were described e
arlier in the chapter
100 A=NOT((3+4)=6)
110 B=("AA"="AB") OR ((8*2)=(4^2))
```

DATA and READ Statements

When a number of variables need data assignments in an ATARI BASIC program, you can use the DATA and READ statements rather than the type of assignment statement described earlier. Consider the following example:

```
5 REM Initialize all variables
10 DATA 10, 20, -4, 300
20 READ A,B,C,D
```

The statement on line 10 specifies four numeric data values. These four values are assigned to four numeric variables by the statement on line 20. After the statement on line 20 is executed, A = 10, B = 20, C = -4, and D = 300.

All the DATA statements in your program construct a single list of values (Figure 3-8). For example, a DATA statement that specifies ten values would construct a ten-entry list. Two DATA statements each specifying five of the ten data entries would construct exactly the same list.

READ statements use a pointer to the list of DATA statement values. The pointer starts at the beginning of the list. Each time a READ statement uses a value from the list, it moves the pointer ahead to the next value (Figure 3-9). The first READ statement executed in a program starts with the first value on the list and takes values sequentially, assigning them to variables named in the READ statement. The second READ statement executed starts with the next unassigned list value. The third READ statement executed picks up where the second one left off, and so forth.

The DATA list can contain both numeric and string values. The values must be constants, not expressions. The ATARI computer will *not* evaluate expressions. You can use scientific notation to express numeric constants. Do *not* enclose string constants in quotation marks. The ATARI computer includes them as part of the string value.

What you see is what you get. Look at these two statements:

```
10 DATA 0, -0.8,1.2558E3
20 DATA A+B, TOTAL,NAME$
```

The statement on line 10 has three numeric values: 0, -0.8, and 1255.8 (note the use of scientific notation). The statement on line 20 has three string values. The first value is three characters long: A + B. The second value is six characters long; the

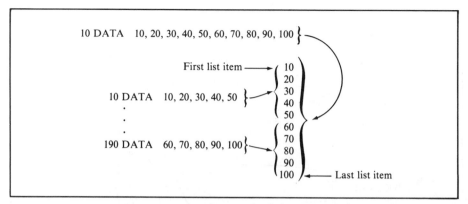

FIGURE 3-8. Building a list of values with a DATA statement

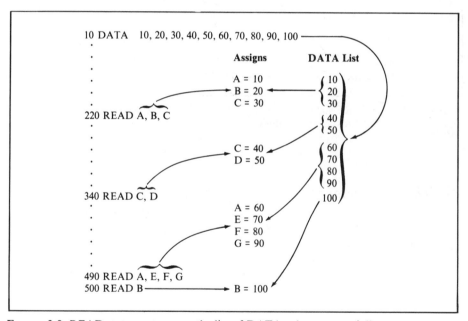

FIGURE 3-9. READ statements access the list of DATA values sequentially

blank space ahead of the word TOTAL is part of the string value. The third string value is the five characters NAME$.

When you assign values to variables using a READ statement, each variable must be the same type (string or numeric) as the corresponding value it is assigned from the DATA statement list. Any character can be assigned to a string variable, so no possibility of a type mismatch error exists. An error will occur if there is an attempt to assign a string value to a numeric variable.

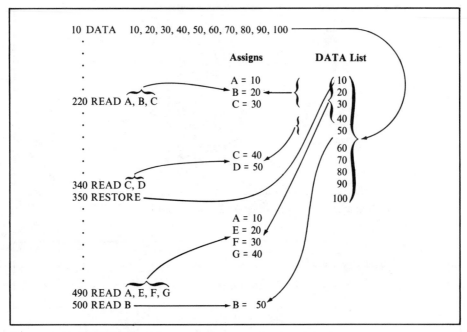

FIGURE 3-10. RESTORE statement starts over at the top of the list
of DATA statement values

RESTORE Statement

You can at any time send the pointer back to the beginning of the list of DATA
statement values by executing a RESTORE statement (Figure 3-10). A variation of
the RESTORE statement lets you put the pointer at the first data value on a specific
line number. Here is an example:

```
10 DATA 1,2,3,4,5
20 DATA 10,20,30,40,50
30 READ A
40 PRINT A
49 REM Move DATA pointer to line 20
50 RESTORE 20
60 READ A
70 PRINT A
```

The READ statement on line 30 assigns the first value on the list of DATA
statement values to variable A. The RESTORE statement on line 50 moves the
pointer to the start of line 20. The next READ statement (line 60) picks up the first
value there and assigns it to variable A.

DIM Statement

If you plan to use arrays or string variables in your program, you need to declare their maximum sizes (or dimensions) in DIM statements. One DIM statement can provide dimensions for any number of arrays and string variables, as long as the statement fits on a standard program line. The computer must first encounter a string variable or array in a DIM statement. Error 9 occurs if you try to use a string variable or array without first dimensioning it.

You dimension an array or string variable by stating its name and then specifying its maximum size. Enclose the size in parentheses. Only one- or two-dimension numeric arrays are allowed — no string arrays or numeric arrays with three or more dimensions. The following example dimensions a five-character string, a numeric array of 13 elements (0 through 12), and a second array of 20 elements:

```
10 DIM S1$(5), NB(12), BOWLER(1,9)
```

The number following a string variable name in a DIM statement is the maximum length that string can be during the program. The number (or numbers) following an array name in a DIM statement is equal to the largest index value that can occur in that particular index position. But remember that indexes begin at 0. Therefore SCORE(10) dimensions array SCORE( ) to have 11 values, not 10, since indexes 0, 1, 2, 3, 4, 5, 6, 7, 8, 9, and 10 will be allowed. BOWLER(8,10), likewise, specifies a two-dimension variable with 99 elements, since the first dimension can have values 0, 1, 2, 3, etc., while the second dimension can have values 0 through 10.

You cannot use an array index higher than the number of elements you declared; each index must have a value between 0 and the number of elements dimensioned. You can assign a string variable a value that's too long. The ATARI computer assigns the first part of the value to the variable. It disregards the extra characters at the end of the value.

Redimensioning Arrays and Strings

Once you have dimensioned an array or string variable you cannot redimension it unless you first clear it. ATARI BASIC lets you undimension every string variable and array, all at once. The CLR command does this. It also sets every simple numeric variable to 0 and resets the pointer to the list of DATA statement values, like the RESTORE statement does. This is shown in the following example:

```
X=37

READY
PRINT X
37

READY
10 DATA 1,2,3,4,5
READ A,B
```

```
READY
PRINT A,B
1          2

READY
CLR

READY
PRINT X
0

READY
READ A,B

READY
PRINT A,B
1          2

READY
▓
```

BRANCH STATEMENTS

Statements within a BASIC program are normally executed in ascending order of
line numbers (Figure 3-1). Branch statements change this execution sequence.

GOTO Statement

GOTO is the simplest branch statement. It allows you to specify the statement
which will be executed next. Consider this program fragment:

```
20  A=4
30  GOTO 100
40  B=5
50  C=6
100 PRINT A
110 PRINT B*C
```

The statement on line 20 is an assignment statement; it assigns a value to variable A.
The next statement is a GOTO; it specifies that program execution must branch to
line 100. Therefore, the instruction execution sequence surrounding this part of the
program will be line 20, then line 30, then line 100. Of course, some other statement
must branch back to line 40. Otherwise the statements on lines 40 and 50 will never
be executed.

You can branch to any line number, even if the line has nothing but a remark on
it. However, the computer ignores the remark, so the effect is the same as branching
to the next line. For example, consider the following branch:

```
20  A=4
30  GOTO 70
40  B=5
70  REM This line is only a remark.
80  PRINT A,B
```

Program execution branches from line 30 to line 70. There is nothing but a remark on line 70, so the computer moves on to line 80, executing the statement there. Even though you can branch to a remark, you might as well branch to the next line, like this:

```
20 A=4
30 GOTO 80
40 B=5
70 REM This line is only a remark.
80 PRINT A,B
```

The ATARI computer will calculate the line number to branch to. Instead of an actual line number, use a numeric expression, like this:

```
10 DATA 0,1,2,3,4
20 READ A
30 PRINT A
40 GOTO 30*A+50
50 PRINT "LINE 50"
60 GOTO 20
80 PRINT "LINE 80"
90 GOTO 20
110 PRINT "LINE 110"
120 RESTORE
130 GOTO 20
```

The computer has to evaluate the expression on line 40 before it knows where to go. It branches to line 50 if variable A is 0, to line 80 if A is 1, or to line 110 if A is 2.

Attempting to branch to a nonexistent line number causes an error. This is true whether the computer has to calculate the line number or not.

To test the calculated GOTO statement, type in the following program, then execute it by typing RUN:

```
9 REM Initialize variable B
10 B=4
20 PRINT B
30 A=B-3
40 GOTO 30*A+50
50 END
79 REM B=4
80 PRINT B
90 B=5
100 GOTO 20
109 REM B=5
110 PRINT B
120 B=3
130 GOTO 20
```

Can you account for the sequence in which digits display (4, 4, 5, 5, 3)? Try rewriting the program so it displays the repeating sequence 3, 4, 5, 3, 4, 5, 3, 4, 5, etc.

Computed GOTO Statement

There is another kind of GOTO statement that uses an expression and a list of line numbers. The following program segment illustrates this type of statement:

```
10 DATA 0,1,2,3,4
20 READ A
30 PRINT A
40 ON A+1 GOTO 50,80,110
50 PRINT "LINE 50"
60 GOTO 20
80 PRINT "LINE 80"
90 GOTO 20
110 PRINT "LINE 110"
120 RESTORE
130 GOTO 20
```

The statement on line 40 is a *computed* GOTO. If variable A is 0, the program branches to line 50. If A is 1, the program goes to line 80; if A is 2, execution continues at line 110.

The ON-GOTO statement contains a numeric expression and a list of line numbers. The ATARI computer evaluates the expression. If its value is 1, the computer branches to the first line number on the list; if 2, to the second; if 3, to the third; and so forth. If the value is 0, or greater than the number of line numbers in the list, the program just executes the statement right after the ON-GOTO statement.

The expression can't have a negative value or a value greater than 255, or an error results. The line numbers in the list can be numeric constants or expressions.

The following ATARI BASIC program demonstrates how the computed GOTO statement works.

```
10 B=4
20 PRINT B
30 A=B-2
40 ON A GOTO 180,70,150
49 REM Value is zero or large
50 PRINT "ONCE AGAIN"
59 REM Start over
60 GOTO 10
69 REM B=4
70 PRINT B
80 B=5
90 GOTO 30
149 REM B=5
150 PRINT B
160 B=3
170 GOTO 20
179 REM B=1
180 PRINT B
190 B=6
200 GOTO 30
```

LOOPS

GOTO and ON-GOTO statements let you create any sequence of statement execution that your program logic may require. But suppose you want to reexecute an instruction (or a group of instructions) many times. For example, suppose array variable A( ) has 100 elements, and each element needs to be assigned a value ranging from 0 to 99. Writing 100 assignment statements would be incredibly tiresome. Even using DATA and READ statements would be tedious. It is far simpler to reexecute one statement 100 times in a loop.

FOR and NEXT Statements

You can create a loop using the FOR and NEXT statements, like this:

```
10 DIM A(99)
20 FOR N=0 TO 99 STEP 1
30 A(N)=1
40 NEXT N
```

Statements between FOR and NEXT are executed repeatedly. In the above example, a single assignment statement appears between FOR and NEXT; therefore this single statement is executed repeatedly. This kind of program structure is called a *FOR-NEXT loop*.

So you can see the workings of FOR-NEXT loops, the following program displays the values it assigns to array A( ) within the loop:

```
10 DIM A(99)
20 FOR N=0 TO 99 STEP 1
30 A(N)=N
35 PRINT A(N)
40 NEXT N
50 END
```

When you run the program, it displays 100 numbers, starting at 0 and ending at 99.

Statements between FOR and NEXT are reexecuted the number of times specified by the *index variable* appearing directly after the keyword FOR; in the illustration above this index variable is N. N is specified as going from 0 to 99 in *steps* of 1. Variable N also appears in the assignment statement on line 30. Therefore, the first time the assignment statement is executed, N will equal 0 and the assignment statement will be executed as follows:

```
30 A(0)=0
```

The value of N starts at 0 and increases by the step value, which is specified on line 20 as 1. N therefore equals 1 the second time the assignment statement on line 30 is executed. The assignment statement has effectively become this:

```
30 A(1)=1
```

Index variable N continues to be incremented by the specified step value until the maximum value, 99 in this case, is reached or exceeded.

The step does not require a value of 1; it can have any numeric value. Change the step to 5 on line 20 and reexecute the program. Now the assignment statement is executed just 20 times. Incrementing the index variable 19 times by 5 will take it to 95. The 20th increment will take it to 100, which is more than the specified maximum value of 99. Keeping the step at 5, you can cause the assignment statement to be executed 100 times by increasing the maximum value of N to 500. Try it. (Remember to change the DIM statement as well.)

The step size does not have to be positive. If the step size is negative, however, the initial value of N must be larger than the final value of N. For example, if the step size is -1 and we want to initialize 100 elements of A( ) with values ranging from 0 to 99, then the statement on line 20 would have to be rewritten as follows:

```
10 DIM A(99)
20 FOR N=99 TO 0 STEP -1
30 A(N)=N
35 PRINT A(N)
40 NEXT N
50 END
```

Execute this program to test the negative step.

If the step size is 1 (and this is frequently the case), you do not have to specify a step size definition. Simply omit the keyword STEP and the step value. In the absence of any definition, BASIC assumes a step size of 1.

You may specify the initial and final index values and the step size using expressions.

Nested Loops

The FOR-NEXT structure is referred to as a *program loop* since statement execution loops around from FOR to NEXT, then back to FOR. This loop structure is very common. Almost every BASIC program you write will include one or more such loops. Loops are so common that they are frequently *nested* one inside the other like a set of mixing bowls. There can be any number of statements between FOR and NEXT. Frequently there are tens, or even hundreds of statements. And within these tens or hundreds of statements additional loops may occur. Figure 3-11 shows an example of a single level of nesting.

Complex loop structures appear frequently, even in relatively short programs. Figure 3-12 shows an example with the FOR and NEXT statements but none of the intermediate statements. In this example, the outermost loop uses index variable N. It contains three nested loops that use indexes X, Y, and Z. The X loop contains two additional loops that use indexes A and B. The Y loop contains one nested loop that uses index P. The Z loop contains no nested loops.

Loop structures are very easy to visualize and use. There is only one error which you must avoid: do not terminate an outer loop before you terminate an inner loop. Figure 3-13 illustrates such an illegal loop structure.

The ATARI computer makes a note in its memory of the location of each FOR statement it executes. That way it knows where to loop back to when it encounters a

```
10 DIM A(99)
20 FOR N=0 TO 99 STEP 1
30 A(N)=N
40 REM Print all values of A() so far
50 FOR J=0 TO N
60 PRINT A(J)
70 NEXT J
80 NEXT N
90 END
```

FIGURE 3-11. Single-level FOR-NEXT nesting

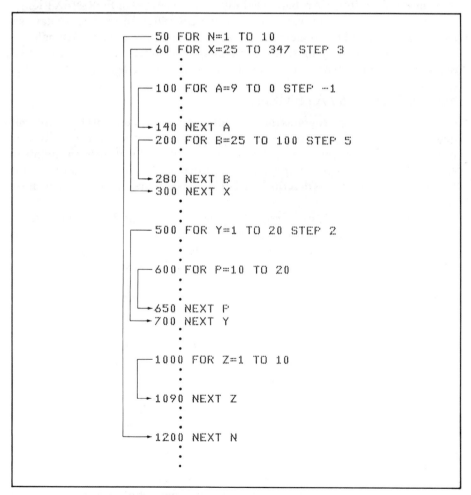

FIGURE 3-12. Complex FOR-NEXT loop nesting
          (Intermediate program lines omitted for clarity)

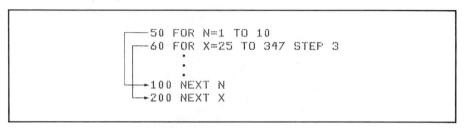

```
       ┌───50 FOR N=1 TO 10
       │┌──60 FOR X=25 TO 347 STEP 3
       ││         •
       ││         •
       ││         •
       │└►100 NEXT N
       └──►200 NEXT X
```

FIGURE 3-13. Illegal FOR-NEXT loop nesting

NEXT statement. When the loop terminates, the computer erases the notation from its memory. Therefore, if a program habitually branches out of FOR-NEXT loops, memory gradually fills up with unexpunged FOR statement location notations. Eventually there will be no memory left, and the program will come to a halt.

Every NEXT statement must have a matching FOR statement. An error occurs if the computer cannot pair up a NEXT statement with an earlier FOR statement.

SUBROUTINE STATEMENTS

Once you start writing programs that are more than a few statements long, you will find short sections of program that are used repeatedly. Suppose you have an array variable (A( ), for example) that is reinitialized frequently at different points in your program. Would you simply repeat the three instructions that constitute the FOR-NEXT loop that was described earlier? Since there are just three instructions, you may as well do so.

Suppose the loop has 10 or 11 instructions that process array data in some fashion before it initializes the array. If you had to use this loop many times within one program, rewriting the same 10 to 15 statements each time you wished to use the loop would take time, but more importantly it would waste a lot of computer memory (Figure 3-14).

You could separate out the repeated statements and branch to them. The group of statements is then referred to as a *subroutine.*

A problem arises, however. Branching from the main program to the subroutine is simple enough. The subroutine has a specific starting line number, so you could execute a GOTO statement whenever you wish to branch to a subroutine. But at the end of the subroutine, to where do you return (Figure 3-15)? If two GOTO statements branch to the subroutine, the subroutine may have to return to either one. The solution is to use special subroutine statements. Instead of a GOTO, use a GOSUB statement.

GOSUB and RETURN Statements

The GOSUB statement branches in the same way as a GOTO, but in addition it remembers the location to which it should return (Figure 3-16). In computer jargon, we say GOSUB *calls* a subroutine.

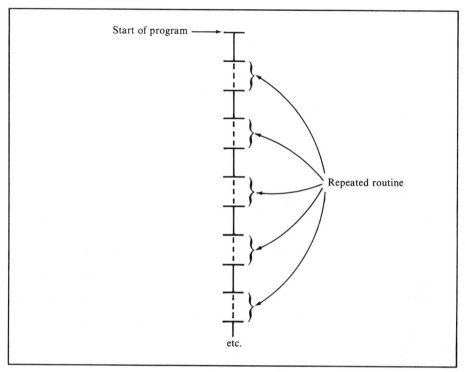

FIGURE 3-14. Duplicate routines use up memory

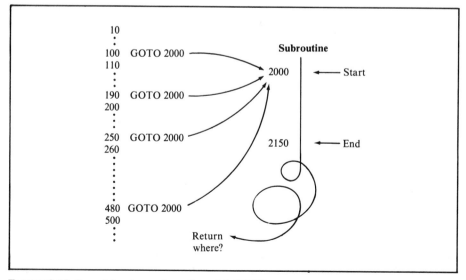

FIGURE 3-15. Branching to a subroutine with GOTO

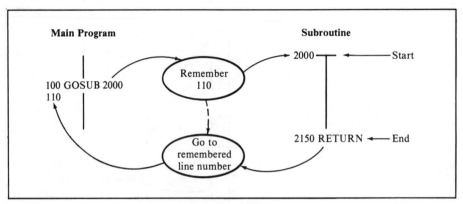

FIGURE 3-16. Branching to a subroutine with GOSUB

You end the subroutine with a RETURN statement. It causes a branch back to the statement that follows the GOSUB statement. If the GOSUB statement is the last one on the line, the program returns to the first statement on the next line.

The three-statement loop which initializes array A( ), if it were converted into a subroutine, would look like lines 2000 through 2050 below:

```
10 REM Main Program
20 REM It is a good idea to
30 REM dimension all variables
40 REM together at the start of
50 REM the main program
60 DIM A(99)
70 GOSUB 2000
80 REM Display proof of return
90 PRINT "RETURNED"
100 END
2000 REM Subroutine starts
2010 FOR N=0 TO 99
2020 A(N)=N
2030 PRINT A(N)
2040 NEXT N
2050 RETURN
```

POP Statement

Under some circumstances you will not want a subroutine to return to the statement following the GOSUB statement. You might be tempted to just use a GOTO statement to return, but that can cause a problem because BASIC is still remembering to where it should return. In cases like this, use the POP statement. Otherwise you risk an error caused by the accumulation of unused return locations. All POP does is make BASIC forget the most recent return location. You can then use a GOTO statement to branch somewhere else in the program.

Bypass the RETURN statement sparingly. Using POP excessively to enable GOTO branching out of subroutines leads to tangled, confusing programs.

Nested Subroutines

Subroutines can be nested. That is, a subroutine can itself call another subroutine, which in turn can call a third subroutine, and so on. You do not have to do anything special in order to use nested subroutines. Simply branch to the subroutine using a GOSUB statement and end the subroutine with a RETURN statement. BASIC will remember the correct line number for each nested return.

The following program illustrates nested subroutines:

```
10 REM Main Program
20 REM It is a good idea to
30 REM dimension all variables
40 REM together at the start of
50 REM the main program
60 DIM A(99)
70 GOSUB 2000
80 REM Display proof of return
90 PRINT "RETURNED"
100 END
2000 REM Subroutine starts
2010 FOR N=0 TO 99
2020 A(N)=N
2029 REM Subr. displays value
2030 GOSUB 3000
2040 NEXT N
2050 RETURN
3000 REM Nested subroutine start
3010 PRINT A(N)
3020 RETURN
```

This program moves the PRINT A(N) statement out of the subroutine at line 2000 and puts it into a nested subroutine at line 3000. Nothing else changes.

While it is perfectly acceptable and even desirable for one subroutine to call another, a subroutine cannot call itself. Neither can a subroutine call another subroutine which in turn calls the first subroutine. This is called *recursion,* and is not allowed in BASIC on the ATARI computer.

You can specify the line number in a GOSUB statement with a numeric expression, as follows:

```
100 GOSUB A*500+2000
110 REM
```

The ATARI computer evaluates the expression on line 100, then branches to the line number that results.

Calling a nonexistent subroutine causes an error. This is true whether or not the computer has to calculate the line number.

Computed GOSUB Statement

GOTO and GOSUB statement logic is very similar. It should be no surprise that there is a computed GOSUB statement akin to the computed GOTO statement. The ON-GOSUB statement contains an expression and a list of line numbers. The

ATARI computer evaluates the expression. If its value is 1, the computer calls the first subroutine on the list; if 2, the second; and so forth. If the value is 0, or greater than the number of line numbers on the list, the program just executes the statement right after the ON-GOSUB statement. The expression can't have a negative value or a value greater than 255, or an error results.

The program remembers where the ON-GOSUB statement is. No matter which subroutine gets called, the next RETURN statement branches back to the remembered line number.

You can nest subroutines using ON-GOSUB statements, just as you can nest subroutines using standard GOSUB statements.

Here is an example of an ON-GOSUB statement:

```
100 ON A GOSUB 1000,500,5000,2300
110 REM
```

If A is 1, a subroutine beginning at line 1000 is called. If A is 2, a subroutine beginning at line 500 is called. If A is 3, a subroutine beginning at line 5000 is called. If A is 4, a subroutine beginning at line 2300 is called. If A has any value other than 1 through 4, program execution falls through to line 110 (no subroutine is called).

CONDITIONAL EXECUTION

ON-GOTO and ON-GOSUB are *conditional* statements. That is, the exact flow of program execution depends on the values of one or more variables which can change as the program is running. The exact program flow depends on the condition of the variables.

IF-THEN Statement

The IF-THEN statement is another conditional statement. It has the general form

IF *expression* THEN *statement*

If the *expression* is true, then the *statement* is executed. Relational and Boolean expressions are most common with IF-THEN statements, but numeric expressions can be used as well. This statement gives a BASIC program real decision-making capabilities. Here are three simple examples of IF-THEN statements:

```
10 IF A=B+5 THEN PRINT MSG$
40 IF CC$="M" THEN IN=0
50 IF Q<14 AND M<M1 THEN GOTO 66
```

The statement on line 10 causes a PRINT statement to be executed if the value of variable A is five more than the value of variable B. The PRINT statement will not be executed otherwise. The statement on line 40 sets numeric variable IN to 0 if string variable CC$ is the letter M. The statement on line 50 causes program execution to branch to line 66 if variable Q is less than 14, and variable M is less than variable M1. Both conditions must be true or program execution will continue with the statement on the next line. If you do not understand the evaluation of expressions following IF, then refer to the discussion of expressions given earlier in this chapter.

An IF-THEN statement can be followed by other statements on the same program line. ATARI BASIC executes statements that follow an IF-THEN statement on the same line only if the expression in the IF-THEN statement is true. If the expression is false, program execution drops down to the first statement on the next program line. Consider the following program segment:

```
10 IF V>100 THEN PRINT "DEWEY WINS":GO
SUB 2000
20 T=T+V:PRINT T
```

The program will print the message DEWEY WINS and call the subroutine at line 2000 only if the value of variable V is greater than 100. If V is less than or equal to 100, the program will not print the message *or* call the subroutine, but will instead proceed directly to the first statement on line 20.

A second form of the IF-THEN statement is available in ATARI BASIC. Whenever the conditionally executed statement is a GOTO statement, you can omit the word GOTO if you wish. The following two statements are equivalent:

```
10 IF MM$=DD$ THEN GOTO 100
```

```
10 IF MM$=DD$ THEN 100
```

INPUT AND OUTPUT STATEMENTS

There are a variety of BASIC statements that control the transfer of data to and from the computer. Collectively these are referred to as *input/output statements*. The simplest input/output statements control data input from the keyboard and data output to the display screen. These simple input/output statements will be discussed in the paragraphs that follow. But there are also more complex input/output statements that control data transfer between the computer and peripheral devices such as the program recorder, disk drives, and printers. These more complex input/output statements are described in Chapters 4 through 7. Chapters 8 and 9 cover output statements to the display screen for graphics. Chapter 10 investigates outputting sound to the television.

We have already encountered the PRINT statement, which outputs data to the display screen. We will discuss this statement first, before looking at input statements.

PRINT Statement

Why use the word PRINT instead of DISPLAY or some abbreviation of the word "display"? In the early 1960s, when the BASIC programming language was being created, displays were very expensive and generally unavailable on medium- or low-cost computers. The standard computer terminal had a keyboard and a printer. Information was printed where today it is displayed; hence the use of the word PRINT to describe a statement which causes a display.

The PRINT statement will display text or numbers. For example, this statement will display the single word TEXT:

```
10 PRINT "TEXT"
```

To display a number, you place the number, or a variable name, after PRINT, like this:

```
10 A=10
20 PRINT 5,A
```

The statement above displays the numbers 5 and 10 on the same line.

You can display a mixture of text and numbers by listing the information to be displayed after the word PRINT. Use commas to separate individual items. The following PRINT statement displays the words ONE, TWO, THREE, FOUR, and FIVE, interspersed with the numerals that correspond to each word:

```
10 PRINT "ONE",1,"TWO",2,"THREE",3,"FO
UR",4,"FIVE",5
20 END
```

If you separate variables with commas, as we did above, then the ATARI computer automatically allocates a fixed number of spaces for each item displayed. Try executing the program above to prove this. If you want the display to remove spaces, separate the variables and constants using semicolons, like this:

```
10 PRINT "ONE";1;"TWO";2;"THREE";3;"FO
UR";4;"FIVE";5
20 END
```

Run this program to see how the semicolons work.

You will recall from Chapter 2 that the cursor is the white square that marks the location where the next character you type will appear on the display screen. The PRINT statement also uses it. The first item in a PRINT statement is displayed at the location of the cursor.

A PRINT statement will automatically return the cursor to the left margin as its last action. In computer jargon, this is called a *carriage return*. When the PRINT statement performs the carriage return, it also drops the cursor down one line. This is called a *line feed*. You can suppress the carriage return and line feed by putting a comma or a semicolon after the last value in the PRINT list. A comma occurring after the last value will move the cursor to where the next value would be displayed, if there were one. The next PRINT statement starts there. To illustrate this, type in the following three-statement program and run it:

```
10 PRINT "ONE",1,"TWO",2
20 PRINT "THREE",3,"FOUR",4
30 END
```

Output occurs on two lines. Add a comma to the end of the statement on line 10 and again execute the program. The two lines of display now occur on a single line.

Now replace the comma at the end of line 10 with a semicolon and again run the program. The display occurs on a single line, but the space between the numeral 2 and the word THREE has been removed. By changing other commas to semicolons you can selectively remove additional spaces.

Numerals have been displayed thus far by inserting them directly into the PRINT statement. You can, if you wish, display the values of variables instead. The following program does the same thing as the first PRINT statement example, but uses array A( ) to create digits. Enter and run this program.

```
5 DIM A(5)
10 FOR N=1 TO 5
20 A(N)=N
30 NEXT N
40 PRINT "ONE";A(1);"TWO";A(2);"THRE
;A(3);"FOUR";A(4);"FIVE";A(5)
50 END
```

You can put the displayed words into a string variable and move the PRINT statement into a FOR-NEXT loop by changing the program as follows:

```
10 DIM N$(5)
20 DATA ONE,TWO,THREE,FOUR,FIVE
30 FOR N=1 TO 5
40 READ N$
50 PRINT N$;N;
60 NEXT N
69 REM Return cursor to left margin
70 PRINT
80 END
```

Notice the simple PRINT statement on line 70. It performs a carriage return and line feed, returning the cursor to the left margin.

INPUT Statement

When the computer executes an INPUT statement, it waits for input from the keyboard. Until the computer gets the input it requires, nothing else will happen.

In its simplest form, an INPUT statement begins with the word INPUT and is followed by a variable name. Data entered from the keyboard is assigned to the named variable. The variable name type determines the type of data that must be entered. A numeric variable name can be satisfied only by numeric input. To demonstrate numeric input, key in the following short program and run it (try entering some alphabetic data and see what happens):

```
10 INPUT A
20 PRINT A
25 REM End program if 0 entered
30 IF A=0 THEN END
40 GOTO 10
```

Upon executing an INPUT statement, the computer displays a question mark, then waits for your entry. The program above displays each key as you press it. In computer jargon, the display screen *echoes* the keyboard. Press the RETURN key to end your entry for the INPUT statement. The PRINT statement on line 20 displays the number you entered, so the number actually appears twice in this program. The first display occurs when the INPUT statement on line 10 is executed and you make an entry at the keyboard. The second display is in response to the PRINT statement on line 20.

The INPUT statement can input more than one value at a time. To do this, list all the variables for which you want to input values following the word INPUT. Separate the variables with commas. When such an INPUT statement is executed, you must respond with a separate value for each variable. Press the RETURN key after each value. Be sure each value is the same type as the variable to which it will be assigned.

When you respond to an INPUT statement, do not use commas as punctuation in large numbers; enter 1000, not 1,000.

The following example inputs two numeric values then displays these inputs:

```
20 INPUT A,B
30 PRINT A,B
35 REM End program if 0 is entered
40 IF A=0 OR B=0 THEN END
50 GOTO 20
```

Run the program above and enter one number followed by a comma, then another number, and then press RETURN. Now try something a bit different. Enter one number and press RETURN. As you can see, the ATARI computer reminds you to enter the next value. Enter another number and press RETURN. Thus, when an INPUT statement calls for more than one numeric value, you have a choice of entering all the values on one line, separated by commas, or entering them on separate lines.

The INPUT statement works somewhat differently with string variables. Try this example:

```
10 DIM A$(9)
20 INPUT A$
29 REM End program if null entry
30 IF A$="" THEN END
40 PRINT A$
50 GOTO 20
```

String variable A$ is only dimensioned for nine characters. Try entering more. ATARI BASIC ignores the extra characters.

You have to enter each string value on a separate line. If an INPUT statement specifies a list of variables and there are string variables in the list, the associated string values must be entered on separate lines. This is because ATARI BASIC lets you include commas as part of a string value. You can prove this for yourself by running the example program above and entering the string value DOE, JOHN.

The following program illustrates what happens when a string variable is one of several variables in an INPUT statement list. Experiment with this program. Try to enter all four values on the same line, separated by commas. What happens? Try entering each value on a separate line. See what happens if you enter a numeric value or a comma as part of a string value.

```
10 DIM A$(10),B$(10)
20 INPUT A$,A,B$,B
30 PRINT A$,A,B$,B
35 REM End program if null entry
40 IF A$="" THEN END
50 GOTO 20
```

Editing During INPUT

You can use all the regular editing keys when responding to an INPUT statement: the arrow keys, the INSERT and DELETE keys, the TAB key, and the BACK S key. They all work with responses to INPUT as they would when changing program lines. Bear in mind that the line at which you press RETURN is the line that the INPUT statement gets. Try using the editing keys with the last example program.

INPUT Statement Prompts

The INPUT statement is very fussy; its syntax is too demanding for any normal human operator. Imagine some poor person who knows nothing about programming. On encountering the kind of error message that can occur if one comma happens to be out of place, he or she will give up in despair. You are therefore likely to spend a lot of time writing "idiot-proof" data entry programs. These are programs which are designed to watch out for every type of mistake that a person can make when entering data. An idiot-proof program will cope with errors in a way that anyone can understand.

One simple trick is to display a short message that describes the expected input. You do this with a PRINT statement just before the INPUT statement. The displayed message is called a *prompt message*. It appears in the PRINT statement as a string constant or variable. The message will be displayed on the same line as the input request if you end the PRINT statement with a semicolon. Here is an example:

```
9 REM Test multiplication facts
10 FOR N=1 TO 9
20 PRINT "HOW MUCH IS ";N*9;
30 INPUT ANS
39 REM If wrong answer, try again
40 IF ANS<>N*9 THEN GOTO 20
49 REM Else do next problem
50 PRINT "ABSOLUTELY RIGHT!"
60 NEXT N
70 END
```

This certainly beats trying to guess which INPUT statement you are supposed to answer.

HALTING AND RESUMING PROGRAM EXECUTION

If a program is running and you want to stop it, press BREAK. You will see a message like this:

```
STOPPED AT LINE 1200
```

Instead of 1200, the ATARI computer displays the actual line number at which program execution halted. The computer then returns to immediate mode. It finishes only the statement it was executing; it will begin no new statement.

You can continue program execution by typing the command CONT. The computer does not pick up exactly where it left off. Execution resumes at the start of the next program line. For example, suppose you are running the Expense Analysis program (Figure 3-17), and press BREAK while the computer is executing the INPUT statement on line 50. When you type CONT, the program resumes at line 60. The computer does not complete line 50. This causes problems later in the program. Try it yourself.

If you are already in immediate mode, BREAK merely cancels the line you were typing.

```
 9 REM Analyze monthly expenses
10 DIM EXPNS$(10),SPENT(4)
19 REM Expense category names
20 DATA RENT,PHONE,GAS,ELECTRIC,FOOD
29 REM Enter expenses
30 FOR N=0 TO 4
40 READ EXPNS$:PRINT EXPNS$;
50 INPUT X:SPENT(N)=X
60 NEXT N
69 REM Enter income
70 PRINT :PRINT "INCOME";
80 INPUT INCOME
89 REM Now compare inc. & exp.
90 PRINT :PRINT :PRINT "ANALYSIS---"
100 PRINT
110 RESTORE
120 FOR N=0 TO 4
130 READ EXPNS$
139 REM Calc. & print percentages
140 PRINT EXPNS$;" IS ";SPENT(N)/INCOM
E*100;" % OF INCOME"
150 NEXT N
160 END
```

FIGURE 3-17. Expense Analysis program listing

The SYSTEM RESET Key

You can of course interrupt your program at any time by pressing the SYSTEM RESET key. This is, however, a drastic measure. The program stops dead in its tracks. The display screen clears. The computer goes through an initialization process and returns to immediate mode. You can try continuing the program with the CONT command. As with the BREAK key, execution resumes with the program line after the one where the reset occurred. The more complex the program, the smaller your chances of continuing successfully after a reset.

The END Statement

The program will halt execution when it encounters an END statement, as de- scribed earlier in this chapter. The **READY** message appears on the display screen. The computer returns to immediate mode.

As with the BREAK key, you can continue program execution by typing the command CONT. Execution resumes at the program line after the one containing the END statement. Add the following line to the Expense Analysis program (Figure 3-17):

```
65 END:? "WALRUS"
```

Run the program. When it stops, type CONT and press RETURN. Execution continues at line 70; the PRINT statement at the end of line 65 is never executed.

The STOP Statement

ATARI BASIC has another statement which will halt program execution: the STOP statement. The STOP statement displays a message like this:

```
STOPPED AT LINE 1200
```

Instead of 1200, the computer displays the actual line number of the STOP state- ment, then returns to immediate mode.

You can continue program execution by typing the command CONT. Execution resumes at the start of the program line after the STOP statement. To see how this works, add the following line to the Expense Analysis program (Figure 3-17):

```
65 STOP:? "MOOSE"
```

Run the program. Use the CONT command to continue the program when it stops at line 65. The second statement on line 65 is not executed. The computer resumes execution at the beginning of line 70.

FUNCTIONS

Another element of BASIC is the *function*. In some ways functions look like variables. In other ways they act more like BASIC statements. The discussion that follows shows you how to use functions. Chapter 11 has a complete list of functions, in alphabetical order.

Consider the following assignment statement:

```
10  A=SQR(B)
```

The variable A is set equal to the square root of the variable B. The keyword SQR specifies the square root function.

Here is a string function:

```
20  L=LEN(D$)
```

In this example the numeric variable L is set equal to the length of string variable D$.

All functions except one have the same format (Figure 3-18). You specify a function with a keyword (like SQR for square root). In this respect functions are similar to statements. But functions are always followed by one argument. (The exception is USR, which can have more than one argument.) The argument is enclosed in parentheses.

The function performs standard calculations or other operations on the argument. It comes up with a value which can be used exactly like any variable or constant. Some functions yield numeric values, while others yield strings. For example, the SQR function always calculates the square root of its single numeric argument. The LEN function always counts the number of active characters in its single string argument.

Functions can be substituted for variables or constants anywhere in a BASIC statement, except to the left of an equal sign. In other words, you can say that A = SQR(B), but you cannot say that SQR(A) = B.

Every function in a BASIC statement is reduced to a single numeric or string value before any other parts of the BASIC statement are evaluated. Function arguments can be constants, variables, or expressions. Therefore, before the computer can perform the function, it may have to evaluate the function argument. It can then apply the function to the argument, yielding the final numeric or string value. Not until all functions in a given expression are evaluated is the expression itself evaluated. For example, consider the following statement:

```
10  B=24.7*(SQR(C)+5)-SIN(0.2+D)
```

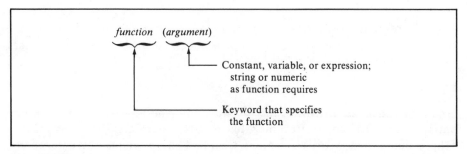

FIGURE 3-18. Function format

The ATARI computer evaluates the SQR function as soon as it retrieves the value of variable C. Then it evaluates the expression 0.2 + D and applies the SIN function to it. Finally it uses the function results in evaluating the entire expression. Suppose SQR(C) = 6.72 and SIN(0.2 + D) = 0.625. The expression is first reduced to 24.7 * (6.72 + 5) - 0.625. Then this simpler expression is evaluated. Variable B, then, is 288.859.

Numeric Functions

Here is a list of the numeric functions that you can use in ATARI BASIC:

SGN   Returns the sign of an argument: +1 for a positive argument, -1 for a negative argument, 0 for a zero argument.

ABS   Returns the absolute value of an argument. A positive argument does not change; a negative argument is converted to its positive equivalent.

RND   Generates a random number between 0 and 1.

INT   Truncates the fractional part of the argument value.

SQR   Computes the square root of the argument.

EXP   Raises the constant e (2.71828179) to the power of the argument (e^{arg}).

LOG   Returns the natural logarithm of the argument.

CLOG   Returns the common logarithm of the argument.

SIN   Returns the trigonometric sine of the argument.

COS   Returns the trigonometric cosine of the argument.

ATN   Returns the trigonometric arctangent of the argument.

Using Numeric Functions

Use functions freely wherever they make your programming job easier. You need not bother with numeric functions you do not already understand, however. For example, if you do not understand trigonometry, you are unlikely to use SIN, COS, and ATN functions in your programs.

The following short program uses a numeric function:

```
10 PRINT "Enter a number";
20 INPUT A
29 REM Determine sign of entry
30 B=SGN(A)
40 PRINT A;" is ";
50 IF B=1 THEN PRINT "positive.":GOTO
10
60 IF B=-1 THEN PRINT "negative.":GOTO
10
69 REM IF B isn't 1 or -1, must be 0
70 PRINT "neither positive nor negativ
e."
80 GOTO 10
```

This program figures out whether a number entered at the keyboard is positive, negative, or neither.

Degrees and Radians in Trigonometric Functions

The three trigonometric functions normally measure angles in radians. You can change to degrees by executing the DEG statement before using the trigonometric functions. Executing the RAD statement switches back to radians. Here are some examples:

```
DEG

READY
? SIN(90)
1

READY
RAD

READY
? SIN(1.571)
0.9999999833

READY
▓
```

String Functions

String functions allow you to manipulate string data in a variety of ways. Here is a list of the string functions that you can use in ATARI BASIC (see Chapter 4 for more information).

ADR   Determines where in memory a string is stored.

ASC   Converts a string character to its standard numeric code (ATASCII) equivalent.

LEN   Counts the number of characters contained in a text string.

STR$ Converts a numeric value to a string of digits.

VAL   Converts a string of digits to its equivalent numeric value.

CHR$ Converts a numeric (ATASCII) code to its equivalent text character.

String functions let you determine the length of a string and convert numeric values, numeric (ASCII) codes, and string characters. Here are some examples:

STR$(14)   Converts 14 to "14".

LEN("ABC")   Determines the length of the string, in this case, 3.

VAL("14")   Converts "14" to 14.

System Functions

Some functions give you access to the ATARI computer on a more fundamental level than does BASIC in general. Chapter 4 discusses how to use these functions.

PEEK   Fetches the contents of a memory location.

FRE   Returns available free space—the number of unused RAM memory bytes.

USR   Transfers control of the ATARI computer to a machine language program.

PADDLE   Reports the position of the paddle controller knob.

PTRIG   Indicates whether the paddle controller button is being pushed.

STICK   Reports which way the joystick controller is leaning.

STRIG   Indicates whether the joystick controller button is being pushed.

4

ADVANCED BASIC PROGRAMMING

This chapter carries on from Chapter 3 in describing how to program the ATARI computer in BASIC. It covers many new BASIC statements and explores new facets of some familiar ones. Chapter 3 taught you enough to let you make your computer do some fancy tricks; this chapter shows you how to make it a useful tool.

USING STRINGS

The earliest computers were only able to use numbers. This made it difficult for the average user to communicate with them. ATARI BASIC makes it easy to use characters, not just numbers, in string values. To write a truly effective program, you need to learn as many string handling techniques as you can.

How Strings are Stored

In order to make full use of strings, you must understand how characters are stored in the ATARI computer's memory. This concept is really very simple. Computer memory can store numbers, but not characters. Characters are therefore converted to numbers. The ATARI computer uses a special numeric code, a variation of the standard code that most computers use. The standard code is called ASCII (American Standard Code for Information Interchange). The ATARI computer uses a slightly different code, called ATASCII (ATARI ASCII). For example, the ATASCII code for the letter A is 65, for B it is 66, C is 67, and so on. You will find a complete table of ATASCII codes and characters in Appendix D.

The ASC function converts the first character of a string to its ATASCII code. To see how this works, try the following program:

```
10 DIM A$(1)
20 PRINT "Enter one character";
30 INPUT A$
40 PRINT "The ATASCII code for ";A$;"
is:"
50 PRINT ASC(A$)
59 REM Use BREAK key to stop program
60 GOTO 20
RUN
Enter one character?A
The ATASCII code for A is:
65
Enter one character?8
The ATASCII code for 8 is:
56
Enter one character? ▓
```

Escape Sequences

Have you tried to assign any of the cursor movement characters, like ← (CTRL-+), to a string variable? Or have you tried to put them in a PRINT statement string constant? Unless you divined the way to do it from Appendix D, you probably met with no success.

There is a way to get special characters into a string. First press the ESC key, then type the keystroke that yields the special character. This process is called an *escape sequence*. We designate an escape sequence by prefixing the name of the second keystroke with ESC\. For example, ESC\CTRL-+ means press the ESC key, release it, then press the CTRL and + keys simultaneously. The cursor doesn't move left, as it would had you not pressed the ESC key. Instead, the escape sequence generates a single character. In this case, the character is ATASCII code 30. If you print that character, then the cursor moves left. Table 4-1 lists all the escape sequences and the characters they produce.

What you see when you type an escape sequence is not exactly what you get as a string character. For example, type ESC\CTRL-+ and you will see the character ←. Strictly speaking, this is not the character that goes in the string. You can see this for yourself in immediate mode. Try the following example (where you see the ← character in the PRINT statement, type ESC\CTRL-+):

```
PRINT "ART←←N"
ANT

READY
▓
```

TABLE 4-1. Escape Sequences

Keystroke	Echoed Character	ATASCII Code	String Character
ESC\ESC	⿃	27	Escape code
ESC\BACK S	◀	126	Cursor left, replace with blank space
ESC\TAB	▶	127	Cursor right to next tab stop
ESC\CTRL--	↑	28	Cursor up
ESC\CTRL-=	↓	29	Cursor down
ESC\CTRL-*	←	30	Cursor right
ESC\CTRL-+	→	31	Cursor left
ESC\CTRL-BACK S	◀	254	Delete character
ESC\CTRL->	▶	255	Insert character
ESC\CTRL-<	◥	125	Clear screen
ESC\CTRL-TAB	◀	158	Clear tab stop
ESC\CTRL-2	◤	253	Sound built-in speaker
ESC\SHIFT-BACK S	↑	156	Delete line
ESC\SHIFT->	↓	157	Insert line
ESC\SHIFT-<	◥	125	Clear screen
ESC\SHIFT-TAB	→	159	Set tab stop

It is possible to display the exact characters you see when you type an escape sequence. You simply precede each escape sequence character with the special escape sequence ESC\ESC. Try the following example (where you see ↓, type ESC\CTRL- =; where you see ⿃ , type ESC\ESC):

```
PRINT "⿃↓⿃↓"
↓↓

READY
▓
```

The CHR$ Function

In ATARI BASIC, you can produce a character directly from its ATASCII code number. The CHR$ function translates an ATASCII code number into its character equivalent. For example, to create the symbol "$", first find its ATASCII code in Appendix D. Then use the code with CHR$, as follows:

```
PRINT CHR$(36)
$

READY
▓
```

The CHR$ function works equally well with any ATASCII code. Experiment in immediate mode using numbers between 0 and 255.

You can use the CHR$ function in conjunction with regular strings in a PRINT statement, as follows:

```
? CHR$(34);"Queen of ";CHR$(123);CHR$(
34);CHR$(253)
"Queen of ♠"

READY
▓
```

The CHR$ function lets you include otherwise unavailable characters like quotation marks as part of a string value.

Substrings

There is a way to extract only part of a string variable's value. Pieces of string values are called *substrings*. To designate a substring, first specify the string variable name. Immediately following that, in parentheses, state the position of the first and last characters to use. For example, suppose the present value of string variable A$ is the six characters ABCDEF. A$(2,4) specifies the substring BCD, the second through the fourth characters in the string. Substrings may look like array elements, but remember that ATARI BASIC does not allow string arrays.

Specifying the position of the last character in a substring is optional. If the last character is not specified, BASIC assumes you want the entire right-hand portion of the string. For example, if A$ is ABCDEF as before, A$(2) specifies the substring BCDEF. In this case, the end of the substring is the same as the end of the whole string.

You can specify the first and last character positions with a numeric constant, variable, or expression.

A substring can be on the left-hand side of an equal sign in an assignment statement, as shown in the following example:

```
10 DIM A$(20)
20 A$="FIRST NAME"
30 A$(7,9)="BAS"
40 ? A$
RUN
FIRST BASE

READY
▓
```

Error number 5 occurs if there is any problem with the substring specification. The last substring character cannot come before the first. For example, with A$ still ABCDEF, substrings A$(4,3) and A$(7,1) will cause error 5. Neither the first nor the last character numbers can be 0.

String Concatenation

You can join strings together to form one longer string. This is called *concatenation* (Figure 4-1). With concatenation, you can develop strings of any length. The only

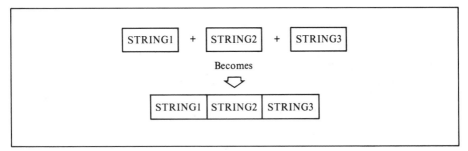

FIGURE 4-1. String Concatenation

limit is the amount of RAM available. The LEN function allows you to concatenate strings in ATARI BASIC. Here is an example:

```
10 DIM A$(10),B$(10),C$(10)
20 A$="WIND"
30 B$="PIPE"
40 C$="LINE"
50 A$(LEN(A$)+1)=B$
60 PRINT A$
70 B$(LEN(B$)+1)=C$
80 PRINT B$
90 END
RUN
WINDPIPE
PIPELINE

READY
※
```

If you wish to concatenate strings for output only, it is just as easy to use the PRINT statement with semicolon separators between strings. The previous program could be rewritten as follows:

```
10 DIM A$(4),B$(4),C$(4)
20 A$="WIND"
30 B$="PIPE"
40 C$="LINE"
50 PRINT A$;B$
60 PRINT B$;C$
70 END
RUN
WINDPIPE
PIPELINE

READY
※
```

This version produces exactly the same output as the first version, but uses fewer statements and shorter string variables to do it. This is definitely an improvement, unless of course you want to use the concatenated strings again in the same program.

Graphics Characters

The ATARI computer has 29 special graphics characters you can generate from the keyboard by using the CTRL key in conjunction with other keys. These are listed in Appendix D. You can use these characters in string values just as you would use any other character. By combining graphics characters in the right sequence, you can draw pictures. For example, you can use them to draw a playing card. Use the / and \ characters (CTRL-F and CTRL-G) for the corners. The ⁻ character (CTRL-M) will draw the top of the card, the _ character (CTRL-N) the bottom, I (CTRL-V) the left edge, and the I character (CTRL-B) the right edge. CTRL-; is the ♣ character. The following program will draw the ace of spades.

```
100 ? "/‾‾‾‾‾‾‾‾‾‾‾‾‾\"
110 ? "I A            I"
120 ? "I             I"
130 ? "I             I"
140 ? "I             I"
150 ? "I             I"
160 ? "I             I"
170 ? "I       ♣     I"
180 ? "I             I"
190 ? "I             I"
200 ? "I             I"
210 ? "I             I"
220 ? "I             I"
230 ? "I         A I"
240 ? "_____/"
```

Notice that many of the lines in this program print exactly the same string. It would be much more efficient to establish a string variable with a value equal to the string printed on line 120. Then instead of repeating the string constant, the program could simply print the string variable.

Numeric Strings

A *numeric string* is a string whose contents can be evaluated as a number. Numeric values can be converted to numeric strings using the STR$ funcion. The general rule is that a numeric value is converted to a string in the same format in which it would appear in PRINT statement output. If the numeric value would display with a minus sign, the first character of the string is a minus sign. If the numeric value is very large or very small, it is expressed in scientific notation when it is either displayed or converted to a numeric string. This is illustrated in the following program:

```
10 DIM N$(20)
20 ? "Enter a number";
30 INPUT N
```

```
40  N$=STR$(N)
50  ? "Numeric ";N
60  ? " String ";N$
69  REM Use BREAK key to end
70  GOTO 20
RUN
Enter a number?-.0098
Numeric -9.8E-03
 String -9.8E-03
Enter a number?1234567899
Numeric 1234567890
 String 1234567890
Enter a number? ▓
```

Run the program and enter some positive and negative numbers. Try a number with more than ten digits, and a number with more than ten nonzero digits after the decimal point.

It is possible to concatenate numeric strings using the LEN function. Try entering a few numbers in the following program:

```
10  DIM N$(100)
20  ? "Enter a few digits";
30  INPUT N
39  REM Append the latest input
40  N$(LEN(N$)+1)=STR$(N)
50  ? "The new number is:"
60  ? N$
70  ?
79  REM Use BREAK key to end
80  GOTO 20
RUN
Enter a few digits?1234
The new number is:
1234

Enter a few digits?5678
The new number is:
12345678

Enter a few digits?9098
The new number is:
123456789098

Enter a few digits? ▓
```

Initializing String Variables

There is a trick you can employ to assign the same value to every character of a string variable. This is illustrated in the following program:

```
10  DIM S$(100)
19  REM Assign character to propagate
20  S$="@"
```

```
29 REM Establish end of propagation
30 S$(100)=S$
39 REM Propagation to end of string
40 S$(2)=S$
50 PRINT S$
60 END
RUN
@@@@@@@@@@@@@@@@@@@@@@@@@@@@@@@@@@@@@@@@@@
@@@@@@@@@@@@@@@@@@@@@@@@@@@@@@@@@@@@@@@@@@
@@@@@@@@@@@@@@@@@@@@@@@@@@@

READY
▓
```

First, assign a value to the first character of a string (line 20). You can use any value; use the CHR$ function if you like. Next, you must establish the end of the propagation (line 30). This can be anywhere up to the maximum dimensioned length of the string. Then a single assignment statement propagates the first character through the string, stopping at the point you just established (line 40).

The propagation trick on line 40 works as follows. The computer assigns the value of the string on the right side of the equal sign to the string on the left side. It does this one character at a time. The first character of the left-hand string is S$(2). The first character of the right-hand string is S$(1). So S$(2) gets the value of S$(1). Now the program moves on to the second character of each string: S$(3) on the left, S$(2) on the right. The new value of S$(2) is assigned to S$(3). The assignment continues character by character. The left-hand string starts out one step ahead of the right, and stays that way. The assignment on line 40 ends when the last character of the left-hand string receives a value from the right-hand string. This happens when S$(100) receives the value of S$(99).

Simulating String Arrays

ATARI BASIC does not allow string arrays. You can simulate a string array with a string variable. We will call this arrangement a *pseudo-array*. What you do is divide the string into substrings of equal lengths, and treat each substring as an element of the pseudo-array (Figure 4-2). To compute the starting position of a pseudo-array element, you need to know its element number and the length of each array element.

There are two limitations to string psuedo-arrays:

· All elements of the pseudo-array must have the same length. The length is fixed at its maximum. If you want to assign a short string value to one element, you have to fill out the unused part of the element with blanks. The LEN function will not work with pseudo-array elements, since element length doesn't vary.

· The process of calculating the starting location of a pseudo-array element is time-consuming. You may notice delays in your program execution.

The following program uses a string pseudo-array:

```
10 DIM A$(100),TEMP$(10),BL$(10)
19 REM Ten string values
```

```
20 DATA Ricky,Lucy,Fred,Ethel,,1234567
8901,+++,A+B=1E100,♥♣,abracadabra
29 REM Initialize BL$ to blanks
30 BL$=" ":BL$(10)=BL$:BL$(2)=BL$
39 REM Assign pseudo-array values
40 FOR N=1 TO 10
49 REM 1st, put value in temp. string
50 READ TEMP$
59 REM Get length of new value
60 TL=LEN(TEMP$)
69 REM Pad short values with blanks
70 IF TL<10 THEN TEMP$(TL+1)=BL$
79 REM Compute start of array element
80 START=(N-1)*10+1
89 REM Assign value to array element
90 A$(START)=TEMP$
100 NEXT N
109 REM display assigned values
110 FOR N=1 TO 10
119 REM Compute start of element
120 START=(N-1)*10+1
130 ? "Element ";N;" is: ";A$(START,ST
ART+9)
140 NEXT N
150 END
RUN
Element 1 is: Ricky
Element 2 is: Lucy
Element 3 is: Fred
Element 4 is: Ethel
Element 5 is:
Element 6 is: 1234567890
Element 7 is: +++
Element 8 is: A+B=1E100
Element 9 is: ♥♣
Element 10 is: abracadabr

READY
▓
```

In this program, string array A$ plays host to the pseudo-array. The pseudo-array has ten elements of ten characters each, for a total of 100 characters (line 10). Each element gets one of the string values from the DATA statement list (line 20). Included among these is a null value and two values that are too long to fit in one array element. The program assigns string variable BL$ a blank value (line 30). You could eliminate variable BL$ by using blank string constants instead, but this way is neater. The program assigns each string value from the DATA statement list to a temporary string variable (line 50). This is necessary because ATARI BASIC doesn't allow subscripted variables in READ statements. The program concatenates blanks onto a short value to remove the remains of the previous value (lines 60 and 70). Finally, the program computes the index of the pseudo-array element and

String variable X$

Element 1	Element 2	Element 3	Element 4	Element 5

1   - - - -   10   - - - -   20   - - - -   30   - - - -   40   - - - -   50

NOTE: String variable X$ is divided into ten elements of equal lengths. Element 1 is X$(1,10), element 2 is X$(11,20), element 3 is X$(21,30), element 4 is X$(31,40), and element 5 is X$(41,50).

FIGURE 4-2. String pseudo-arrays

assigns it the value built up in the temporary variable (lines 80 and 90). When you run the program, notice what happens to the null string value and the values that are too long.

VARIABLE STORAGE

There is a limit to the number of variables you can have in one ATARI BASIC program. The maximum is 128. Each numeric variable name, string variable name, and array name you use counts toward the limit. An entire array only counts as one name, no matter how many elements it contains.

ATARI BASIC maintains a list of variable names. This list is called the *variable name table* (VNT). The variable name table has room for 128 variable names, hence the 128-variable limit. Each time you use a new variable name in immediate mode, it is added to the variable name table. Variables in programmed mode are added to the variable name table as they are encountered during program execution.

Variable names stay in the variable name table until a NEW command is executed. Then the entire variable name table is cleared. Merely deleting all references to a variable will not remove it from the variable name table.

When you record a program on cassette using the CSAVE statement, the variable name table is saved along with the program lines. When you read the program back in with the CLOAD statement, the recorded variable name table takes the place of the variable name table currently in memory. Chapter 5 explains a way to record programs on cassette without recording the variable name table. Chapter 7 discusses what happens to the variable name table when you save and load programs from diskette.

DIRECT ACCESS AND CONTROL

A number of statements allow you direct access to the ATARI computer's memory and its communication channels to input and output devices. As BASIC programs become more complex, they tend to need this direct access. Several of the programs in this chapter require direct access. Later chapters rely even more heavily on direct access and control statements. For example, you need these statements in order to exercise the ATARI computer's full graphics capabilities.

Memory and Addressing

The ATARI computer can have as many as 65,536 individually addressable memory locations. They are addressed by number, 0 through 65535. Each usable memory location can hold one number ranging between 0 and 255. Everything in memory must be converted to a number in this range. The ATARI computer uses different coding schemes to convert programs and data to sequences of numbers that are stored in this fashion. It has one scheme for BASIC keywords, and others for general character data, numeric values, graphics displays, machine language code—the list goes on. The computer knows by context how to decode memory contents. When you see memory contents in their raw form, as numbers between 0 and 255, you will have to decide what they mean. Appendix D will help you decode ATASCII codes to characters.

PEEK and POKE

The PEEK function lets you examine the value stored in any memory location. Consider the following statement:

```
10 A=PEEK(200)
```

This statement assigns the contents of memory location 200 to variable A.

The POKE statement puts a value into a memory location. For example, the following statement takes the value of variable A and stores it in memory location 8000:

```
20 POKE 8000,A
```

You can specify the address for PEEK and POKE with a number, a variable, or an expression. In any case, its value must be between 0 and 65535 or error number 3 occurs. No error results from using PEEK or POKE with a memory location that is outside the available memory on your computer. For example, an ATARI computer with 16K of RAM has no memory at location 24000. In this case, a PEEK or POKE to that location would be meaningless but would not cause an error.

You can use the PEEK function with RAM or ROM. You can use the POKE statement with either kind of memory, but it will only affect RAM that actually exists. By definition, ROM can only be read. It cannot be changed with the POKE statement.

Appendix G lists useful memory locations to use PEEK and POKE with.

PROGRAM OUTPUT AND DATA ENTRY

The most inexperienced programmer quickly discovers that the input and output sections of a program are its most difficult parts.

Nearly every program uses data which must be entered at the keyboard. Will a few INPUT statements suffice? In most cases the answer is "no." What if the operator accidentally presses the wrong key? Or worse, what if the operator discovers that he or she input the wrong data—after entering two or three additional data items? A usable program must assume that the operator is human, and is likely to make any conceivable human error.

Results, likewise, cannot simply be displayed or printed haphazardly by a group of unplanned PRINT statements. A human being will have to read this output. Unless the output is carefully designed, it will be very difficult to read. As a consequence, information could be misread, or entirely overlooked. This chapter will explore some ways of arranging information on the display screen for best readability. Chapter 6 addresses the same topic for the printer.

DISPLAY SCREEN OUTPUT

We use the word *formatting* to describe the process of arranging information on a display screen so that the information is easier to understand or more pleasing to the eye. The basic tool for displaying information is the PRINT statement. We've already used it to print numeric and string data, one or more items per line.

The key to formatting output on the display screen is cursor control. PRINT statement output starts wherever the cursor is located. Each character that displays on the screen affects the position of the cursor. After displaying most characters, the cursor moves one column to the right. A few characters, notably escape sequences, move the cursor in other directions. The PRINT statement may end with a carriage return, moving the cursor to the beginning of the next display line. A new statement, POSITION, can move the cursor to any spot on the display screen. Let's see how we can use these facts to control display screen output.

Carriage Return

It is natural to associate a carriage return with the RETURN key. When you press the RETURN key, the cursor advances to the beginning of the next display line. This happens because the RETURN key generates an ATASCII *end-of-line* (EOL) character, which causes a carriage return. A carriage return occurs whenever the display screen receives an ATASCII EOL character. The PRINT statement can also generate an EOL character.

Normally, a PRINT statement outputs an EOL character as its last action. That explains why the cursor advances to the next display line at the end of a PRINT statement. For example, this program displays a column of 20 Z's in the first position of each display line:

```
190 DIM C$(1)
200 C$="Z"
210 FOR I=1 TO 20
220 PRINT C$
230 NEXT I
```

```
240 PRINT "PHEW!"
250 END
```

Of course, a semicolon or comma at the end of a PRINT statement suppresses the carriage return; or does it? Try this variation on the last program:

```
190 DIM C$(1)
200 C$="Z"
210 FOR I=1 TO 760
220 PRINT C$;
230 NEXT I
240 PRINT "PHEW!"
250 END
```

The screen fills with 20 lines of Z's. The word "PHEW!" appears at the beginning of the 21st line. Where did those 20 carriage returns come from? The semicolon at the end of the PRINT statement on line 20 is supposed to suppress the EOL character. It doesn't seem to work at the end of a display line.

Whenever anything is displayed in the last column of any row, it triggers a carriage return. This is a feature of the display screen. Rather than lose the characters off the screen to the right, the display screen performs a carriage return and continues the same output line on the next display line.

The computer is doing more than moving the cursor down to the next display line. It is actually tacking another whole display line onto the end of the logical line started by the first display line. There is no way to stop this; commas and semicolons won't work in this instance. This doesn't matter in most cases. Letters and digits always appear as letters and digits. The cursor control characters, ↓, ↑, ←, and → (ATASCII codes 28 through 31), always move the cursor the same way. But the delete-line and insert-line characters (ATASCII codes 156 and 157) work on logical lines, not just physical lines. The tab characters (ATASCII codes 127, 158, and 159), which we will investigate soon, also work with logical lines. If you use any characters that work on logical lines, it is best to simply avoid displaying anything in the last column. That way no logical line will be longer than one physical display line.

Suppose something is displayed in the last column of the last line on the screen. A carriage return occurs, but there is no next line to advance to. The computer forces the entire first logical line off the screen so the cursor will have a place to go. The following program illustrates this:

```
300 PRINT "first logical line, which i
s so long, it takes two display lines"

309 REM Skip down to bottom line
310 FOR N=1 TO 21
320 PRINT
330 NEXT N
339 REM Space over to last character
340 FOR N=1 TO 37
350 PRINT "-";
360 NEXT N
```

```
369 REM Ring the bell awhile
370 FOR N=1 TO 25
380 PRINT CHR$(253);
390 NEXT N
399 REM Display last col., last line
400 PRINT "@";
409 REM Loop until BREAK key hit
410 GOTO 410
```

This program first displays the "first line" message (line 300). Then it outputs 21 EOL characters, moving the "first line" message to the top of the screen, and leaving the cursor at the beginning of the bottom line (lines 310 to 330). Next it outputs 37 hyphens, moving the cursor to the penultimate column of the last row (lines 340 to 360). After that, it sounds the console speaker for a few seconds (lines 370 to 390). This gives you a chance to watch the top line carefully. Finally, the program displays a character in the last column of the bottom display line (line 400). A carriage return occurs. The "first line" message is instantly pushed off the top of the screen so the cursor can advance to the next display line. Notice that the whole logical line scrolls off the top, not just the top display line. The program loops indefinitely to suppress the **READY** message that would occur if it ended (line 410). Press the BREAK key to end the program.

Were you surprised that sounding the speaker did not cause a carriage return? After all, the PRINT statement on line 380 looks like it should display a character in the last column of the bottom line. It doesn't, because the bell character, ATASCII code 253, is a *nonprinting* character. It has no effect on the cursor position.

Technically, the automatic carriage return signals the end of a physical line only, not necessarily the end of a logical line. The logical line ends only when an EOL character occurs. But a logical line can comprise at most three display lines. Therefore, if three automatic carriage returns happen with no intervening EOL character, an EOL character automatically occurs along with the third carriage return.

Columnar Output

It is usually much easier to scan a list of items if they are organized in columns. This is true of both numbers and characters. ATARI BASIC has two ways to produce output in columnar form. One is to use commas between values in PRINT statements. The other is to use the TAB key with escape sequences.

If the computer finds a comma after a PRINT statement value, it moves the cursor to the right. It fills in blank spaces between the end of the value just displayed and the next *column stop*. The first column stop is ten spaces from the left margin. Additional column stops occur every ten spaces after that. The program in Figure 4-3 uses two of the three available column stops, as shown in the sample output in Figure 4-4.

There is a catch to using commas. The two spaces just ahead of a column stop must be blank. If these spaces are not blank, that stop is deactivated for the current

```
9 REM Display gas cost table
10 PRINT "How much per gallon";
20 INPUT CPG
30 PRINT "Average miles per gallon";
40 INPUT MPG
50 PRINT "MILES","GALLONS","COST"
60 PRINT "--------","----------","------"
70 FOR MI=100 TO 1700 STEP 100
79 REM Compute gal. to nearest 10th
80 GAL=INT(MI/MPG*10)/10
89 REM Compute cost to nearest cent
90 COST=INT(CPG*GAL*100)/100
100 PRINT MI,GAL,COST
110 NEXT MI
120 PRINT
130 PRINT ,"MPG=";MPG,"$";CPG;" per ga
1."
140 END
```

NOTE: Sample output shown in Figure 4-4.

FIGURE 4-3. Gas Cost program listing

```
MILES        GALLONS      COST
--------     ----------   ------
100          4.5          7.74
200          9            15.48
300          13.6         23.39
400          18.1         31.13
500          22.7         39.04
600          27.2         46.78
700          31.8         54.69
800          36.3         62.43
900          40.9         70.34
1000         45.4         78.08
1100         50           86
1200         54.5         93.74
1300         59           101.48
1400         63.6         109.39
1500         68.1         117.13
1600         72.7         125.04
1700         77.2         132.78

             MPG=22       $1.72 per gal.

READY
▓
```

FIGURE 4-4. Sample output from Gas Cost program (Figure 4-3)

display line. The next EOL character reactivates the stop. In the following program, the second PRINT statement value is nine characters long. It encroaches on one of the spaces ahead of a column stop, disabling the stop.

```
PRINT "NAME","TELEPHONE","PARTY"
NAME        TELEPHONE            PARTY

READY
▓
```

The Tab Feature

The tab feature on the ATARI computer is much like the tab feature on a typewriter. It allows you to move the cursor rapidly from left to right to the next established tab stop. A number of tab stops are preset when you turn on the ATARI computer. They occur across the entire length of a logical line. On the standard 38-column screen, there are tab stops at the left margin (column 2) and at columns 7, 15, 23, and every eight columns after that (Figure 4-5). The tab feature is similar in function to commas in PRINT statements. The two are completeley independent, however. The locations of column stops have no bearing on the locations of tab stops, and vice versa.

The TAB key advances the cursor to the next tab stop on the screen. To tab the cursor in immediate mode, simply press the TAB key. The cursor moves past anything already displayed, without erasing it. If you press the TAB key with the cursor at or beyond the last tab stop, the cursor advances to the beginning of the next logical line.

To tab the cursor in programmed mode, display ATASCII code 127. You can do this with the CHR$ function or by using ESC\TAB in a string value. We can rewrite the program in Figure 4-3 to display columnar output using the tab feature instead of commas. Change the program as shown below; where you see the character ▶ , type ESC\TAB.

```
50  PRINT "▶MILES▶GALLONS▶COST"
60  PRINT "▶------▶----------▶----"
100 PRINT "▶";MI;"▶";GAL;"▶";COST
130 PRINT "▶▶MPG=";MPG;"▶$";CPG;" per
gal."
140 END
```

The modified program displays the same table as the original (Figure 4-4), but the spacing is a bit different.

You can set additional tab stops in any column. To set a tab stop in immediate mode, move the cursor to the desired column, then press SHIFT-TAB.

You can set tab stops using a PRINT statement. The PRINT statement has to display a string which moves the cursor to the desired column, then displays the tab-set character. You can place the tab-set character in a string with the escape sequence ESC\SHIFT-TAB or with CHR$(159). The following program sets a tab

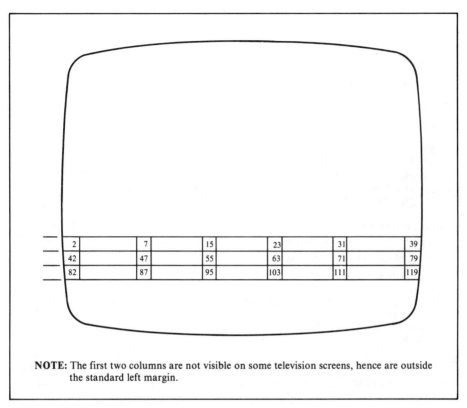

2		7		15		23		31		39
42		47		55		63		71		79
82		87		95		103		111		119

NOTE: The first two columns are not visible on some television screens, hence are outside the standard left margin.

FIGURE 4-5. Standard display screen tab stops

stop in the fifth space to the right of the left margin, then displays a message starting there:

```
110 PRINT "    ";CHR$(159)
120 PRINT CHR$(127);"THIS MESSAGE IS I
NDENTED FIVE SPACES FROM THE LEFT MARG
IN"
RUN

     THIS MESSAGE IS INDENTED FIVE SPA
CES FROM THE LEFT MARGIN

READY
▓
```

To clear a tab stop in immediate mode, move the cursor to the desired column and press CTRL-TAB. To clear a tab stop in programmed mode, move the cursor to the desired column and display ATASCII code 158. You can display this code with the CHR$ function or with the escape sequence ESC\CTRL-TAB. The following program clears all the preset tab stops. Where you see ↑, type ESC\CTRL‑‑. For ▶ type ESC\TAB, and for ← type ESC\CTRL-TAB.

```
498 REM ***Clear preset tab stops***
499 REM 1st, create a long line
500 FOR N=1 TO 114
510 PRINT "H";
520 NEXT N
529 REM Move cursor back up
530 PRINT "↑↑↑";
539 REM Clear all stops
540 FOR N=1 TO 16
550 PRINT "▶←";
560 NEXT N
570 END
```

There is one thing to watch out for when you use the tab feature. If you print anything in the space just before a tab stop, you temporarily inactivate that stop. The next EOL character reactivates the stop. Here is an example of this aspect of tabbing (type ESC\TAB where you see ▶):

```
50 PRINT "MILES▶GALLONS▶COST"
60 PRINT "――――▶――――――▶――――"
70 PRINT 100;"▶";4.5;"▶";7.74
80 END
```

Both lines 50 and 60 display something in the space just ahead of the first tab stop, inactivating it. Line 70 does not. As a result, the columns do not line up as intended. Press the SYSTEM RESET key before you run this program to clear any nonstandard tab stops you may have set.

Right-Justified Output

Both of ATARI BASIC's methods for aligning output in columns line values up on the left edge of the column. This is called *left-justified* output, and is fine for words and other alphabetic values. Numbers, on the other hand, are easier to read if they line up on the right. We can add a subroutine to the Gas Cost program (Figure 4-3) to right-justify its three columns. Figure 4-6 shows the new version of the program.

The main program uses the following new variables:

· N, the numeric value that will be right-justified
· NS, the number of spaces available in the column
· BL$, a string full of blanks
· T$, a string variable used temporarily
· N$, the output string.

The main program has changed in order to add the subroutine. It now dimensions BL$, T$, and N$ to have at least as many characters as the widest column (line 5). It fills BL$ with blanks (line 7). The single PRINT statement now uses three lines (lines 100, 102, and 104). Notice that the PRINT statements on lines 100 and 102 end with

```
4 REM String needed for subroutine
5 DIM N$(10),T$(10),BL$(40)
6 REM Fill BL$() with blanks
7 BL$(1)=" ":BL$(40)=BL$:BL$(2)=BL$
9 REM Display gas cost table
10 PRINT "How much per gallon";
20 INPUT CPG
30 PRINT "Average miles per gallon";
40 INPUT MPG
50 PRINT "MILES","GALLONS","  COST"
60 PRINT "-----","-------","------"
70 FOR MI=100 TO 1700 STEP 100
79 REM Compute gal. to nearest 10th
80 GAL=INT(MI/MPG*10)/10
89 REM Compute cost to nearest cent
90 COST=INT(CPG*GAL*100)/100
100 NS=5:N=MI:GOSUB 11000:PRINT N$(1,N
S),
102 NS=7:N=GAL:GOSUB 11000:PRINT N$(1,
NS),
104 NS=6:N=COST:GOSUB 11000:PRINT N$(1
,NS)
110 NEXT MI
120 PRINT
130 PRINT ,"MPG=";MPG,"$";CPG;" per ga
l."
140 END
10995 REM *****************************
10996 REM *    Subroutine aligns      *
10997 REM *numeric values on right    *
10998 REM *****************************
10999 REM Convert to left-just string
11000 T$=STR$(N)
11009 REM Erase stale value of N$
11010 N$=BL$
11019 REM Right-justify
11020 N$(NS-LEN(T$)+1,NS)=T$
11030 RETURN
```

NOTE: Shading shows lines changed from Figure 4-3. Sample output shown in Figure 4-8.

FIGURE 4-6. Right-justified Gas Cost program listing

a comma. This advances the cursor to the left edge of the next column.

The subroutine needs individual access to each digit of the number to be justified. BASIC allows such access only in string variables, so the subroutine converts the number to a numeric string (line 11000). Next, it fills the output string with blanks (line 11010). That guarantees a reliable, benign value in parts of the string that don't end with a digit. Finally, it right-justifies the number (line 11020). It figures out how long the number is and how close to the right edge of the column that number has to start in order to fit (Figure 4-7).

As an exercise, try changing the program to use the tab feature instead of commas.

The right-justified output (Figure 4-8) is a definite improvement over the original output (Figure 4-4). This is especially true in the left-hand column, where none of the numbers have decimal points.

Decimal-Aligned Output

It would be easier to read columns of numbers with decimal points if the numbers lined up on the decimal point. To do this, we have to decide where to fix the decimal point in each column. Then we have to figure out where the decimal point is in each number. This is not a trivial task, because BASIC uses floating point numbers. The decimal point could be anywhere. Once we find it, we have to shift it right or left so it lines up properly. This may mean truncating extra digits from the right or filling in extra blanks on the right. To do all these things, we have to change the main program and the subroutine, as Figure 4-9 shows.

The new subroutine has all the requirements of the old one, plus a few new ones. Variable DD must specify the number of decimal digits. The subroutine also uses variables DP, NL, and J. The main program must assume that the subroutine will change their values before it returns.

The subroutine must discover the position of the decimal point in the number. It begins by assuming there is no decimal point (line 11030), then uses a FOR-NEXT loop to search through the numeric string until it finds one (lines 11040 to 11060). If no decimal point turns up, the subroutine sticks with its initial assumption: the decimal point follows the last digit. At this point (line 11070), variable DP has the number of digits up to and including the decimal point. The number is going to take

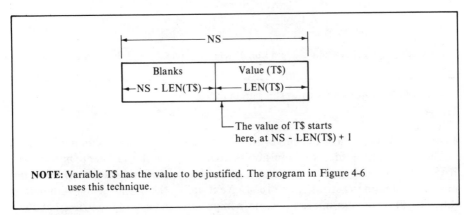

NOTE: Variable T$ has the value to be justified. The program in Figure 4-6 uses this technique.

FIGURE 4-7. Right-justifying a string value

```
        MILES       GALLONS       COST
        -----       -------       ----
          100           4.5        7.74
          200             9       15.48
          300          13.6       23.39
          400          18.1       31.13
          500          22.7       39.04
          600          27.2       46.78
          700          31.8       54.69
          800          36.3       62.43
          900          40.9       70.34
         1000          45.4       78.08
         1100            50          86
         1200          54.5       93.74
         1300            59      101.48
         1400          63.6      109.39
         1500          68.1      117.13
         1600          72.7      125.04
         1700          77.2      132.78

                     MPG=22     $1.72 per gal.

        READY
        ▓
```

FIGURE 4-8. Sample output from Right-justified Gas Cost program (Figure 4-6)

that many characters, plus the number of post-decimal digits specified by variable DD.

Compare the output from this version (Figure 4-10) with the output from the last version (Figure 4-8). Now all columns are easy to scan.

Notice that BASIC does not print a decimal point with whole numbers. Neither does it print *trailing zeros,* that is, zeros at the end of a number which don't change the value. A decimal point and trailing zeros can be added to numbers that need them. Add these lines to the end of the program in Figure 4-9:

```
11089 REM Decimal digits requested?
11090 IF DD=0 THEN RETURN
11099 REM Ensure decimal point's there

11100 N$(NS-DD,NS-DD)="."
11109 REM Replace trailing blanks with
zeros
11110 FOR J=NS-DD+1 TO NS
11120 IF N$(J,J)=" " THEN N$(J,J)="0"
11130 NEXT J
11140 RETURN
```

```
4 REM String needed for subroutine
5 DIM N$(10),T$(10),BL$(40)
6 REM Fill BL$() with blanks
7 BL$(1)=" ":BL$(40)=BL$:BL$(2)=BL$
9 REM Display gas cost table
10 PRINT "How much per gallon";
20 INPUT CPG
30 PRINT "Average miles per gallon";
40 INPUT MPG
50 PRINT "MILES","GALLONS","   COST"
60 PRINT "------","-------","-------"
70 FOR MI=100 TO 1700 STEP 100
79 REM Compute gal. to nearest 10th
80 GAL=INT(MI/MPG*10)/10
89 REM Compute cost to nearest cent
90 COST=INT(CPG*GAL*100)/100
100 NS=6:DD=0:N=MI:GOSUB 11000:PRINT N
$(1,NS),
102 NS=7:DD=1:N=GAL:GOSUB 11000:PRINT
N$(1,NS),
104 NS=7:DD=2:N=COST:GOSUB 11000:PRINT
 N$(1,NS)
110 NEXT MI
120 PRINT
130 PRINT ,"MPG=";MPG,"$";CPG;" per ga
l."
140 END
10995 REM ******************************
10996 REM *    Subroutine aligns     *
10997 REM *numeric values on decimal*
10998 REM ******************************
10999 REM Convert to left-just string
11000 T$=STR$(N)
11009 REM Erase stale value of N$
11010 N$=BL$
11029 REM Assume dec. point at end
11030 DP=LEN(T$)+1
11039 REM Look for real dec. point
11040 FOR J=1 TO LEN(T$)
11050 IF T$(J,J)="." THEN DP=J:J=NS
11060 NEXT J
11069 REM Compute number length
11070 NL=DP+DD
11079 REM Right-justify
11080 N$(NS-NL+1,NS)=T$
11090 RETURN
```

NOTE: Shading shows lines changed from Figure 4-6. Sample output
      shown in Figure 4-10.

FIGURE 4-9. Decimal-aligned Gas Cost program listing

```
    MILES        GALLONS        COST
 .... .... .... ....   .... .... .... .... ....   .... .... .... ....
       100         4.5        7.74
       200         9         15.48
       300        13.6       23.39
       400        18.1       31.13
       500        22.7       39.04
       600        27.2       46.78
       700        31.8       54.69
       800        36.3       62.43
       900        40.9       70.34
      1000        45.4       78.08
      1100        50         86
      1200        54.5       93.74
      1300        59        101.48
      1400        63.6      109.39
      1500        68.1      117.13
      1600        72.7      125.04
      1700        77.2      132.78

                  MPG=22    $1.72 per gal.

    READY
    ▓
```

FIGURE 4-10. Sample output from Decimal-aligned Gas Cost program (Figure 4-9)

What happens if you enter unrealistic values for gas price and mileage? Try entering $14.98 per gallon, and 2 miles per gallon. Error 5 occurs on line 11080 because the cost figure is too large for the last column. There are three ways to guard against this error: the subroutine can check, the calling program can check, or the calling program can carefully set the column width to make the error unlikely. At this point, we are using the latter alternative. We designed the columns to handle the largest probable values.

The most foolproof way to forestall an error like this is to have the subroutine check. Then no matter what the program user enters or how the program calls the subroutine, the error is blocked. Add this to the subroutine in Figure 4-9:

```
11019 REM Check for too-large numbers
11020 IF ABS(N)>=10^(NS-DD-2) THEN N$=
T$: N$(NS)="*": RETURN
```

Line 11020 makes sure the number will fit in the column. It assumes a sign character will occupy one space (a minus sign for negative numbers, a blank space for positive ones). If the number is too large, the subroutine generates as many digits as will fit. The last character becomes an asterisk to announce the overflow condition.

Try running the program with line 11020 added. The modified program displays much more slowly, which is quite a price to pay to avoid an error that careful output design will all but eliminate. Error checking has its place, but clearly not here.

CURSOR CONTROL

Semicolons, commas, and tab characters are fine for controlling the cursor in simple tables like those shown so far. More complicated displays demand more cursor control. ATARI BASIC offers two ways of directly controlling the cursor. One is to program the cursor movement characters, using the CHR$ function or escape sequences. The other way is to use the POSITION statement.

Clearing the Display Screen

Sometimes a program needs to erase everything on the display screen. Displaying ATASCII code 125 clears the screen and puts the cursor in the upper left-hand corner, its *home* position. You can use either CHR$(125), ESC\CTRL-<, or ESC\SHIFT-< to generate the necessary character.

Cursor Movement

It is possible to move the cursor to any space on the screen by programming the ↑, ↓, ←, and → characters. These cursor movement characters do not erase any characters they pass over. They behave exactly the same in programmed mode as they do in immediate mode.

The Future Value program (Figure 4-11) figures out what an investment you make today will be worth some years from now. After computing a future value, the program moves the cursor on top of your last inputs, one at a time. That lets you enter a new number or just press RETURN to leave the last entry unchanged.

The POSITION Statement

The POSITION statement places the cursor at any location on the screen. You just specify the column number and row number where you want the cursor positioned. The next PRINT statement starts at that screen location. Try this:

```
9 REM Clear screen
10 ? CHR$(125);
20 FOR J=1 TO 23
30 POSITION J,J
40 ? "*";
50 POSITION 24-J,J
60 ? "*";
70 NEXT J
79 REM Loop until BREAK pressed
80 GOTO 80
```

```
10 DIM R$(1),CU$(24),CR$(40)
19 REM Fill strings w/ cursor movement
 characters
20 CU$=CHR$(28):CU$(24)=CU$:CU$(2)=CU$

30 CR$=CHR$(31):CR$(40)=CR$:CR$(2)=CR$

40 PRINT CHR$(125);"FUTURE VALUE OF AN
 INVESTMENT"
50 PRINT
60 PRINT "Amount invested"
70 PRINT "Nominal interest rate"
80 PRINT "Compounded how many times ea
ch year"
90 PRINT "How many years";CU$(1,4)
100 PRINT CR$(1,15);:INPUT AMT
110 PRINT CR$(1,21);:INPUT IR
120 PRINT CR$(1,35);:INPUT CMP
130 PRINT CR$(1,14);:INPUT YR
139 REM Calc. intr. rate per period
140 IP=IR/CMP/100
149 REM Calculate future value
150 FV=AMT*(1+IP)^(CMP*YR)
159 REM Round to nearest cent, print
160 PRINT "Future value: $";INT(FV*100
+0.5)/100
170 PRINT
180 PRINT "Change investment";
190 INPUT R$
200 IF R$="Y" THEN PRINT CU$(1,7);:GOT
O 100
210 END
RUN
FUTURE VALUE OF AN INVESTMENT

Amount invested?6800
Nominal interest rate?9.5
Compounded how many times each year?4
How many years?10
Future value: $17388.64

Change investment?Y
```

FIGURE 4-11. Future Value program listing and sample output

When you run this program, the screen clears and a cross appears.

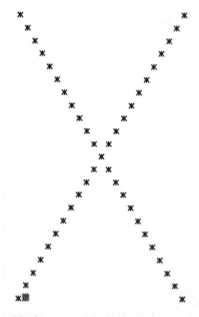

Notice how the leftmost parts of the cross are one space to the left of the normal left margin. Also, the top line of the screen is blank. How can this be? The first time the POSITION statement on line 30 is executed, it should put the cursor at column 1 on row 1. This is actually the case. There are usually only 38 usable columns on each line. But remember, the screen actually has 40 columns; the first two are normally unused because they are outside the standard left margin.

The POSITION statement ignores margins and treats the screen as a 40 × 24 grid. It numbers columns from 0 at the left edge to 39 at the right, and it numbers rows from 0 at the top of the screen to 23 at the bottom (Figure 4-12).

As a further example, try changing the Future Value program (Figure 4-11) so it uses the POSITION statement instead of cursor movement characters. You can eliminate the cursor movement string variables, CU$ and CR$. That makes lines 20 and 30 unnecessary. Lines 100, 110, 120, 130, and 200 all change to use the POSITION statement instead of the PRINT statement.

Determining Cursor Position

The POSITION statement does not move the cursor. It updates certain locations in the computer's memory with the new cursor position. The next time something is displayed on the display screen, it appears at the position dictated by those memory locations. The new row number is in location 84. The new column is in location 85. You can use the PEEK function at any time to find out where the cursor will be next: PEEK(84) for the row number, PEEK(85) for the column number. In some screen graphics modes, which we will cover in Chapters 8 and 9, the ATARI computer uses

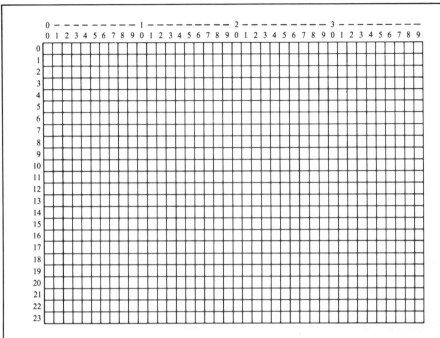

NOTE: The first two columns are not visible on some television screens, hence are outside the standard left margin.

FIGURE 4-12. POSITION statement column and row numbering

two locations for the column number. In this case, PEEK(86) * 256 + PEEK(85) gives the column number.

Each time the PRINT statement displays something, it updates two other memory locations with the last cursor position. Location 90 has the row number; 91 has the column number. PEEK(91) gives the last cursor column. PEEK(90) gives the last cursor row. Rows are numbered from 0 to 23, columns from 0 to 39, as with the POSITION statement (Figure 4-12).

Resetting Margins

You can change the display screen margins with the POKE statement. The ATARI computer uses memory location 82 to keep track of the left margin, and location 83 for the right margin. The standard left margin is at column 2. To change it to column 0, use this statement:

```
POKE 82, 0
```

The standard right margin is at column 39, the far right edge of the screen. The following statement changes it to column 38:

```
POKE 83, 38
```

When you reset margins, remember that the PRINT statement observes the margins. There is no character you can display with a PRINT statement that will move the cursor outside the margins. When output reaches the right margin, a carriage return occurs. To prove this for yourself, try the following program:

```
10 POKE 83, 10:REM Right Margin
20 FOR J=1 TO 10
30 PRINT CHR$(31);:REM Cursor right
40 NEXT J
50 PRINT "PUCE"
60 POKE 83, 39:REM Right Margin
RUN
  PUCE

READY
```

The cursor starts off at the left margin, in column 2. The PRINT statement inside the FOR-NEXT loop (lines 20 through 40) advances it nine spaces to the right margin, column 10. There it circles back to the left margin. The loop advances the cursor another two spaces, where a word is printed (line 50).

The POSITION statement can put the cursor outside the established margins. If the cursor is to the right of the right margin, only the first character of the next PRINT statement appears there. The computer displays the first character, then does an immediate carriage return. The following program illustrates this.

```
10 POKE 83, 10:REM Right margin
20 PRINT CHR$(125):REM clr. screen
30 POSITION 20,8
40 PRINT "SAFFRON"
50 POKE 83, 39:REM Right margin
```

The letter "S" appears at column 20, row 8. The rest of the PRINT statement output appears on row 9, starting at the left margin.

Widening the margins reduces the length not only of the physical display line, but of the logical line as well. A logical line never contains more than three physical lines, no matter what their lengths.

PROGRAMMING INPUT

Nearly every program requires some kind of input from the person using it. The goal of any program should be to minimize input errors and make it easy for someone using the program to spot and correct errors that do occur. There are ways to organize input which tend to minimize input errors. This section discusses the following methods:

· Display helpful messages
· Expect natural, intuitive responses
· Check inputs for reasonableness and range
· Use an error-handling subroutine

· Group inputs logically
· Allow review and change of grouped inputs
· Restrict responses: use game controllers
· Restrict choices: use menus.

Prompt Messages

Prompt messages were introduced in Chapter 3. Many of the example programs in this chapter have used them. As the examples have illustrated, prompt messages should be succinct. Space on the display screen is usually at a premium, so verbosity is a luxury. Keep the prompt brief. Try to leave enough room on the same line for the entire input response. When this is impossible, put the prompt message on one line and input the response on the next. Since the INPUT statement always displays a question mark, it's best to phrase prompt messages as questions.

Amplifying Input Instructions

Sometimes it is impossible to phrase a prompt message satisfactorily. Either it is too cryptic or it takes up too much room. In a case like this, you can display an amplified prompt message elsewhere on the screen. Here's how it works. The program displays a short prompt message next to the input. The program lets the user enter "H" if he needs help. If he does, the program displays amplified instructions. It puts the instructions in some standard location on the screen, say the bottom four lines. All it takes is a few PRINT statements to display the instructions. After displaying the instructions, the program must return to the input where the call for help originated. Figure 4-13 provides an example.

The program in Figure 4-13 inputs a single-letter command on the second line of the screen. It expands the command letter to a command word and displays the word on the right side of the top line. A complete program would do more than print the command, of course.

Figure 4-13 has a strange subroutine at line 32767. The subroutine does absolutely nothing but return. This technique is often useful with the ON-GOSUB statement. In this program, for example, there is no command "B." If the user enters a B, the program branches to the "do nothing" subroutine, then returns to get another command. The same thing happens to commands F and G. When the command is anything past H, the expression in the ON-GOSUB statement is larger than the number of lines on its list. Therefore, program execution falls through to the next program line, 390. Line 390 checks for the one remaining valid command, P.

The subroutine at line 1400 ends with POP and GOTO statements. If this were a RETURN statement, the program would branch back through line 380 to line 310. There the screen would be cleared, erasing the amplified instructions before anyone could read them.

```
10 DIM BL$(40),CMD$(1),R$(1)
49 REM Fill BL$ with blanks
50 BL$=" ":BL$(40)=BL$:BL$(2)=BL$
299 REM Amplified instr. line no.
300 AMPSUB=2000
310 PRINT CHR$(125):REM clear scrn
320 POSITION 2,1
330 PRINT "COMMAND (ACDEP, H for help)
";
340 INPUT CMD$
359 REM Process entry here
360 POSITION 20,0
370 PRINT "Command is ";
380 ON ASC(CMD$)-64 GOSUB 600,32767,80
0,1000,1200,32767,32767,1400:GOTO 310
390 IF CMD$<>"P" THEN 310
400 PRINT "Print":RETURN
600 PRINT "Add":RETURN
800 PRINT "Change":RETURN
1000 PRINT "Delete":RETURN
1200 PRINT "End":POSITION 2,10:END
1400 PRINT "Help"
1410 GOSUB 2000
1420 POP:GOTO 320
1994 REM ****************************
1995 REM *  Subroutine to explain *
1996 REM *  prompt message        *
1997 REM ****************************
1998 REM Clear dedicated area, then
1999 REM Position cursor
2000 GOSUB 2300
2009 REM Now display instructions
2010 PRINT "_____Command Summary__
_____"
2020 PRINT
2030 PRINT "   A=add    C=change   D=
delete"
2040 PRINT "   E=end    P=print     H=
help";
2050 RETURN
2296 REM ****************************
2297 REM *  Subroutine to clear   *
2298 REM *  instructions area     *
2299 REM ****************************
2300 POSITION 2,19
2310 FOR J=20 TO 23
2320 PRINT
2330 PRINT BL$(1,38);
2340 NEXT J
2350 POSITION 2,20
2360 RETURN
32767 RETURN:REM Do-nothing subr.
```

FIGURE 4-13. Command Input program listing

Any character or word could trigger the instructions; our choice, H, is arbitrary. You can put the instructions anywhere on the screen, but it is preferable to display every set of instructions in the same area.

In fact, you can display instructions of almost any length and complexity in just a few lines, if you do it one piece at a time. Of course the program must wait for the user to finish reading each piece of the instructions before it goes on to the next piece. A single INPUT statement takes care of that. At the same time, the program can allow the user to interrupt the instructions and return to the regular input sequence. Replace the subroutine at line 2000 in Figure 4-13 with the one in Figure 4-14.

Another common place to put instructions is at the beginning of a program. The displayed instructions will not replace well-written printed instructions, but they are often a sufficient reminder for someone who is a bit rusty. You may recognize Figure 4-15 as the instructions for the Future Value program (Figure 4-11).

Input Masks

Some limit always exists on the length of a response. The program can display a string of characters which demarcate the response length. Such a string is called an *input mask.*

Any character will do for the input mask. Underline characters, asterisks, and number signs are common choices. The program can use one kind of character for string input masks and a different kind of character for numeric input masks. That gives the user even more information about the expected response. The following program uses underline characters for string input and number signs for numeric input:

```
10 DIM NMSK$(40),SMSK$(40),R$(40),CL$(
40)
19 REM Fill input mask strings
20 NMSK$="#":NMSK$(40)=NMSK$(1):NMSK$(
2)=NMSK$(1)
30 SMSK$="_":SMSK$(40)=SMSK$(1):SMSK$(
2)=SMSK$(1)
39 REM Fill cursor movement string
40 CL$=CHR$(30):CL$(40)=CL$(1):CL$(2)=
CL$(1)
90 PRINT CHR$(125);"ENTERING BILLS REC
EIVED"
100 PRINT "EXPENSE ACCOUNT CODE IS ";S
MSK$(1,6);CL$(1,7);
110 INPUT R$
120 PRINT "AMOUNT OF BILL IS ";NMSK$(1
,8);CL$(1,9);
130 INPUT R
140 END
```

Each PRINT statement that prints an input mask also prints a string of characters

```
1994 REM ******************************
1995 REM *  Subroutine to explain *
1996 REM *  prompt message           *
1997 REM ******************************
1998 REM Clear dedicated area, then
1999 REM Position cursor
2000 GOSUB 2300
2009 REM Now display instructions
2010 PRINT "_____Command Summary__
     "
2020 PRINT "More detail (ACDP, N for n
one)"
2030 PRINT "   A=add    C=change   D=
delete"
2040 PRINT "   E=end    P=print    H=
help";
2049 REM More detail?
2050 POSITION 31,21
2060 INPUT R$
2070 IF R$="N" THEN RETURN
2080 ON ASC(R$)-64 GOTO 2150,32767,221
0,2210
2090 IF R$<>"P" THEN GOTO 2050
2099 REM Display instr. for Print
2100 GOSUB 2300:REM Clear instr. area
2110 PRINT "_____Command: Print__
     _____"
2120 PRINT "   Prints a list of expense
 categories"
2130 PRINT "and their numbers."
2140 RETURN
2149 REM Display instructions for Add
2150 GOSUB 2300:REM Clear instr. area
2160 PRINT "_____Command:   Add_
     _____"
2170 PRINT "   To add an expense catego
ry, you"
2180 PRINT "must assign it a 5 digit n
umber, a"
2190 PRINT "1 to 5 character name, and
 frequency"
2200 RETURN
2209 REM Display instructions for Chan
ge, Delete
2210 GOSUB 2300:REM Clear instr. area
2220 PRINT "_____Command: Change or D
elete_____"
2230 PRINT "   To change or delete an e
xpense cat-"
```

NOTE: Shading shows changes from Figure 4-13.

(continued)

FIGURE 4-14. Extended Amplified Instructions subroutine listing

```
2240 PRINT "egory, you must know its n
umber. Use"
2250 PRINT "command P to list names an
d numbers"
2260 RETURN
```

NOTE: Shading shows changes from Figure 4-13.

FIGURE 4-14. Extended Amplified Instructions subroutine listing (continued)

which back the cursor up to the beginning of the input mask (lines 100 and 120). They actually back up one space behind the first mask character; that is where the INPUT statement will display a question mark (lines 110 and 130).

Choosing Input Responses

You can decrease the chance of error just by choosing input responses carefully. Your program should allow and expect its user to respond in a natural, intuitive way. It is convenient when you write a program to insist that the user code all input, but this forces the user to perform a mechanical task every time he or she wants to use the program. Since the computer excels at mechanical tasks, why not let it do the coding? If the natural response is a word or letter which the program will eventually need converted to a number, let the program make the conversion.

This is exactly what we did on lines 310 through 390 of Figure 4-13. The user enters a mnemonic command code: A, C, D, E, P, or H (line 340). The program figures out which subroutine to call (line 380) in order to carry out the command. Imagine how much easier it would be to write a program that required the user to input a numeric command, but how much harder it would be to use that program.

Checking Input Responses

It doesn't matter how carefully you design your input requests; you can't be sure how people will respond. If a bad input could cause a problem, the program should check for it. Are string entries too long? Are numeric entries within range? Does the entry make sense in context? Will it cause an error later in the program?

If you want to write a thorough program, you will make every effort to anticipate errors that someone using your program might make. Your program will catch entry errors and force the user to reenter values that would cause the program to halt abnormally.

It is true that BASIC will catch some kinds of data entry errors for you. It will not accept alphabetic entry when inputting a numeric value with a statement like INPUT A. If you try to enter letters in response to such a statement, the computer issues an error message and stops the program.

Built-in error checking capabilities are limited, though. It is possible to enter a

```
10 DIM R$(1)
40 GOSUB 300:REM Display instructions
290 END
300 PRINT CHR$(125);"FUTURE VALUE OF A
N INVESTMENT"
310 PRINT
320 PRINT "This program calculates a f
uture"
330 PRINT "value of an investment when
 interest"
340 PRINT "is a factor. You must provi
de the"
350 PRINT "amount of the initial inves
tment, the"
360 PRINT "nominal interest rate, the
number of"
370 PRINT "compounding periods per yea
r, and the"
380 PRINT "number of years of investme
nt."
390 PRINT
400 PRINT "Assuming there are no addit
ional"
410 PRINT "deposits or withdrawals, th
e future"
420 PRINT "value is based on this form
ula:"
430 PRINT
440 PRINT ,"FV=AMT*(1+IR/CMP)^(CMP*YR)
"
450 PRINT "where: FV = total value aft
er YR years"
460 PRINT "        AMT= initial investm
ent"
470 PRINT "        IR = nominal interes
t rate"
480 PRINT "        CMP= compounding fre
quency"
490 PRINT "        YR = number of years
"
500 PRINT
510 PRINT "Press the RETURN key to beg
in";
520 INPUT R$
530 PRINT CHR$(125);"FUTURE VALUE OF A
N INVESTMENT"
540 RETURN
```

FIGURE 4-15. Future Value Instructions program listing

value of the correct type that has an unacceptable value. That is, the value may cause a program error further down the line. Here is a short program that illustrates this problem:

```
100 INPUT X
200 PRINT 100/X
300 END
```

If you enter 0 in response to the INPUT statement (line 100), the program will fail when it tries to divide by 0 in the PRINT statement (line 200). It is easy enough to avoid this. Add the following lines to the program above to check the input to make sure it is not 0, and request reentry if it is.

```
110 IF X<>0 THEN 200
120 PRINT "NOT ALLOWED...RE-ENTER"
130 GOTO 100
```

By extending the principle illustrated in this example, you can see how easy it is to check an entry for problem values. Depending on the circumstances, it may make sense to check input with the ON-GOTO or ON-GOSUB statements, rather than a series of IF-THEN statements.

Sometimes checking for errors is expensive. It can take a lot of programming time, program space, and program execution time. Consider a typical yes-or-no question, for example. The program should allow any of the correct "natural" responses. They are: yes, no, Yes, No, YES, NO, y, n, Y, or N. There are ten answers in all; that's quite a few for a program to have to check. You can easily reduce the number of input tests: simply check the first character input. If the response is not allowed, the program repeats the input request. Try this program:

```
10 DIM R$(40)
200 PRINT
210 PRINT "ENTER ANOTHER BILL";
220 INPUT R$:R$=R$(1,1)
230 IF R$="Y" OR R$="y" THEN 90
240 IF R$="N" OR R$="n" THEN END
250 GOTO 210
```

The TRAP Statement

ATARI BASIC has a special statement that allows you to trap errors that it catches before it displays an error message and halts program execution. Here is an example:

```
100 TRAP 20000
```

Once such a statement has been executed, ATARI BASIC will branch to the specified line number if it detects an error. It will also place a numeric code describing the error in memory location 195, which you may inspect with the PEEK function. Appendix A explains what each error code number means. ATARI BASIC also saves the line number where the error occurred. The expression

PEEK(187) * 256 + PEEK(186) reveals the line number.

The TRAP statement is deactivated each time an error occurs. The program must execute another TRAP statement to reactivate it. To negate an active TRAP statement and restore the ATARI computer to its normal automatic error handling state, use the statement TRAP 40000.

An Error-Handling Routine

The usual procedure for handling errors with the TRAP statement is to write an error-handling routine. ATARI BASIC branches to the routine when an error occurs. At the end of the routine, the program can branch back to the beginning of the line where the error occurred, or to any other program line. The error-handling routine can take different actions depending on the nature of the error and the current state of the program, which can usually be determined by inspecting the values of key variables.

The following program demonstrates the TRAP statement. This program treats errors that are unrelated to keyboard entries as fatal errors. It reports the error number and error-causing line, and halts the program. Entry errors are not fatal. The program announces them and requests reentry.

```
10 DIM X$(10)
50 TRAP 8000
200 PRINT "ENTER A STRING VALUE";
210 INPUT X$
220 IF X$="E" THEN 500:REM End progr?
230 PRINT "ENTER A NUMERIC VALUE";
240 INPUT X
249 REM Error occurs if entry = 0
250 X=X/X
499 REM End Program
500 PRINT "LAST ENTRIES WERE: ";X$;" A
ND ";X
510 TRAP 40000:REM Turn off TRAP
520 END
7998 REM +++++ Error handler +++++
7999 REM Get error number
8000 E=PEEK(195)
8009 REM Get line no. where error was
8010 EL=PEEK(187)*256+PEEK(186)
8020 IF E=3 OR E=8 THEN 8100
8029 REM Non-input error occurred
8030 PRINT "ARRGH! ERROR NO. ";E;" FOU
ND"
8040 PRINT "ON LINE NO. ";EL
8050 PRINT "WRITE THIS INFO. DOWN, ALO
NG WITH"
8060 PRINT "WHAT YOU WERE DOING."
8070 PRINT "CONSULT THE USER'S MANUAL
FOR HELP"
8080 END
8100 REM Input error occurred
```

```
8110 PRINT CHR$(253);:REM Ring bell
8120 PRINT "ERROR...TRY AGAIN"
8130 TRAP 8000:REM Reset TRAP
8140 GOTO EL
```

Input Utility Subroutines

At this point we can develop a general input subroutine. It will use all the input techniques we have discussed so far: prompt messages, amplified instructions, input masks, response checking, and an error-handling routine.

The input subroutine will use several other subroutines. One of them clears lines on the display screen (Figure 4-16). It uses variable BL$ to clear all but the last column of each line. Clearing the last column would force a carriage return. If that happens on the last line, the screen scrolls up one line. Extra programming could overcome this, at the expense of memory and execution speed. In most cases, this simpler solution is adequate. The main program must dimension and fill BL$ with blanks.

Another auxiliary subroutine flashes an error message in the top right corner of the display screen (Figure 4-17). The message to display must be in variable ERM$,

```
97 REM ********************************
98 REM *  Clear Display Lines        *
99 REM ********************************
100 FOR J=L1 TO L2
110 POSITION 0,J
120 PRINT BL$(1,39);
130 NEXT J
140 RETURN
```

FIGURE 4-16. Clear Display Lines subroutine listing

```
167 REM ********************************
168 REM *    Display Error Message   *
169 REM ********************************
170 FOR J=1 TO 3
180 POSITION 20,0
190 PRINT ERM$;" ERROR";CHR$(253);
200 FOR J1=1 TO 100:NEXT J1:REM Delay
210 POSITION 20,0
220 PRINT BL$(1,19):REM Erase mesg.
230 NEXT J
240 RETURN
```

FIGURE 4-17. Display Error Message subroutine listing

which the main program must dimension. The subroutine always appends the word "ERROR" to the message. It also beeps the console speaker each time the message flashes. It uses an empty FOR-NEXT delay loop, so the message stays on the screen for a few seconds.

We also need a subroutine to clear the area at the bottom of the screen where the amplified instructions go (Figure 4-18). All this subroutine does is call the subroutine that clears display lines (Figure 4-17) and position the cursor to the start of the instruction area.

Figure 4-19 shows the input subroutine itself. First the subroutine makes sure the error handler is active (line 600). Then it displays the input mask at the specified column and row (lines 630 and 640). Input is always into a string variable R$ (line 660). This allows the user to enter a question mark to cue amplified instructions (line 670), even during numeric entry. It also allows the user to just press the RETURN key during a numeric entry; the subroutine treats it as a 0 (line 700). The input subroutine checks for numeric range (line 720) or string length (line 750). It does not enforce any length restrictions on numeric entries, nor does it truncate or round numeric responses to some number of decimal places. These latter two functions usually vary from one input to the next, so they are better done outside the input subroutine.

The input subroutine uses two variable line numbers, ERRHDL (line 600) and AMPSUB (line 670). This allows the calling program to provide its own routines and thereby vary the way it treats error-handling and amplified instructions. AMPSUB must be a real line number. The line can consist of only a RETURN statement, but it must exist. ERRHDL, on the other hand, can have an illegally high line number like 40000. If it does, ATARI BASIC handles errors itself.

We also need a subroutine that inputs with a prompt message (Figure 4-20). It displays a prompt message on the second line of the screen and calls the input subroutine (Figure 4-19) to input a value on the line after that.

The last utility routine is the error handler (Figure 4-21). If an input error occurs, it uses the Display Error Message subroutine (Figure 4-17) to flash a message. Then it returns to the *beginning* of the line where the error occurred. If a non-input error occurs, the error handler displays an advisory message and ends the program.

```
247 REM ****************************
248 REM *Clear Instr. Area of Screen*
249 REM ****************************
250 L1=20:L2=23:GOSUB 100
260 POSITION 2,20
270 RETURN
```

NOTE: Requires the Clear Display Lines subroutine (Figure 4-16).

FIGURE 4-18. Clear Instruction Area subroutine listing

```
596 REM *******************************
597 REM *  General Input Subroutine *
598 REM *******************************
599 REM Enable error-handler
600 TRAP ERRHDL
609 REM Clear ampl. instr. lines
610 GOSUB 250
630 POSITION IC+1,IR
640 PRINT MSK$(1,IL)
650 POSITION IC,IR
659 REM Input and check response
660 INPUT R$
663 FOR J1=1 TO IL
664 REM Strip out extra mask chars.
665 FOR J1=1 TO IL:IF R$(J1,J1)<>MSK$(
1,1) THEN NEXT J1
666 R$=R$(1,J1-1)
669 REM Amplify instructions?
670 IF R$="?" THEN GOSUB AMPSUB:GOTO 6
30
680 IF LO>HI THEN GOTO 750:REM string
690 REM Null entry = numeric 0
700 IF R$="" THEN R$="0"
709 REM Process numeric response
710 R=VAL(R$)
720 IF R>=LO AND R<=HI THEN RETURN
729 REM Numeric Range error
730 ERM$="NUMERIC RANGE"
740 GOSUB 170:GOTO 620
749 REM String Input
750 IF LEN(R$)<=IL THEN RETURN
759 REM String length error
760 ERM$="STRING LENGTH"
770 GOSUB 170:GOTO 620
```

NOTE: These subroutines must be present: Clear Display Lines (Figure 4-16),
Display Error Message (Figure 4-17), and Error Handler (Figure 4-21).

FIGURE 4-19. General Input subroutine listing

Table 4-2 lists all the utility subroutines by line number. It shows which subroutines use which variables, and which subroutines require other subroutines to be present. A program that uses any of these subroutines has to do a number of things. It must dimension string variables which the selected subroutines use, as described in Table 4-3. It must assign values to the variables these subroutines use, as described in Table 4-4.

Have you noticed how the subroutines assume that the main program dimensions variables such as PRMT$ and MSK$ correctly? They could check that

```
796 REM ******************************
797 REM *     Input with Prompt      *
798 REM ******************************
799 REM Clear prompt & input lines
800 L1=1:L2=2:GOSUB 100
809 REM Print prompt message
810 POSITION 2,1
820 PRINT PRMT$
829 REM Input value
830 IC=2:IR=2:GOSUB 600
840 RETURN
```

NOTE: Requires the following subroutines: Clear Display Lines (Figure 4-16)
       and General Input (Figure 4-19).

FIGURE 4-20. Input with Prompt subroutine listing

```
7996 REM ++++++++++++++++++++++++++++
7997 REM +        Error handler      +
7998 REM ++++++++++++++++++++++++++++
7999 REM Get error number
8000 E=PEEK(195)
8009 REM Get line no. where error was
8010 EL=PEEK(187)*256+PEEK(186)
8020 IF E=3 OR E=8 THEN 8100
8029 REM Non-input error occurred
8030 PRINT "ARRGH! ERROR NO. ";E;" FOU
ND"
8040 PRINT "ON LINE NO. ";EL
8050 PRINT "WRITE THIS INFO. DOWN, ALO
NG WITH"
8060 PRINT "WHAT YOU WERE DOING."
8070 PRINT "CONSULT THE USER'S MANUAL
FOR HELP"
8080 END
8100 REM Input error occurred
8110 ERM$="INPUT"
8120 GOSUB 170:REM Flash Message
8130 TRAP ERRHDL:REM Reset TRAP
8140 GOTO EL
```

NOTE: Requires the Display Error Message subroutine (Figure 4-17).

FIGURE 4-21. Error Handler program listing

TABLE 4-2. Utility Subroutine Requirements

Line	Figure and Title	Variables	Subroutines
100	4-16. Clear Display Lines	BL$, J, L1, L2	None
170	4-17. Display Error Message	BL$, ERM$, J, J1	None
250	4-18. Clear Instruction Area	L1, L2	100
600	4-19. General Input	AMPSUB, ERM$, ERRHDL, HI, IC, IL, IR, J1, LO, MSK$, R, R$	ERRHDL, AMPSUB, 170, 250
640	4-37. String Input	IC, IL, IR, J, R, R$, X	None
800	4-20. Input with Prompt	IC, IR, L1, L2, PRMT$	100, 600
850	4-38. Disable BREAK Key	J	None
6000	4-33. Move Cursor with Stick	BR, DLY1, J, LC, RC, SC, SR, TR	None
6500	4-31. Numeric Input with Joystick	BL$, HI, IC, IL, INC, IR, J, LO, R, SD	None
8000	4-21. Error Handler	E, EL, ERM$, ERRHDL	170
8200	4-36. Enter Valid Date	D, DAT$, IC, IR, M, MSK$, R$, Y	8400
8400	4-36. Input Two Digits	J1, R, R( )	None

TABLE 4-3. Utility Subroutine String Variable Dimensions*

Variable	Minimum	Maximum
BL$	39	None
DAT$	8	8
ERM$	13	13
MSK$	0**	39
R$	1**	39
PRMT$	0	39

  * Used in Figures 4-16 through 4-21, 4-31, 4-33, and 4-36 through 4-38.
** Must accommodate the largest input.

IL<= LEN(PRMT$) and that IL<= LEN(MSK$). But these are programming errors, not user errors. Once discovered and corrected, a programming error will almost never reappear. It would be a waste of computer memory and execution speed for the program to check for such errors.

Let's use the utility subroutines (Figures 4-16 through 4-21) in a program. Type them all in together, then use the CSAVE statement to record them on a cassette. That way you can use the CLOAD statement to get them back in memory when future example programs need them, rather than retyping them each time.

Once you have all the subroutines in memory, type in the listing shown in Figure 4-22. The resulting program first dimensions and initializes the variables that the

TABLE 4-4. Input Utility Subroutine Variable Usage

Variable	Value Change?*	Use
AMPSUB	No	Line number of the subroutine that amplifies the prompt message
BL$	No	Blank characters for erasing the screen
BR	No	Bottom row cursor limit
D	Yes	Day entered
DAT$	Yes	Date entered, with punctuation
DLY1	No	Cursor speed
E	Yes	BASIC error number
EL	Yes	Line number where error occurred
ERRHDL	No	Line number of the error handler; if none, let ERRHDL = 40000
HI**	No	The largest number that can be entered
IC	No	The input column number, 0 to 38. Avoid column 39, since it forces a carriage return
IL	No	The input length
INC	No	Increment
IR	No	The input row number, 0 to 23
J	Yes	Temporary
J1	Yes	Temporary
L1	Yes	First display line to clear, 0 to 23
L2	Yes	Last display line to clear, L1 to 23
LC	No	Left-hand column cursor limit
LO**	No	The smallest number that can be entered
M	Yes	Month entered
MSK$	No	Input mask characters
PRMT$	No	The prompt message; it can be null
R	Yes	Returns the numeric value input, if any
R( )	Yes	Temporary
R$	Yes	Returns the string value input, or string equivalent of numeric input
RC	No	Right-hand column cursor limit
SC	Yes	Stick-directed cursor column
SD	No	Delay between incrementing
SR	Yes	Stick-directed cursor row
TR	No	Top row cursor limit
Y	Yes	Year entered

* The subroutines change the values of only the indicated variables.

** If LO > HI, the subroutine inputs a string value. If not, it inputs a numeric value.

subroutines use (lines 10 to 40). Then it branches around the subroutines to start the main execution sequence (line 90). It sets up a 20-character string input (lines 1010 to 1040) and a numeric input (lines 1050 to 1110). The prompt message for the numeric input includes the response to the string input (lines 1050 to 1070). Notice that the string input has no amplified instructions—AMPSUB is 32767, the "do-nothing" subroutine. There are amplified instructions for numeric entry, however (lines 7000 to 7040).

```
10 DIM PRMT$(40),MSK$(40),BL$(40),ERM$
(13),R$(20)
19 REM Fill BL$ with blanks
20 BL$=" ":BL$(40)=BL$:BL$(2)=BL$
29 REM Fill MSK$ with input mask char
30 MSK$="_":MSK$(40)=MSK$:MSK$(2)=MSK$
(1)
39 REM Error-handler starting line
40 ERRHDL=8000
89 REM branch to  start of program
90 GOTO 1000
999 REM --- Main Program ---
1000 PRINT CHR$(125):REM clr. screen
1009 REM Input string value
1010 PRMT$="What is the bowler's last
name?"
1020 IL=20:LO=1:HI=0
1030 AMPSUB=32767
1040 GOSUB 800
1049 REM Enter numeric value
1050 PRMT$="What did "
1060 PRMT$(LEN(PRMT$)+1)=R$
1070 PRMT$(LEN(PRMT$)+1)=" score?"
1080 IL=7:LO=0:HI=300
1090 AMPSUB=7000
1100 GOSUB 800
1110 GOTO 1010
6997 REM --- Numeric Input Instr. ---
6998 REM Clear dedicated area, then
6999 REM position cursor
7000 GOSUB 250
7010 PRINT "Enter a positive numeric v
alue,"
7020 PRINT "less than 300."
7030 RETURN
32767 RETURN :REM do-nothing subr.
```

NOTE: Shows the input utility subroutines (Figures 4-16 through 4-21) in action.

FIGURE 4-22. Enter Bowling Scores program listing

Group Inputs

Very often a program needs several pieces of information, not just one or two. It can input the data items in a number of different ways. One way is to input each item in turn at the same place on the screen, using a different prompt for each item to guide the operator. This is the approach the last example program (Figure 4-22) used to enter names and scores. That program reminded you whose score to enter by incorporating the name into the prompt message for the score. Imagine the confusion that would occur without this aid. You would always have to remember the last name you entered.

That program could display the most recent entries on the unused part of the screen. Try changing it so it displays the most recent name and score on lines 5 and 6 of the screen (Figure 4-23).

The best way of handling multiple-item data entry is to display a form on the screen, and fill in the form as data is entered. Related data items stay on the screen until all items are entered. To do this, the program first displays the form. This consists of a label for each item and enough space next to the label for the entry (Figure 4-24). The labeled items are called *fields*. Each field has a number. You enter data sequentially, starting with the first field and ending with the last.

Only minimal programming effort is required to accomplish this. Suppose you want to input a name and address. There are five items to enter: name, street, city, state, and ZIP code. The input utility subroutines we just developed will do most of the work (see Tables 4-2, 4-3, and 4-4 and Figures 4-16 through 4-21). If you recorded them on cassette as we suggested, load them into memory now. Otherwise you will have to retype them. Be sure none of the program lines from the last

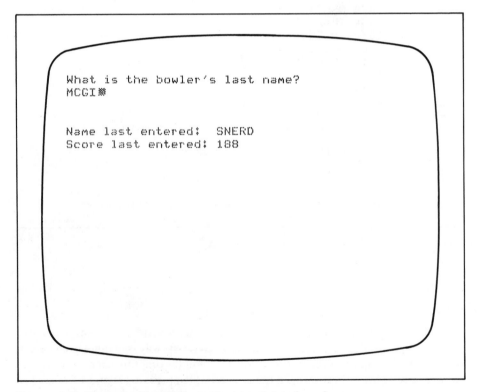

FIGURE 4-23. Displaying the most recently entered data for reference

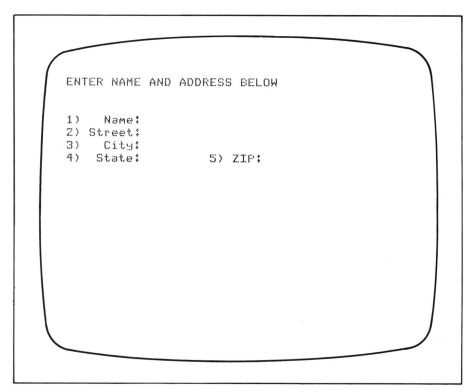

FIGURE 4-24. Displaying a form for data entry

example program (Figure 4-22) remain. Add the following program lines to clear
the screen and display the initial form:

```
9 REM Initialize variables
10 DIM PRMT$(40), MSK$(40), BL$(40),ER
M$(13)
19 REM Fill BL$ with blanks
20 BL$=" ":BL$(40)=BL$:BL$(2)=BL$
29 REM Fill MSK$ with input mask char
30 MSK$="_":MSK$(40)=MSK$:MSK$(2)=MSK$

39 REM Error-handler starting line
40 ERRHDL=8000
89 REM Branch to start of program
90 GOTO 1000
999 REM Clear screen & display form
1000 PRINT CHR$(125);"ENTER NAME AND A
DDRESS BELOW"
1010 PRINT:PRINT
1020 PRINT "1)    Name:"
1030 PRINT "2) Street:"
1040 PRINT "3)    City:"
```

```
1050 PRINT "4)  State:"
1060 POSITION 20,6
1070 PRINT "5) ZIP:"
1900 END
```

Next, the program has to input the name, street, city, state, and ZIP code. Add a separate subroutine to input each field:

```
50 DIM NA$(20),STT$(20),CI$(20),ST$(2)
,ZI$(9),R$(20)
1099 REM Enter all 5 fields
1100 FOR F=1 TO 5
1110 GOSUB 2000
1120 NEXT F
1130 GOTO 1100
1996 REM ++++++Subroutine 2000+++++++
1997 REM Branch to entry routine
1998 REM for field F
1999 REM Input string w/ no amplif.
2000 LO=1:HI=0:AMPSUB=32767
2010 ON F GOTO 2100,2200,2300,2400,250
0
2097 REM
2098 REM Enter 20-char name
2099 REM
2100 IC=13:IR=3:IL=20:GOSUB 600
2110 NA$=R$:RETURN
2197 REM
2198 REM Enter 20-char street
2199 REM
2200 IC=13:IR=4:IL=20:GOSUB 600
2210 STT$=R$:RETURN
2297 REM
2298 REM Enter 20-char city
2299 REM
2300 IC=13:IR=5:IL=20:GOSUB 600
2310 CI$=R$:RETURN
2397 REM
2398 REM Enter 2-char state
2399 REM
2400 IC=13:IR=6:IL=2:GOSUB 600
2410 ST$=R$:RETURN
2497 REM
2498 REM Enter 9-char ZIP
2499 REM
2500 IC=28:IR=6:IL=9:GOSUB 600
2510 ZI$=R$:RETURN
32767 RETURN :REM do-nothing subr.
```

Run the program. If it does not run correctly, check your listing carefully. In particular, look for missing subroutines and for semicolon errors in PRINT statements.

When you run the Name-and-Address program, it displays an entry mask for each of the five fields in turn. This tells you which field to enter. Note how easy it is to see what you are entering.

Reviewing and Changing Input

When you finish entering everything on a form, the program can easily allow changes to any individual field. All it needs to know is the number of the field to change.

You can add the ability to make changes to the Name-and-Address program. When initial form entry is complete, the program will need to ask whether you want to make changes. If so, it must input the field number you want to change and use an ON-GOSUB statement to call the appropriate input subroutine. Figure 4-25 shows the complete program with statements added to allow changes (lines 1130 through 1230), and all subroutines.

Study the Name-and-Address program carefully. Be sure you understand the data entry aids which it uses. These aids are listed below.

- By labeling each field and juxtaposing an entry mask at the appropriate time, the program clearly indicates what data is expected, and how many entry spaces are available.
- If you exceed the allowed entry length, the program reports an error.
- When you enter the number of a field to change, the entry mask again quickly tells you whether you specified the correct field number.
- When the program asks questions, it only recognizes meaningful responses: Y or N for yes or no, or a number between 1 and 5 to select a field.

The following are data entry features which have not been included but could be added:

- The program could check the ZIP code for any nondigit entry. (Note that similar codes in some countries do allow both letters and numbers, however.)
- Many cautious programs ask the question "Are you sure?" when you answer no in response to the question "Do you want to make any changes?". This gives the program user a second chance to make changes in the event that he or she accidentally pressed the wrong key.
- The program could recognize a special character which, when input, retains the prior value. For example, if the you choose the wrong field to change, the example program now forces you to reenter the field. The program could easily recognize a character which retains the previous field value.

Try modifying the Name-and-Address program yourself to include the additional safety features described above.

Using Game Controllers to Restrict Responses

One problem with all forms of input is the multitude of choices the user has. Every extraneous choice is a potential error. The program must check for inappropriate responses. If it neglects to check, some user will make the mistake that crashes the

```
9 REM Initialize variables
10 DIM PRMT$(40),MSK$(40),BL$(40),ERM$
(13)
19 REM Fill BL$ with blanks
20 BL$=" ":BL$(40)=BL$:BL$(2)=BL$
29 REM Fill MSK$ with input mask char
30 MSK$="_":MSK$(40)=MSK$:MSK$(2)=MSK$

39 REM Error-handler starting line
40 ERRHDL=8000
50 DIM NA$(20),STT$(20),CI$(20),ST$(2)
,ZI$(9),R$(20)
89 REM Branch to start of program
90 GOTO 1000
97 REM ********************************
98 REM *   Clear Display Lines       *
99 REM ********************************
100 FOR J=L1 TO L2
110 POSITION 0,J
120 PRINT BL$(1,39);
130 NEXT J
140 RETURN
165 REM *******************************
166 REM *     Display Error Message  *
169 REM *******************************
170 FOR J=1 TO 3
180 POSITION 20,0
190 PRINT ERM$;" ERROR";CHR$(253);
200 FOR J1=1 TO 100:NEXT J1:REM Delay
210 POSITION 20,0
220 PRINT BL$(1,19):REM Erase mesg.
230 NEXT J
240 RETURN
247 REM *******************************
248 REM *Clear Instr. Area of Screen*
249 REM *******************************
250 L1=20:L2=23:GOSUB 100
260 POSITION 2,20
270 RETURN
596 REM *******************************
597 REM *   General Input Subroutine *
598 REM *******************************
599 REM Enable error-handler
600 TRAP ERRHDL
619 REM Clear ampl. instr. lines
620 GOSUB 250
630 POSITION IC+1,IR
```

NOTE: Demonstrates forms data entry. Uses all input utility subroutines (Figures 4-16 through 4-21). Can be modified to create a mailing list data file on cassette (see Figure 5-2).

(continued)

FIGURE 4-25. Name-and-Address program listing

```
640 PRINT MSK$(1,IL)
650 POSITION IC,IR
659 REM Input and check response
660 INPUT R$
663 FOR J1=1 TO IL
664 REM Strip out extra mask chars.
665 FOR J1=1 TO IL:IF R$(J1,J1)<>MSK$(
1,1) THEN NEXT J1
666 R$=R$(1,J1-1)
669 REM Amplify instructions?
670 IF R$="?" THEN GOSUB AMPSUB:GOTO 6
30
680 IF LO>HI THEN GOTO 750:REM string
690 REM Null entry = numberic 0
700 IF R$="" THEN R$="0"
709 REM Process numeric response
710 R=VAL(R$)
720 IF R>=LO AND R<=HI THEN RETURN
729 REM Numeric Range error
730 ERM$="NUMERIC RANGE"
740 GOSUB 170:GOTO 620
749 REM String Input
750 IF LEN(R$)<=IL THEN RETURN
759 REM String length error
760 ERM$="STRING LENGTH"
770 GOSUB 170:GOTO 620
796 REM ********************************
797 REM *     Input with Prompt      *
798 REM ********************************
799 REM Clear prompt & input lines
800 L1=1:L2=2:GOSUB 100
809 REM Print prompt message
810 POSITION 2,1
820 PRINT PRMT$
829 REM Input value
830 IC=2:IR=2:GOSUB 600
840 RETURN
999 REM Clear screen & display form
1000 PRINT CHR$(125);"ENTER NAME AND A
DDRESS BELOW"
1010 PRINT :PRINT
1020 PRINT "1)   Name:"
1030 PRINT "2) Street:"
1040 PRINT "3)   City:"
1050 PRINT "4)  State:"
1060 POSITION 20,6
```

NOTE: Demonstrates forms data entry. Uses all input utility subroutines (Figures 4-16 through 4-21). Can be modified to create a mailing list data file on cassette (see Figure 5-2).

(continued)

FIGURE 4-25. Name-and-Address program listing (continued)

```
1070 PRINT "5) ZIP:"
1099 REM Enter all 5 fields
1100 FOR F=1 TO 5
1110 GOSUB 2000
1120 NEXT F
1129 REM Allow changes
1130 PRMT$="Do you want to make any ch
anges"
1140 LO=1:HI=0:AMPSUB=32767
1150 IL=1:GOSUB 800
1159 REM Analyze response
1160 IF R$="N" OR R$="n" THEN 1100
1170 IF R$="Y" OR R$="y" THEN 1200
1180 ERM$="Y or N please":GOSUB 170
1190 GOTO 1130
1199 REM Get field number
1200 PRMT$="Which field"
1210 LO=1:HI=5:AMPSUB=32767
1220 IL=1:GOSUB 800
1230 F=R:GOSUB 2000:GOTO 1130
1900 END
1996 REM ++++++Subroutine 2000+++++++
1997 REM Branch to entry routine
1998 REM for field F
1999 REM Input string w/ no amplif.
2000 LO=1:HI=0:AMPSUB=32767
2010 ON F GOTO 2100,2200,2300,2400,250
0
2097 REM
2098 REM Enter 20-char name
2099 REM
2100 IC=13:IR=3:IL=20:GOSUB 600
2110 NA$=R$:RETURN
2197 REM
2198 REM Enter 20-char street
2199 REM
2200 IC=13:IR=4:IL=20:GOSUB 600
2210 STT$=R$:RETURN
2297 REM
2298 REM Enter 20-char city
2299 REM
2300 IC=13:IR=5:IL=20:GOSUB 600
2310 CI$=R$:RETURN
2397 REM
2398 REM Enter 2-char state
2399 REM
```

NOTE: Demonstrates forms data entry. Uses all input utility subroutines (Figures 4-16 through 4-21). Can be modified to create a mailing list data file on cassette (see Figure 5-2).

(continued)

FIGURE 4-25. Name-and-Address program listing (continued)

```
2400 IC=13:IR=6:IL=2:GOSUB 600
2410 ST$=R$:RETURN
2497 REM
2498 REM Enter 9-char ZIP
2499 REM
2500 IC=28:IR=6:IL=9:GOSUB 600
2510 ZI$=R$:RETURN
7996 REM ++++++++++++++++++++++++++++
7997 REM +       Error handler       +
7998 REM ++++++++++++++++++++++++++++
7999 REM Get error number
8000 E=PEEK(195)
8009 REM Get line no. where error was
8010 EL=PEEK(187)*256+PEEK(186)
8020 IF E=3 OR E=8 THEN 8100
8029 REM Non-input error occurred
8030 PRINT "ARRGH! ERROR NO. ";E;" FOU
ND"
8040 PRINT "ON LINE NO. ";EL
8050 PRINT "WRITE THIS INFO. DOWN, ALO
NG WITH"
8060 PRINT "WHAT YOU WERE DOING."
8070 PRINT "CONSULT THE USER'S MANUAL
FOR HELP"
8080 END
8100 REM Input error occurred
8110 ERM$="INPUT"
8120 GOSUB 170:REM Flash Message
8130 TRAP ERRHDL:REM Reset TRAP
8140 GOTO EL
32767 RETURN :REM do-nothing subr.
```

NOTE: Demonstrates forms data entry. Uses all input utility subroutines (Figures 4-16 through 4-21). Can be modified to create a mailing list data file on cassette (see Figure 5-2).

FIGURE 4-25. Name-and-Address program listing (continued)

program. The solution to this problem is to eliminate the keyboard as the input device and use the game controllers instead. The joystick is the easiest to adapt. It is not always possible to use a game controller instead of the keyboard, but the number of ways in which game controllers can be used is surprising.

The STICK function reads the joystick in ATARI BASIC. It returns a value between 5 and 15, depending on the direction the stick is pointed (Figure 4-26). The STRIG function reads the joystick trigger button. It returns a 0 value only if the trigger is being pressed. You can hook up as many as four joysticks to an ATARI computer at once. Therefore you must state which stick you want the STICK or STRIG function to read. Sticks are numbered 0 through 3 for these functions. Stick

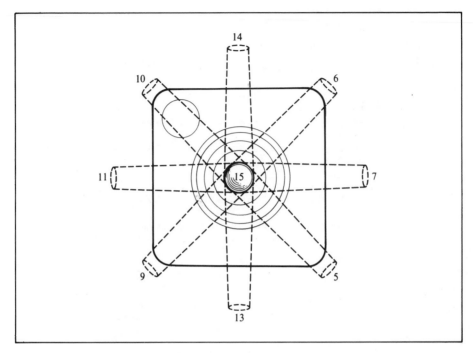

FIGURE 4-26. STICK function values

0 plugs into socket 1 (the leftmost socket) on the front of the ATARI computer, stick 1 plugs into socket 2, and so on. The following program shows how these two functions work:

```
10 PRINT CHR$(125)
20 POSITION 2,5
29 REM Use BREAK key to stop program
30 PRINT "STICK 0 VALUE:    ";STICK(0);
"  ";
40 PRINT "STICK 0 TRIGGER: ";
50 IF STRIG(0)=0 THEN PRINT "ON ":GOTO
 20
60 PRINT "OFF":GOTO 20
```

ATARI BASIC reads the paddle with the PADDLE function. It returns a value between 1 and 228, depending on the amount of rotation (Figure 4-27). The PTRIG function reads the paddle trigger button. It returns a 0 value only if the trigger is being pressed. Paddles come in pairs. You can hook up as many as four pairs to an ATARI computer at once. Therefore you must state which of the eight paddles you want either of these functions to read. Paddles are numbered 0 through 7 for these functions. Paddles 0 and 1 plug into socket 1 on the front of the ATARI computer, paddles 2 and 3 plug into socket 2, and so on. The following program shows how

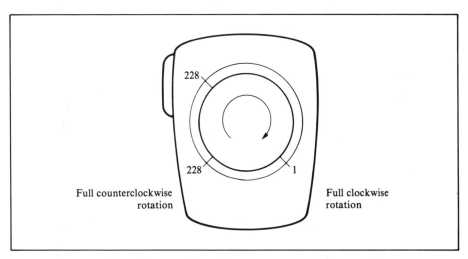

FIGURE 4-27. PADDLE function values

these two functions work:

```
10 PRINT CHR$(125)
20 POSITION 2,5
29 REM Use BREAK key to stop program
30 PRINT "PADDLE 0 VALUE:    ";PADDLE(0
);"   ";
40 PRINT "PADDLE 0 TRIGGER: ";
50 IF PTRIG(0)=0 THEN PRINT "ON ":GOTO
 20
60 PRINT "OFF":GOTO 20
```

Joystick Control of the Display

When dealing with large quantities of data, the display screen can only show a small amount of the data at one time. One way to do this is to use the display screen as a window on the data. At any time it shows only part of the data available. Viewing data in this way is easy if the data is in the form of numeric array variables or even string pseudo-arrays (described earlier in this chapter). Imagine that the array data is written on a large chalkboard and you are looking at the chalkboard through the viewfinder of a camera. The chalkboard is large enough that you cannot get it all in the viewfinder at one time, but you can view any part of the chalkboard by moving the viewfinder up, down, right, or left. The display screen can imitate the viewfinder, and the joystick can control its movement over the field of data.

We will now show how to implement this technique with a two-dimension numeric array. As the value of each array element, we will assign a four-digit number which identifies the array indexes, like this:

$X(i,j) = 0i0j$

For example:

    X(3,2) = 0302
    X(19,8) = 1908
    X(11,12) = 1112

This numeric array can be initialized very simply with some nested FOR-NEXT loops, as follows:

```
10 DIM X(50,14)
49 REM Initialize array
50 PRINT CHR$(125);"PLEASE WAIT--INITI
ALIZATION IN PROCESS";
60 FOR K=0 TO 14
70 FOR J=0 TO 50
80 X(J,K)=(J+1)*100+K+1
90 NEXT J
100 NEXT K
```

The computer takes about ten seconds to execute these lines. This is a long time to leave the program user in suspense, so the program displays an advisory message about the initialization. Without such a message, the program user may well assume that the computer is not working. It is a good idea to display a prominent message whenever such periods of apparent inactivity occur.

The fourth and fifth rows of the display will show column headings. The first ten spaces of each line will show row headings (Figure 4-28). We deliberately created a window that is smaller than the entire screen in order to better illustrate the concept of a window on data. There is nothing to prevent you from creating a window that occupies your entire screen, but there will be occasions when you want a small window so that other data can appear on the screen concurrently.

As the part of the array that is visible changes, the program will have to change the row and column numbers in the headings. The following subroutine accomplishes that:

```
998 REM +++++ Subroutine 1000+++++
999 REM      Display headings
1000 FOR J=1 TO 3
1010 POSITION 3+J*10,3
1020 PRINT "COLUMN";
1030 NEXT J
1040 FOR J=0 TO 2
1050 POSITION 16+J*10,4
1059 REM right-justify one-digit no
1060 IF C+J+1<10 THEN PRINT " ";
1070 PRINT C+J+1;
1080 NEXT J
1090 FOR J=0 TO 9
1100 POSITION 3,J+5
1110 PRINT "ROW ";
1119 REM right-justify one-digit no.
1120 IF R+J+1<10 THEN PRINT " ";
1130 PRINT R+J+1;
```

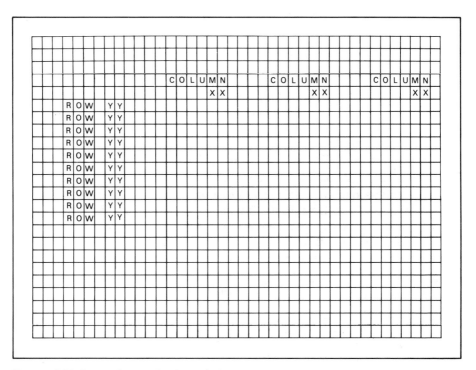

FIGURE 4-28. Screen format for data window program

```
1140 NEXT J
1150 RETURN
```

Note that lines 1070 and 1130 add 1 to the row and column numbers as they are displayed. ATARI BASIC arrays have elements with 0 indexes, but most people start counting with 1, not 0. Therefore, the program makes this minor translation to make it easier to use.

The following lines display array values starting with X(25,7) in the upper left corner of the window:

```
20  DIM X$(10),BL$(40)
29  REM Fill BL$ with blanks
30  BL$=" ":BL$(40)=BL$:BL$(2)=BL$
200 R=24:C=6:REM array center
210 GOSUB 1000:REM Headings
219 REM Fill in values
220 FOR K=1 TO 10
230 FOR J=1 TO 3
240 POSITION J*10-1,K+4
250 X$=STR$(X(R+K-1,C+J-1))
260 PRINT BL$(1,10-LEN(X$));X$;
270 NEXT J
```

```
280 NEXT K
290 POSITION 2,1
350 END
```

Variable R determines the topmost column in the window. Variable C determines the leftmost column. Each array value is converted into a numeric string on line 250 before being printed. This conversion simplifies display formatting. It makes it easy to right-justify the array values in the columns, as shown by the PRINT statement on line 260.

Our program takes great care to terminate the display on the 39th column of the display, rather than the 40th and last column. If you run displays out to the 40th column, you will run afoul of the wrap-around logic, whereby lines that are more than 40 characters long automatically continue on the next line. You should do your best to avoid the display formatting nightmare that can result from the interaction between carriage returns generated by printing in column 40 and your own formatting carriage returns.

These lines monitor joystick 0:

```
299 REM Move window right
300 IF STICK(0)=7 AND C<12 THEN C=C+1:
GOTO 210
309 REM Move window left
310 IF STICK(0)=11 AND C>0 THEN C=C-1:
GOTO 210
319 REM Move window down
320 IF STICK(0)=13 AND R<41 THEN R=R-1
:GOTO 210
329 REM Move window up
330 IF STICK(0)=14 AND R>0 THEN R=R-1:
GOTO 210
339 REM Use BREAK key to stop program
340 GOTO 290
```

If the stick is moved right, left, down, or up, and the window is not already as far as it can go in that direction, the program adjusts variables R and C. Then it redisplays the window, starting with these new array indexes.

The complete program, illustrated in Figure 4-29, is a relatively primitive program. It has only one speed: slow. It takes about two seconds to redisplay the window each time the row or column number changes; that's 20 seconds to move the window ten rows. You could fine tune the program and possibly cut this time in half, but ten seconds is still a long time. Instead of redisplaying the window as often as possible while the stick is held in one direction, the program could redisplay only when the stick is centered. That way the window redisplays just one time for each nonstop move. We have reduced the time it takes to move the window to two seconds, plus the length of time the stick is off-center. Of course, the program has to update the column numbers as it moves the window horizontally, and the row numbers as it moves vertically, so the user knows where the window is. That small overhead will take very little time. Try making these changes to Figure 4-29 yourself.

```
10 DIM X(50,14)
20 DIM BL$(40),X$(4)
29 REM Fill BL$ with blanks
30 BL$=" ":BL$(40)=BL$:BL$(2)=BL$
49 REM Initialize array
50 PRINT CHR$(125);"PLEASE WAIT--INITI
ALIZATION IN PROCESS";
60 FOR K=0 TO 14
70 FOR J=0 TO 50
80 X(J,K)=(J+1)*100+K+1
90 NEXT J
100 NEXT K
199 REM Main program
200 PRINT CHR$(125);"Use stick to move
 window";
205 R=25:C=7:REM array center
210 GOSUB 1000:REM Headings
219 REM Fill in values
220 FOR K=1 TO 10
230 FOR J=1 TO 3
240 POSITION J*10-1,K+4
250 X$=STR$(X(R+K-1,C+J-1))
260 PRINT BL$(1,10-LEN(X$));X$;
270 NEXT J
280 NEXT K
290 POSITION 2,1
299 REM Check Joystick
300 IF STICK(0)=7 AND C<12 THEN C=C+1:
GOTO 210
310 IF STICK(0)=11 AND C>0 THEN C=C-1:
GOTO 210
320 IF STICK(0)=13 AND R<41 THEN R=R+1
:GOTO 210
330 IF STICK(0)=14 AND R>0 THEN R=R-1:
GOTO 210
340 GOTO 290
998 REM +++++ Subroutine 1000 +++++
999 REM Display headings
1000 FOR J=1 TO 3
1010 POSITION 3+J*10,3
1020 PRINT "COLUMN";
1030 NEXT J
1040 FOR J=0 TO 2
1050 POSITION 16+J*10,4
1059 REM right-justify one-digit no.
1060 IF C+J+1<10 THEN PRINT " ";
1070 PRINT C+J+1;
1080 NEXT J
1090 FOR J=0 TO 9
1100 POSITION 3,J+5
```

(continued)

FIGURE 4-29. Screen Data Window program listing

```
1110 PRINT "ROW ";
1119 REM right-justify one-digit no.
1120 IF R+J+1<10 THEN PRINT " ";
1130 PRINT R+J+1;
1140 NEXT J
1150 RETURN
```

FIGURE 4-29. Screen Data Window program listing (continued)

You can also move the window diagonally. The STICK function can detect diagonal stick positions (Figure 4-26). Try expanding the program between lines 300 and 330 to enable diagonal window movement. If the program detects a diagonal joystick position, it must change both row and column, variables R and C. Furthermore, when the window moves diagonally, it might run into both the top (or bottom) and side of the array at the same time. Be sure to check for this condition. Figure 4-30 summarizes the effects of the various joystick positions on the row and column variables.

Numeric Input with the Joystick

We can write a program that uses the joystick to input a numeric value. The program starts by displaying a number on the screen. Then it monitors the joystick. Move the stick to the left and the program decreases the number. Move the stick to the right and the number increases. Center the stick and the number stops changing. When the number you want to input is on the screen, press the trigger button. Here is a simple program to input a number between 1 and 10:

```
1000 R=1
6509 REM Erase old value, pos. curs.
6510 PRINT CHR$(125)
6519 REM Display current value
6530 PRINT R;
6539 REM Quit when trigger pressed
6550 IF STRIG(0)=0 THEN END
6579 REM Move ahead?
6580 IF STICK(0)=11 AND R<>LO THEN R=R
-1:GOTO 6510
6589 REM Move back?
6590 IF STICK(0)=7 AND R<>HI THEN R=R+
1:GOTO 6510
6599 REM No change
6600 GOTO 6550
```

The program works, but it is hard to stop at a particular number. The program is too sensitive to joystick movement. It is checking the stick position too often. Delay

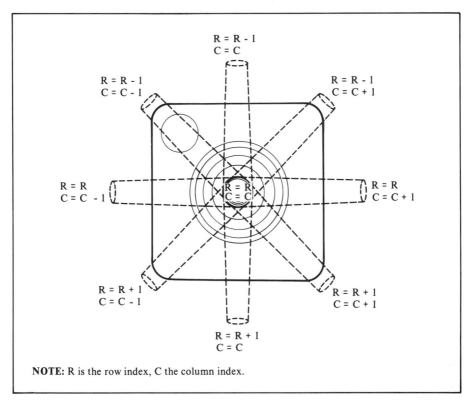

NOTE: R is the row index, C the column index.

FIGURE 4-30. Joystick position affects data window indexes

it with a FOR-NEXT loop, like this:

```
6559 REM Delay before checking stick
6560 FOR J=1 TO 30:NEXT J
```

The number of loop iterations determines the delay time. A long delay makes it easier to step from one value to the next, but it takes longer to get from a low value to a high one. A short delay has the opposite effect.

This program is even more useful as a subroutine (Figure 4-31). It uses the same variables as the General Input subroutine (Figure 4-19) to specify input range (LO and HI), cursor position (IR and IC), and field size (IL). It also returns the input value in variable R. Variable INC is the amount to increment or decrement the value each time it changes (lines 6580 and 6590). The subroutine employs a two-speed delay loop to control the speed with which the number changes (line 6560). It starts out with a small delay (line 6570) for maximum speed and minimum control. As soon as the stick centers, the subroutine shifts to low speed (line 6600). So if you move the stick either right or left and hold it there, the number changes at high speed. Quickly tap the stick right or left and the change occurs slowly.

```
10 DIM BL$(40)
19 REM Fill BL$ with blanks
20 BL$=" ":BL$(40)=BL$:BL$(2)=BL$
1000 PRINT CHR$(125)
1199 REM Set range, start val, incrmt
1200 LO=0:HI=200:R=100:INC=.5
1209 REM Set cursor pos. & field size
1210 IC=10:IR=11:IL=3
1220 GOSUB 6500
1230 PRINT
1240 PRINT "Number selected: ";R
1900 END
6496 REM ******************************
6497 REM * Numeric Input w/ Joystick*
6498 REM ******************************
6499 REM Erase input field
6500 POSITION IC,IR
6510 PRINT BL$(1,IL)
6519 REM Display current value
6520 POSITION IC,IR
6530 PRINT R;
6539 REM Quit when trigger pressed
6550 IF STRIG(0)=0 THEN RETURN
6559 REM Delay before checking stick
6560 FOR J=1 TO SD:NEXT J
6569 REM Assume min. delay
6570 SD=1
6579 REM Move ahead?
6580 IF STICK(0)=11 AND R<>LO THEN R=R
-INC:GOTO 6510
6589 REM Move back?
6590 IF STICK(0)=7 AND R<>HI THEN R=R+
INC:GOTO 6510
6599 REM No change:max. delay factor
6600 SD=30:GOTO 6550
```

NOTE: Sample main program (lines 10 through 1900) demonstrates the use of this subroutine.

FIGURE 4-31. Numeric Input with Joystick subroutine listing

Using Menus to Restrict Choices

The easiest way to eliminate user errors is to carefully design your program so the user has as few options as possible. The very nature of the questions the program asks can make the user's job easy or difficult. So far, the example programs have asked the user to fill in the blank. Sometimes fill-in questions are the only choice. At other times a multiple-choice question will do. Instead of "What do you want to do?". the program asks "Which option do you choose?". That is what a menu does.

You may recall the program in Figure 4-13; it inputs a command. The choices were A, C, D, E, P, or H. You can fashion a menu to do the same input (Figure 4-32). Using the input utility subroutines (Figures 4-16 through 4-21), you could easily write a program to display the menu and input the command.

The menu approach is better for both the user and the programmer. The user doesn't have to remember or look up the allowable options. The programmer doesn't have to write complicated program lines which display amplified instructions. There is no guarantee the user will only enter a displayed option, though, so the program must still check for the proper input.

Almost all input can be broken down into a series of multiple-choice questions. Each multiple-choice question can be presented as a menu. The user works his way through the menus to arrive at an answer to the final question.

Using a Joystick for Menu Selection

The computer can be programmed to move the cursor around on the screen under the control of a joystick. If there is a menu displayed on the screen, the user moves the cursor until it rests on one of the menu selections. He or she then presses the

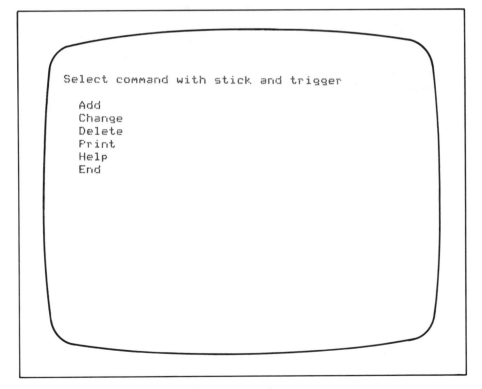

FIGURE 4-32. Designing a menu to input commands

trigger button on the joystick to make the selection. The BASIC program senses this, figures out where the cursor is, and determines which menu selection that location corresponds to.

The subroutine in Figure 4-33 harnesses the joystick to the cursor. First it checks the joystick trigger (line 6000). If it is being pressed, the subroutine ends, leaving the cursor at its last position. The subroutine uses a delay loop to control its sensitivity to the joystick (line 6010). Variable DLY1 determines the number of iterations. The number of iterations affects the cursor speed. More iterations slow the cursor down; less speed it up. The balance of the subroutine senses the stick position, displays appropriate cursor movement characters, and adjusts the cursor position variables so they always match the actual cursor position (lines 6020 through 6060). Variables SC and SR keep track of the cursor column and row position. The cursor can only move inside a box defined by four variables:

- LC, the left column limit
- RC, the right column limit
- TR, the top row limit
- BR, the bottom row limit.

To see how the subroutine works, type it in along with the following program:

```
999 REM Clear screen & display grid
1000 PRINT CHR$(125)
1010 POSITION 0,11
1020 PRINT "01234567890123456789012345
67890123456789"
1030 FOR J=0 TO 23
1040 POSITION 21,11
1050 PRINT J-INT(J/10)*10;
1060 NEXT J
1069 REM Start cursor at grid int.
1070 POSITION 21,11
1080 PRINT CHR$(253);
1089 REM Variables match curs. pos.
1090 SC=21:SR=11
1099 REM Establish cursor range
1100 LC=2:RC=39:TR=0:BR=23
1109 REM Set stick speed
1110 DLY1=20
1119 REM Have stick move cursor
1120 GOSUB 6000
1900 END
```

This program begins by displaying cross hairs to help you gauge cursor movement (lines 1000 through 1060). Then it moves the cursor to the center of the cross hairs (line 1070). There it "displays" the nonprinting character which sounds the console speaker (line 1080). Finally, it assigns the necessary variables and calls the Move Cursor with Stick subroutine (lines 1090 through 1120).

```
5996 REM ********************************
5997 REM * Move cursor with stick    *
5998 REM ********************************
5999 REM Push trigger to stop cursor
6000 IF STRIG(0)=0 THEN RETURN
6009 REM Slow cursor down
6010 FOR J=1 TO DLY1:NEXT J
6019 REM Check stick position
6020 IF STICK(0)=7 AND SC<>RC THEN SC=
SC+1:PRINT CHR$(31);
6030 IF STICK(0)=11 AND SC<>LC THEN SC
=SC-1:PRINT CHR$(30);
6040 IF STICK(0)=13 AND SR<>BR THEN SR
=SR+1:PRINT CHR$(29);
6050 IF STICK(0)=14 AND SR<>TR THEN SR
=SR-1:PRINT CHR$(28);
6060 GOTO 6000
```

FIGURE 4-33. Move Cursor with Stick subroutine listing

The program below uses the Move Cursor with Stick subroutine (Figure 4-33) to input a menu choice. If the last example is still in the computer's memory, you can avoid retyping the subroutine. Delete lines 1000 through 1900 and add the following lines:

```
999 REM Clear screen & display menu
1000 PRINT CHR$(125)
1010 PRINT "Select command with stick
and trigger"
1020 PRINT
1030 PRINT "   Add"
1040 PRINT "   Change"
1050 PRINT "   Delete"
1060 PRINT "   Print"
1070 PRINT "   Help"
1080 PRINT "   End"
1089 REM Start cursor at 4,3
1090 POSITION 4,2
1100 PRINT CHR$(29);
1110 SC=4:SR=3
1119 REM Establish cursor range
1120 LC=4:RC=4:TR=3:BR=8
1129 REM Cursor speed
1130 DLY1=30
1140 GOSUB 6000
1900 END
```

This program displays a menu of commands (lines 1000 through 1080). Then it places the cursor over the first letter of the first command (lines 1090 and 1100). The stick can move the cursor up and down over the first letters of the commands, but it cannot move the cursor from side to side (line 1120). As before, pressing the trigger button stops the cursor; variables SC and SR then have the cursor coordinates.

The only thing left to do is to translate the cursor position into the chosen command and act on that command. The lines below show how the translation takes place. All they do is display the name of the selected command. An actual program would do more, of course. Add these lines to the last example program:

```
1149 REM Cursor row tells command
1150 POSITION 2,0
1160 ON SR-2 GOSUB 2000,2500,3000,3500
,4000:GOTO 1900
1170 POSITION 2,10
1900 END
2000 PRINT "Add   ":RETURN
2500 PRINT "Change":RETURN
3000 PRINT "Delete":RETURN
3500 PRINT "Print ":RETURN
4000 PRINT "Help  ":RETURN
```

ADVANCED INPUT AND OUTPUT

A program can go just so long before it must either input or output information. Until now we have used statements that automatically choose the output device. The CLOAD and CSAVE statements always use the program recorder. In our examples so far, the INPUT statement has always used the keyboard, and the PRINT statement has always used the display screen. ATARI BASIC supports input and output beyond simple INPUT and PRINT statements. There are additional variations on PRINT and INPUT, and there are new input and output statements. This chapter will describe these new features as they pertain to the keyboard and display screen. Later chapters will describe how these new features make input and output possible with the program recorder, printer, and disk drive.

Device Names

Every input and output device has a name. The simplest names consist of one capital letter followed by a colon. For example, the display screen is device S:, and the keyboard is device K:.

In immediate mode, the ATARI computer consolidates the screen and keyboard and calls the result the *editor,* device E:. The INPUT statement also uses the editor. When you press a key, the corresponding character appears on the screen automatically. Your program does not have to echo each character back to the screen.

The other devices also have names. These will be discussed later.

Input/Output Channels

The ATARI computer communicates with all input and output devices indirectly, by means of *input/output channels.* There are eight channels in all, numbered 0 through 7. In order to communicate with a specific input or output device, a BASIC program first links the device to one of the channels. If the program requests input from that channel, it comes from the desired device. Similarly, the program directs output to a channel, which pipes it to the previously selected output device. A program uses input/output channels the same way you use the channel selector on a television set. You set the channel selector to link the television to a specific station. The television then displays the show sent by the station you selected.

We use the term *channel* in this book, but elsewhere you may see channels called input/output control blocks, IOCBs, file numbers, or logical unit numbers.

BASIC reserves channels 0, 6, and 7 for specific activities. Channel 0 is permanently reserved for the editor (device E:). Command input from the keyboard in immediate mode uses channel 0. All simple INPUT and PRINT statements use channel 0. Channel 7 is used for some printer operations and for program loading and saving. The special ATARI BASIC screen graphics statements use channel 6; Chapters 8 and 9 describe those statements.

Channels 1 through 5 are completely available to a BASIC program. Channels 6 and 7 are available on a limited basis. If the program uses none of the special screen graphics statements, it can use channel 6. If it does not load or save programs nor use the LPRINT statement (see Chapter 6), it can use channel 7.

Opening a Channel

The OPEN statement links a channel to a device. Subsequent input or output statements can then access that device by means of the channel number.

The OPEN statement consists of the keyword OPEN followed by four parameters. It looks like this:

```
OPEN #1,12,0,"E:"
```

The first number after the keyword OPEN is the channel number. The last parameter is the device name. In the example above, channel 1 is opened to the editor (device E:).

The second number in the OPEN statement specifies the kind of action that will be allowed on the channel. The action can be input, output, or both. The action must make sense. For example, a program cannot open the keyboard for output, because it cannot output to a keyboard. Generally speaking, action 4 is input, action 8 is output, and action 12 is input and output. Some devices support other actions, which will be described when those devices are discussed.

There is one more parameter, the one just ahead of the device name. It is used in different ways, depending on the device. When the device is the keyboard (K:) or editor (E:), it is ignored. With the display screen (S:), it selects the screen mode, which can be text or graphics. In this chapter we will discuss only text mode.

Opening a channel to the editor (device E:) or the text mode screen (device S:, third parameter 0), always clears the display screen. The following program illustrates this.

```
10 DIM R$(1)
20 PRINT "PRESS RETURN TO EXECUTE OPEN
   STATEMENT"
25 INPUT R$
30 OPEN #1,4,0,"S:"
40 PRINT "OPEN CLEARED SCREEN"
```

Closing a Channel

Once open, a channel stays open until the end of the program or until explicitly closed. When a program ends by executing an END statement, all channels are closed. The same thing happens if the program ends by running out of statements. But if the program halts as a result of a STOP statement, the BREAK key, or an error, all open channels remain open.

The CLOSE statement explicitly closes one channel. Here is an example:

```
CLOSE #1
```

The PRINT # Statement

A new form of the PRINT statement lets you direct its output to any open channel. It is identical to the regular PRINT statement in every way, except the first item on its list is the channel number. Consider these two statements:

```
10 PRINT #1;R$;R
20 PRINT R$;R
```

Both of these produce the same output. The second (line 20) goes to the display screen, while the first (line 10) is directed to the device linked to channel 1. Device and channel must be linked by a previously executed OPEN statement.

Notice that we used a semicolon after the channel number in the PRINT # statement (line 10). A comma will work, but it causes the output of enough blank characters to move the cursor to the start of the next column stop. A PRINT # statement with only a channel number outputs only an EOL character.

It so happens that any channel open to the display screen is always open for output, no matter what the action parameter is. Therefore action 4, normally input only, is the same as action 8, output only. This program illustrates:

```
10 OPEN #1,4,0,"S:"
20 PRINT #1,"EVEN THOUGH THE ACTION CA
LLS FOR INPUT ONLY, THE CHANNEL IS STI
LL OPEN FOR OUTPUT"
```

The OPEN statement (line 10) clears the screen and opens channel 1, nominally for input only. But a PRINT # statement to channel 1 produces output on the display screen anyway.

The INPUT # Statement

The INPUT # statement is not limited to the keyboard. It can receive input from any channel that is open for input. The new format looks like this:

```
INPUT #1,R
```

You can use either a comma or a semicolon after the channel number; the result is the same.

The INPUT # statement works almost the same with or without a channel number present. It continues to input characters until you press RETURN, generating an EOL character. Then it attempts to assign the entry to the next variable on its list. An error occurs if it finds anything wrong. Try this program:

```
10 OPEN #1,12,0,"E:"
20 INPUT #1,A
```

Notice anything different? This form of the INPUT statement does not display a question mark on the screen. That is the only difference.

The General Input subroutine was developed earlier in this chapter (Figure 4-19). It uses a standard INPUT statement to receive keyboard entry. That means it always displays a question mark just ahead of the input mask. Sometimes that is not appropriate. Try changing the subroutine to use the INPUT # statement instead. The main program will have to open an input channel for the subroutine, of course. If you use a variable to specify the channel number in the INPUT # statement, the main program can use any channel.

The PUT Statement

The PUT statement outputs a single numeric value to an open output channel. When the channel is open to the text display screen, the numeric value is interpreted as an ATASCII code (see Appendix D). The corresponding character appears on the screen. The following example illustrates this:

```
10 OPEN #1,8,0,"E:"
20 PRINT "WHAT IS THE ATASCII CODE";
30 INPUT R
40 PRINT "THAT CHARACTER IS: ";
50 PUT #1,R
60 PUT #1,155:REM EOL (carriage ret.)
69 REM Use BREAK key to stop program
70 GOTO 20
```

Like the PRINT statement, PUT determines where to display by looking at memory locations 84 (row) and 85 (column). Unlike the PRINT statement, the PUT statement does not output an EOL character when it finishes. Therefore, the program has to do it explicitly (line 60). The PUT statement requires a comma after the channel number. A semicolon will cause an error.

The GET Statement

The GET statement inputs a single character from an open channel. It does not display the character on the screen. You do not press RETURN after typing the character. The entry always results in a numeric value, the ATASCII code of the input character. Type in the following program and run it:

```
10 OPEN #1,4,0,"K:"
20 PRINT "HIT ANY KEY ";
30 GET #1,R
40 PRINT "YOU HIT ";CHR$(R);",ATASCII
CODE ";R
49 REM Use BREAK key to stop program
50 GOTO 20
```

A program can be made to wait for a specific character, like this:

```
10 OPEN #1,4,0,"K:"
20 GET #1,R
30 IF R<>ASC("X") THEN GOTO 20
40 END
```

The program inputs one character (line 20) and tests to see if it is the specific character it wants (line 30). The user must enter the letter X. Nothing else will do.

Programs frequently use the GET statement with the keyboard or editor when generating dialogue with the user. For example, the program may wait for the user to indicate he or she is there by pressing a specific key. The following program waits for the user to press the RETURN key:

```
10 OPEN #1,4,0,"K:"
20 PRINT "Are you there?"
30 PRINT "Press RETURN if so."
40 GET #1,R
50 IF R<>155 THEN GOTO 40
60 PRINT "OK, let's get on with it.
```

Notice that this sequence never displays the character entered at the keyboard.

Entering a Valid Date

In this section we will develop a program that inputs a valid date using the GET statement. You must take more care with such simple data entry than might at first appear necessary. In all probability the date will be just one item in a data entry sequence. If you carefully design data entry for each small item, the user won't have to restart or back up in a long data entry sequence whenever he or she makes a mistake in a single entry.

The user will have to enter the month, day of the month, and year as two-digit numbers (Figure 4-34). The program supplies the dashes that separate the entries. Depending on your personal preferences, you may substitute slashes or any other character for the dashes.

The user should be able to see immediately where to enter the next data. Therefore, the program will use an entry mask (Figure 4-35). The following program lines create such a mask:

```
10 DIM MSK$(2),R$(2),DAT$(8),R(1)
20 MSK$="__"
```

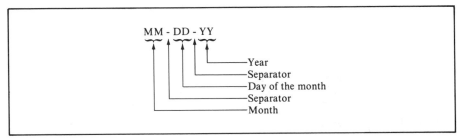

FIGURE 4-34. Format for date entry

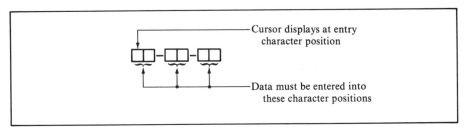

FIGURE 4-35. Entry mask for date entry

```
1000 PRINT CHR$(125);"Enter a valid da
te"
1010 IC=15:IR=4
1020 GOSUB 8200:REM Input date
1050 END
8200 POSITION IC,IR:PRINT CHR$(253);
8210 PRINT MSK$(1,2);"-";MSK$(1,2);"-"
;MSK$(1,2);
8220 POSITION IC,IR:PRINT CHR$(253);
8470 RETURN
```

The program clears the screen so that residual garbage on the screen does not surround the request for a date (line 1000). It starts date entry at column 15 and row 4 (lines 1010 and 8200). After displaying the date entry mask, the cursor moves back to the first character of the mask, although this is not apparent because of the END statement (line 1050).

Try using an INPUT statement on line 8400 to input the month. Add the following statement and run the program:

```
8400 INPUT R$
```

The INPUT statement will not do. A question mark displaces the first input mask character. An INPUT # statement would remedy that, but the user could still enter too many characters and ruin the display.

This is an occasion to use the GET statement. Add the following program lines:

```
59 REM Open keyboard input channel
60 OPEN #1,4,0,"K:"
```

```
8400 FOR J1=0 TO 1
8410 GET #1,R
8440 PRINT CHR$(R);:REM Echo input
8450 NEXT J1
```

These statements accept a two-digit input. The input appears in the first part of the entry mask. The program automatically terminates the data entry after two characters have been entered. The user does not have to press RETURN.

Three two-digit entries are needed: month, day, and year. Rather than repeating statements on lines 8400 through 8460, we will put these statements into a subroutine and go to it three times, as follows:

```
8230 GOSUB 8400:REM Month
8270 PRINT CHR$(31);
8280 GOSUB 8400:REM Day
8340 PRINT CHR$(31);
8350 GOSUB 8400:REM Year
8380 RETURN
8397 REM ***************************
8398 REM *    Input Two digits     *
8399 REM ***************************
8400 FOR J1=0 TO 1
8410 GET #1,R:R(J1)=R
8440 PRINT CHR$(R);:REM Echo input
8450 NEXT J1
8460 R$=CHR$(R(0));R$(2)=CHR$(R(1))
8470 RETURN
```

There are three ways to help the user avoid errors while entering a date:

· Accept only numeric characters (digits)
· Test for valid month, day, and year entries
· Provide a means of restarting the date entry.

Figure 4-36 shows the complete Enter Valid Date subroutine, including improvements. Only numeric entries are allowed (line 8430). The month must be between 1 and 12 (line 8250). The program does not take leap years into account, but otherwise it checks for the maximum number of days in the specified month (lines 8290 through 8320). Any year from 00 through 99 is allowed (line 8360). Entering an invalid date restarts the entire date entry sequence. If the user presses the BACK S key, the entire date entry sequence restarts (line 8420).

Notice that the date is built up in the eight-character string DAT$ as month, day, and year are entered (lines 8260, 8330, and 8370).

It takes extra time to write a good data entry program that displays information in a pleasing manner and checks for valid data input, allowing the user to restart at any time. It is certainly worthwhile to spend the extra time at this stage. You will write a program once. A user may have to run the program hundreds or thousands of times. Therefore, you spend extra programming time once in order to save users hundreds or thousands of delays.

```
10 DIM MSK$(2),R$(2),DAT$(8),R(1)
20 MSK$="__"
59 REM Open keyboard input channel
60 OPEN #1,4,0,"K:"
1000 PRINT CHR$(125);"Enter a valid da
te"
1010 IC=15:IR=4
1020 GOSUB 8200:REM Input date
1030 POSITION 15,6
1040 PRINT DAT$
1050 END
8197 REM ******************************
8198 REM *      Enter Valid Date      *
8199 REM ******************************
8200 POSITION IC,IR:PRINT CHR$(253);
8210 PRINT MSK$(1,2);"-";MSK$(1,2);"-"
;MSK$(1,2);
8220 POSITION IC,IR:PRINT CHR$(253);
8230 GOSUB 8400:REM Month
8240 M=VAL(R$)
8250 IF M<1 OR M>12 THEN 8200
8260 DAT$(1,2)=R$:DAT$(3,3)="-"
8270 PRINT CHR$(31);
8280 GOSUB 8400:REM Day
8290 D=VAL(R$)
8300 IF D<1 THEN 8200
8310 IF M=2 AND D>29 THEN 8200
8320 IF (M=4 OR M=6 OR M=9 OR M=11) AN
D D>30 THEN 8200
8325 IF D>31 THEN 8200
8330 DAT$(4,5)=R$:DAT$(6,6)="-"
8340 PRINT CHR$(31);
8350 GOSUB 8400:REM Year
8360 IF Y<0 OR Y>99 THEN 8200
8370 DAT$(7,8)=R$
8380 RETURN
8397 REM ******************************
8398 REM *      Input Two digits      *
8399 REM ******************************
8400 FOR J1=0 TO 1
8410 GET #1,R:R(J1)=R
8419 REM BACK S Key means restart
8420 IF R=126 THEN POP :GOTO 8200
8429 REM Ignore nondigit entries
8430 IF R<48 OR R>57 THEN 8410
8440 PRINT CHR$(R);:REM Echo input
8450 NEXT J1
8460 R$=CHR$(R(0)):R$(1)=CHR$(R(1))
8470 RETURN
```

FIGURE 4-36. Enter Valid Date subroutine listing

A String Input Subroutine

The General Input subroutine (Figure 4-19) developed earlier in this chapter has a serious shortcoming. You may have noticed that it lets the user type in entries that are longer than the input mask. Worse yet, the user can move the cursor all over the display screen with the arrow keys. All this adds up to a high probability that sooner or later the user will ruin the display. If you use the GET statement instead of the INPUT statement, you can control the input much more closely. You also rid the program of the irksome question mark that the INPUT statement displays.

Figure 4-37 shows a bare-bones subroutine that inputs a string value. It begins by setting the input value to null, just in case an obsolete value was there (line 600). To keep the display neat, it turns the cursor off (line 610). It then displays the input mask (lines 630 and 640). Note that the calling program must dimension and assign the mask variable, MSK$, must assign the screen location to variables IC (column) and IR (row), and must assign the input length to variable IL. The subroutine inputs one character with the GET statement (line 660). Here it assumes the main program has opened channel 1 for input from the keyboard. It then computes the current input length (line 670). After that, it analyzes the character just input. The RETURN key generates an EOL character, which terminates entry (line 680). Digits, capital letters, and punctuation marks are added to the input string, if space permits (line 690). The BACK S key causes the subroutine to back up one character. It redisplays the input mask (lines 710 and 720) and removes the last character from the input string (lines 740 and 750).

There are a number of ways in which the String Input subroutine (Figure 4-37) could be improved. Here are some ideas:

- Use a variable to specify the input channel.
- Allow upper- and lower-case letters (ATASCII codes 97 through 122).
- Add a TRAP statement at the beginning to enable an error handler at line ERRHDL.
- Call a subroutine at line number AMPSUB to display amplified instructions if a particular character is entered. This is a bit trickier than in the General Input subroutine (Figure 4-19) if the subroutine checks for the special character as each character is input.
- Allow numeric input with range checking ($LO < = R < = HI$). As a last step before returning from the subroutine, check whether the input is to be numeric. If so, convert the string value to a numeric value and check the numeric value for range. Rely on the TRAP statement and your error handler to take care of non-numeric entry errors. Do not try to check the string before converting it.

The program below shows the String Input subroutine (Figure 4-37) in use. If you want to run the program, be sure you type the subroutine in along with these program lines.

```
9 REM Initialize variables
10 DIM MSK$(40)
29 REM Fill MSK$ with input mask char
30 MSK$="_":MSK$(40)=MSK$:MSK$(2)=MSK$
```

```
597 REM *******************************
598 REM *   String Input Subroutine   *
599 REM *******************************
600 R$=""
610 POKE 755,0:REM Cursor off
629 REM Display input mask
630 POSITION IC,IR
640 PRINT MSK$(1,IL)
649 REM Position to start of field
650 POSITION IC,IR
659 REM Input next character
660 GET #1,R
670 J=LEN(R$)
679 REM Cursor on & quit if RETURN
680 IF R=155 THEN POKE 755,2:RETURN
689 REM If character OK, add to input
690 IF R>=32 AND R<=95 AND J<IL THEN R
    $(J+1,J+1)=CHR$(R):PRINT CHR$(R);:GOTO
    660
699 REM Check for valid backspace
700 IF R<>126 OR J=0 THEN GOTO 660
709 REM Renew mask & erase last char.
710 POSITION IC+J-1,IR
720 PRINT MSK$(1,1);
730 POSITION IC+J-1,IR
740 IF J>1 THEN R$=R$(1,J-1)
750 IF J=1 THEN R$=""
760 GOTO 660
```

FIGURE 4-37. String Input subroutine listing

```
49 REM Open keyboard input channel
50 OPEN #1,4,0,"K:"
89 REM Branch to start of main program

90 GOTO 1000
1000 PRINT CHR$(125):REM Clr screen
1010 POSITION 2,4
1020 PRINT "NAME"
1030 IC=7:IR=4:IL=20:GOSUB 600
1040 POSITION 2,8
1050 PRINT "ENTERED: ";R$
1060 CLOSE #1
1070 END
```

Disabling the BREAK Key

The most carefully designed program is still vulnerable. The BREAK key can stop the program. A message automatically appears on the screen, ruining the display. It will probably be impossible to continue the program right where the break occurred, because the CONT statement resumes at the *start* of the program line where the halt occurred when the BREAK key was pressed. If that happens to be a multiple-statement program line, some statements at the beginning of the line will be reexecuted.

There is a way to disable the BREAK key (Figure 4-38). Unfortunately, it is not foolproof. Several things reenable the BREAK key, including the SYSTEM RESET key, the first PRINT statement that displays on the screen, any OPEN statement with the display screen (device E: or S:), the first PRINT statement after such an OPEN statement, and the GRAPHICS statement (see Chapter 8). The easiest way around these limitations is to frequently execute the Disable BREAK Key subroutine (Figure 4-38). A good place to do that is in the input subroutine. You can do this in either the General Input subroutine (Figure 4-19) or the String Input subroutine (Figure 4-37) on line 620 with a GOSUB 850 statement.

The LOCATE Statement

ATARI BASIC includes a statement which figures out the ATASCII code number of a character at any particular screen location. It is the LOCATE statement. This statement has the following format:

```
LOCATE 3,4,AC
```

The numeric variable name (AC in the example) is assigned the ATASCII code of the character at the column and row specified by the first two numbers. In order to use LOCATE, channel 6 must be open for input from the display screen.

The LOCATE statement not only interrogates the screen, it moves the cursor one position to the right. If this happens at the end of a row, the cursor moves to the first column of the next row down. The cursor doesn't actually move until the next PRINT or PUT statement outputs something to the screen. The LOCATE statement moves the cursor in the same manner as the POSITION statement, by updating memory locations 84 (row) and 85 (column). You can defeat the cursor advance feature of the LOCATE statement by saving the contents of memory locations 84 and 85 before the LOCATE statement and restoring them after it, like this:

```
1000 OPEN #6,12,0,"S:"
1400 P84=PEEK(84):P85=PEEK(85)
1410 LOCATE C,R,CODE
1420 POKE 84,P84:POKE 85,P85
```

The LOCATE statement is used in a somewhat different way with a graphics display.

Joystick Character Entry

Earlier in this chapter we looked at a way to input numeric values with the joystick, completely independent of the keyboard. By using the LOCATE statement in conjunction with the joystick, a program can input any character directly from the screen. The program first displays the characters to choose from. The user moves

```
847 REM *******************************
848 REM *      Disable BREAK Key      *
849 REM *******************************
850 J=PEEK(128)-128
860 IF J<0 THEN RETURN
870 POKE 16,J
880 POKE 53774,J
890 RETURN
```

FIGURE 4-38. Disable BREAK Key subroutine listing

the cursor from one character to the next with the joystick. When the cursor rests on
the desired character, the user presses the trigger button. The program reads the
value from the screen with a LOCATE statement. The next program illustrates this
technique. It requires the Move Cursor with Stick subroutine (Figure 4-33).

```
19 REM ATASCII codes of game tokens
20 DATA 0,16,19,20,96,123
999 REM Open screen input/output chan
1000 OPEN #6,12,0,"S:"
1010 PRINT CHR$(125):REM Clr. screen
1019 REM Display token choices
1020 PRINT "Choose your token"
1030 RESTORE 20
1040 FOR J=3 TO 8
1050 READ TOKEN
1060 POSITION 4,J
1070 PRINT CHR$(TOKEN)
1080 NEXT J
1089 REM Start cursor at 4,3
1090 POSITION 4,2
1100 PRINT CHR$(29);
1110 SC=4:SR=3
1119 REM Establish cursor range
1120 LC=4:RC=4:TR=3:BR=8
1129 REM Cursor speed
1130 DLY1=30
1140 GOSUB 6000:REM Move cursor
1149 REM Read char. off screen
1150 LOCATE SC,SR,TOKEN
1159 REM Reverse cursor out of token
1160 TOKEN=TOKEN-128*SGN(TOKEN-127)
1170 POSITION 2,12
1180 PRINT "You chose ";CHR$(TOKEN)
1900 END
```

The program begins by displaying a choice of six game tokens (line 20 and lines 1000
through 1070). Then it positions the cursor over the first token (lines 1090 and
1100), establishes the portion of the screen in which the cursor can roam (line 1120),
and the speed at which the stick will move the cursor (line 1130). It lets the user move

the cursor with the joystick until it covers the token he wants (line 1140). It uses a LOCATE statement to determine the ATASCII code of the token that the cursor covers (line 1150). Because the cursor is covering the token, the ATASCII code is the inverse of the token's actual code, so the program has to reverse the cursor out of the code (line 1160).

DEBUGGING PROGRAMS

A new program never seems to work quite the way you expect it to. Even if there are no errors in the BASIC syntax, there may be errors in the program logic. Either kind of error is a *bug*. The process of finding and eliminating program errors is called *debugging*. There are several approaches you can take to debugging a program.

This is an appropriate place for the usual warning: take your time, plan it out, get it right the first time. Don't sit down at the keyboard with a half-baked notion about what you want your program to do and start typing away. If you are new to programming, supplement this book with one of the BASIC primers listed in Appendix I to get some pointers on good programming practices.

Surprisingly, the PRINT statement is a very useful debugging tool. You can temporarily put extra PRINT statements in your program at strategic points to display messages which tell you that the program has reached a certain point without failing. This helps you trace the flow of program execution. The extra PRINT statements can display intermediate values of variables as well. This gives you more information about program progress. It also helps you figure out which part of a multiple-part calculation is faulty.

PROGRAM OPTIMIZATION

Traditionally, the optimal program is the one that runs the fastest and uses the least memory. A better measure of a program's merit is its usefulness. It is all too easy to get caught up in the quest for quintessential program efficiency and forget why you wrote the program in the first place: to get a job done. Of course, useful programs can be efficient, and vice versa. A fast program is less tiring and requires less patience to use than a slow one. Avoiding memory waste leaves room for more program features which make the program easier to use. In this spirit, we will describe a few ways to write programs that are faster and use less memory.

Some of the techniques for making a program run faster will make it take more space, while some ways of decreasing space requirements will increase program execution time. When a conflict arises, you will have to decide which is more important in your particular program.

Faster Programs

Spend time carefully designing your program before you write a single program statement. Keep these tips in mind:

· Identify the time-consuming parts of the program: array and string initialization, lengthy calculations, screen displays, and so on. Use the fastest methods you know of to accomplish these tasks.

· Place the most frequently used subroutines on the lowest line numbers. Do the same with popular FOR-NEXT loops. Whenever BASIC looks for a line number, it starts at the beginning of the program. It will find the lowest line numbers faster than the highest ones.

· When you use nested FOR-NEXT loops, try to put the loops with the most iterations furthest inside the loop. This minimizes the bouncing back and forth between loops.

· Instead of repeating a calculation, do it once, assign the value to a variable, and use the variable.

· Simplify calculations. Addition and subtraction take less time than multiplication and division. Exponentiation takes the longest. Functions, especially nested functions, are slow. You may avoid needless calculations inside a FOR-NEXT loop by clever use of the index variable or step value.

· Put FOR-NEXT loops on the same program line.

Once you get your program working, go back and rewrite it. BASIC does not lend itself to efficient programming. During debugging you probably added pieces of code and used some new variables. Consolidate those fragments and reuse existing variables. Cleaning up the program also makes it easier to change in the future.

More Compact Programs

The time to start saving space is during the design phase of your program. Use the methods listed below, but use them with caution. Many of them lead to programs that are hard to decipher. Figuring out how to make the program work the first time is hard enough. It's even worse to have rediscover how the program works every time you look at it.

· Avoid using constants (e.g., 0, 100, "Y," "ENTER"). Instead, assign the value of the constant to a variable early in your program. Then use the variable where you would have used the constant. As a side benefit, it will be easier to change the one assignment statement than to hunt down and change every occurrence of the constant.

· Use subroutines to avoid duplicating program lines. This will also improve the readability, reliability, and changeability of your program.

· Use the zero elements of arrays (for example, X(0), B(0)).

· Use READ and DATA statements rather than simple assignment (LET) statements to initialize variables. Better yet, use INPUT and GET statements and data files (see Chapters 5 and 7).

· Branch using variables instead of constants for line numbers.

· Be thrifty with the use of variables. Reuse standard variables for FOR-NEXT loop indexes, intermediate calculations, and the like. Don't overdo it, though. Some unique variables enhance program readability (for example, R$ is always user response).

· Put more than one statement on a program line. Note, however, that compound program lines are hard to edit and harder still to read and understand.

· Use REM statements judiciously; abbreviate comments. But be careful; the fewer remarks your program has, the harder it will be to understand when you come back to it later on.

Rewrite the program once it is working. This will not only speed it up, but will save space as well.

MACHINE LANGUAGE PROGRAMMING

In a manner of speaking, the ATARI computer does not understand BASIC statements. It has to translate BASIC into a more primitive language, called *machine language*. Machine language instructions are not words, like PRINT or OPEN, but numbers. It takes many machine language instructions to equal one BASIC statement. Each machine language instruction has a name, but the computer uses the number, not the name. What's more, machine language doesn't use variables, only constants.

Programming in machine language is much more complicated than programming in BASIC, so why bother? Machine language gives you more control over the computer's actions. It is similar to the control you get with the PEEK function and the POKE statement, but is more flexible and powerful.

There is another kind of computer language closely related to machine language. It is called *assembly language*. Instead of numeric instructions, assembly language uses mnemonic abbreviations of the machine language instruction names. Each assembly language instruction corresponds to one machine language instruction. In most cases, people write assembly language programs and let the computer assemble them into machine language equivalents. It is also possible to write programs directly in machine language.

There are many machine languages. The ATARI computer understands one of them, 6502 machine language.

This book will not attempt to teach you assembly language or machine language programming. If you need to learn or brush up on assembly language or machine language programming, consult one of the books in Appendix I before reading the rest of this chapter.

The USR Function

ATARI BASIC allows you to transfer to a machine language program and return back to the BASIC program. The USR function does this. Here is an example:

```
1500 A=USR(1664)
```

USR is a function, not a statement. This means you have to use it like a variable or an expression. This also means it returns a numeric value.

There must always be at least one parameter inside the parentheses of a USR function; there can be many. The first parameter is the memory location where the machine language program starts. Other parameters are separated by commas. They must have values between 0 and 65535. BASIC passes the parameter values to the machine language subroutine via the 6502 hardware stack. The following example shows four USR parameters in use, including the machine language program address:

```
1550 PRINT USR(MLA,2,RND(0)*255,100)
```

The Hardware Stack

When ATARI BASIC encounters a USR function, it pushes its current location within the BASIC program onto the hardware stack. Then, starting with the last parameter on the list, BASIC converts each parameter to a hexadecimal integer between 0 and 65535, and pushes the two-byte value onto the hardware stack. In each case, the low byte precedes the high byte. The first parameter, which is the starting address of the machine language program, is not placed on the hardware stack. After pushing the last value on the stack, BASIC pushes a one-byte count of the number of two-byte parameters, not including the address parameter. Figure 11-4 illustrates how the USR function uses the hardware stack.

The USR function always affects the 6502 hardware stack, even if only the address parameter is present. In that case, it pushes only the one-byte count of parameters, which is 0, onto the stack.

The machine language program must always remove these entries from the hardware stack, or the computer will not be able to return to the BASIC program. A single assembly language instruction like PLA removes one byte from the hardware stack. The PLA instruction is equivalent to machine language instruction 68 hexadecimal, or 104 decimal.

The machine language program can transfer an integer value between 0 and 65535 back to the BASIC program. It must place the low byte of the value in memory location 212 and the high byte in location 213. BASIC converts the hexadecimal integer stored there into a numeric value, the value of the USR function.

To return to the BASIC program, the machine language program must execute an assembly language RTS instruction. That is machine language instruction 60 hexadecimal, or 96 decimal.

5

THE
PROGRAM
RECORDER

The ATARI 410 Program Recorder can store BASIC programs or data outside the computer's memory, on cassettes. Later, it can read the programs or data back into memory.

PROGRAM STORAGE

There are three ATARI BASIC statements — CSAVE, LIST, and SAVE — that save programs on cassette. Each of these statements has a counterpart — CLOAD, ENTER, and LOAD — that loads a program back into memory.

Saving a Program

CSAVE is a special statement for saving programs on cassette only. LIST and SAVE are general statements that output a program to any device, the program recorder being just one. Any of the following statements will record a program on the program recorder:

```
CSAVE
LIST "C:"
SAVE "C:"
```

Notice that you must specify the program recorder (device C:) for the LIST and SAVE statements.

Both the CSAVE and SAVE "C:" statements always save the entire program from memory. The LIST "C:" statement can save all or part of the program. As with other forms of the LIST statement, you can specify the first and last lines to be listed. For example, the following statement records only program lines with line numbers between 100 and 1000.

```
LIST "C:",100,1000
```

The CSAVE, LIST "C:", and SAVE "C:" statements all cause the same sequence of events. First, the computer beeps its built-in speaker twice. This is your signal to put a cassette into the program recorder. With the REWIND and FAST FORWARD levers, cue the tape to the spot where you want the recording to start, generally the beginning of the tape. Then depress the RECORD and PLAY levers. The ATARI computer cannot tell when you finish setting up the tape in the program recorder. You must signal it when the cassette is ready by pressing the RETURN key on the keyboard. The tape starts moving. If you turn up the volume on the television, you will hear the recording taking place. First there is a steady, high-pitched tone. This is followed by one or more bursts of sound. Each sound burst means the program recorder is saving another block of the program on the cassette. The longer the program, the more blocks it takes, and the more sound bursts you will hear. The sound bursts stop when the recording is complete. The tape stops as well. You can now press the STOP lever.

Loading a Program

The CLOAD statement loads programs saved on cassette by the CSAVE statement. ENTER and LOAD are general statements that input a program from any device. ENTER "C:" can only load programs saved by the LIST "C:" statement. LOAD "C:" can only load programs saved by the SAVE "C:" statement.

Both the CLOAD and the LOAD statements erase the program currently in memory before loading a new one. The ENTER statement, on the other hand, merges the program it loads with the program in memory. If there are incoming lines with the same line numbers as existing lines, the incoming lines replace the existing ones. To circumvent the merging, type NEW before using the ENTER statement.

The CLOAD, ENTER "C:", and LOAD "C:" statements all cause the same sequence of events. First, the computer beeps its built-in speaker once. This is your signal to put the cassette containing the program you want to load into the program recorder. Use the REWIND and FAST FORWARD levers to cue the tape to the spot where the program starts, generally the beginning of the tape. Depress the PLAY lever. The ATARI computer cannot tell when you finish setting up the tape in the program recorder. You must signal it when the cassette is ready by pressing the RETURN key on the keyboard.

The tape starts moving. If you turn up the volume on the television, you will hear the program load taking place. First there is a period of silence, typically lasting 20 seconds. This is followed by one or more bursts of sound. Each sound burst means the program recorder is loading another block of the program from the cassette. The longer the program, the more blocks there are, and the more sound bursts you will hear. The sound bursts stop when the whole program is in memory. The tape stops as well. You can now press the STOP lever.

The Tape Counter

A program is usually recorded starting at the beginning of the tape. That way it is always easy to find: just rewind the tape completely. A program can start anywhere on the tape, as long as you can find it again. If you can't find it, you can't load it.

You can use the tape counter to mark the start of a program. You must remember to *always* reset the tape counter whenever you rewind the tape. It must always start at 0 when the tape is fully rewound. *Never* reset the counter at any other time. If you put a new tape in the program recorder, don't assume it is rewound. Depress the REWIND lever just to be sure, then reset the counter. If you observe these precautions, a recording that started at a certain tape counter reading will always start at that reading.

Tape counter speed varies from one recorder to the next. Thus, tape counter readings noted on one recorder may not match those on another.

One-Step Program Load and Run

A new form of the RUN statement lets you load and run a program from cassette in one step. It looks like this:

```
RUN "C:"
```

This is essentially a combination of the LOAD "C:" and RUN statements. Therefore it works only with programs recorded on cassette by the SAVE "C:" statement.

Chaining Programs

The RUN statement works just as well in programmed mode as it does in immediate mode. A program that contains a RUN "C:" statement will run and load another program when that statement is executed. This process of one program loading another is called *chaining*.

To see how this works, put a cassette in the program recorder, rewind it all the way, and type in the following statements:

```
NEW

READY
10 PRINT "PROGRAM ONE"
20 PRINT "PRESS RETURN WHEN THE TAPE I
S READY"
30 RUN "C:"
SAVE "C:"

READY
▓
```

That puts the first program on tape. Notice that the program includes instructions to the user (line 20) so he will know what to do when the RUN "C:" statement (line 30) beeps the built-in speaker.

The program is still in memory. Change it to become the second program, and save the result on tape.

```
10 PRINT "PROGRAM TWO"
SAVE "C:"

READY
```

Now there are two programs on the tape. Make a few changes to the second program, which is still in memory, to create the third and final program, and save it on tape.

```
10 PRINT "PROGRAM THREE"
20 END
30
SAVE "C:"

READY
```

The cassette now has three programs on it, one right after another. The first will load and run the second, and the second will load and run the third. Rewind the tape and try it:

```
RUN "C:"
PROGRAM ONE
PRESS RETURN WHEN THE TAPE IS READY
PROGRAM TWO
PRESS RETURN WHEN THE TAPE IS READY
PROGRAM THREE

READY
```

Chained programs look to the user much like one long program. When programs are chained, the user must press RETURN to continue with the next program module. This interrupts program continuity somewhat, but not as much as having to type RUN "C:" between every module.

The main drawback to chaining programs with the RUN statement is that it clears all variables before it loads the next program. Therefore, one program cannot use values that were input or calculated by an earlier program in the chain.

Subroutine Libraries

Review the utility subroutines developed in Chapter 4 (Figures 4-16 through 4-21, 4-31, 4-33, and 4-36 through 4-38). They are useful subroutines in many programs, but it is certainly inconvenient having to retype them every time you want to use them. One way to get around this is with the CSAVE and CLOAD statements. Type in all the subroutines together and record them with the CSAVE statement. Then when you start to write a new program, the first thing you do is load the whole subroutine package with the CLOAD statement. Delete the lines you won't need, and you are left with the subroutines you want. This method works well unless you have two subroutines that use the same line numbers, or more subroutines than will fit in memory at once.

The LIST "C:" and ENTER "C:" statements make it easy to incorporate subroutines into programs. All you do is record each subroutine as a separate program with the LIST "C:" statement. It usually works best if you put only one or two subroutines on each side of a tape. Then when you write a new program, you can merge subroutines at any time by using ENTER "C:" statements.

Program Recording Formats

Recording a program is outwardly the same no matter which statement you use, CSAVE, LIST "C:", or SAVE "C:". But the three statements each record programs in a different format.

The LIST statement outputs programs in the same format regardless of the device. It sends out the ATASCII code of every character in the program listing.

Both the CSAVE and SAVE statements abbreviate keywords with one-character tokens. Thus, instead of storing five ATASCII characters for the keyword PRINT, the tokenized format stores just one character, the token for PRINT. The CLOAD and LOAD statements load tokenized programs. It doesn't matter what the codes for the tokens are, since the computer encodes and decodes them for you.

The ATARI computer records programs in blocks. The difference between the CSAVE and SAVE "C:" statements is the space between those blocks on the tape. The CSAVE statement records programs more densely than the SAVE "C:" statement. Thus loading and saving proceed a bit faster with CSAVE and CLOAD than with SAVE "C:" and LOAD "C:".

Variable Name Table

ATARI BASIC keeps a table of all the variable and array names you have used in programmed or immediate mode. The CSAVE and SAVE statements record this variable name table along with the program lines. The CLOAD and LOAD statements load the variable name table back into memory, replacing the current variable name table.

The LIST statement does not record the variable name table, nor does the ENTER statement load a variable name table. The existing variable name table remains. When you run the program, variables and arrays it uses are added to the variable name table.

Over a period of time, the variable name table can become cluttered with obsolete variable names. It is easy to clear out the deadwood. First, record the program with the LIST statement. Then clear the variable name table completely with the NEW statement. Of course, this erases the program as well. Load the program back into memory with the ENTER statement.

STORING DATA

Many computer applications involve large amounts of data, more than the computer can possibly store in its memory at once. ATARI BASIC lets you store data on cassette with the PRINT # and PUT statements. The INPUT # and GET statements read the data back in.

Data Files, Records, and Fields

The computer stores data on a cassette in *files*, much as you might store information in a filing cabinet. Each cassette is the equivalent of a filing cabinet; each cassette file is the equivalent of a file drawer. A cassette can have one file or many files, just as a filing cabinet can have one drawer or many. A cassette file, like a filing cabinet drawer, can be full or empty.

Data files are divided into *records* and *fields*. These can be compared to the file folders and their contents in a file drawer. There can be any number of records in a data file, as long as the tape is long enough to hold them all. A record can have any number of fields, though all records in the same file generally have the same number of fields. If a field is unused, its value is zero or blank. The computer writes a special record, called the *end-of-file* (EOF) record, to mark the end of the file.

Cassette data files do have one limitation: data in them can only be accessed sequentially. You must always start at the beginning of the file and read through to the end. You cannot add or delete records.

The Cassette Buffer

Rather than transfer data to and from the program recorder character by character, the ATARI computer does it in 128-character blocks. It sets aside part of its memory to hold one block of cassette data. This area is called the *cassette buffer*.

Cassette File Format

Every cassette data file has three components: the leader, data blocks, and an end-of-file record (Figure 5-1). The 20-second leader gives the program recorder and the computer a chance to synchronize and prepare for data transfer. All data blocks except the last one contain 128 characters (bytes) of data. The last data block contains the last few characters in the file, usually less than 128. The very last block on the file is the special end-of-file block.

A record may take more than one block, exactly one block, or less than one block, depending on its length. Generally speaking, the program does not have to worry about how the data records are blocked. The computer takes care of that automatically. The only exception will be discussed in the next section.

Opening a Data File

When you open a file, the information in it becomes accessible. The information remains accessible until you close the file. Use the OPEN statement to open a cassette data file, like this:

```
OPEN #1,8,0,"C:"
```

This statement opens channel 1 for output to the program recorder.

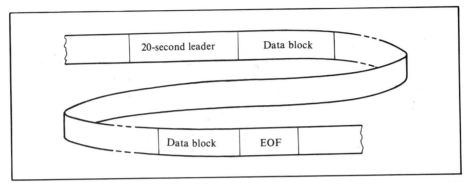

FIGURE 5-1. Cassette data file format

As with other devices, the second parameter of the OPEN statement determines whether the specified channel is open for input or output. A value of 4 means input, 8 means output. A cassette file cannot be open for input and output simultaneously. The third OPEN statement parameter is 0 for normal data files.

When you open a cassette data file, the computer goes through its tape-cueing process. It beeps the speaker once for input, twice for output. Then it waits while the user positions the tape to the proper starting point with the REWIND and FAST FORWARD levers. When the user presses a key on the keyboard, the program recorder starts the tape moving.

It is a good idea to display some instructions for the user just before opening a cassette data file. That way the speaker beeping won't take the user by surprise. Here is an example:

```
10 PRINT "Cue tape; press RETURN when
ready";
20 OPEN #2,4,0,"C:"
```

As soon as the tape starts moving, the computer starts to read or write the 20-second file leader. If the channel is open for output, it writes the leader. If the channel is open for input, it reads the leader. During this time, the computer will execute no other statements.

When the program recorder finishes reading or writing the leader, the program must immediately read or write the first data. If the file is open for output, the program must write 128 characters out to the program recorder. If it fails to do so, an error may result when the file is subsequently read. If there is no real data ready to go, the program can write a dummy block of zeros or blanks. If the file is open for input, the program must read the first data value from the file. If it does not, an error may occur when it tries to read data later in the program. Examples will be provided later in this chapter.

Closing a Data File

Closing an inactive data file is important because it frees a channel for other use.

The CLOSE statement closes a data file. Here is an example:

```
CLOSE #1
```

It is especially important to close a file that has been open for output. Failure to do so may result in loss of data. The cassette buffer may be partially full of data. Closing the file outputs the partially full buffer to the last data block on the cassette file. If the file is not closed, the partially full cassette buffer is never output.

Both the END and RUN statements automatically close all open channels. The computer also closes all open channels when it runs out of programmed mode statements to execute.

Writing to Data Files

Either a PRINT # or a PUT statement can output data to a cassette file. Both statements direct output to an open channel. It makes no difference to which device the the output channel is linked. If an OPEN statement has linked the output channel to the program recorder (device C:), that is where the data ends up. The following program demonstrates this:

```
10 PRINT "Cue tape; press RETURN when
ready";
20 OPEN #3,8,0,"C:"
30 PRINT #3;"This message is written t
o the program recorder."
40 CLOSE #3
```

The PRINT # statement outputs numeric and string values in ATASCII code. Always use semicolons, rather than commas, to separate items in a PRINT # statement to the program recorder. Commas are perfectly legal, but only result in extra spaces being recorded.

Each separate data value sent to the program recorder must end with an EOL character. When the value is read back, the EOL character determines where it ends. One way to guarantee that the EOL character occurs is to output each value with a separate PRINT # statement. Never end such PRINT # statements with a semicolon or comma. Another way to output the EOL character is with the CHR$ function, as follows:

```
10 PRINT "Cue tape; press RETURN when
ready";
20 OPEN #3,8,0,"C:"
30 PRINT #3;A;CHR$(155);B;CHR$(155);C
40 CLOSE #3
```

Each PUT statement outputs a single numeric value between 0 and 255. Each value takes the same space as one ATASCII character. The following program outputs a dummy record right after it opens an output channel to the cassette.

```
10 PRINT "Cue tape; press RETURN when
ready";
20 OPEN #3,8,0,"C:"
29 REM Dummy cassette record
30 FOR J=1 TO 128
40 PUT #3,0
50 NEXT J
60 PRINT #3,"First actual data"
70 CLOSE #3
```

Reading Data Files

The INPUT # statement reads values stored by the PRINT # statement. The channel number it specifies must be open for input from the program recorder. To see how it works, first use the following program to create a data file:

```
10 DIM A$(120)
20 PRINT "What message do you want rec
orded?"
30 INPUT A$
40 PRINT
50 PRINT "Cue tape; press RETURN when
ready";
60 OPEN #3,8,0,"C:"
70 PRINT #3;A$
80 CLOSE #3
```

The next program uses the INPUT # statement to read back the message recorded by the previous program. Don't forget to rewind the tape.

```
10 DIM A$(120)
20 PRINT "Cue tape; press RETURN when
ready";
30 OPEN #3,4,0,"C:"
40 INPUT #3;A$
50 PRINT A$
60 CLOSE #3
```

The INPUT # statement interprets data from a cassette file as ATASCII codes. Every time it encounters an EOL character (ATASCII code number 155), it assigns the characters it has read since the last EOL character to the next variable on its list. If the variable is numeric, the INPUT # statement converts the characters it has read into a numeric value. If the value is not numeric, error 8 occurs.

Each GET statement reads one numeric value. Your program must decide how to interpret that value. For example, it can interpret the value as an ATASCII code with the help of the CHR$ function. The next program uses the GET statement to read the same file as the last program.

```
10 PRINT "Cue tape; press RETURN when
ready";
20 OPEN #3,4,0,"C:"
30 GET #3,A
39 REM Print chars. until EOL
40 IF A<>155 THEN ? CHR$(A);:GOTO 30
50 ? :REM Force carriage return
60 CLOSE #3
```

Notice that this program has to watch for the EOL character itself (line 40).

A Practical Example

Consider a practical use of cassette files: a mailing list. Two programs will be needed. One will input names and addresses from the keyboard and save them on cassette. The other will read the names and addresses from the tape and display them on the screen. In Chapter 6 we will develop a program to print mailing labels from the cassette file.

Records on the mailing list file will each have five fields: name, street, city, state, and ZIP code. Our programs will always use the same string variables to reference each field: NA$, STT$, CI$, ST$, and ZIP$.

The program that creates the mailing list file must first dimension the record variables and open an output channel to the program recorder. The program should output a dummy record after it opens the output channel. The first real data will not be ready until the user enters it, and there is no telling how long that will be. The following program lines do all that:

```
50 DIM NA$(20),STT$(20),CI$(20),ST$(2)
,ZI$(9),R$(20),EOL$(1)
60 EOL$=CHR$(155):REM EOL character
69 REM Open file, write dummy record
70 GOSUB 3000
1900 END
2999 REM Open for cassette output
3000 PRINT CHR$(125);"Cue tape, press
RETURN, and stand by."
3010 OPEN #1,8,0,"C:"
3019 REM Output a dummy record
3020 FOR J1=1 TO 128:PUT #1,0:NEXT J1
3030 RETURN
```

Next, the program must enter the data for one record, as follows:

```
1000 PRINT CHR$(125);"ENTER NAMES AND
ADDRESSES"
1010 PRINT:PRINT
1020 PRINT "    Name:";
1030 INPUT NA$
1040 PRINT "  Street:";
1050 INPUT STT$
1060 PRINT "    City:";
1070 INPUT CI$
```

```
1080 PRINT "    State:";
1090 INPUT ST$
1100 POSITION 20,6
1110 PRINT "ZIP:";
1120 INPUT ZI$
```

If the user makes a mistake, the program should at least allow him to start over again. The following lines do that:

```
1130 POSITION 2,1
1140 PRINT "Reenter this?"
1150 INPUT R$:R$=R$(1,1)
1160 IF R$="N" OR R$="n" THEN 1300
1170 IF R$="Y" OR R$="y" THEN 1000
1180 GOTO 1130
```

When the user indicates that the data is correct, the program can output it to the program recorder. The output goes to the program recorder via the cassette buffer. If there is room in the cassette buffer for all of it, the output occurs very quickly. But the cassette buffer may become full and have to be recorded on the cassette. That will take a few seconds. Just to be safe, the program should advise the user to stand by while the output occurs. Add the following program lines:

```
1300 POSITION 8,21
1310 PRINT "* * *  PLEASE STAND BY * *
 *";
1319 REM Output cassette record
1320 PRINT #1;NA$;EOL$;STT$;EOL$;CI$;E
OL$;ST$;EOL$;ZI$
```

With the output completed, the program can now erase the advisory message and check with the user to see if there is more data. Add the following lines:

```
1329 REM Erase advisory message
1330 PRINT CHR$(156):REM Delete line
1340 POSITION 2,1
1350 PRINT "Add another name and addre
ss"
1360 INPUT R$:R$=R$(1,1)
1370 IF R$="Y" OR R$="y" THEN 1000
1380 IF R$<>"N" AND R$<>"n" THEN 1340
```

When the user finishes entering names and addresses, the program outputs one more record, then closes the file. The extra record is called a *trailer record*. It marks the end of the file. It has special values in all five fields — values the user is unlikely to enter. A program which reads the file can watch for these special field values and stop reading when they appear. These lines finish the program:

```
1389 REM Output trailer record
1390 FOR J=1 TO 5:REM 5 fields
1400 PRINT #1;CHR$(253);EOL$;
1410 NEXT J
1420 CLOSE #1
1900 END
```

```
50 DIM NA$(20),STT$(20),CI$(20),ST$(2)
,ZI$(9),R$(20),EOL$(1)
60 EOL$=CHR$(155):REM EOL character
69 REM Open file, write dummy record
70 GOSUB 3000
1000 PRINT CHR$(125);"ENTER NAMES AND
ADDRESSES"
1010 PRINT :PRINT
1020 PRINT "     Name:";
1030 INPUT NA$
1040 PRINT "  Street:";
1050 INPUT STT$
1060 PRINT "    City:";
1070 INPUT CI$
1080 PRINT "   State:";
1090 INPUT ST$
1100 POSITION 20,6
1110 PRINT "ZIP:";
1120 INPUT ZI$
1130 POSITION 2,1
1140 PRINT "Reenter this?"
1150 INPUT R$:R$=R$(1,1)
1160 IF R$="N" OR R$="n" THEN 1300
1170 IF R$="Y" OR R$="y" THEN 1000
1180 GOTO 1130
1300 POSITION 8,21
1310 PRINT "* * *  PLEASE STAND BY * *
 *";
1319 REM Output cassette record
1320 PRINT #1;NA$;EOL$;STT$;EOL$;CI$;E
OL$;ST$;EOL$;ZI$
1329 REM Erase advisory message
1330 PRINT CHR$(156):REM Delete line
1340 POSITION 2,1
1350 PRINT "Add another name and addre
ss"
1360 INPUT R$:R$=R$(1,1)
1370 IF R$="Y" OR R$="y" THEN 1000
1380 IF R$<>"N" AND R$<>"n" THEN 1340
1389 REM Output trailer record
1390 FOR J=1 TO 5:REM 5 fields
1400 PRINT #1;CHR$(253);EOL$;
1410 NEXT J
1420 CLOSE #1
1900 END
2999 REM Open for cassette output
3000 PRINT CHR$(125);"Cue tape, press
```

NOTE: Demonstrates cassette data file output. Shaded lines can be added to Figure 4-25 to add output capability to it.

(continued)

FIGURE 5-2. Mailing List Entry program listing

```
RETURN, and stand by."
3010 OPEN #1,8,0,"C:"
3019 REM Output a dummy record
3020 FOR J1=1 TO 128:PUT #1,0:NEXT J1
3030 RETURN
```

NOTE: Demonstrates cassette data file output. Shaded lines can be added to Figure 4-25
to add output capability to it.

FIGURE 5-2. Mailing List Entry program listing (continued)

The complete program appears in Figure 5-2. You probably noticed that the data
entry section is fairly crude. One of the programs in Chapter 4 inputs the same data,
name and address, but uses many more data entry aids (Figure 4-25). Compare lines
1000 through 1180 in Figure 5-2 with lines 1000 through 1230 in Figure 4-25. You
may wish to combine the cassette output portions of Figure 5-2 (lines 50, 60, 70,
1300 through 1420, and 3000 through 3030) with Figure 4-25 (all lines except 50) for
the best program.

A program to read the cassette file starts out by dimensioning the variables used
to read a data record. Then it opens an input channel to the program recorder, and
reads past the dummy record at the beginning of the file. Use the following lines:

```
50 DIM NA$(20),STT$(20),CI$(20),ST$(2)
,ZI$(9),R$(20)
69 REM Open file, read dummy record
70 GOSUB 3100
1900 END
3099 REM Open for cassette input
3100 PRINT CHR$(125);"Cue tape, press
RETURN, and stand by."
3110 OPEN #1,4,0,"C:"
3119 REM Input a dummy record
3120 FOR J1=1 TO 128:GET #1,R:NEXT J1
3130 RETURN
```

Next, the program displays some instructions for the user. The display can be
stopped by pressing CTRL-1, a standard ATARI computer feature. Pressing CTRL-1
again restarts the display. The following lines display the instructions:

```
1000 PRINT CHR$(125):REM Clr screen
1010 PRINT "DISPLAY MAILING LIST"
1020 POSITION 2,21
1030 PRINT "Press CTRL-1 to stop displ
ay."
1040 PRINT "Press CTRL-1 again to resu
me."
1050 POSITION 2,2
1060 PRINT "Press RETURN when ready to
 begin"
1070 INPUT R$
```

```
50 DIM NA$(20),STT$(20),CI$(20),ST$(2)
,ZI$(9),R$(20)
69 REM Open file, read dummy record
70 GOSUB 3100
1000 PRINT CHR$(125):REM Clr screen
1010 PRINT "DISPLAY MAILING LIST"
1020 POSITION 2,21
1030 PRINT "Press CTRL-1 to stop displ
ay,"
1040 PRINT "Press CTRL-1 again to resu
me."
1050 POSITION 2,2
1060 PRINT "Press RETURN when ready to
 begin"
1070 INPUT R$
1079 REM Display mailing list
1080 OPEN #4,8,0,"S:"
1089 REM Read next record
1090 INPUT #1,NA$,STT$,CI$,ST$,ZI$
1099 REM Watch for trailer record
1100 IF NA$=CHR$(253) THEN 1200
1110 PRINT #4;NA$
1120 PRINT #4;STT$
1130 PRINT #4;CI$
1140 PRINT #4;ST$;"   ";ZI$
1150 PRINT :PRINT
1160 GOTO 1090
1199 REM Trailer record found; quit
1200 CLOSE #1
1210 CLOSE #4
1900 END
3099 REM Open for cassette input
3100 PRINT CHR$(125);"Cue tape, press
RETURN, and stand by."
3110 OPEN #1,4,0,"C:"
3119 REM Input a dummy record
3120 FOR J1=1 TO 128:GET #1,R:NEXT J1
3130 RETURN
```

NOTE: Demonstrates cassette data file input. Can be modified to print a mailing list on
a printer (see Figure 6-4).

FIGURE 5-3. Mailing List Display program listing

The program will display the mailing list on the screen, so it opens an output
channel to the screen. Then, one by one, it reads records from the cassette and
displays them on the screen. Each time it reads a record, it checks to see if it is the
trailer record. Without this check, the program would eventually read the end-of-
file record, which would cause error 136. The following lines finish the program.

```
1079 REM Display mailing list
1080 OPEN #4,8,0,"S:"
1089 REM Read next record
1090 INPUT #1,NA$,STT$,CI$,ST$,ZI$
1099 REM Watch for trailer record
1100 IF NA$=CHR$(253) THEN 1200
1110 PRINT #4;NA$
1120 PRINT #4;STT$
1130 PRINT #4;CI$
1140 PRINT #4;ST$;"   ";ZI$
1150 PRINT:PRINT
1160 GOTO 1090
1199 REM Trailer record found; quit
1200 CLOSE #1
1210 CLOSE #4
```

The complete program listing appears in Figure 5-3. Chapter 6 has a modified version of this program that prints the mailing list instead of displaying it (Figure 6-4).

6
ATARI PRINTERS

When you turn on an ATARI computer, output automatically goes to the display screen. It is easy to divert the output to a printer instead.

This chapter will concentrate on programming output on the three ATARI printers: the ATARI 820 Printer, the ATARI 822 Printer, and the ATARI 825 Printer. When it comes to printing ordinary text and numbers, there is very little difference between the three ATARI printers. The main difference is in the width of the print line. The ATARI 820 and 822 Printers both have 40-column lines, just like the display screen. The ATARI 825 Printer has a nominal 80-column line; it can print as many as 132 characters per line. It also has a number of programmable features which will be covered at the end of this chapter. Until then, everything applies equally to all three printers unless stated otherwise.

Before going any further, make sure your printer is properly connected and turned on. The ATARI 825 Printer must be hooked up through the ATARI 850 Interface Module, and both components must be turned on. Refer to the operator's manual for detailed installation instructions.

PRINTING PROGRAM LISTINGS

If you type the LIST command at the keyboard, the BASIC program in the ATARI computer's memory will be listed on the display screen. A variation of the LIST command lets you divert the listing to a printer. It looks like this:

```
LIST "P:"
```

P: is the printer's device name. By explicitly stating the device name with the LIST command, you tell the computer where output goes. You can also specify starting and ending line numbers to be listed. The following command lists all program lines between lines 10 and 100 on the printer:

```
LIST "P:",10,100
```

No matter which device it goes to, the listing looks much the same. One exception is line length. The output device, not the LIST statement, determines the maximum line width. The display screen, the ATARI 820 Printer, and the ATARI 822 Printer all have a 40-column limit. Program lines longer than 40 characters will wrap around to the next display or printer line. Normally, the ATARI 825 Printer has an 80-column limit. On this printer, a program line will not wrap around unless it is more than 80 characters long.

None of the printers can print graphics characters, such as ♥ and ♣. On the ATARI 820 and 822 Printers, graphics characters appear as blank spaces in a printed listing. On the ATARI 825 Printer, some graphics characters do not print at all, while others cause strange special effects. These will be described at the end of this chapter.

PROGRAMMING PRINTER OUTPUT

Programming output on the printer is almost the same as programming output on the display screen. It is certainly no harder, although some differences do exist. For example, the printer has no cursor. The POSITION statement will move the cursor around on the screen display, but it will not move a print head around on a piece of paper. The printer prints an entire line at a time. Lines print sequentially, one line after another. On the screen, you can display the headings on a form (see Figure 4-24), then go back and fill in values for each heading. You cannot do this on the printer. Instead, you must print all the headings and values for one line before you go on to the next.

The LPRINT Statement

ATARI BASIC has a special statement for sending output to the printer. This statement, LPRINT, is designed to work with the 40-column printers in exactly the same way a PRINT statement works with the display screen. LPRINT, however, prints on the printer, rather than displaying on the screen. Here are some examples:

```
10 LPRINT "LPRINT STATEMENT DEMONSTRATION"
20 LPRINT
30 LPRINT "NO. ONE","NO. TWO","NO. THREE"
40 LPRINT 2.2E+44,-100.76,
50 LPRINT 1234567890
```

The LPRINT statement does not work quite right under all circumstances on the ATARI 825 Printer. If an LPRINT statement generates 40 characters or fewer and ends with a semicolon or comma, the output of the next LPRINT statement begins in column 41 of the same print line. Run the above program, and you will see that lines 40 and 50 demonstrate this phenomenon. If an LPRINT statement generates between 41 and 80 characters and ends with a semicolon or comma, the output of the next LPRINT statement starts at the beginning of the next print line.

The LPRINT statement automatically uses channel 7 for output. No OPEN statement is necessary. If the channel is already open to some other device, an error occurs, closing channel 7 in the process. Subsequent LPRINT statements will work fine.

PRINT # and PUT with a Printer

Either a PRINT # or PUT statement can send output to the printer. Both of these statements direct output to an open output channel. They do not care which device the output channel is linked to. In order for the output to go to the printer, you need only link the output channel to the printer (device P:). The following is an OPEN statement which does that:

```
10 OPEN #2,8,0,"P:"
```

After executing this statement, any PRINT # or PUT statement to channel 2 will send output to the printer.

The following program prints two lines of text on a printer:

```
10 REM OUTPUT 2 LINES TO A PRINTER
20 REM Open a printer output channel
30 OPEN #3,8,0,"P:"
40 PRINT #3;"Nice guys finish last"
50 PRINT #3;"Cheaters never prosper"
60 CLOSE #3
```

Output is much slower on the printer, but is otherwise identical to screen output. No matter what the output device is, PRINT # statements (lines 40 and 50 in the example) always format output the same way. In fact, the PRINT # statement itself knows only which channel to put the output on. It has no idea to which device the output is going. Try changing the OPEN statement so that it opens channel 3 to the display screen (device S:). Rerun the program, and the same two lines of text appear on the screen instead of on the printer.

Mixing Screen and Printer Output

A program can alternate its output between the printer and the display screen. Plain PRINT statements, without channel numbers, always go to the screen. The LPRINT statement always goes to the printer. You can mix these statements freely in any program. Use PRINT for output that will always go to the display screen. Use LPRINT for output that will always go to the printer.

What about output that may go to either the printer or the screen? By using the PRINT # statement, you can let the program user decide where program output will appear. Of course, the program must display its output in a manner that will work on either the screen or the printer. It must start at the top of the page and print each line completely before it moves on to the next. It must print lines no more than 38 characters long. It can print at most 24 lines at a time, or some lines will scroll off the top of the screen and be lost. Here is an example:

```
10 DIM N$(12)
20 PRINT "OUTPUT ON SCREEN OR PRINTER
(S OR P)";
30 INPUT N$
40 IF N$(1,1)="S" THEN N$="S:":GOTO 70

50 IF N$(1,1)="P" THEN N$="P:":GOTO 70

60 GOTO 20:REM Didn't respond S or P
69 REM Open output chan. per request
70 OPEN #4,8,0,N$
79 REM Input data
80 PRINT "ENTER A NAME";
90 INPUT N$
99 REM Output to chosen device
100 PRINT #4;N$;" backwards is ";
110 FOR J=LEN(N$) TO 1 STEP -1
120 PRINT #4;N$(J,J);
130 NEXT J
140 PRINT #4:REM EOL
150 IF N$<>"END" THEN 80
160 CLOSE #4:END
```

The program asks the user where program output should appear (lines 20 through 60). It assigns the appropriate device name, S: or P:, to a string variable (line 40 or 50). The OPEN statement that opens channel 4 uses the string variable to specify the device name (line 70). Program output goes out over channel 4 to its final destination (lines 100, 120, and 140).

Line Length

Remember that if you display anything in the last column of the display screen (column 39), a carriage return occurs automatically. The same thing happens if you print in the last column of a printer line. Print a 40-character line on the ATARI 820 or 822 Printer, or an 80-character line on the ATARI 825 Printer, and an automatic carriage return occurs on the printer. Screen margins, however, reduce screen width to 38 columns. Therefore, a full line on the display screen is normally shorter than a full line on a printer. A 38-character line will cause a carriage return on the screen but not on a printer. The following program demonstrates this feature:

```
10 REM Open output channels
20 OPEN #2,8,0,"S:"
30 OPEN #3,8,0,"P:"
39 REM Print on display and printer
40 FOR J=2 TO 3
49 REM Print a 39-character line
50 PRINT #J;"THIS LINE EXCEEDS DISPLAY
WIDTH BY ONE!"
60 NEXT J
70 END
```

The program displays the same message on the screen and the printer. It is too long for one screen line, but fits on one printer line. If the message were one character longer, it would also produce an automatic carriage return on a 40-column printer. On the ATARI 825 Printer, the output line must be 80 characters long before the automatic carriage return occurs.

Line length considerations are the same with the LPRINT statement as with the PRINT # statement.

The Printer Line Buffer

The printer has enough memory of its own to hold one line of print. This printer memory is called a *printer line buffer*. As PRINT #, LPRINT, and PUT statements send characters to the printer, those characters go into the printer line buffer. The printer does not display them immediately upon receipt. It waits until it gets an EOL (end-of-line) character. Then it prints the entire line and advances to the next line. If the line buffer fills up before an EOL character arrives, the printer prints the line, clears the buffer, and advances to the next line on its own. This happens when you print 40 characters or more (80 characters or more on the ATARI 825 Printer). The following program demonstrates this.

```
9 REM Open printer output channel
10 OPEN #3,8,0,"P:"
20 FOR J=0 TO 99
29 REM Print digits 0 thru 9
30 PRINT #3;J-INT(J/10)*10;
39 REM Display no. of each digit
40 PRINT J
50 NEXT J
59 REM Force output of last line
60 PRINT #3
70 CLOSE #3
```

The program prints the digit pattern 0123456789 ten times (lines 20, 30, and 50). It displays the number of the digit as it outputs each one to the printer (line 40). Notice that the digits do not print each time a number displays on the screen, which is when they are output. Nothing prints until the line buffer is full. The program prints 100 digits; the last few do not exactly fill a line. Therefore, the program must print an EOL character to force the printer to empty its buffer (line 60).

The printer line buffer does not care where the characters it gets come from. They may come from LPRINT, PRINT #, or PUT statements, on any output channel. The printer line buffer simply takes each character, puts it in the line buffer, and waits patiently for an EOL character or a full buffer.

Formatted Printer Output

Formatting output for the printer is similar to formatting output for the display screen. You can use commas in PRINT # or LPRINT statements to align columns. Review the Gas Cost program (Figure 4-3) for the display screen method. By

```
4 REM Strings needed for subroutine
5 DIM N$(10),T$(10),BL$(40)
6 REM Fill BL$() with blanks
7 BL$(1)=" ":BL$(40)=BL$:BL$(2)=BL$
9 REM Display gas cost table
10 PRINT "How much per gallon";
20 INPUT CPG
30 PRINT "Average miles per gallon";
40 INPUT MPG
42 PRINT "Output on Screen or Printer
(S or P)"
44 INPUT T$
46 IF T$(1,1)="P" THEN OPEN #5,8,0,"P:
":GOTO 50
48 OPEN #5,8,0,"S:"
50 PRINT #5;"MILES","GALLONS","    COST
"
60 PRINT #5;"-----","------","-------
"
70 FOR MI=100 TO 1700 STEP 100
79 REM Compute gal. to nearest 10th
80 GAL=INT(MI/MPG*10)/10
89 REM Compute cost to nearest cent
90 COST=INT(CPG*GAL*100)/100
100 NS=6:DD=0:N=MI:GOSUB 11000:PRINT #
5;N$(1,NS),
102 NS=7:DD=1:N=GAL:GOSUB 11000:PRINT
#5;N$(1,NS),
104 NS=7:DD=2:N=COST:GOSUB 11000:PRINT
#5;N$(1,NS)
110 NEXT MI
120 PRINT #5
130 PRINT #5,"MPG=";MPG,"$";CPG;" per
gal."
140 END
10995 REM *****************************
10996 REM *    Subroutine aligns     *
10997 REM *numeric values on decimal*
10998 REM *****************************
10999 REM Convert to left-just string
11000 T$=STR$(N)
11009 REM Fill output str with blanks
11010 N$=BL$
11029 REM Assume dec. point at end
11030 DP=LEN(T$)+1
11039 REM Look for real dec. point
```

NOTE: Shading shows lines changed from Figure 4-9. Output similar to Figure 4-10.

(continued)

FIGURE 6-1. Decimal-aligned Printer Output program listing

```
11040 FOR J=1 TO LEN(T$)
11050 IF T$(J,J)="." THEN DP=J:J=NS
11060 NEXT J
11069 REM Compute number length
11070 NL=DP+DD
11079 REM Right-justify
11080 N$(NS-NL+1,NS)=T$
11090 RETURN
```

FIGURE 6-1. Decimal-aligned Printer Output program listing (continued)

changing the PRINT statements on lines 50, 60, 100, 110, 120, and 130 to LPRINT statements, you can generate the same output on the printer. None of the printers supports the programmed tab feature, so you cannot use it to align columnar output.

The methods presented in Chapter 4 for right justification and decimal alignment also work with printer output. Figure 6-1 shows a new version of the Decimal-aligned Gas Cost program (compare this figure with Figure 4-9). This new version gives the user a choice between screen and printer output. If the user enters "P," output goes to the printer (lines 42 through 46). Any other entry sends output to the screen (line 48). The program uses PRINT # statements instead of the original PRINT statements (lines 50, 60, 100, 102, 104, 120 and 130). There are no other changes.

Paging

ATARI printers pay no attention to page length. They assume they are printing on an endless roll of paper, with no page boundaries.

There is a way to print program listings page by page. Use a separate LIST statement to list one page-sized chunk at a time. Explicitly specify a starting and ending line number for each chunk, so that the program lines within that chunk will fit on one page.

Paging program output is much less tedious. The program must count output lines. It must regularly check the line count against a maximum number of lines per page. If the count equals or exceeds the maximum, the program prints blank lines to advance the paper to the top of the next page. There it can print a title and column headings, if desired. The following program uses a special subroutine (Figure 6-2) to do the testing and handle the top-of-page ritual. Type in both the subroutine and these program lines:

```
90 GOTO 1000
993 REM --- Start of Main Program ---
999 REM Open printer output channel
1000 OPEN #4,8,0,"P:"
```

```
1010 PRINT CHR$(125):REM Clr. screen
1020 PRINT "Align printer at top of pa
ge"
1030 PRINT "How many lines"
1040 INPUT L
1049 REM Force new page
1050 PL=61:GOSUB 900
1060 PRINT
1070 PRINT "Printing, please stand by
. . .";
1080 FOR J=1 TO L
1090 FOR K=1 TO 4
1100 PRINT #4;INT(RND(0)*799)+200;"-";
INT(RND(0)*999)+1000,
1110 NEXT K
1119 REM Output EOL to print line
1120 PRINT #4
1129 REM Page full yet?
1130 PL=PL+1:GOSUB 900
1140 NEXT J
1150 END
```

This program prints four columns of seven-digit numbers. It assumes that before starting the program, the user sets the printer so it is ready to print on the first line at the top of a page. By setting PL to 61 (line 1050), the Top of Page subroutine (line 900) will leave five blank lines at the top of the first page before it prints the title. The program then outputs one column at a time (lines 1090 through 1110). Then it

```
897 REM *******************************
898 REM *  Top of Page Subroutine   *
899 REM *******************************
900 IF PL<55 THEN RETURN
909 REM Advance to next page
910 FOR J1=1 TO 66-PL
920 LPRINT :NEXT J1
929 REM Print title
930 LPRINT ,,"TITLE"
940 LPRINT
949 REM Print column headings
950 LPRINT "COL 1","COL 2","COL 3","CO
L 4"
959 REM Reset line count
960 PL=3:RETURN
```

NOTE: Title (line 930) and column headings (line 950) are only samples.

FIGURE 6-2. Top of Page subroutine listing

outputs an EOL character to force the printer to print its line buffer (line 1120). Each time a line is printed, the program increments the line counter and uses the subroutine to see how full the page is (line 1130). The subroutine will skip to the top of the next page if the program has printed 56 lines on the current page.

A Practical Example

In Chapter 5 we introduced a program to enter names and addresses for a mailing list and to build a mailing list file on cassette (Figure 5-2). Another program read the file and displayed the names and addresses on the display screen (Figure 5-3). It would be more useful to print the addresses on labels. Pressure-sensitive labels on continuous fan-fold carrier paper (Figure 6-3) are widely available.

The changes required to make the program in Figure 5-3 print labels are quite simple. First, line 1080 must open an output channel to the printer instead of to the display screen. Second, the output format must fit the labels.

The label forms (Figure 6-3) are one label wide, 12 labels per 12-inch page. The first line of the second label is one inch below the first line of the first label. There are

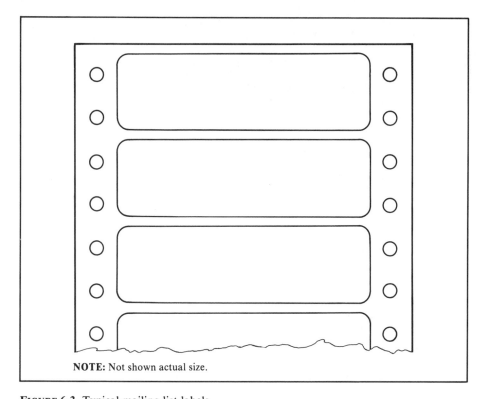

NOTE: Not shown actual size.

FIGURE 6-3. Typical mailing list labels

five lines of name and address data to print. The printer prints six lines to an inch. That leaves one blank line between labels. Therefore, line 1150 must print one blank line between addresses. Printer output cannot be stopped by pressing CTRL-1, so the instructions on lines 1030 and 1040 need revision. Figure 6-4 shows the final program.

```
50 DIM NA$(20),STT$(20),CI$(20),ST$(2)
,ZI$(9),R$(20)
69 REM Open file, read dummy record
70 GOSUB 3100
1000 PRINT CHR$(125):REM Clr screen
1010 PRINT "PRINT MAILING LABELS"
1020 POSITION 2,21
1030 PRINT "Place continuous labels in
printer."
1040 PRINT "Align at top of first label."
1050 POSITION 2,2
1060 PRINT "Press RETURN when ready to
begin"
1070 INPUT R$
1079 REM Display mailing list
1080 OPEN #4,8,0,"P:"
1089 REM Read next record
1090 INPUT #1,NA$,STT$,CI$,ST$,ZI$
1099 REM Watch for trailer record
1100 IF NA$=CHR$(253) THEN 1200
1110 PRINT #4;NA$
1120 PRINT #4;STT$
1130 PRINT #4;CI$
1140 PRINT #4;ST$;"   ";ZI$
1150 PRINT #4
1160 GOTO 1090
1199 REM Trailer record found; quit
1200 CLOSE #1
1210 CLOSE #4
1900 END
3099 REM Open for cassette input
3100 PRINT CHR$(125);"Cue tape, press
RETURN, and stand by."
3110 OPEN #1,4,0,"C:"
3119 REM Input a dummy record
3120 FOR J1=1 TO 128:GET #1,R:NEXT J1
3130 RETURN
```

NOTE: Shading shows lines changed from Figure 5-3. Prints labels from cassette data file prepared using the program in Figure 5-2.

FIGURE 6-4. Mailing List Labels program listing

PRINTER CHARACTER SETS

All ATARI printers can print numbers, punctuation, upper-case letters, and lower-case letters. None of them can print graphics characters like ▀, ▄, or ▬, nor can they print inverse characters.

The printers have a slightly different character set than does the display screen because they use a slightly different character code. The printers use the ASCII code to define their character sets, while the display screen uses the ATASCII code. The two codes are very similar for code numbers between 32 and 127. Appendix D lists both codes side by side. Table 6-1 summarizes the standard character set for the ATARI 820 and 822 Printers. Table 6-2 summarizes the ATARI 825 Printer character set. The ATARI 825 Printer interprets many of the codes lower than 32 as special control characters. These are discussed in more detail at the end of this chapter.

TABLE 6-1. ATARI 820 and 822 Printers Standard
Character Set Summary

Decimal Code	Character
0-31	Space
32-95	Same as display screen*
96	\
97-122	Same as display screen*
123	{
124	¦
125	}
126	~
127	Space

*Display screen characters are listed in Appendix D.

TABLE 6-2. ATARI 825 Printer Character Set Summary

Decimal Code	Character
0-31	Control characters (see Table 6-4)
32-95	Same as display screen*
96	\
97-122	Same as display screen*
123	{
124	¦
125	}
126	~
127	Non-printing

*Display screen characters are listed in Appendix D.

TABLE 6-3. Sideways Character Set (ATARI 820 Printer)

Decimal Code	Character	Decimal Code	Character	Decimal Code	Character	Decimal Code	Character	Decimal Code	Character
48	0	64	@	80	P	96	@	112	P
49	1	65	A	81	Q	97	A	113	Q
50	2	66	B	82	R	98	B	114	R
51	3	67	C	83	S	99	C	115	S
52	4	68	D	84	T	100	D	116	T
53	5	69	E	85	U	101	E	117	U
54	6	70	F	86	V	102	F	118	V
55	7	71	G	87	W	103	G	119	W
56	8	72	H	88	X	104	H	120	X
57	9	73	I	89	Y	105	I	121	Y
58	:	74	J	90	Z	106	J	122	Z
59	;	75	K	91	[	107	K	123	[
60	<	76	L	92	\	108	L	124	\
61	=	77	M	93	]	109	M	125	]
62	>	78	N	94	←	110	N	126	←
63	?	79	O	95	↓	111	O	127	↓

Printing Sideways Characters (ATARI 820 Printer)

In addition to normal characters, the ATARI 820 Printer can also print most of its
character set sideways. This is accomplished by opening a printer output channel
with a third parameter of 83, like this:

```
OPEN #4,8,83,"P:"
```

Subsequent PRINT# and PUT statement output to channel 3 will appear sideways
on the ATARI 820 Printer.

The sideways character set is somewhat different from the normal set. It has no
lower-case characters. Table 6-3 lists the sideways character set.

There are 29 characters per line in sideways mode.

PRINTER CONTROL CHARACTERS (ATARI 825 Printer)

The ATARI 825 Printer has a number of special features. The rest of this chapter
will describe them; you need not read on unless you have an ATARI 825 Printer.
The features include the following:

· Advance paper one line
· Advance paper one-half line
· Back paper up one line
· Back paper up one-half line
· Backspace

- Microspace forward and backward
- Underline
- Print subscripts and superscripts
- Print elongated characters
- Print condensed characters
- Print proportionally sized characters
- Print boldface characters
- Justify the right margin.

All these features are activated by control characters. Table 6-4 lists control characters for the ATARI 825 Printer. You send the ATARI 825 Printer a control character the same way you send it any regular character: with an LPRINT, PRINT #, or PUT statement. Of course, you have to generate the control character somehow, and there are no keys with the control functions printed on them. The simplest way to generate control characters is with the CHR$ function. For exam-

TABLE 6-4. Printer Control Characters (ATARI 825 Printer)

Decimal Code(s)	Graphics Character(s)	Keystroke(s)	ATARI 825 Printer function
10		CTRL-J	Line feed
27 & 10		ESC\ESC & CTRL-J	Reverse line feed
27 & 28		ESC\ESC & ESC\CTRL - -	Half-line feed
27 & 30		ESC\ESC & ESC\CTRL - +	Reverse half-line feed
13		CTRL-M	Carriage return with automatic line feed
15		CTRL-O	Start underlining
14		CTRL-N	Stop underlining
27 & 14		ESC\ESC & CTRL-N	Start double-wide printing
27 & 15		ESC\ESC & CTRL-O	Stop double-wide printing
27 & 19		ESC\ESC & CTRL-S	Select standard (10 cpi) characters
27 & 20		ESC\ESC & CTRL-T	Select condensed (16.7) characters
27 & 17		ESC\ESC & CTRL-Q	Select proportionally sized characters
27 & 1		ESC\ESC & CTRL-A	One dot blank space
27 & 2		ESC\ESC & CTRL-B	Two dot blank spaces
27 & 3		ESC\ESC & CTRL-C	Three dot blank spaces
27 & 4		ESC\ESC & CTRL-D	Four dot blank spaces
27 & 5		ESC\ESC & CTRL-E	Five dot blank spaces
27 & 6		ESC\ESC & CTRL-F	Six dot blank spaces
8 & nn*		CTRL-H & *keystroke**	Backspace nn* dots

* The character that follows the backspace control character (ASCII code 8) is interpreted as the number of dots to backspace. Use Appendix D to select the *keystroke* which produces the ATASCII character whose code number equals *nn*, the number of dots to backspace.

ple, the control character that advances the paper one full line, the *line feed* character, is ASCII code 10. The following program advances the paper ten lines.

```
9 REM Advance paper 10 lines
10 FOR J=1 TO 10
20 LPRINT CHR$(10)
30 NEXT J
```

You can also generate control characters directly with certain keystrokes, just like you do for cursor control and graphics characters on the display screen. Table 6-4 lists the keystrokes that generate each control character. When you type these keystrokes, certain graphics characters echo on the screen. This is because the screen interprets the keystroke as an ATASCII character (see Appendix D), and displays it accordingly. When the character is sent to the ATARI 825 Printer, it will interpret the same code as a control character and will respond accordingly. For example, look at the keystroke CTRL-J. It generates the ◣ graphics character on the display screen, but it advances the paper one full line on the ATARI 825 Printer. Try this new version on the last example (where you see ◣, type CTRL-J):

```
9 REM Advance paper 10 lines
10 FOR J=1 TO 10
20 LPRINT "◣"
30 NEXT J
```

Many of the ATARI 825 Printer features require a pair of control characters in tandem. In all but one case, the first character is ASCII code 27, the ASCII *escape character*. You can generate the ASCII escape character with CHR$(27) or with the ESC\ESC keystroke. (Recall from Chapter 4 that the notation ESC\ESC means press the ESC key, release it, then press it again.) As an example of a pair of control characters, consider ASCII codes 27 and 10. Together they make the ATARI 825 Printer back up the paper one full line, that is, perform one *reverse line feed*. The following program backs up the paper five lines. It uses the CHR$ function to create each reverse line feed.

```
9 REM Back paper up 5 lines
10 FOR J=1 TO 5
20 LPRINT CHR$(27);CHR$(10)
30 NEXT J
```

Most of the special features on the ATARI 825 Printer are produced by control character pairs like this. Two features, right margin justification and boldface characters, require more BASIC programming than just printing a control character or two. These will be discussed in more detail later in this chapter.

Listings Containing Control Characters

Don't be surprised if strange things happen when you list a program in which you typed control characters directly inside quotation marks. The display screen translates them into harmless graphics characters. The ATARI 825 Printer, though, cannot tell it is just printing a program listing. It obeys the control characters and ruins the listing in the process. Suppose, for example, you have a program that contains the statement PRINT #2; "◣;". When this statement is executed, the ATARI 825 Printer performs a line feed. The character also causes a line feed when you list it.

If you use the CHR$ function to generate control characters, your program will list with no surprises. The control characters are created only when the CHR$ function is executed. That happens only when the program is run. At program listing time, the CHR$ function is just a benign series of normal, everyday characters: C, H, R, and so on.

Vertical Paper Movement

Four control characters control vertical paper movement. They move the paper forward and backward one full line or one-half line at a time. The paper moves up and down, but the print head does not move at all. It takes one control character to move the paper, and another to move the paper back. Try the following program:

```
10 LPRINT "How dry. I";CHR$(27);CHR$(10
);" hic ";CHR$(10);"am."
```

The program prints this:

```
          hic
How dry I       am.
```

Notice that the ATARI 825 Printer prints the line in three parts. After each part it returns the print head to the left margin.

Aside from novelties like this, the principal use of the line feed character (ASCII code 10) is rapid paper advance. True, a plain LPRINT or PRINT # statement (one with no items to print and no terminating semicolon) will advance the paper one line. But plain LPRINT and PRINT # statements move the print head, while line feed characters do not. Therefore, a succession of line feed characters will advance the paper faster than a series of plain LPRINT or PRINT # statements.

Subscripts and Superscripts

Printing subscripts and superscripts is easy. Here's how to print a subscript:

1. Roll the paper forward one-half line with one pair of control characters: ASCII codes 27 and 28. This puts the print head one-half line *below* the main text line.
2. Print the subscript text.
3. Roll the paper back one-half line with another pair of control characters: ASCII codes 27 and 30. This puts the print head back over the main text line.

To print a superscript, just reverse the first and last steps:

1. Roll the paper back one-half line with one pair of control characters: ASCII codes 27 and 30. This puts the print head one-half line *above* the main text line.
2. Print the superscript text.
3. Roll the paper forward one-half line with another pair of control characters: ASCII codes 27 and 28. This puts the print head back over the main text line.

The following program demonstrates superscripts:

```
10 PRINT "Compute 1.5 to what power";
20 INPUT R
30 LPRINT "(1.5)";CHR$(27);CHR$(30);R;
CHR$(27);CHR$(28);"=";1.5^R
```

If you enter 5 in response to the INPUT statement (line 20), the program prints this:

$(1.5)^5$=7.59374994

Underlining

One control character (ASCII code 15) starts character underlining. The ATARI 825 Printer continues to underline characters until instructed to stop by another control character (ASCII code 14). Turning off the printer also cancels underlining mode. Here is an underlining example:

```
LPRINT CHR$(15);"War and Peace";CHR$(1
4);", by Leo Tolstoy"
```

Printed output of this immediate mode program looks like this:

War and Peace, by Leo Tolstoy

Character Size and Line Length

Standard character size on the ATARI 825 Printer is ten characters per inch. Condensed characters are also available; they print 16.7 characters per inch. In either case, character width is uniform. The ATARI 825 Printer can also print proportionally sized characters. In this mode, an "I" or an "l" is narrower than an "M" or a "W." On the average, proportionally sized characters print 14 to the inch. However, all proportionally sized *digits* are the same size; numbers will print 12.5 characters per inch.

Different pairs of control characters switch from one character size to another. When one of these pairs occurs, character size changes with the next non-control character. However, if the characters in the print line are standard sized, character size will not change to condensed or proportional until the start of the next print line. Similarly, if the characters in the print line are condensed or proportionally sized, character size will not change to standard until the start of the next print line. Thus, you can mix proportional and condensed characters on the same print line, but you cannot mix either of those sizes with standard characters.

Once a character size is in effect, it stays in effect until another control character occurs to change it. Character size reverts to standard when you turn the printer off and back on again.

In addition to all this, the ATARI 825 Printer can take any character and print it twice its normal width, or *double-width*. You activate double-wide character mode with one pair of control characters (ASCII codes 27 and 14). Characters continue to print in double-wide mode until you deactivate it with another pair of control characters (ASCII codes 27 and 15), or until a carriage return occurs.

The following program demonstrates the different character sizes. (Table 6-4 tells you which keystrokes produce the graphics characters you see below.)

```
10 DIM STD$(2),CDS$(2),PRP$(2),CW$(2)
19 REM Assign printer control chars.
20 STD$="[E][+]":REM 10 cpi characters
30 CDS$="[E][●]":REM 16.7 cpi characters
40 PRP$="[E][r]":REM Proportional char.
99 REM Open printer output channel
100 OPEN #3,8,0,"P:"
110 PRINT #3;STD$;"Standard Characters
"
120 GOSUB 1000
130 PRINT #3;CDS$;"Condensed Character
s"
140 GOSUB 1000
150 PRINT #3;PRP$;"Proportional Charac
ters"
160 GOSUB 1000
200 END
999 REM Print entire character set
1000 CW$="":REM Start w/1-wide char.
1010 FOR L=1 TO 2
1020 FOR K=32 TO 96 STEP 32
1029 REM Select char. width
1030 PRINT #3;CW$;
1039 REM Print next 32 characters
1040 FOR J=1 TO 31
1050 PRINT #3;CHR$(J+K);
1060 NEXT J
1069 REM Force printer buffer output
1070 PRINT #3
1080 NEXT K
1089 REM Select 2-wide characters
1090 CW$="[E][_]"
1099 REM And repeat character set
1100 NEXT L
1110 PRINT #3:REM Blank line
1120 RETURN
```

Character width on the ATARI 825 Printer is measured in terms of *dots*. It varies from six dots for the narrowest proportionally sized character to 36 dots for the widest double-wide, proportionally sized character. Standard and condensed characters are between these extremes, at a nominal ten and nine dots each, respectively. Table 6-5 summarizes character widths. Table 6-6 lists specific widths for all proportionally sized characters.

Maximum line length on the ATARI 825 Printer is always eight inches. Remember that when a line is full, an automatic carriage return occurs. A full line of standard characters contains 80 characters. A full line of condensed characters contains 132 characters. Since proportionally sized character widths differ, you

TABLE 6-5. Summary of Character Widths (ATARI 825 Printer)*

Character Size	Dots per Character
Standard	10
Condensed	9
Proportional	6 to 18

*Double-wide characters are twice the width shown.

TABLE 6-6. Widths of Proportionally Sized Characters (ATARI 825 Printer)*

Decimal Code	Character	Dots	Decimal Code	Character	Dots	Decimal Code	Character	Dots
32	Space	7	64	@	14	96	`	7
33	!	7	65	A	16	97	a	12
34	"	10	66	B	15	98	b	12
35	#	15	67	C	14	99	c	10
36	$	12	68	D	16	100	d	12
37	%	16	69	E	14	101	e	12
38	&	14	70	F	14	102	f	10
39	'	7	71	G	16	103	g	12
40	(	7	72	H	16	104	h	12
41	)	7	73	I	10	105	i	8
42	*	12	74	J	14	106	j	6
43	+	12	75	K	16	107	k	12
44	,	7	76	L	14	108	l	8
45	-	12	77	M	18	109	m	16
46	.	7	78	N	16	110	n	12
47	/	12	79	O	16	111	o	12
48	0	12	80	P	14	112	p	12
49	1	12	81	Q	14	113	q	12
50	2	12	82	R	15	114	r	10
51	3	12	83	S	12	115	s	12
52	4	12	84	T	14	116	t	10
53	5	12	85	U	16	117	u	12
54	6	12	86	V	16	118	v	12
55	7	12	87	W	18	119	w	16
56	8	12	88	X	16	120	x	12
57	9	12	89	Y	16	121	y	12
58	:	7	90	Z	10	122	z	10
59	;	7	91	[	12	123	{	10
60	<	12	92	\	12	124	l	7
61	=	12	93	]	12	125	}	10
62	>	12	94	^	12	126	~	12
63	?	12	95	—	12	127	None	0

* Double-wide characters are twice the width shown.

cannot simply count characters to see when the line is full. You have to count dots. There are 1200 dots per line, but the printer considers the line full when it contains 1185 dots. At that point, it will accept one more character, of any width, as the last character on that line. It then performs a carriage return. To avoid the automatic carriage return, do not print more than 1185 dots per line.

Half as many double-wide characters of any kind fit on one line. Therefore, 40 double-wide standard characters, 66 double-wide condensed characters, or 600 double-wide dots fill one line and cause an automatic carriage return.

Microspacing Forward and Backward

You can space forward on the print line in fixed amounts with the space character (ASCII code 32). A standard space character is ten dots wide, a condensed space character is nine dots wide, and a proportional space character is seven dots wide. There are also six pairs of control characters which add blank space to the print line in amounts of one to six dots. ASCII code 27 is always the first of the control character pair for this operation. The ASCII code of the second control character specifies the number of blank dots to add (one to six). The most straightforward way to specify this is with the CHR$ function. The number inside the parentheses is the number of dots to space forward. The following programs show how this works:

```
9 REM Open printer output channel
10 OPEN #5,8,0,"P:"
19 REM 1 to 6 dots between words
20 FOR J=1 TO 6
30 PRINT #5;"HO";CHR$(27);CHR$(J);
40 NEXT J
50 PRINT #5;"HUM"
```

The program prints this:

```
HOHOHO HO HO HO HO HUM
```

Forward microspacing is primarily useful in printing boldface characters and in justifying the right margin, two topics we will address shortly.

The ATARI 825 Printer can also backspace on the print line. It backspaces only in dot increments. Backspacing over a standard or condensed character is possible; just specify the appropriate number of dots (see Table 6-5 for dot equivalents).

The backspace control character is ASCII code 8. The printer interprets the character after the ASCII backspace code as the number of dots to backspace. The number of dots equals the ASCII code of the character. It can be any number between 0 and 127. Consider this program:

```
9 REM Open printer output channel
10 OPEN #5,8,0,"P:"
20 PRINT #5;"Print strikeouts";
29 REM Overprint the last 10 chars.
30 PRINT #5;CHR$(8);CHR$(100);
40 PRINT #5;"---------- with the backs
pace character"
```

The program outputs a backspace character, then immediately outputs the number of dots to backspace (line 20). It backspaces 100 dots, the equivalent of ten standard characters. Right after that, it prints ten hyphens. Because of the back-spacing, they end up printing over the last ten characters printed, like this:

```
Print strikeouts with the backspace character
```

The ATARI 825 Printer does not backspace by literally moving the print head backward along the print line. Instead, it returns the print head to the left margin, then moves it right back to the spot where it was, less the number of backspace dots. The net effect is to backspace the print head.

Instead of using the CHR$ function to specify the number of dots, you can use the equivalent ASCII character. In the last example, you could replace CHR$(100) with its ASCII equivalent, the letter "d." Line 30 would then look like this:

```
30 PRINT #5;CHR$(8);"d";
```

You cannot backspace over the last character of a full print line. By the time the backspace control character gets to the printer, the full line will have printed.

Boldface Characters

It is possible to darken printed characters for additional emphasis. The simplest way to do this is to overprint them two or more times. Here is an example:

```
9 REM Open printer output channel
10 OPEN #5,8,0,"P:"
20 PRINT #5;"This line printed once."
30 FOR J=1 TO 2
40 PRINT #5;"This line printed twice f
or added emphasis."
49 REM Back up one line
50 PRINT #5;CHR$(27);CHR$(10);
60 NEXT J
69 REM Cancel last reverse line feed
70 PRINT #5
80 END
```

The program uses a FOR-NEXT loop to print a message twice (lines 40 through 60). Each time the printer finishes the message, it advances the paper to the next line (line 40). The program backs the paper up one line (line 50). That way the next printing will overprint the first printing. When the loop ends, the program has just backed the paper up one line. Therefore it must advance the paper one line to cancel that extra reverse line feed (line 70). Here is the result:

```
This line printed once.
This line printed twice for added emphasis.
```

The boldface effect can be enhanced by staggering the second printing one dot. Add these lines to the last example:

```
80 FOR J=1 TO 2
90 PRINT #5;"This line printed boldfac
e for maximum emphasis."
99 REM Back up one line
100 PRINT #5;CHR$(27);CHR$(10)
109 REM Microspace one dot
110 PRINT #5;CHR$(27);CHR$(1);
120 NEXT J
129 REM Cancel last reverse line feed
130 PRINT #5
140 END
```

This is what you get:

```
This line printed once.
This line printed twice for added emphasis.
This line printed boldface for maximum emphasis.
```

Right Margin Justification

Dot spacing makes right margin justification possible. You must determine the number of dots between the last character on the line and the right margin. Then you must find new places somewhere else on the line for every one of those dots. This means sneaking in one or two blank dots between each character. You have to do it evenly across the line, or the line will look unbalanced. You may be able to put a few more dots between words than between letters. A good program recognizes where it can best add extra space, and where it will look ugly.

Writing even a simple justification program is not a trivial task. It can be done in BASIC, but it will be very slow. You may wish to experiment with it as an exercise. Right margin justification is best programmed in assembly language.

7
THE ATARI
810 DISK DRIVE

The disk drive is one of the most important components of a computer system. Disk drives allow almost instantaneous access to a large block of information. The ATARI 810 Disk Drive can store about 90,000 characters on a single diskette. That is nearly twice as much information as can be held in the computer in 48K of RAM. When you turn off the computer, all of the information in RAM disappears, but information stored on a diskette remains intact.

DISKS

Disks store information magnetically, the same way a tape recorder does. The biggest difference between a disk and tape is that a disk is round, like a record. A disk spins in the disk drive, much like a record spins on a turntable. Inside the disk drive there is a magnetic head that can read and write information on the disk. The head operates on the disk drive like a needle does on a record player. You can put the needle anywhere you want on a record. It is just as easy to place it in the middle or at the end of the record as it is to place it at the beginning. The computer, likewise, can direct the read/write head to any location on the surface of the disk. This ability is called *random access*. Thus, the disk is a random access storage device.

There are three kinds of disks: hard disks, Winchester disks, and diskettes. Currently, diskettes are the most common type of disk used with microcomputers like the ATARI 400/800 computers. We will describe all three types of disks.

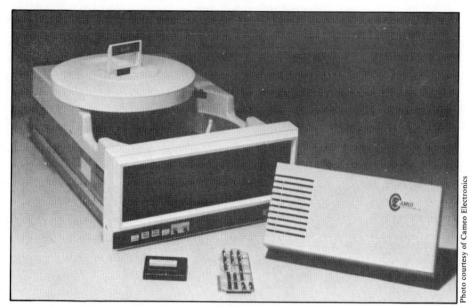

FIGURE 7-1. Typical hard disk drive and removable disk cartridge

Hard Disks

Hard disks are made of a rigid material, such as aluminum, that has been coated with a magnetic substance. Hard disks typically store 5 to 10 million characters. Usually the hard disk comes in a cartridge which is inserted in the drive (Figure 7-1). The disk and disk drive are separate so that you can change disks. Hard disks cost about $150 each; hard disk drives cost $3000 to $10,000.

Winchester Disks

Winchester disk drives (Figure 7-2) use a special technology that allows six to ten times more data to be stored on a disk than on conventional hard disks. Winchester disks are extremely susceptible to dust and dirt—even cigarette smoke. Because they must be kept very clean, the disk surfaces are sealed inside the drive and cannot be changed easily. Winchester disk drives cost from $2500 to $8000.

Diskettes

A diskette consists of a vinyl disk enclosed in a stiff plastic envelope. The flexible vinyl disk is very fragile. The stiff envelope protects the diskette from damage during normal handling and use. Never remove the diskette from its protective envelope. Figure 7-3 shows what a 5 ¼-inch diskette looks like inside its envelope.

   The diskette spins freely inside the envelope. Openings in the envelope allow the

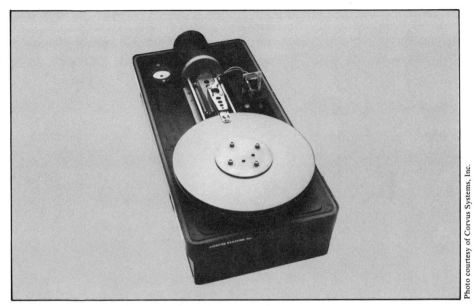

Photo courtesy of Corvus Systems, Inc.

FIGURE 7-2. Winchester disk drive (Shown with cover removed)

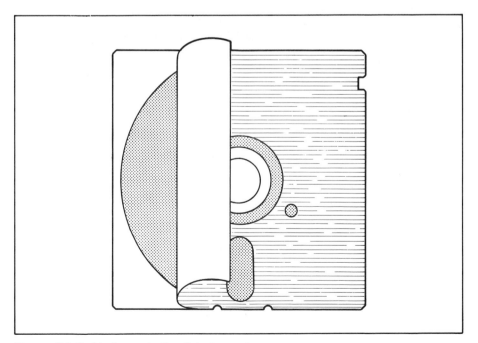

FIGURE 7-3. Inside the protective diskette envelope

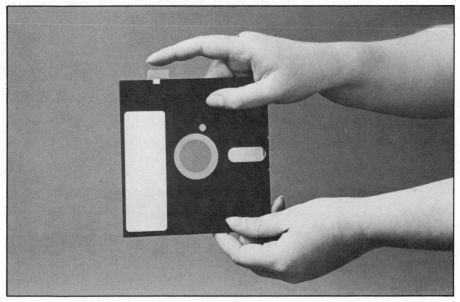

FIGURE 7-4. Write-protecting a 5¼-inch diskette

center of the diskette where the drive can grip and spin the diskette.

Diskettes are also known as *floppy disks* or *flexible disks*. They come in two sizes: 8-inch diameter and 5 ¼-inch diameter. The smaller ones are also called *mini-disks* or *mini-diskettes*. The ATARI 810 Disk Drive uses 5 ¼-inch diskettes; it can store 92,160 characters on a single diskette.

Write-Protecting Diskettes

There is a notch on the side of the diskette that is used to allow or prevent information from being written on a diskette. This notch is called a *write enable notch*, because the disk drive will not write on a diskette unless the notch is present.

Some diskettes have no notch. They are permanently protected against accidental writing. You can protect a notched diskette by covering the notch with a write-protect label or a piece of opaque tape (Figure 7-4).

DISK FILES

The disk drive stores information in *files*, much as you might store information in a filing cabinet. Each diskette is the equivalent of a file drawer; each file is the equivalent of a file folder. A diskette can contain many files, or it can contain no files. The maximum number of files per diskette is 64; however, if some of the files are long, the diskette may become full with fewer than 64 files. A single file can have any length that can be physically accommodated by the diskette.

A disk file can contain a BASIC program, a machine language program, or data. The techniques for reading and writing each kind of file are different, as you will discover later in this chapter.

File Names

Every file has a name, which is used to distinguish it from other files on the diskette. File names can contain up to eight characters. The characters can be any combination of capital letters and numbers, but the first character must be a capital letter. No blank spaces, special characters (such as $, @, or #), or punctuation marks of any kind are allowed in file names.

File Name Extensions

A file name can have a suffix of one, two, or three characters. The suffix is called a *file name extension.* File name extensions can contain any combination of letters and numbers. The first character can be a number; it is not restricted to letters, as is the file name itself. You specify a file name extension by adding a period to the end of the file name, then the extension. For example, FILENAME with the extension TXT would be written as FILENAME.TXT.

The extension is sometimes called the *file type,* because of the common practice of using it to indicate the type of file. Table 7-1 lists some common conventions for file name extensions and the types of files they imply. Avoid the extension .SYS, since it is reserved for system files.

TABLE 7-1. Common File Name Extensions

Extension	Implied File Type
SYS	System files. Files which contain system programs like the disk operating system, or language interpreters like Microsoft BASIC.
BAS	Files which contain BASIC programs in tokenized (SAVE statement) format.
LST	BASIC programs stored as ATASCII characters (LIST statement format).
ASM	Assembly language programs in source (text) form.
DAT	Data files. DTA is also used.
TXT	Text files.
OBJ	Object files. Assembly language programs assembled into machine language.
BAK	Backup files. Copies of a file made in case the original version is accidentally destroyed.
TMP	Temporary files which contain information that will be needed for only a short time.

The Disk Directory

Part of every diskette is set aside for a directory. The directory contains the name, location, and size of every file on the diskette. When you specify a file name, the computer looks up the file name in the directory. That is how it determines whether the file already exists and, if so, where it is on the disk.

THE DISK OPERATING SYSTEM

The *disk operating system* (DOS) is a computer program that controls the operations of the disk drive. When a BASIC program needs to use the disk for any reason, the disk operating system performs the actual disk operation and returns the results to the BASIC program. The disk operating system program is written in machine language, not in BASIC.

Versions of the Disk Operating System

There are currently two versions of the disk operating system. DOS 1.0 was the first version released by Atari, Inc. It was shipped with all ATARI 810 Disk Drives through the end of 1981. It has now been replaced by DOS 2.0S. The version you are using should be marked on the diskette label. Later in this chapter we will describe characteristics of the two versions that will enable you to tell them apart without looking at the label.

This chapter will describe both DOS 1.0 and DOS 2.0S. The descriptions of DOS 2.0S are accurate as of December 1981.

The two versions of the disk operating system are very similar, but not identical. DOS 2.0S can *read* a diskette prepared by DOS 1.0, but DOS 1.0 will have mixed success reading diskettes prepared by DOS 2.0S; errors may occur at random. In any event, *do not write information on a diskette with a discrepant version of the disk operating system.* Doing so can destroy data on the diskette. To be safe, place a write-protect label on any diskette before you use it with a discrepant version of the disk operating system.

The Two Parts of the Disk Operating System

There are two parts to the disk operating system program. One part records and loads BASIC programs and reads and writes data files. The other part is a package of utilities that assist in disk maintenance activities. These utilities also allow you to read and write machine language program and data files.

In DOS 1.0, the two parts of the disk operating system are treated as one program. They are stored on disk in one file, named DOS.SYS. In DOS 2.0S, the two parts of the disk operating system are treated as two programs. They are stored on disk in two files. The two parts are divided in DOS 2.0S to make better use of the computer's memory. The first part (file name DOS.SYS) is needed whenever you use the disk drive, but the second part (file name DUP.SYS) is not required unless you are using the disk utility package. Separating these functions means that your program can use the memory that would otherwise be occupied by the disk utility package.

Program and Data Transfer

The disk operating system controls the flow of all information between the disk drive and the computer. It does this in 128-character blocks. It sets aside part of the computer's memory to hold one block of disk data. This is called the *disk buffer*. There are actually four disk buffers, one for each of the four disk drives that can be attached simultaneously to the ATARI computer.

When the disk operating system receives a request for more program lines or data, it tries to fill the request from the disk buffer. If the buffer runs out, the disk operating system replenishes it by reading another block from the disk.

Recording a program or writing to a data file also proceeds one block at a time. As the disk operating system receives program lines or data to go to the disk, it puts them in the disk buffer. When the buffer becomes full, the disk operating system writes it out to the disk.

STARTING UP WITH A DISK DRIVE

Before the ATARI computer can execute any disk command, the disk operating system program must be in memory. If you had a lot of time, you could type it into memory using the keyboard. But there is an easier way: it is called *booting* the disk. Booting the disk, or booting DOS, reads a copy of the disk operating system program from a diskette and places it in the computer's memory.

How to Boot DOS

Chapter 2 has complete instructions for booting DOS. If you follow the standard power-on procedure (page 14), you will boot DOS as a matter of course. To recapitulate, these are the three key steps required to boot DOS:

- Turn on Drive 1. To determine which is Drive 1 on a multiple-drive system, look in the access hole at the back of each drive. The drive with both the black and white switches all the way to the left is Drive 1 (Figure 2-5).
- Place a diskette containing a copy of the disk operating system program (file name DOS.SYS) into Drive 1. The diskettes labeled "Disk File Manager Master Copy" (DOS 1.0) and "Disk File Manager II Master Copy" (DOS 2.0S) have copies of DOS on them.
- Turn the console power off and on. The disk drive whirrs as it transfers DOS from the diskette to the computer's memory.

While the boot is in progress, you will hear beeping sounds from the television speaker if the sound level is turned up. After about 20 seconds, the BASIC **READY** prompt will appear.

To all appearances, nothing unusual has occurred. What you can't see is that during those 20 seconds the disk operating system program was loaded into

```
DISK OPERATING SYSTEM II   VERSION 2.0S
COPYRIGHT 1980 ATARI

A. DISK DIRECTORY  I. FORMAT DISK
B. RUN CARTRIDGE.  J. DUPLICATE DISK
C. COPY FILE       K. BINARY SAVE
D. DELETE FILE(S)  L. BINARY LOAD
E. RENAME FILE     M. RUN AT ADDRESS
F. LOCK FILE       N. CREATE MEM.SAV
G. UNLOCK FILE     O. DUPLICATE FILE
H. WRITE DOS FILES
```

FIGURE 7-5. DOS 2.0S menu

memory. The computer can now interpret references to the disk drive.

You can boot DOS from any diskette that has file DOS.SYS. Booting DOS transfers the machine language disk operating system program from file DOS.SYS into the computer's memory. With DOS 1.0, this includes both parts of the disk operating system. With DOS 2.0S, it includes only the first part; it does not include the disk utility package. In either case, the contents of file DOS.SYS remain in memory until you turn off the computer.

THE DISK UTILITY PACKAGE (DOS MENU)

After you boot DOS, you can use any of the disk statements. The first one to use is the DOS command. Simply type the following command and press RETURN:

```
DOS
```

The DOS menu appears on the display screen (Figure 7-5 or 7-6). If you are using DOS 1.0, the menu appears immediately. If you are using DOS 2.0S, the disk utility package must be loaded from disk; you must wait several seconds while this takes place.

The DOS command transfers control of the computer from BASIC to the DOS menu. If you boot DOS without a ROM cartridge inserted in the computer, you will never see the BASIC **READY** message. Instead, the DOS menu appears as soon as DOS is booted.

Executing the DOS statement with DOS 2.0S transfers the disk utility package into memory from disk file DUP.SYS. That file must be present on the diskette in Drive 1 when the DOS statement is executed. The contents of file DUP.SYS go into the area of memory where BASIC programs reside. This destroys any BASIC program present in memory. When you leave the DOS menu and return to BASIC, your program will be gone, just as if you had issued a NEW command. At that point there is no way to retrieve the program unless you saved it on diskette or cassette. Later in this chapter we will discuss a way to have the computer automatically preserve your BASIC program when it executes the DOS statement.

With DOS 1.0, the disk utility package is transferred into memory when you boot DOS. Since it is present in memory when the DOS statement is executed, file DUP.SYS is not used. In this case, the disk utility package resides in an area of memory that does not conflict with a BASIC program. With DOS 1.0, therefore, executing the DOS statement will not affect your program.

Determining the DOS Version

The time it takes for the DOS menu to appear is a foolproof way to determine whether you are using DOS 1.0 or DOS 2.0S. If Drive 1 becomes active before the menu appears, you are using DOS 2.0S. The version number also appears in the upper right-hand corner of the DOS 2.0S menu (Figure 7-5).

The MEM.SAV File

When the computer executes the DOS statement under DOS 2.0S, it loads the disk utility package from disk file DUP.SYS into memory. In the process it writes over part of the memory area where BASIC programs reside. This section describes how the computer can automatically preserve the contents of the overwritten memory

```
DISK OPERATING SYSTEM      9/24/79
COPYRIGHT 1979 ATARI

A. DISK DIRECTORY  I. FORMAT DISK
B. RUN CARTRIDGE   J. DUPLICATE DISK
C. COPY FILE       K. BINARY SAVE
D. DELETE FILE(S)  L. BINARY LOAD
E. RENAME FILE     M. RUN AT ADDRESS
F. LOCK FILE       N. DEFINE DEVICE
G. UNLOCK FILE     O. DUPLICATE FILE
H. WRITE DOS FILE
```

NOTE: Item N, DEFINE DEVICE, is not implemented.

FIGURE 7-6. DOS 1.0 menu

area with the special file MEM.SAV. This does not apply to DOS 1.0, so skip this section if you are using that version of DOS only.

With DOS 2.0S, whenever the computer executes the DOS statement it searches the diskette in Drive 1 for file MEM.SAV. If the file exists, the computer saves everything in the memory area that will be used by the disk utility package onto file MEM.SAV. Then it loads the disk utility package from file DUP.SYS and transfers control to the DOS menu. When you return to BASIC, the contents of file MEM.SAV are restored to memory, leaving your program intact.

The disadvantage of using MEM.SAV is the time it takes to save and restore the memory area. Usually, it takes about ten seconds to load the disk utility package from the DUP.SYS disk file. If there is a MEM.SAV file, it takes an additional 20 seconds to save the program area; you must wait three times as long before you will see the DOS menu. Later, when you return to BASIC, it takes another seven seconds to restore the program area.

Both MEM.SAV and DUP.SYS must be on the same diskette, in Drive 1, when the DOS statement is executed. If you want to use all of the space on a diskette for your own files, put DUP.SYS and MEM.SAV on a separate diskette (possibly on the same diskette that has the DOS.SYS file), and put that diskette in Drive 1 before you type the DOS command. That same diskette must be in Drive 1 when you return to BASIC, or the program from memory cannot be restored.

One of the disk utilities creates special file MEM.SAV specifically to save, and later restore, the contents of the memory area used by the disk utility package. Instructions for creating a MEM.SAV file are provided later in this chapter.

The MEM.SAV file also works with non-BASIC programs. If the MEM.SAV file is present, the contents of the memory area that the disk utility package will occupy are saved on it and then restored when you finish with the disk utilities. It does not matter what the memory area was used for.

Ambiguous File Names

Many of the disk utilities ask you to enter one or more file names. You can always enter an explicit file name. Sometimes, however, it is easier to use an ambiguous file name. For example, you may be unable to explicitly state a file name because you only remember the first three letters. You can have the disk operating system use any file name it finds that starts with the characters you specify. As another example, you may wish to copy all files with a certain extension from one disk to another. In DOS 2.0S, you can do this without typing each individual file name.

The disk operating system treats the asterisk (*) and question mark (?) characters as "wild card" characters. An asterisk represents an entire file name or extension. For example, the file name *.BAS is interpreted to mean "all files which have a .BAS extension." Similarly, the file name DATAFILE.* refers to all files named DATAFILE, regardless of their extensions.

In a file name, characters to the right of an asterisk are ignored. For example, *FILE.TXT is treated as *.TXT, but the name GAME*.BAS will match all file names that begin with GAME and have a .BAS extension. The asterisk works in the opposite way when it is part of an extension; characters to the left of the asterisk are ignored. Thus the extension .A* is interpreted as .*, but .*A will match all extensions that end in the letter A.

A question mark can represent any single character. For example, the file name GAME?.BAS matches any five-character file names which begin with the four letters GAME and have the extension .BAS.

The ambiguous file name ????????.TXT is equivalent to *.TXT. Each question mark represents one character position, so eight question marks represent all possible file names.

If you use a consistent system in naming your files, the wild card characters will provide you with a very powerful programming aid. This feature is even more useful when combined with the conventions for extensions given in Table 7-1.

DOS MENU SELECTIONS

The DOS menu (Figures 7-5 and 7-6) offers many selections which manipulate information stored on diskettes. This part of the chapter describes the selections which are most useful to a BASIC programmer. A few of the items pertain mostly to machine language programming; they are described at the end of the chapter.

When the DOS 2.0S menu first appears you will see this prompt message near the bottom of the screen:

```
SELECT ITEM OR [RETURN] FOR MENU
▓
```

The prompt for DOS 1.0 is similar:

```
SELECT ITEM
▓
```

Whenever you see either of these prompt messages, you can choose an item on the DOS menu. Each item is preceded by a single letter. To choose an item, type the appropriate letter and press RETURN. Then proceed as described in the paragraphs that follow. Most selections will ask you for additional information, such as a file name or drive number. If you do not enter a letter now, but just press RETURN, the menu is redisplayed.

The various menu items are all valid with any diskette you use with your ATARI 810 Disk Drive. You can switch diskettes any time the disk drive BUSY lamp is off.

You can abort any selection at any time by pressing the BREAK key. You will be asked to choose another menu item.

If at any time you press the SYSTEM RESET key, the DOS menu releases control of the computer. If the BASIC cartridge is installed, control returns to BASIC. You will see the **READY** message. If there is no cartridge installed, DOS is rebooted and the DOS menu reappears.

```
DIRECTORY--SEARCH SPEC, LIST FILE?
```

FIGURE 7-7. Directory listing prompt

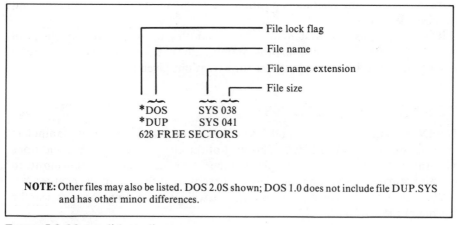

NOTE: Other files may also be listed. DOS 2.0S shown; DOS 1.0 does not include file DUP.SYS
      and has other minor differences.

FIGURE 7-8. Master diskette directory

What Is on a Diskette

To display the names of all the files on a diskette, choose DOS menu item A, DISK
DIRECTORY. When you select it, a prompt message appears on the screen (Figure
7-7). If you press RETURN in response to this prompt, the computer will search for all
file names on the diskette in Drive 1, and list them on the screen. If you are using
DOS 2.0S, the directory will contain at least files DOS.SYS and DUP.SYS (Figure
7-8). If you have DOS 1.0, the directory listing will not include file DUP.SYS.

Parts of the Directory

Each file in the directory is listed on a separate line. There are four parts to a
directory entry: the lock flag, the file name, the file name extension, and the file size
(Figure 7-8).

The *lock flag* is an asterisk which appears before the file names of some files. The
presence of an asterisk indicates that the file is locked. Locked files cannot be
changed or deleted. This safety feature lets you protect valuable files from accidental change or erasure. Other DOS menu selections lock and unlock files; these will
be described shortly.

The file name and file name extension (if any) appear side by side in the directory listing. Note that the directory does not put a period between them. File names less than eight characters long are padded on the right with trailing spaces. Extensions always appear at the ninth character position. You must include a period whenever you type an extension, however.

File size is reported in the right-hand column of the directory listing. The number listed is the number of 128-character blocks that the file uses. Large files use more blocks than small files. The smallest files use only one block.

The last line of a directory listing displays the number of 128-character blocks that are available on the diskette. This will be 707 on a blank DOS 2.0S diskette, and 709 on a blank DOS 1.0 diskette. The number listed is obtained by adding up the sizes of all the files on a diskette and subtracting that sum from 707 (DOS 2.0S) or 709 (DOS 1.0). You will receive a "disk full" error if you try to store more data than can fit in the available free space on a diskette.

Listing the Directory from Any Drive

You can get the directory listing of any drive connected to your ATARI computer. When the directory listing prompt appears (Figure 7-7), type the drive number and a colon before pressing RETURN. The following example lists the names of files on the diskette in Drive 2:

```
DIRECTORY--SEARCH SPEC, LIST FILE?
D2:
```

The capital letter D is optional.

Restricted Directory Listing

You can instruct the computer to display only those names which fit a particular format. You do this with the help of ambiguous file names. For example, you can list only those file names which start with the letter E, as follows:

```
DIRECTORY--SEARCH SPEC, LIST FILE?
E*.*
```

When the disk operating system displays the directory listing prompt (Figure 7-7), it is requesting two things, the search specification (SEARCH SPEC) and the output device name (LIST FILE). If you just press RETURN to answer this prompt, you are accepting the default specifications. The disk operating system will search for all files on Drive 1, and output them to the display screen.

You may specify your own ambiguous file name as the search specification. For example, if you want to see all file names that have the extension .BAS, respond like this:

```
DIRECTORY--SEARCH SPEC, LIST FILE?
D1:*.BAS
```

Since D1: is the default drive, you can leave it off, like this:

```
DIRECTORY---SEARCH SPEC, LIST FILE?
*.BAS
```

Either way, you get a listing of only those files that have the extension .BAS.

In the most extreme case, you can specify an exact file name you want to search for. If the file is not on the diskette, its name will not be listed. In that case, the directory listing will show only the available free space on the diskette.

Directory Listing on Any Device

The directory listing prompt (Figure 7-7) also requests entry of an output device, or LIST FILE. Thus far we have not explicitly stated an output device. The disk operating system has been using the default output device, the display screen. To specify an output device, type a comma, the device name, and a colon, and press RETURN. The following response would list all files from Drive 1 on the printer:

```
DIRECTORY--SEARCH SPEC, LIST FILE?
D1:*.*,P:
```

You can omit the file specification entirely. You will get a listing of all files on Drive 1. The following response generates the same directory listing as the last response:

```
DIRECTORY--SEARCH SPEC, LIST FILE?
,P:
```

Remember to type a comma before the P:. The comma tells the disk operating system that the P: is a response to the second item requested, the output device (LIST FILE). If you omit the comma, the disk operating system will think you want to search for all the file names on the diskette in the specified output device. In this case that device is the printer; the task is clearly impossible.

To print the directory of a diskette in a drive other than Drive 1, type the drive number and a colon before the comma, like this:

```
DIRECTORY--SEARCH SPEC, LIST FILE?
2:,P:
```

LEAVING THE DOS MENU

To transfer control of the computer from the DOS menu to the the ROM cartridge, choose DOS menu item B, RUN CARTRIDGE. Pressing the SYSTEM RESET key has the same effect. If the BASIC cartridge is installed, the **READY** message appears. If the Editor/Assembler cartridge is installed, the **EDIT** prompt appears. If there is no ROM cartridge in the computer, the message **NO CARTRIDGE** appears; you must choose another menu item.

If the MEM.SAV file is active (DOS 2.0S only), *do not* use DOS menu item B to return to BASIC. Instead, press the SYSTEM RESET key. This will insure that the memory area is correctly restored from file MEM.SAV.

COPYING FILES

To copy the contents of a file to a different file, choose DOS menu item C, COPY FILE. Both files can be on the same diskette as long as the file names are different. Both files can be on different diskettes as long as both diskettes are accessible simultaneously. In other words, you must have two disk drives in order to copy a file from one diskette to another. If you have only one disk drive and wish to copy a file to a different diskette, you must use DOS menu item O, DUPLICATE FILE.

When selected, DOS menu item C displays a prompt message. It asks you to specify the source and destination disk drive numbers and file names. Here is an example:

```
COPY FILE--FROM,TO?
FILE1.BAS,FILE1.BAK
```

In this example no drive number is specified for either file. The disk operating system will use Drive 1 for both. Notice that the file names are separated by a comma.

If the destination file already exists, it is overwritten by the contents of the source file. If the destination file does not exist, it is created.

If the source file does not exist, error number 170 occurs. Other error messages appear if there is not enough room on the destination diskette (error 162) or if the destination diskette directory is full (error 169).

A message appears if the MEM.SAV file is in use (DOS 2.0S only). It requests permission to use the entire program area of memory for the copy operation (Figure 7-9). If you agree, the contents of file MEM.SAV will *not* be restored to memory when you leave the DOS menu; any program you hoped to preserve by means of the MEM.SAV file will be gone when you return to BASIC. To allow this, type Y and press RETURN. Any other response aborts the file copy operation, preserving the integrity of file MEM.SAV. You can use the file copy operation and still preserve

```
        TYPE "Y" IF OK TO USE PROGRAM AREA
        CAUTION: A "Y" INVALIDATES MEM.SAV
        ▓
```

FIGURE 7-9. Prompt requesting permission to use program area

a program in memory. Simply leave the DOS menu and save the program onto cassette or diskette. Then you can let the file copy operation invalidate file MEM.SAV, knowing that you can always reload your program from diskette or cassette.

The file named DOS.SYS is a special file. The file copy operation, DOS menu item C, cannot copy it. An error occurs if you try.

Copy with Ambiguous File Names

DOS 2.0S allows wild card characters in the name (or extension) of the file to be copied from. If they are present, the destination can be a disk drive number only. Do not specify a destination file name or extension. Here is an example:

```
COPY FILE--FROM,TO?
*.BAK,D2:
```

This response will copy all files with .BAK extensions from Drive 1 to Drive 2.

Files that have a .SYS extension are not copied during any ambiguous file name copy operation. To copy a .SYS file, specify the entire file name explicitly, using no wild card characters.

The Copy Append Option

In DOS 2.0S, the file copy operation (DOS menu item C) can append one file to the end of another. To do this, type the two characters / A directly after the destination file name. Here is an example:

```
COPY FILE--FROM,TO?
D2:NAMES.TXT,D3:NUMBERS.TXT/A
```

The destination file must already exist. The / A suffix prevents the destination file from being overwritten by the contents of the source file. Instead, the contents of the source file are added to the end of the destination file.

Do not use the / A suffix to append BASIC programs stored with the SAVE statement. It will not work. The first program will be tacked onto the end of the second, but the LOAD statement will not recognize it. In effect, nothing happens.

You can append BASIC programs only if both programs are stored with the LIST statement. Lines in the first file will be tacked onto the end of the second file. Then when you issue an ENTER command to load the second file, BASIC merges the two sets of program lines. It is just as if, starting with the second program in memory, you typed in every line from the first file. Lines already in memory will be replaced by later lines with the same line number. You may want to save the program back into the file with the LIST statement. Doing so will eliminate duplicate lines, which waste disk space.

File Copy with One Drive, Two Diskettes

If you have only one disk drive attached to your ATARI computer and wish to transfer files from one diskette to another, you must use DOS menu item O,

DUPLICATE FILE. It requests the name of the file you wish to transfer.

```
NAME OF FILE TO MOVE?
▓
```

Type the name of the file you wish to transfer. Enter only one file name; the source and destination file names are the same. Do not specify a drive number. DOS menu item O always uses Drive 1 for both source and destination.

You can use wild card characters in the file name. In this case, all files that match the ambiguous file name will be transferred, one at a time. However, files that have a .SYS extension will not be transferred. If you want to transfer a .SYS file, you must specify the entire file name explicitly.

Next, a message appears if the MEM.SAV file is in use (DOS 2.0S only). It requests permission to use the entire program area of memory for the file duplicate operation (Figure 7-9). If you agree, the contents of file MEM.SAV will *not* be restored to memory when you leave the DOS menu; any program you hoped to preserve via the MEM.SAV file will be gone when you return to BASIC. To allow this, type Y and press RETURN. Any other response preserves the integrity of file MEM.SAV and the program area of memory. The file transfer will still take place, but at a much slower pace.

With the preliminaries out of the way, the transfer begins. Messages appear on the display screen, asking you to insert first the source disk and then the destination disk. You may have to swap disks several times. Each time you insert a disk, you must signal that it is ready by pressing RETURN on the keyboard.

When you insert the source disk, the computer reads part of the source file into its memory. When you substitute the destination disk, the computer writes that piece of the file onto the destination file. You may have to change diskettes several times if the file is very large, or if you are moving more than one file.

CAUTION: Using DOS menu item O with DOS 1.0 effectively erases the program area of memory. If you had a BASIC program in memory, it will be gone when you return to BASIC after duplicating files.

REMOVING UNNEEDED FILES

After a while, you will probably end up with a number of files you no longer need. To remove files from a diskette and make the space they used available for other files, choose DOS menu item D, DELETE FILE(S). When you select it, the following prompt message appears:

```
DELETE FILE SPEC
▓
```

You must enter the disk drive number and file name of the file you wish deleted. You may use wild card characters to specify an ambiguous file name and extension.

Next, this message appears:

```
TYPE "Y" TO DELETE...
```

The diskette is searched for all the file names that match your specification. Whenever a match is found, the file name is printed, followed by a question mark. If you wish to delete the file, type the letter Y and press RETURN. Type any other letter if you do not want the file deleted.

You may not delete any file that is locked. If you try to delete a locked file, error number 167 occurs, and the delete selection is aborted.

To erase all files from a diskette, use *.* as the delete file specification, like this:

```
DELETE FILE SPEC
*.*
```

Disabling Delete Confirmation

Normally, DOS menu item D requires that you confirm every file name to be deleted. This is a good way to avoid accidentally deleting the wrong file, but becomes somewhat tedious when you use an ambiguous file name in order to delete a large number of files. If you want to circumvent the confirmation step for each file, type the characters / N right after the file name. For example, the following response deletes all files on Drive 1, without asking "yes" or "no" for each file:

```
DELETE FILE SPEC
*.*/N
```

Be very careful when you use the / N suffix, since you cannot recover a file once it is erased.

CHANGING FILE NAMES

To change the name of any file on a diskette, choose DOS menu item E, RENAME FILE. The following prompt message appears:

```
RENAME - GIVE OLD NAME, NEW
▓
```

Enter the old file name, a comma, and the new file name. You may specify a drive number for the old file name, but not for the new name. Use DOS menu item C to move a file to a different drive.

Error 170 occurs if the old file name you specify does not exist. Error 167 occurs if it is locked.

CAUTION: If the new file name already exists on the diskette, you will end up with two files with the same name. If this happens, future references to one file will also affect the other. If you try to rename one, the other will be renamed also. The only way to recover from duplicate file names is to delete both files and start over. If you are not sure whether a file name is in use, list the file directory with DOS menu item A before you rename a file.

Ambiguous file names are allowed. Here is an example:

```
RENAME - GIVE OLD NAME, NEW
*.DAT,*.TXT
```

This will change all .DAT extensions to .TXT. The following response changes all file extensions to .ZZZ:

```
RENAME - GIVE OLD NAME, NEW
*.*,*.ZZZ
```

Be very careful with ambiguous file name changes. It is all too easy to end up with duplicate file names.

Do not change the name of file DOS.SYS, or the diskette will not boot. If you change the name of the DUP.SYS file (DOS 2.0S only), you will not be able to load the DOS menu from that diskette.

LOCKING FILES

Locking a file prevents any action that changes the information stored for that file, including changing the file name. To lock files, choose DOS menu item F, LOCK FILE. When you select it, this prompt appears:

```
WHAT FILE TO LOCK?
▓
```

Enter the disk number and file name of the file you want locked. The following example locks the DOS boot file, on Drive 1:

```
WHAT FILE TO LOCK?
DOS.SYS
```

You may use wild card characters to specify an ambiguous file name to be locked. For example, *.* will lock every file. Similarly, *.BAS will lock all files with .BAS extensions.

It is a good idea to lock the DOS.SYS file, and the DUP.SYS file if it exists. That prevents you from accidentally changing their names or contents.

REMOVING FILE LOCKS

To unlock files, choose DOS menu item G, UNLOCK FILE. When you select it, this prompt appears:

```
WHAT FILE TO UNLOCK?
▓
```

Enter the disk number and file name of the file you want unlocked. The following example unlocks file MAILLIST.DAT, on Drive 2:

```
WHAT FILE TO UNLOCK?
D2:MAILLIST.DAT
```

You may use wild card characters to specify an ambiguous file name to be unlocked. For example, *.* will unlock every file. Similarly, *.BAS will unlock all files with .BAS extensions.

WRITING NEW DOS FILES

The disk operating system program is stored on one or two files. DOS 1.0 is on file DOS.SYS, while DOS 2.0S uses two files, DOS.SYS and DUP.SYS. To write a copy of these files onto a diskette in a specific drive, choose DOS menu item H, WRITE DOS FILES. The programs are copied from the computer's memory, not from another diskette. The procedure is slightly different for DOS 1.0 and DOS 2.0S.

Write DOS 2.0S Files

In DOS 2.0S, this prompt message appears after you select DOS menu item H:

```
DRIVE TO WRITE FILES TO?
```

Enter Drive number 1, 2, 3, or 4.
    Now a prompt message appears asking you to confirm your choice by typing Y:

```
DRIVE TO WRITE FILES TO?
1
TYPE "Y" TO WRITE DOS TO DRIVE 1
```

If you type anything other than a capital Y, the operation will be aborted.

Write DOS 1.0 File

DOS 1.0 always writes file DOS.SYS to Drive 1. You cannot choose the drive. This prompt message appears:

```
TYPE "Y" TO WRITE NEW DOS FILE
```

FORMATTING DISKETTES

Before you can use a new diskette it must be formatted. The formatting procedure writes timing marks and other information on the diskette. The disk operating system uses this information to ascertain where it is on the diskette. Because formatting writes over everything previously on the disk, it will erase a used diskette. This can be disastrous if you accidentally format the wrong diskette.
    To format a diskette, choose DOS menu item I, FORMAT DISK. The following prompt message appears:

```
WHICH DRIVE TO FORMAT?
```

    Enter the number of the drive that contains the diskette you wish to format. Since formatting a diskette will erase anything stored on it, you will be asked to confirm your choice, as follows.

```
WHICH DRIVE TO FORMAT?
1
TYPE "Y" TO FORMAT DRIVE 1
※
```

This is your last opportunity to avoid erasing the wrong diskette. It is a good time to double-check the diskette in the drive to make sure it is the one you wish to erase.

When you respond with a Y to the above prompt, the drive will become active, and you may hear beeps from the TV speaker. Any other response will abort the selection. The format operation takes about one minute.

COPYING ENTIRE DISKETTES

Although DOS menu item C allows you to copy files as needed, you will frequently wish to copy the contents of an entire diskette. To do that, choose item J, DUPLICATE DISK. It copies all files on a diskette, even files with .SYS extensions. It can copy from one drive to another. It can also copy using just one drive.

When you select DOS menu item J, this prompt message appears:

```
DUP DISK--SOURCE,DEST DRIVES?
※
```

> **CAUTION:** Using DOS menu item J with DOS 1.0 effectively erases the program area of memory. If you had a BASIC program in memory, it will be gone when you return to BASIC after duplicating a disk.

Single-Drive Duplication

If you have only one drive, respond like this:

```
DUP DISK--SOURCE,DEST DRIVES?
1,1
```

Now this prompt appears:

```
INSERT SOURCE DISK, TYPE RETURN
※
```

If the diskette you wish to copy is not already in the disk drive, insert it now. Press RETURN. The computer will read part of the diskette's contents into its memory. It will then ask you to insert the destination disk, with this prompt:

```
INSERT DESTINATION DISK,TYPE RETURN
※
```

Place a formatted diskette into the drive, close the drive door, and press RETURN. A few seconds later, the **INSERT SOURCE DISK** message will reappear. You must change diskettes again. This process will repeat several times, depending on how much memory your computer has and how much data is stored on the source diskette. The diskette-swapping cycle will repeat until the entire disk is copied.

Right after you first insert the source disk, another message will appear, but only if the MEM.SAV file is in use (DOS 2.0S only). The message requests permission to use the entire program area of memory for the duplicate disk operation (Figure 7-9). If you agree, the contents of file MEM.SAV will *not* be restored to memory when you leave the DOS menu; any program you hoped to preserve via the MEM.SAV file will be gone when you return to BASIC. To allow this, type Y and press RETURN. Any other response aborts the duplicate disk operation, preserving the integrity of file MEM.SAV. It is possible to duplicate a diskette and still preserve a program in memory. Simply leave the DOS menu and save the program onto cassette or diskette. Then you can let the disk duplication invalidate file MEM.SAV, knowing that you can always reload your program from diskette or cassette.

Multiple-Drive Duplication

Duplicating diskettes is much easier if you have two disk drives connected to your ATARI computer. Specify one drive as the source drive and the other drive as the destination. When you use two drives to duplicate, there is no need to swap diskettes. The following example will copy from the diskette in Drive 1 to the diskette in Drive 2:

```
DUP DISK--SOURCE,DEST DRIVES?
1,2
INSERT BOTH DISKETTES, TYPE RETURN
▓
```

As with single-drive duplication, you will see another prompt message (Figure 7-9) if file MEM.SAV is active (DOS 2.0S only). Reply with a Y if it is all right to use the entire program area of memory for the disk duplication. If it is not, reply with an N; the disk duplication will be aborted.

CREATING A MEM.SAV FILE

To create the special file called MEM.SAV (DOS 2.0S only), choose DOS menu item N, CREATE MEM.SAV. The file will be created on the diskette in Drive 1. The following prompt message will appear:

```
TYPE "Y" TO CREATE MEM.SAV
▓
```

Enter Y to proceed with MEM.SAV file creation; any other entry aborts the file creation.

If the file already exists on the diskette, the message **MEM.SAV FILE ALREADY EXISTS** appears and the operation is aborted.

BASIC PROGRAMS ON DISK

Five BASIC statements form a very useful connection between BASIC and the disk operating system. The SAVE and LIST statements store programs on a diskette. The LOAD, ENTER, and RUN statements retrieve programs from a diskette.

Storing a Program

When you type a program into the computer, it will remain in memory until the power is turned off, or until it is erased by a statement such as NEW. The SAVE and LIST statements allow you to store a program in a diskette file of your choice. You must specify the disk drive number, the file name, and any file name extension. Either of the following statements will store a program on the diskette in Drive 1:

```
SAVE "D1:MYPROG.BAS"
LIST "D1:MYPROG.LST"
```

You can omit the drive number, but not the device name (D: is the disk drive device name). Drive 1 is assumed unless you specify otherwise. The following statements will also write to the diskette in Drive 1:

```
SAVE "D:MENU.BAS"
LIST "D:MENU.LST"
```

Notice that we use extension .BAS with the SAVE statement and extension .LST with the LIST statement. That makes it easy to identify whether we used LIST or SAVE to store a particular file. This is important because the two statements do not use the same recording format.

The LIST statement outputs in the same format regardless of the device. It sends out the ATASCII code of every character in the program listing.

The SAVE statement abbreviates keywords with one-character *tokens*. Thus, instead of storing five ATASCII characters for the keyword INPUT, it stores just one character, the token for INPUT.

The SAVE statement always stores the entire program from memory. The LIST statement can store all of the program or any part of it. You can specify the first and last lines to be stored. For example, the following statement stores only lines with line numbers between 10 and 50:

```
LIST "D:DATASTMT.LST",10,50
```

Retrieving a Program

The LOAD statement retrieves programs that were stored in tokenized format by the SAVE statement. The ENTER statement retrieves programs that were stored in straight ATASCII code by the LIST statement. Because of the different formats, you cannot use LOAD and ENTER interchangeably.

You must specify a disk drive number, file name, and file extension. If the drive number is absent, Drive 1 is used. The following statement retrieves a program stored by a SAVE statement:

```
LOAD "D2:MAILLIST.BAS"
```

The following statement retrieves a program stored by a LIST statement:

```
ENTER "D:CHESS.BAS"
```

The file name and extension must be the same as the ones you used to store the program. Both LOAD and ENTER check to see if the file name you specify actually exists on the diskette in the drive you specify. If not, error 170 results. If the file is present, the new program is read in from the diskette, and BASIC displays the **READY** message when program retrieval is finished.

The LOAD statement erases any program currently in memory. The new program replaces the old one. The ENTER statement, on the other hand, merges the program it retrieves with the program in memory. If there are incoming lines with the same line numbers as existing lines, the incoming lines replace the existing lines. To circumvent the merging, type NEW before using the ENTER statement.

The RUN Statement

Frequently, the first thing you will want to do after loading a program is to run it. Normally this takes two commands, as in the following example:

```
LOAD "D:PAYROLL.BAS"
READY
RUN
```

You can abbreviate this two-step process by adding the file name to the RUN statement. Shorten the previous example like this:

```
RUN "D:PAYROLL.BAS"
```

The program will run as soon as it is loaded. The LOAD command becomes an implicit step.

Chaining Programs

When executed, a programmed mode RUN statement will load and run another program. Chapter 5 explained how this chaining process works with cassettes. It works even better with diskettes.

To see how chaining works, we will create three small programs on a diskette. The first program will load and run the second, and the second will load and run the third. To begin, enter and save the first program:

```
NEW

READY
10 PRINT "PROGRAM ONE"
20 RUN "D1:P2.BAS"
SAVE "D1:P1.BAS"

READY
※
```

That stores the first program in file P1.BAS, on the diskette in Drive 1.

The program is still in memory. Change it to become the second program, and store the result in file P2.BAS.

```
10 PRINT "PROGRAM TWO"
20 RUN "D1:P3.BAS"
SAVE "D1:P2.BAS"

READY
※
```

Now you have stored two programs on the diskette in Drive 1. Make a few changes to the second program, which is still in memory, to create the third and final program, and store it in file P3.BAS.

```
10 PRINT "PROGRAM THREE"
20 END
SAVE "D1:P3.BAS"
READY
※
```

The diskette now has three chained programs on it. The first will load and run the second, and the second will load and run the third. Use the RUN statement to load and run the first program.

```
RUN "D1:P1.BAS"
PROGRAM ONE
PROGRAM TWO
PROGRAM THREE

READY
※
```

The other two programs run automatically, with no action on your part.

Chained programs look to the user very much like one long program. Recall from Chapter 5 that the user has to press the RETURN key to continue with each successive program module on cassette. There is no need to do this with programs on disk.

The main drawback to chaining programs with the RUN statement is that it clears all variables before it loads the next program. This means that one program cannot use values that were input or calculated by an earlier program in the chain.

Subroutine Libraries

Over a period of time, programmers develop general purpose subroutines which they use in one program after another. Chapter 4 introduced several such subroutines (Figures 4-16 through 4-21, 4-31, 4-33, 4-36, 4-37, and 4-38). Using subroutines like these saves programming time, but somehow you must enter the subroutines every time you use them. You can type them in, but that is dull and time-consuming. You can avoid the retyping by building a library of subroutines on disk.

It is extremely easy to create and use a library of subroutines on disk. Every time you write a subroutine, store in on disk with the LIST statement. Later, when you want to include the subroutine in a program you are writing, use the ENTER statement to retrieve it. It will merge with the program in memory.

Variable Name Table

Recall from earlier chapters that ATARI BASIC keeps a table of all the variable and array names you have used in programmed or immediate mode. The SAVE statement stores this variable name table along with the tokenized program lines. The LOAD statement replaces the current variable name table with the one it retrieves from the disk file.

The LIST statement does not store the variable name table, nor does the ENTER statement restore one to memory. The existing variable name table remains, unless you use the NEW statement.

Over a period of time, the variable name table can become cluttered with obsolete variable names. It is easy enough to remove these unwanted names. First, store the program with the LIST statement. Then use the NEW statement to clear the variable name table completely. Of course, this also erases the program lines. Load the program back into memory with the ENTER statement.

USING DISK DATA FILES

The disk drive is ideally suited to storing large quantities of data. The BASIC statements PRINT # and PUT store data on disk. The INPUT # and GET statements read data back in.

Data Files, Records, and Fields

From the computer's perspective, a data file is no different from a program file. Both are simply collections of numbers. What makes the difference is the way in which the numbers are interpreted. From the user's standpoint, a program file contains program lines and a data file contains numeric and string values. Files are generally arranged in some kind of logical order. For example, one file might contain a mailing list, which is nothing more than a collection of names and addresses. Each name and address is called a *record*. Any name-and-address record contains several items: name, street, city, state, and ZIP code. These specific data items are called *fields*. Every record usually has the same fields. Only the values in the fields vary.

File Accessing Methods

There are two ways to access disk files. One is called *sequential access*. A sequential file is just like a file on cassette. To read or write the last item in the file, you must read or write all previous items. For some applications, sequential access is acceptable.

Random access allows more flexibility than does sequential access. You may read or write any record in the file with equal ease, regardless of its location. For many applications, random access is the best solution.

DOS 2.0S supports both sequential and random access. DOS version 1.0 supports only sequential access.

How Data is Stored

To quickly find one particular character among the thousands stored on a diskette, the disk operating system divides storage space on a diskette into 720 parts, called *sectors*. Each sector holds exactly 128 characters.

DOS 2.0S reserves 13 sectors of each diskette. Sectors 1, 2, and 3 store the program that boots the disk operating system itself into memory. Sectors 361 through 368 are used for the diskette directory. Sector 360 keeps track of which sectors are in use, and which are free, on the whole diskette. This is called the *Volume Table of Contents*. The last sector of every diskette, sector 720, is also reserved. DOS 2.0S leaves 707 sectors free for you to use.

DOS 1.0 uses only sector 1 for the DOS boot program, leaving two additional sectors for data storage. DOS 1.0 uses the other sectors reserved by DOS 2.0S for the same purposes.

Tracks

To make it easier to find a particular sector, the 720 sectors of a diskette are arranged into 40 concentric circles of 18 sectors each, called *tracks* (Figure 7-10). By moving the read/write head to a particular track, a maximum of 18 sectors will be read before the desired one is found.

OPENING DATA FILES

Disk files must be opened before they can be used. Opening a file causes the disk operating system to retrieve information about the file. You are informed whether the file is on the disk, and if so, where it is on the disk. Opening a file also sets aside an area of memory to be used as a *file buffer*. The file buffer is similar to the disk buffer, but it is dedicated to the file. It allows you to access a small portion of the file without activating the disk drive for every item accessed, and that saves a good deal of time.

The OPEN statement opens an input/output channel to a disk file. It looks like this:

```
OPEN #2,8,0,"D1:FILENAME.EXT"
```

This statement opens channel 2 for output to file FILENAME.EXT on Drive 1.

The first parameter in the OPEN statement is the channel number. As Chapter 4 explains, channels 1 through 5 are always available for your BASIC program. Channels 6 and 7 are also available under some circumstances. The BASIC graphics statements use channel 6 (see Chapters 8 and 9). The CLOAD, CSAVE, and LPRINT statements use channel 7. If you use any of these statements, they will automatically take over channel 6 or 7.

After a program opens a channel to a disk file, it refers to the channel number, not to the file itself. The OPEN statement must occur in the program before any other reference to the file occurs.

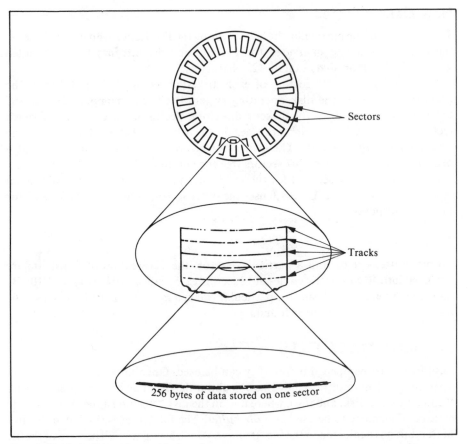

FIGURE 7-10. A diskette's recorded surface

There are five disk access modes: input (mode 4), output (mode 8), update (mode 12), append (mode 9), and directory input (mode 6). The value of the second OPEN statement parameter determines the access mode. We will describe the different modes shortly.

The third OPEN statement parameter is ignored. Make this parameter 0.

The fourth and final OPEN statement parameter specifies the drive number and file name. If you omit the drive number, Drive 1 will be used, but you must always specify the disk drive with a capital D and a colon. You may specify any drive, file name, and extension you like. Do not use DOS.SYS, MEM.SAV, or DUP.SYS, however, as these files are needed for proper operation of the disk operating system.

If you open a file for anything other than mode 8 output, the file name must exist on the drive as specified. If it does not, error 170 occurs.

Access mode 8 is the only mode that will cause a file to be created. The other modes expect the file to already exist. If the file does exist, access mode 8 will first delete, then recreate the file. This will erase all information already in the file.

Normally, no more than three disk files can be open simultaneously. Each one must use a different channel, of course. In DOS 2.0S there is a way to extend the limit so there can be seven files open simultaneously. You must make a minor change to the disk operating system. The procedure is described at the end of this chapter.

CLOSING DATA FILES

There are many ways to close a channel. The END statement will close all open channels. The following program opens a channel for output to a disk data file and closes it implicitly with an END statement:

```
100 PRINT "NOW OPENING FILE..."
200 OPEN #1,8,0,"D1:DATAFILE.TMP"
300 PRINT "THE FILE IS NOW OPEN."
400 END
```

This program has a major flaw: it does not explicitly close the file. The best way to close a channel that is open to a disk data file is with the CLOSE statement. The best time to do it is right after you are finished with the file. This is especially important with a file that has been opened for output. Not closing output files can result in loss of data, or even destruction of data on another diskette.

Correct the last program by adding line 390, as follows:

```
100 PRINT "NOW OPENING DATA FILE..."
200 OPEN #1,8,0,"D1:DATAFILE.TMP"
300 PRINT "THE FILE IS NOW OPEN."
390 CLOSE #1
400 END
```

WRITING TO DATA FILES

Just opening and closing files is a fairly useless activity. Disk files are supposed to store information. This section will show you how to modify the last program so it will store information.

Information is sent to disk files in the same way it is sent to the program recorder or printer: by means of the PRINT # statement. Anything you can print can be sent to a file. In fact, you might visualize a sequential file as paper in the printer. The printer puts each character it receives into the printer buffer. When the buffer is full, the printer prints the buffer's contents on the paper. Similarly, when information is sent to a disk file, it goes into the file buffer. When the buffer is full, its contents are written on the disk.

To direct the PRINT # statement to a disk file, use the channel that you assigned in the OPEN statement for that file. The last example program assigned channel 1 to the file DATAFILE.TMP. The following program writes some text on that file.

```
100 PRINT "NOW OPENING DATA FILE..."
200 OPEN #1,8,0,"D1:DATAFILE.TMP"
300 PRINT "THE FILE IS NOW OPEN."
310 PRINT #1;"WORDS CANNOT DESCRIBE"
320 PRINT #1;"HOW SPEECHLESS I FELT"
390 CLOSE #1
400 END
```

When you run this program, the old file DATAFILE.TMP on your disk is deleted,
then recreated as a new, empty file. This happens because the OPEN statement
specifies access mode 8 (line 200). The OPEN statement also sets a pointer to the
beginning of the file buffer (line 200). At this point the file buffer looks like Figure
7-11.

The first PRINT# statement outputs 21 text characters to the file (line 310). They
end up in the file buffer. The file buffer pointer moves to the 22nd position. Since the
PRINT # statement does not end with a semicolon or comma, it also outputs an
EOL character. That moves the file buffer pointer to position 23. The file buffer now
looks like Figure 7-12.

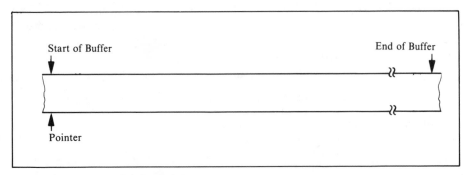

FIGURE 7-11. Empty disk file buffer

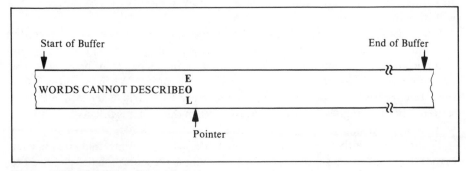

FIGURE 7-12. Disk file buffer with data

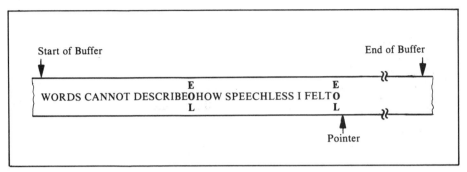

FIGURE 7-13. Disk file buffer with two fields

The next PRINT # statement outputs another 21 text characters, plus an EOL character (line 320). These characters also end up in the file buffer. The pointer now points to the 46th position. The file buffer looks like Figure 7-13. The program has stored two fields of data in the file buffer. Each field is terminated by an EOL character.

The CLOSE statement forces the contents of the file buffer to be output to channel 1 (line 390). Since channel 1 is linked to file DATAFILE.TMP, the contents of the buffer are stored in it.

The file buffer has a capacity of 125 characters. The buffer actually takes up 128 bytes of memory, but three are not available. The contents of the buffer are written to the diskette each time the buffer fills.

With sequential access, the file pointer can only be moved forward. The only way to move the pointer backward is to close the file, then reopen it. Whenever a file is opened, the pointer is set to the first character in the file.

Experiment with the example program above. Change the PRINT # statements to store different data. Try using string variables and numeric variables and constants. You may add more PRINT # statements, as long as they occur after the OPEN statement and before the CLOSE statement.

Remember that if any PRINT # statement terminates with a semicolon or comma it will not output an EOL character to the file. The characters in the next PRINT # statement become part of the same field. Here is an example:

```
100  OPEN #1,8,0,"D:ONEFIELD.TMP"
200  PRINT #1;"THIS IS THE FIRST";
300  PRINT #1;"AND THIS IS THE SECOND"
400  CLOSE #1
500  END
```

Output from the first PRINT # statement (line 200) is concatenated with output from the second PRINT # statement (line 300). The result is one data field in the file (Figure 7-14).

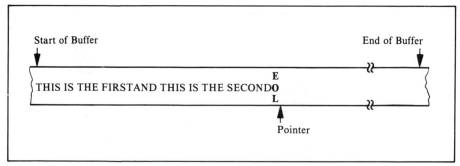

FIGURE 7-14. Concatenated output

Commas in PRINT # Statements

In PRINT # statements, commas can occur as separators between items, like this:

```
745 PRINT #4;"HELLO!","WHAT IS YOUR NA
ME?"
```

They can also occur at the end of a PRINT # statement, like this:

```
9456 PRINT #2;"THE END",
```

The computer does not know the difference between writing data to a disk file and writing data to the screen. On the screen, a comma causes spaces to be output between items until the cursor is at the next column stop. A comma also suppresses the EOL character. For more details, see Chapter 4. In a disk file, the file buffer pointer takes the place of the cursor. Consider the following statement:

```
PRINT #1;1,2,3,
```

Assuming that channel 1 is open for output to a disk file, the statement above will output one field to the file. Because commas separate the items, nine blank spaces are appended to each character. Because a comma ends the statement, no EOL character is output. Figure 7-15 illustrates this.

Because of the blank spaces inserted by commas, you should not use commas in PRINT # statements that output to disk files. If you want items to be concatenated, use a semicolon.

If you do not want items to be concatenated, you should put each field in a separate PRINT # statement. Another solution is to explicitly output an EOL character between fields, as shown below:

```
233 PRINT #5;"YES!";CHR$(155);"WE HAVE
NO BANANAS"
```

CHR$(155) generates an EOL character.

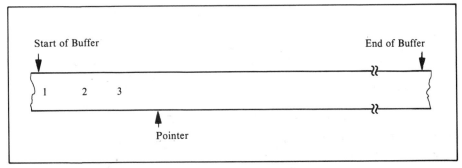

FIGURE 7-15. Commas in PRINT # statements

If you intend to use the above technique extensively, you may wish to define a string variable as an EOL character. Here is an example:

```
5 DIM R$(1)
10 R$=CHR$(155):REM EOL
    •
    •
    •
431 PRINT #2;NAME$;R$;RANK;R$;SERIALNU
MBER
```

Writing with the PUT Statement

A PUT statement can output a single numeric value to a disk file. The value must be between 0 and 255. The value is usually interpreted as an ATASCII character code. Each value takes the same space on the file as one character from a PRINT # statement. The PUT statement does not output an EOL character. The following program will store the text "HELLO" on a file, complete with the enclosing quotes and a terminating EOL character.

```
10 OPEN #5,8,0,"D:HELLO.TXT"
20 PUT #5,34:REM "
30 PUT #5,72:REM H
40 PUT #5,69:REM E
50 PUT #5,76:REM L
60 PUT #5,76:REM L
70 PUT #5,79:REM O
80 PUT #5,34:REM "
90 PUT #5,155:REM (EOL)
100 CLOSE #5
110 END
```

READING SEQUENTIAL DATA FILES

Once data has been stored on a disk file, it can be retrieved, or read from the file. The INPUT # and GET statements read file data and assign the values to variables. To see how these statements work with the disk, first run the following program to create the file DATAFILE.TMP:

```
200 OPEN #1,8,0,"D1:DATAFILE.TMP"
310 PRINT #1;"DAMN THE TORPEDOES!"
320 PRINT #1;"FULL SPEED AHEAD!"
390 CLOSE #1
400 END
```

The next program will read data fields from DATAFILE.TMP and display them on the screen:

```
100 DIM A$(100)
190 REM Open file for input
200 OPEN #1,4,0,"D:DATAFILE.TMP"
300 INPUT #1;A$
400 PRINT A$
500 GOTO 300
600 CLOSE #1
700 END
```

When you run the program, this appears on the screen:

```
DAMN THE TORPEDOES!
FULL SPEED AHEAD!

ERROR-    136 AT LINE 300
```

Error 136 occurred because the program tried to read past the end of the file. Since the program was stopped at line 300 by the error, the CLOSE statement was not executed. In this case that is not important. The program did not write to the file, so the file buffer never contained new data that needed to be written on the disk.

It is not good practice to write programs that end with errors. You can avoid the end-of-file error by using the TRAP statement. Add a new line to the program above, as follows:

```
100 DIM A$(100)
190 REM Open file for input
200 OPEN #1,4,0,"D1:DATAFILE.TMP"
210 TRAP 600
300 INPUT #1;A$
400 PRINT A$
500 GOTO 300
600 CLOSE #1
700 END
```

Now the program ends neatly, without the error message.

To be really safe, the program should check to make sure that the error is in fact an end-of-file error. Without proper checking, the program treats any error as an end-of-file error. Here is a new version of the last program, with more careful error checking:

```
100 DIM A$(100)
190 REM Open file for input
200 OPEN #1,4,0,"D1:DATAFILE.TMP"
```

```
210 TRAP 510
300 INPUT #1;A$
400 PRINT A$
500 GOTO 300
509 REM Get error number
510 ERR=PEEK(195)
519 REM End of file?
520 IF ERR=135 THEN 600
529 REM If not, print error number
530 PRINT "ERROR NUMBER ";ERR;" HAS OC
CURRED!"
600 CLOSE #1
700 END
```

The INPUT # statement reads one data field at a time. It keeps reading characters until it encounters an EOL character. Then it assigns the field value to the next variable on its list. The value type must match the variable type; an error results if you try to read a non-numeric string into a numeric value.

Using GET to Read Files

The GET statement reads a file character by character. Each GET statement reads one numeric value. Your program must decide how to interpret that value. Most often it will use the CHR$ function to interpret the value as an ATASCII character code. The next program uses the GET statement to read the same file as the last program.

```
190 REM Open file for input
200 OPEN #1,4,0,"D1:DATAFILE.TMP"
210 TRAP 510
300 GET #1,A
400 PRINT CHR$(A);
500 GOTO 300
509 REM Get error number
510 ERR=PEEK(195)
519 REM End of file?
520 IF ERR=135 THEN 600
529 REM If not, print error number
530 PRINT "ERROR NUMBER ";ERR;" HAS OC
CURRED!"
600 CLOSE #1
700 END
```

OPEN TO APPEND

When you open a file for output (mode 8), everything in the file is erased, and the pointer is set to the beginning of the file. It is possible to add to information that is already in a file without erasing the old data.

If you specify mode 9 (append) when you OPEN a file, the pointer will be set to the end of the file. The file must exist or error 170 will occur.

Suppose there is a disk file TALE.TXT which contains only the text "ONCE

UPON A TIME" followed by an EOL character. Then the following program is executed:

```
210 OPEN #2,9,0,"D:TALE.TXT"
220 PRINT #2;"THERE WAS A FLOPPY DISK
DRIVE"
230 PRINT #2;"THAT HAD NO DISKETTE"
240 CLOSE #2
250 END
```

Because mode 9 (append) was used in the OPEN statement (line 210), the file buffer pointer is set to the next available position on the file (Figure 7-16). When more text is sent to the file (lines 220 and 230), it is appended to the end of the file (Figure 7-17).

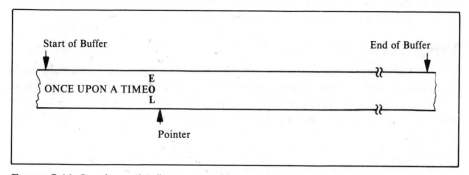

FIGURE 7-16. Opening a disk file to append

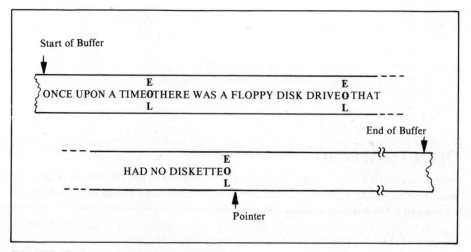

FIGURE 7-17. Appending data to a disk file

Whenever you use append mode, another sector (128 characters) is automatically allocated for the file. This happens every time a mode 9 OPEN statement is executed. A program can consume disk space at a rapid rate if it is not carefully designed. Fortunately, there is another way to add data to an existing file, as the next section describes.

OPEN FOR UPDATE

Mode 8 (output) and mode 9 (append) both permit only writing. Mode 4 (input) permits only reading. In order to both read and write, you must use mode 12 (update). A file must exist before it can be opened for updating.

When a file is opened for update, the pointer is set to the beginning of the file, and the data already in the file is left intact. The file may be read or written to at this time. For each character that is read or written, the file pointer is moved forward one position.

Data written to the file replaces previous data on a character-by-character basis. For example, the next program creates a data file and writes the message "THIS IS THE OLD DATA" on it.

```
100 OPEN #4,8,0,"D:TESTFILE.TMP"
110 PRINT #4;"THIS IS THE OLD DATA"
120 CLOSE #4
130 END
```

This program updates the same file:

```
200 OPEN #3,12,0,"D:TESTFILE.TMP"
210 PRINT #3;"HELLO"
220 CLOSE #3
230 END
```

The OPEN statement leaves the pointer at the beginning of the file (line 200). The PRINT # statement output starts there. The five characters of "HELLO" and the EOL character replace the first six characters of the data previously in the file. Two fields are now stored in the file, demarcated by EOL characters (Figure 7-18).

The data already on file can be read. This moves the pointer forward in the file. Thus you can start writing at any point between the beginning and the end of the file. Simply read along until the pointer is at the desired position, then write. Either an INPUT # statement or a GET statement will read data and move the file pointer forward. INPUT # reads fields, while GET reads single characters. The following example uses the GET statement:

```
100 TRAP 1900:REM In case no file
190 REM Open file for update
200 OPEN #3,12,0,"D:WORDS.TXT"
600 TRAP 1700:REM In case no $
790 REM Read characters until $ found
800 GET #3,A:IF CHR$(A)<>"$" THEN 800
900 REM Dollar sign found
```

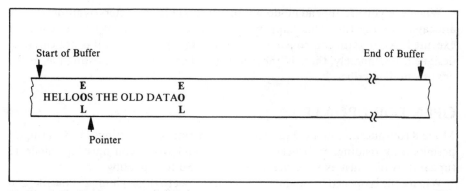

FIGURE 7-18. Writing over existing data

```
1000 PRINT #3;"1234.56";
1100 REM Last semicolon above
1200 REM Inhibits EOL character
1300 CLOSE #3
1400 PRINT "UPDATE COMPLETE"
1500 GOTO 2000
1700 PRINT "NO DOLLAR SIGN IN FILE"
1800 GOTO 2000
1900 PRINT "FILE DOES NOT EXIST"
2000 END
```

The program opens a file for update (line 200). The file must exist or the program will end (lines 100 and 1900). A GET statement reads each character of the file until a dollar sign occurs (line 800). Then the next seven characters are replaced by the number 1234.56 (line 1000).

STORING NUMBERS IN FILES

You may have already experimented with storing numbers in a file. There are several ways to do it. The following program illustrates:

```
100 PRINT "NOW OPENING FILE..."
200 OPEN #1,8,0,"D1:DATAFILE.TMP"
300 PRINT "THE FILE IS NOW OPEN."
310 PRINT #1;"MY ADDRESS IS 1234 NORTH
    STREET"
320 PRINT #1;1,2,3,4,5
330 A=10:B=20:C=30
340 D=40:E=50
350 PRINT #1;A,B,C,D+A,E*B
390 CLOSE #1
400 END
```

You can store numbers as part of a string value (line 310). You can store them directly, either from numeric constants (line 320), or using numeric variables and expressions (line 350).

If you store numbers directly, you may read them back by using an INPUT # statement that contains a numeric variable. The program below illustrates how numbers should be stored and retrieved:

```
99 REM Open disk file for output
100 OPEN #2,8,0,"D:NUMBERS.DAT"
109 REM Enter 10 numbers
110 FOR J=1 TO 10
120 PRINT "ENTER A NUMBER TO STORE";
130 INPUT N
139 REM Store each number on file
140 PRINT #2;N
150 NEXT J
160 CLOSE #2
199 REM Open disk file for input
200 OPEN #2,4,0,"D:NUMBERS.DAT"
209 REM Read 10 numbers
210 PRINT "YOU ENTERED:"
220 FOR I=1 TO 10
230 INPUT #2,N
239 REM Display each stored number
240 PRINT N
250 NEXT I
260 CLOSE #2
300 END
```

The program creates a data file (line 100). It then asks you to enter ten numbers, each of which it stores on the data file (lines 110 through 160). Notice how the CLOSE statement activates the disk drive to write out any numbers that remain in the file buffer (line 160). Finally, the program reopens the data file, this time for input (line 200). Then it reads back and displays each number it stored (lines 220 through 250).

It is important to understand how numbers are read from disk files. As far as the computer is concerned, a number being read from a file continues until the end of a field is reached (as marked by an EOL character). If a comma is found, the number being read will stop at that point, but additional data in the file will be read and discarded until an EOL is reached. None of the characters encountered between the comma and the EOL character have any effect on the numeric value.

A single PRINT # statement can store more than one number when the numbers are separated by commas, as shown here:

```
560 PRINT #3;1,2,3,
```

In this case there will be no EOL or comma stored after any of the values. The commas in the PRINT # statement merely insert extra blank spaces, as described earlier (Figure 7-15).

You cannot read such values into a numeric variable one at a time, as follows.

```
650 INPUT #3;X
660 INPUT #3;Y
670 INPUT #3;Z
```

Nor can you read them in with one INPUT # statement, like this:

```
792 INPUT #3;A,B,C
```

In either case an error will result, since embedded spaces are not allowed in numbers.

If you use semicolons instead of commas to separate the numbers in the PRINT # statement, they are all concatenated in the file. A subsequent attempt to read the numbers back will interpret them as one number.

The way to avoid this problem is to make sure each value is separated by an EOL character. Consider this program:

```
300 OPEN #4,8,0,"D:NUMBERS.DAT"
340 FOR I=1 TO 10
350 PRINT #4;I;
360 NEXT I
370 CLOSE #4
```

The ten values will be stored as one large number. The problem can be corrected by removing the semicolon at the end of the PRINT # statement.

You may store values separated by semicolons, but you must store a comma between each value. A comma can be placed between each value by putting it within quotation marks, like this:

```
270 PRINT #4;QTY;",";PRICE;",";TOTAL
```

You must be very careful to read the values back the same way they are stored, in this case as a set of three. The numbers stored by line 270 above must be read like this:

```
450 INPUT #4;Q,P,T
```

You cannot try to read one value at a time, like this:

```
450 INPUT #4;Q
460 INPUT #4;P
470 INPUT #4;T
```

In this case, the second and third values will be discarded while BASIC looks for an EOL character. The INPUT # statements on lines 460 and 470 will not work as you expect. You can always read every character with a GET statement, searching for commas and EOL characters as you go, but that is a lot of trouble.

In short, you should separate every value with an EOL character. It requires no more space than a comma, and it will result in a file format that is easy to use.

RANDOM FILE ACCESS

Random access allows you to reference any part of a file without regard the the remainder of the file. The BASIC statements that allow you to do this are NOTE and POINT. These statements work only with DOS 2.0S. If you are using DOS 1.0, you may skip this entire section.

The NOTE Statement

The NOTE statement is used to determine the current position of a file pointer. The pointer location is returned as two pieces of information: the number of the last sector referenced, and the number of the last character referenced within that sector. Here is an example:

```
NOTE #2,SECT,CHAR
```

This statement refers to the file opened on channel 2. It assigns the number of the last sector accessed to variable SECT. It also assigns to variable CHAR the number of the last character accessed in that sector.

The sector number returned is not relative to the number of sectors in the file; it is the absolute sector number on the diskette. It may be any number from 1 to 719. The first sector of the file is not necessarily sector number 1, and subsequent sectors of the file may have sector numbers lower than the first. Sector numbers of a file may or may not be sequential. The first sector might be number 148, for example, and the second might be number 153, or 127.

The POINT Statement

The POINT statement is the opposite of NOTE. POINT moves the pointer to the sector and character numbers you specify. A subsequent PRINT #, PUT, INPUT #, or GET statement will start at that point. Here is an example:

```
120 S=250:C=10:POINT #3,S,C
```

These statements move the pointer for the file open on channel 3 to sector 250, character 10.

The sector and character numbers must be specified by numeric variables. They may not be constant values, even though their values are not changed by execution of the POINT statement. The file number specified must refer to an open file.

The sector number should be an actual diskette sector number (1 to 719). The character number must be between 0 and 125 (the number of usable characters in a sector).

No checking is done to see if the sector you specify is part of the file being referenced until the actual read or write operation is performed. When the operation does occur, the disk operating system will check that the sector being accessed is part of the file specified by the channel number. If they do not match, one of the following errors will result.

· Error 170 (end of file) occurs if an INPUT # or GET statement tried to read.

· Error 171 (point invalid) occurs if a PRINT # or PUT statement tried to write.

Using NOTE and POINT

NOTE and POINT allow you to randomly access data stored in files. Efficient use of NOTE and POINT will allow your ATARI computer to perform complex data processing.

The next three sections describe different random access methods. Each method has its strengths and weaknesses. All require fairly long and complex programs. Unfortunately, space does not permit sample programs to illustrate each method.

Indexed Data Files

One way to use NOTE and POINT is to maintain two files in place of one. One file serves to store the actual data for each record your program needs to access. The second file is an index to the first file. It contains a key for each record in the first file. Along with each key, the index file stores the location where the data record starts in the first file. Each location is specified by a sector number and character number. At the start of your program, the keys and their associated sector and character numbers are read into arrays.

To find a record, the program searches through the index until it finds the key for the desired record. Then it uses the associated sector and character numbers with a POINT statement to position the disk to the proper data record. After that, it can read the data record with INPUT # or GET statements or write the data record with PRINT # or PUT statements.

Adding a record between two existing records is a time-consuming chore in an indexed file. You must physically move each record that follows the new record in order to open up a space for the new record. You must add the new key to the index file, and also change the index file so all the keys after it point to the correct new locations. Physically deleting a record requires the same amount of work, but in reverse. You must move all the records that follow the deleted record down in the file, remove the deleted key from the index, and change the pointers for all the keys that follow it.

To save space, your program can store sector and character numbers in a string variable, using the CHR$ and ASC functions to convert between string and numeric values. Only three characters will be needed for each record: two for the sector number (1 to 719), and one for the character number (0 to 125).

The main strength of indexed or keyed file accessing is the speed with which you can find a record. Searching an array of keys in memory is much faster than reading through a file record by record.

Linked List Data Files

Another random access method maintains a *linked list* of records. In a linked list, each data record has a pointer to the next data record. The pointer consists of a sector number and a character number.

To find a record in a linked list, you must start with the first record and read each record in turn until you find the one you want. This is no better than a straight sequential file.

The advantage to a linked list is the ease with which you can add and delete records. To add a record to a linked list file, the program stores the new record on the diskette and notes its location (sector and character numbers). Next, the program locates the record which should precede the new entry. We will call that record the preceding record. The new record is set to point where the preceding record now points. The pointer for the preceding record is changed to point to the new record.

Deleting a record from a linked list is accomplished by setting the pointer in the preceding record equal to the pointer stored in the record to be deleted.

Indexed Linked Data Files

For the fastest record lookup, addition, and deletion, you can use an indexed linked list. This method uses an index file, so a particular record can be located by key. Each data record is linked to the next one, so adding or deleting records only requires changing pointers. The indexed linked list method is quite complex and requires extensive programming to implement. You should probably not attempt it unless you are an advanced programmer.

READING THE DIRECTORY

Another mode that can be specified by the OPEN statement is directory access (mode 6). Directory access lets you read the disk directory as if it were a data file. Each field in the "file" is one line from the directory.

You must specify a file name in the OPEN statement; it may be an ambiguous file name. The "file" pointer will be set to the first character of the first field that matches the file name specified.

When you read from the "file," only the lines containing file names that match the specified file name will be returned. File names that do not match will be automatically skipped. At the end of the "file," the "number of sectors free" line will be returned, regardless of the file name you specified in the OPEN statement, even if there was no match.

The program below will display the entire directory of the diskette in Drive 1, without using the DOS menu:

```
10 DIM A$(20)
19 REM Open disk for directory access
20 OPEN #1,6,0,"D:*.*"
30 TRAP 90:REM For end of directory
40 INPUT #1;A$
50 PRINT A$
60 GOTO 40
90 END
```

If you want to list only those names which have a .BAS extension, change line 20 to read as follows.

```
20  OPEN #1,6,0,"D:*.BAS"
```

Do not execute any other OPEN statement while the directory is open. If you do, the "directory file" pointer will be moved, and subsequent directory file reads will be confused.

MACHINE LANGUAGE PROGRAM FILES

The DOS menu contains a number of selections which facilitate reading, writing, and executing machine language program files. These selections are used to manipulate *object files,* which are files of binary numbers usually created by the ATARI Assembler/Editor. They can also be used to read and write any block of contiguous memory locations without respect to the memory contents.

Many ATARI computer users will not need these selections. If you are not familiar with assembly language or machine language, some of the terms in this section will be foreign to you. You may skip this entire section if you wish.

SAVING BINARY DATA

To save areas of memory onto a diskette or cassette, choose DOS menu item K, BINARY SAVE. This selection is different in DOS 1.0 and DOS 2.0S.

Binary Save from DOS 1.0

When you select DOS menu item K in DOS 1.0, this prompt message appears:

```
SAVE-GIVE FILE,START,END
```

You must enter the file name and the starting and ending locations of the block of memory you wish to save. The starting and ending locations are treated as hexadecimal numbers. Here is a sample response:

```
SAVE-GIVE FILE,START,END
PROGRM1.OBJ,3E00,4AFF
```

This will create an object file named PROGRM1.OBJ on Drive 1. The file will contain the block of memory between locations 3E00 and 4AFF.

You may prefix the file name with a disk drive number, like this:

```
SAVE-GIVE FILE,START,END
D2:PROGRM3.OBJ,3D70,42FF
```

Files created by DOS menu item K are usually read back into memory by DOS menu item L, BINARY LOAD. After loading memory, item L normally returns control of the computer to the DOS menu. If you save the binary file in a special way, it will automatically be run after it is loaded.

To save a file so that DOS menu item L will load and automatically run it, you must first place the program starting address in memory locations 736 and 737 (2E0 and 2E1 hexadecimal). Before entering the DOS menu, use POKE statements to do this. The low byte of the starting address goes in location 736, the high byte in 737. The following statements set up a starting address of 16400 (4010 hexadecimal):

```
A=16400

READY
POKE 736,A-INT(A/256)*256

READY
POKE 737,INT(A/256)
```

After setting up memory locations 736 and 737, enter the DOS menu and choose item K. When you specify the file name, append the suffix /A. This causes the starting address to be saved along with the binary data. Here is an example:

```
SAVE-GIVE FILE,START,END
PROGRM3.OBJ/A,3CFF,4EFF
```

Binary Save from DOS 2.0S

When you select DOS menu item K in DOS 2.0S, this prompt message appears:

```
SAVE---GIVE FILE,START,END(,INIT,RUN)
※
```

You must enter the file name and the starting and ending locations of the block of memory you wish to save. The starting and ending locations are treated as hexadecimal numbers. Here is a sample response:

```
SAVE--GIVE FILE,START,END(,INIT,RUN)
PROGRM1.OBJ,3E00,4AFF
```

This will create an object file named PROGRM1.OBJ on Drive 1. The file will contain the block of memory between locations 3E00 and 4AFF.

You may prefix the file name with a disk drive number, like this:

```
SAVE--GIVE FILE,START,END(,INIT,RUN)
D2:PROGRM1.OBJ,3D70,42FF
```

You may also specify two additional memory locations. The first, the INIT location, is the starting location of an initialization routine. The second, the RUN location, is the starting location of the main program. These are locations that DOS menu item L will use to automatically execute the program after it loads the program into memory. These two addresses are interpreted as hexadecimal values. Here is a sample response:

```
SAVE---GIVE FILE,START,END(,INIT,RUN)
PROGRM3.OBJ,3CFF,4EFF,4E00,4010
```

The initialization address can be omitted with the run address still specified, like this:

```
SAVE--GIVE FILE,START,END(,INIT,RUN)
PROGRM4.OBJ,3E10,517F,,4800
```

If an initialization address is specified, that routine will be executed first. The routine must end with an assembly language RTS instruction. At that point, execution branches to the run address.

Merging Binary Files

In DOS 2.0S, you can use the / A option of DOS menu item C (COPY FILE) with binary files created by DOS menu item K (BINARY SAVE). The result is a *compound file*. A compound file is simply one or more binary files merged together. Compound files allow you to store information from two or more separate, non-contiguous areas of memory, without affecting all of the memory between those areas.

Initialization and run addresses are handled a bit differently in compound files. Each initialization address is still used, but only the final run address applies. As each part of the compound file is loaded, it is checked for an initialization address. If there is one, the initialization routine is executed before the next part of the compound file is loaded. The final run address is taken from the last part of the compound file.

LOADING BINARY FILES

DOS menu item L, BINARY LOAD, loads a file created by DOS menu item K, or one created by the Assembler/Editor cartridge. It will also automatically execute the loaded file, if the file was saved with a run address.

When you choose DOS menu item L, this prompt appears:

```
LOAD FROM WHAT FILE?
▓
```

You must enter the name of the binary file to be loaded. Here is an example:

```
LOAD FROM WHAT FILE?
PROGRM1.OBJ
```

This will load the binary data from file PROGRM1.OBJ into memory at the locations specified when the file was created. The file may have been saved by DOS menu item K with an automatic execution address. If so, execution begins immediately at that address.

You can specify a disk drive number ahead of the file name, like this:

```
LOAD FROM WHAT FILE?
D2:PROGRM2.OBJ
```

The binary file may conflict with the area of memory used by the DOS menu program in DOS 2.0S. If this happens, file MEM.SAV must exist on the diskette in Drive 1. In this case, the part of the binary file that conflicts with the DOS menu program is saved on file MEM.SAV until the binary file is executed. If the required MEM.SAV is absent, the message **NEED MEM.SAV TO LOAD THIS FILE** appears.

Preventing Automatic Execution

In DOS 2.0S, you can prevent automatic execution of a file that was created with an initialization or run address. All you do is append the suffix / N to the file name. Here is an example:

```
LOAD FROM WHAT FILE?
PROGRM3.OBJ/N
```

EXECUTING A LOADED PROGRAM

To execute a machine language (object) program that is in memory, choose DOS menu item M, RUN AT ADDRESS. This prompt message appears:

```
RUN FROM WHAT ADDRESS?
```

You must enter the starting address of the program. The address you enter is treated as a hexadecimal number. Be very careful. Entering the wrong address could cause the system to hang up. In that case you must turn the system off and back on again.

The DOS menu branches to the machine language program with an assembly language JSR instruction. If the machine language program ends with an assembly language RTS instruction, control returns to the DOS menu.

THE AUTORUN.SYS FILE

DOS 2.0S recognizes a special binary file name, AUTORUN.SYS. If this file is present when you boot DOS 2.0S, it will be loaded automatically. If it was saved with initialization or run addresses, it will be executed automatically as well.

There is a standard AUTORUN.SYS file. It contains a program which establishes an RS-232 serial handler program in memory. The RS-232 handler is required in order to use the serial ports of the ATARI 850 Interface Module.

You can have your own machine language program automatically loaded and run as part of the power-on, DOS boot procedure. Simply use DOS menu item K to save it on a binary file named AUTORUN.SYS. If your program ends with an assembly language RTS instruction, control transfers to a built-in initialization routine. Among other things, the initialization routine enables the use of the SYSTEM RESET key. If your program does not end with an RTS instruction, it should initialize memory location 580 (244 hexadecimal) to 0, and memory location 9 to 1.

MODIFYING DOS 2.0S

This section describes two simple modifications you can make to DOS 2.0S. These modifications are valid only on DOS 2.0S. Do not make them on DOS 1.0.

Freeing Memory with DOS 2.0S

DOS 2.0S is designed to support as many as four ATARI 810 Disk Drives. A separate disk buffer is reserved in memory for each drive. If you have fewer than four drives, you can increase the memory available to your BASIC programs. Each drive you don't use will yield 128 bytes (characters) of memory.

You can free the memory set aside for unused drives. You must change the value stored in memory location 1802 to reflect the actual number of drives connected to your computer.

Make sure the BASIC cartridge is in the computer. Then boot DOS by turning the ATARI 400/800 computer's power off and back on again. When the **READY** message appears, type this command:

```
?PEEK(1802)
```

The computer will print a code number that indicates the number of drives DOS 2.0S is currently set up to use. Table 7-2 translates the code into the number of drives. Use Table 7-2 to determine the code for the number of drives you actually have. Then use a POKE statement to change location 1802 to the code shown in the table. For example, to change to a one-drive system, type this:

```
POKE 1802,1
```

Next, type the DOS command to get the DOS menu. Put a blank diskette in Drive 1. Format the diskette with DOS menu item I if necessary. Then write the disk operating system program out to the diskette with DOS menu item H. You have just created a new version of the disk operating system on diskette. Use this as your new master diskette.

Now every time you boot from the diskette you just created, the memory savings

TABLE 7-2. Disk Drives Allowed by DOS

Number of Drives	Code Value*
1	1
2	3
3	7
4	15

* Values for memory location 1802

will be in effect. If you boot from an old diskette, the memory savings will not be in effect.

Allowing More Files Open at Once

Normally, only three data files can be open simultaneously. When you boot DOS, it looks at memory location 1801. The number it finds there is the limit on files open.

With DOS 2.0S, you can change memory location 1801 to the number of files you want to have open simultaneously. The maximum is seven. Each file requires an input/output channel, and there are only seven of those available. There is a penalty for increasing the limit, however. For each file you add, you lose 128 bytes of memory. The memory is set aside for a file buffer when you boot DOS.

Make sure the BASIC cartridge is in the computer. Then boot DOS by turning the ATARI 400/800 computer power off and back on again. When the **READY** message appears, type this command:

```
?PEEK(1801)
```

The computer will print the number of files it currently allows open at one time. The number will probably be 3. Use a POKE statement to change location 1801 to the number you want; remember, 7 is the practical maximum. For example, to cause seven files to be open simultaneously, type this:

```
POKE 1801,7
```

Next, type the DOS command to get the DOS menu. Put a blank diskette in Drive 1. Format the diskette with DOS menu item I if necessary. Then write the disk operating system program out to the diskette with DOS menu item H. You have just created a new version of the disk operating system on diskette. Use this as your new master diskette.

Now every time you boot from the diskette you just created, the new limit on simultaneous files open will be in effect. If you boot from an old diskette, the old limit will be in effect.

DISK CRASH

To close the chapter, we will describe one of the worst disk calamities that can occur, a *disk crash*. There are two types of disk crashes: hard crashes and soft crashes. Hard crashes happen when the diskette has a physical defect, like a rip or a piece of dirt on it. A hard crash can cause damage to the read/write head inside the drive. The damaged head can, in turn, damage more diskettes. For this reason, always handle diskettes with care.

A soft crash occurs when the data on the diskette becomes garbled. This most frequently happens when one or more files have been written to but not closed, a different diskette is placed in the drive, and the files from the first diskette are closed. To fully appreciate the resulting mess you must experience it.

8

INTRODUCTORY GRAPHICS

Whatever you use your ATARI computer for, its graphics capabilities can enhance any program you write. This chapter describes the various graphics modes you can use with BASIC. In addition, you will learn a few tricks which will help you squeeze more performance out of your computer.

There are nine graphics modes, numbered from 0 to 8, that you can use with BASIC. You activate these graphics modes with the GRAPHICS statement, followed by the number of the mode to activate. You will see later that variations on these nine modes exist. For now, it is best to concentrate on some basic concepts which you will need to know before going any further.

COLOR REGISTERS

In any graphics mode, you can control one or more foreground colors (text or graphics color), the background color, and the border color which frames the background. The ATARI computer has *color registers* — memory locations which set the foreground, background, and border colors. For instance, press the RESET key and enter this:

```
SETCOLOR 2,0,0
```

The background color turns black. Here, the BASIC statement SETCOLOR changed the value of the register controlling the background color. In effect, the screen color changed instantly. The border color will change to green if you enter this:

```
SETCOLOR 4,12,8
```

The following statement turns the text black:

```
SETCOLOR 1,0,0
```

Unlike other personal computers, which give you an irrevocable color choice before drawing graphics, the ATARI computer allows you to change colors on the screen by using the SETCOLOR statement at any time. With this approach it is possible to draw invisibly on the screen, change a color register's value, and illuminate a fully-drawn graphics image in an instant.

Using SETCOLOR

The numbers (or numeric expressions) that follow SETCOLOR select which color register to change, what color to change it to, and what the brightness (or *luminance*) of that color will be. From one graphics mode to the next, however, different registers control foreground, background, and border colors.

The first number after SETCOLOR indicates which register to set; registers are numbered from 0 to 4. The second number selects the color itself; colors are numbered from 0 to 15. Table 8-1 lists the colors available, and their numeric values for use with the SETCOLOR statement. The third and last number sets the luminance from 0 (darkest) to 14 (brightest). Only even-numbered luminance settings are meaningful. This number can actually exceed 14, but the color register will ignore the excess value over 14. With the colors and luminance settings available, up to 128 different shades of color are possible. The following short program will give you some idea of the possible color combinations:

```
10 GRAPHICS 0
20 LIST :REM PUT SOME TEXT ON THE SCRE
EN
30 FOR I=0 TO 15
40 SETCOLOR 2,I,0:REM SET BACKGROUND C
OLOR
50 SETCOLOR 4,15-I,0:REM SET BORDER CO
LOR
60 FOR J=0 TO 14 STEP 2
70 SETCOLOR 2,I,J:REM INCREASE BACKGRO
UND LUMINANCE
80 SETCOLOR 0,0,14-J:REM DECREASE TEXT
  LUMINANCE
90 SETCOLOR 4,15-I,J:REM INCREASE BORD
ER LUMINANCE
100 NEXT J
110 NEXT I
```

The five color registers have preassigned color numbers and luminance values. These are listed in Table 8-2. You can change the color number and luminance values with the SETCOLOR statement.

TABLE 8-1. Color Numbers Used with SETCOLOR

Number	Color	Number	Color
0	Grey	8	Light Blue
1	Gold	9	Blue-Green
2	Orange	10	Aqua
3	Red	11	Green-Blue
4	Pink	12	Green
5	Violet	13	Yellow-Green
6	Blue-Purple	14	Orange-Green
7	Blue	15	Orange

TABLE 8-2. Default (Preassigned) Color Register Settings

Register Number	Color Number	Luminance Value	Actual Screen Color
0	2	8	Orange
1	12	10	Aqua
2	9	4	Blue
3	4	6	Light Red
4	0	0	Black

The COLOR Statement

The COLOR statement should not be confused with the SETCOLOR statement. In some graphics modes, multiple foreground color registers are available. The COLOR statement selects one of the available color registers and uses that color register to draw with. For instance, in graphics mode 7 it is possible to plot or draw graphics in three foreground colors. The COLOR statement selects which of the three possible registers to use when plotting points or drawing lines. Therefore, the COLOR statement is often unnecessary in text modes, or in other modes which have only one possible foreground color register.

The numeric expression after COLOR will often select different color registers, depending on the current graphics mode. One consistent rule with COLOR is that COLOR 0 will always select the background color register, while COLOR 1 will always select the foreground color register. Tables 8-3 and 8-4 enumerate the color registers selected by various COLOR statements in the different graphics modes.

In graphics mode 0 (the normal text mode) you cannot draw lines or plot points. The COLOR statement does not select a color to plot or draw with. Instead, by placing the code number of an ATASCII character after COLOR, you can select a text or graphics character to plot with. For bar graphs, or for extensive use of the mode 0 character graphics, the COLOR statement can be very useful.

TABLE 8-3. Graphics Modes Summary

Display Type	Graphics Mode Number	Colors Available	Screen Size (columns × rows)	Foreground Color Register(s)	Background Color Register	Border Color Register	Register Selection With COLOR	Memory Used (Bytes)
Normal text	0	1 color, 2 luminances	40×24	1 (Color is not selectable)	2	4	*	992
Double-width text	1	5	20×20 (split) 20×24 (full)	0, 1, 2, 3	4	4	(see Table 8-4)	674 (split) 672 (full)
Double-width, double-height text	2	5	10×20 (split) 12×20 (full)	0, 1, 2, 3	4	4	(see Table 8-4)	424 (split) 420 (full)
Four-color graphics	3	4	40×20 (split) 40×24 (full)	0, 1, 2	4	4	COLOR 1: register 0 COLOR 2: register 1 COLOR 3: register 2 COLOR 0: register 4	Mode 3: 434 (split) 432 (full)
	5	4	80×40 (split) 80×48 (full)	0, 1, 2	4	4		Mode 5: 1174 (split) 1176 (full)
	7	4	160×80 (split) 160×96 (full)	0, 1, 2	4	4		Mode 7: 4190 (split) 4200 (full)
Two-color graphics	4	2	80×40 (split) 80×48 (full)	0	4	4	COLOR 1: register 0 COLOR 0: register 4	Mode 4: 694 (split) 696 (full)
	6	2	160×80 (split) 160×96 (full)	0	4	4		Mode 6: 2174 (split) 2184 (full)
High-resolution graphics	8	1 color, 2 luminances	320×160 (split) 320×192 (full)	1 (color is not selectable)	2	4	COLOR 1: register 1 COLOR 0: register 2	8112 (split) 8138 (full)

* In Mode 0, COLOR will accept an ATASCII character to plot with. For example, COLOR ASC("!") in Mode 0, followed by PLOT or DRAWTO statements, will place ! characters on the screen.

TABLE 8-4. Color Register Assignments, Graphics Modes 1 and 2

Characters	ATASCII Values	Color Register Assigned
Upper-case alphabet (A-Z), numbers, special characters (! $ + -)	32-90 160-218	Normal: 0 Inverse*: 2
Lower-case* alphabet	61-122 225-250	Normal: 1 Inverse*: 3

*Lower-case and inverse characters display as normal, upper-case text. They are assigned to different registers, however.

GRAPHICS STATEMENT OPTIONS

Graphics modes 1 through 8 set a split screen when the GRAPHICS statement executes. Graphics mode 0 text is confined to the four lines at the bottom of the screen. This is the *text window,* and it is not always needed for displaying graphics. You can eliminate the text window altogether, thus allowing you more vertical display lines for graphics.

To set up a graphics screen without a text window, add 16 to the expression after GRAPHICS. For instance, the statement GRAPHICS 24 would put the display into high-resolution graphics mode 8, with no text window. This yields 32 more high-resolution lines than the statement GRAPHICS 8. Since the text window is not used, the graphics mode selected makes use of the remaining part of the display normally allocated to the text window.

By adding 32 to the expression after GRAPHICS, you eliminate the automatic screen clearing normally performed by a GRAPHICS statement. However, don't get the idea that you can display normal (mode 0) text, then execute GRAPHICS 40 (graphics mode 8 with 32 added), and have the text stay on the screen. Once the new graphics mode is in effect, anything on the screen is interpreted as being in the new mode. To find out more about mixing graphics modes in your program, consult the section on inserting text into graphics displays later in this chapter.

To combine the options of full-screen graphics without destroying the previous contents of the graphics page, add 48 to the graphics mode desired. A good application of this option is to selectively open and close the text window at particular points in the program, as shown here:

```
10 GRAPHICS 8+16:REM FULL-SCREEN GRAPH
ICS
20 COLOR 1:PLOT 0,0
30 DRAWTO 319,191:REM DRAW A DIAGONAL
40 FOR DLAY=1 TO 200:NEXT DLAY:REM DEL
AY LOOP
50 GRAPHICS 8+32:REM OPEN THE TEXT WIN'
DOW
60 PRINT "A DIAGONAL LINE"
70 FOR DLAY=1 TO 200:NEXT DLAY:REM DEL
AY LOOP
80 GRAPHICS 8+48:REM NOW CLOSE THE TEX
T WINDOW
90 GOTO 40
```

The screen flickers when the ATARI computer switches graphics modes, but the unsightliness may be worth the trouble.

Using the Text Window

PRINT and INPUT statements use the text window for normal data entry and display. The computer will force a program out of a full-screen graphics mode in order to display PRINT statements, accept responses to INPUT statements, or display error messages. The computer erases the screen and returns to graphics mode 0. You can program around this in graphics modes 1 and 2, which normally display text, but other graphics modes will be more difficult to use with full-screen graphics *and* some kind of text display or data entry. The method used earlier to open and close the text window might be useful in this case.

EXPANDED TEXT: MODES 1 AND 2

In graphics modes 1 and 2, the text on the screen is expanded. A GRAPHICS 1 statement sets up a screen 20 characters wide and 20 rows deep. GRAPHICS 2 creates a screen 20 characters wide and 10 rows deep. In full-screen modes 1 and 2, 24 and 12 rows are available, respectively.

Displaying Expanded Text

In graphics modes 1 and 2, lower-case text and inverse video characters display on the screen as normal upper-case text. The two high-order bits of each ATASCII character, normally used to identify lower-case or inverse video text, are used as color register selectors in these modes. In the text window, both upper-and lower-case characters will display. In these expanded text modes, PRINT statements can go to either the screen or the text window; therefore, you have to use different syntax to place data on the screen. Try this short program:

```
10 GRAPHICS 1
20 PRINT #6;"ExPaNdEd TeXt"
30 PRINT "MODE 0 TEXT"
```

Expanded text displays at the top of the screen, and then normal text displays in the text window. The first PRINT statement directs output to the mode 1 area. Any time you want to display expanded text, use PRINT #6 in this mode.

If you want to eliminate the text window and have the entire screen contain expanded text, use GRAPHICS 17 to set up a screen with 24 lines of 20 characters, and use GRAPHICS 18 to display 12 lines of 20 characters.

Color Registers in Modes 1 and 2

Color register 4 is used to control the background and border colors. SETCOLOR doesn't control the colors of the expanded text on the screen, however. Instead, the ATASCII character set is divided among the color registers.

As mentioned earlier, the high-order bits of each byte used for expanded text will assign a color register. Although this appears to be a strange way to assign color registers, you can take advantage of this feature to make screen displays much more dynamic than mode 0 displays. Enter and run the following program.

```
10 GRAPHICS 17:REM FULL-SCREEN
20 PRINT #6;"*█*█*█*█*█*█*█*█*█"
30 PRINT #6;"█              *"
40 PRINT #6;"*    marquee    █"
50 PRINT #6;"█              *"
60 PRINT #6;"*█*█*█*█*█*█*█*█*█"
70 SETCOLOR 2,4,8:REM SET THE NORMAL-V
IDEO ASTERISKS
80 SETCOLOR 0,10,8:REM SET THE REVERSE
 ASTERISKS
90 FOR DLAY=1 TO 50:NEXT DLAY
100 SETCOLOR 0,4,8:REM RESET THE REVER
SE ASTERISKS
110 SETCOLOR 2,10,8:REM RESET THE NORM
AL ASTERISKS
120 FOR DLAY=1 TO 50:NEXT DLAY
130 GOTO 70
```

GRAPHICS PROGRAMMING STATEMENTS

In graphics modes 2 through 8, four BASIC statements — PLOT, DRAWTO,
LOCATE and POSITION — control graphics input and output. You can actually
use these statements in any graphics mode, but you wouldn't normally use them to
display or manipulate text.

PLOT and DRAWTO

The PLOT and DRAWTO statements enable you to plot points and draw lines on
the graphics screen. The PLOT statement illuminates a single point on the screen.
The following example, in graphics mode 3, plots random points on the screen in all
of the available colors:

```
10 GRAPHICS 3+16
20 COLOR RND(0)*4:REM CHOOSE A RANDOM
FOREGROUND REGISTER
30 PLOT RND(0)*39,RND(0)*19:REM PLOT R
ANDOM POINT
40 GOTO 20
```

DRAWTO can best be illustrated by this graphics mode 8 program:

```
10 GRAPHICS 8+16
20 SETCOLOR 2,0,0:REM BLACK BACKGROUND
30 COLOR 1:REM SELECT FOREGROUND REGIS
TER
40 FOR Y=0 TO 191 STEP 3
50 PLOT 0,Y
60 DRAWTO Y,191
70 NEXT Y
80 GOTO 80
```

Because DRAWTO indicates only the column and row to draw to, the PLOT statement at line 40 is necessary in order to show which column and row to draw from when connecting the line.

POSITION and LOCATE

The POSITION statement is functionally similar to PLOT. POSITION, however, sets the coordinates without plotting. In the last example program, line 40 could be rewritten as follows:

```
40 POSITION 0,Y
```

Replacing this statement in the DRAWTO example program would produce a slightly different result. Coordinate (0,Y) would not be illuminated. POSITION can also be used to move the cursor in graphics mode 0, 1, or 2.

The LOCATE statement reads a point that you specify on the graphics screen and passes its value back to a BASIC variable. Here is an example:

```
10 LOCATE 10,14,X
```

This LOCATE statement reads a value from the point at the eleventh row and fifteenth column. This value identifies the color selected for the graphics point. The value corresponds to the color statement value, which determines the color register used for the graphics point. Table 8-3 shows the possible color values that LOCATE will return to the variable.

FOUR-COLOR GRAPHICS: MODES 3, 5, AND 7

Three graphics modes — 3, 5, and 7 — have three foreground color registers available, as well as one color register for the background and border color. The three modes differ in resolution, and therefore in the amount of memory they use.

Notice that you can select the background color register, using a COLOR 0 statement, in order to erase selected parts of a graphics image. Here is an example:

```
10 GRAPHICS 7+16
20 SETCOLOR 2,0,0:REM BLACK BACKGROUND
30 COLOR 1:REM SELECT FOREGROUND REGIS
TER
40 STEPSIZE=1:REM DRAW EVERY LINE
50 GOSUB 100
60 COLOR 0:REM DRAW WITH BACKGROUND CO
LOR
70 STEPSIZE=6:REM UNDRAW EVERY SIXTH L
INE
80 GOSUB 100
90 GOTO 90
100 REM PLOT SUBROUTINE
110 FOR Y=0 TO 95 STEP STEPSIZE:REM DR
AW THE FIGURE
120 PLOT 0,Y
130 DRAWTO Y,95
140 NEXT Y
150 RETURN
```

Color Registers in Modes 3, 5, and 7

Background and border colors are controlled by color register 4. You can select register 0, 1, or 2 for foreground colors. Color register 3 is not used in four-color modes.

Graphics Mode 3

Executing a GRAPHICS 3 statement will turn the screen into 20 rows of 40 graphics cells. This is the lowest-resolution graphics mode on the ATARI computer. This mode allows you to plot points and draw lines in three different foreground colors. You will need to use the COLOR statement to select the color register to plot and draw with. This graphics mode is ideal for displaying large block letters and creating simple games.

TWO-COLOR GRAPHICS: MODES 4 AND 6

Modes 4 and 6 allow one foreground and one background/border color register. These modes have resolution equivalent to that of modes 5 and 7; however, modes 4 and 6 allocate less memory than the four-color modes. Four-color modes need two bits of memory per graphics point for color register selection. In a two-color mode, only one bit is needed. If a bit in the screen memory is set to 1, this selects the foreground color register; otherwise, the background color is assumed. As a result, memory consumption is nearly half that of four-color modes.

HIGH-RESOLUTION GRAPHICS: MODE 8

Graphics mode 8 offers the highest resolution possible on the ATARI computer, but it also costs the most in terms of memory consumption. Resolution in split-screen mode is 160 rows, with 320 points across. In full-screen mode, 192 rows of 320 points are available. In this mode, the foreground color cannot be selected. In other words, the background/border color register controls the color of the graphics points. However, you can set the luminance of the foreground color register.

Extra Colors in Mode 8

Technically, graphics mode 8 allows only one foreground color, and that color really is not unique from that chosen for the graphics screen background. It is possible, however, to obtain other colors by manipulating the patterns of bits which make up each point on the graphics screen.

In graphics mode 8, the screen has 320 separate horizontal positions. Each of these 320 picture cells (or *pixels*) equals one half of a *color cycle*. A color cycle is actually the amount of time the television receiver takes to illuminate two graphics pixels (Figure 8-1).

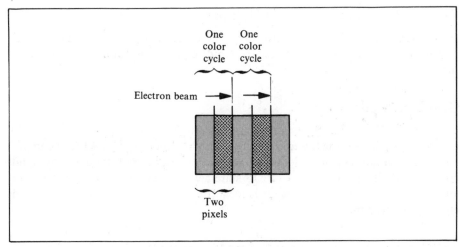

FIGURE 8-1. Color cycles and pixels

By cleverly staggering the illuminated pixels, you will cause a *color phase shift,* which is a by-product of changing the luminance of a television signal across color cycle boundaries. Remember that the computer is not changing the color — only the luminance of the signal. This forces a color change on the television set. Table 8-5 lists the bit patterns that generate colors produced by variations in luminance. The exact color seen on the TV screen will be different for different TV sets.

The following program will generate the luminance-varied colors in horizontal bands down the screen:

```
5 GRAPHICS 8:SETCOLOR 1,0,15
10 REM 4-COLOR MODE 8
20 DATA 85,170,255
30 SCRMEM=PEEK(88)+PEEK(89)*256
40 READ X:PRINT "BIT VALUE=";X
80 FOR I=SCRMEM TO SCRMEM+1000
85 REM CYCLE THROUGH THE COLORS
90 POKE I,X
100 NEXT I
105 SCRMEM=SCRMEM+1000
110 IF X=255 THEN STOP
120 GOTO 40
```

Using PLOT and DRAWTO with Extra Colors

The luminance-varied, or *phase-shifted,* colors can be overdrawn with PLOT and DRAWTO statements. After you run the example program listed above, type in a few PLOT and DRAWTO statements. Then change the plotting color by alternately typing COLOR 1 and COLOR 0. This method is good for setting background colors, but it is unwieldy for more advanced uses.

TABLE 8-5. Bit Patterns for Luminance-Varied Colors

Bit pattern	Color generated
0 0	No illumination (mode 8 background)
0 1	Solid phase-shifted color #1
1 0	Solid phase-shifted color #2
1 1	White (mode 8 foreground)

In order to predictably use graphics plotting statements with extra colors, you can simulate graphics mode 7 when the graphics screen is actually in mode 8. Graphics mode 7 allows four color registers. In this mode, each color register is two bits wide. By loading each color register with the bit pattern desired, you can use COLOR statements to select which of these extra mode 8 colors to use.

By using POKE statements to change a few memory locations, you can retain the mode 8 screen and manipulate it as if you had more colors available, as in mode 7. The following program illustrates this graphics mode 7 simulation with full mode 8 resolution:

```
5 DEG :REM USE DEGREES
10 GRAPHICS 8
20 POKE 87,7:REM POKE MODE 7 TO THE OP
ERATING SYSTEM
30 SETCOLOR 2,14,14:SETCOLOR 1,0,0:REM
 USE THE MODE 8 COLOR REGISTERS
40 X=60:Y=40:REM SET COORDINATES
50 FOR R1=12 TO 36 STEP 3
60 COLOR 1:R=R1:GOSUB 210:REM PLACE BI
NARY '01' DATA ON SCREEN
70 COLOR 2:R=R1+1:GOSUB 210:REM PLACE
BINARY '10' DATA ON SCREEN
80 COLOR 3:R=R1+2:GOSUB 210:REM PLACE
BINARY '11' DATA ON SCREEN
90 NEXT R1
100 STOP
200 REM PLOT A CIRCLE (APPEARS ELLIPTI
CAL DUE TO MODE 7 SIMULATION)
210 PLOT X+R,Y
220 FOR ANG=0 TO 360 STEP 18
230 DRAWTO X+R*COS(ANG),Y+R*SIN(ANG)
240 NEXT ANG
250 RETURN
```

The disadvantage of this method is the error message you get when trying to use PLOT or DRAWTO beyond the screen boundaries that are normal for graphics mode 7. On the horizontal axis, each point plotted is two pixels wide. Therefore, the screen resolution is cut in half on the horizontal axis (to 160 points), even though PLOT and DRAWTO statements can cross the full width of the screen. In mode 7, a maximum of 96 rows are available. In graphics mode 8, 192 rows are available.

Although the effective horizontal resolution is halved in this mode, the screen will still hold 192 rows. This leaves 96 rows that you can't use on the bottom half of the screen. This is an unfortunate side effect, caused by trying to fool the computer. To get around this problem, you have to again deceive the computer with some POKE statements.

Memory location 89 holds a pointer to the beginning memory address of the graphics screen. By modifying this pointer, it is possible to use the lower 96 rows. The program listed below contains a subroutine at lines 1200 to 1290 which enables you to plot or draw on either portion of the screen.

```
10 DEG :REM USE DEGREES
20 GRAPHICS 8
30 SETCOLOR 2,0,0
40 POKE 87,7
50 FOR M=60 TO 120 STEP 60
60 FOR I=1 TO 3
70 COLOR I
80 R=20
90 X=30+I*8+R:Y=M:REM SET RADIUS
100 PLT=1:GOSUB 1200
110 FOR ANG=0 TO 360 STEP 12
120 PLT=0
130 X=I*8+30+R*COS(ANG):Y=M+R*SIN(ANG)
140 GOSUB 1200
150 NEXT ANG
160 NEXT I
170 NEXT M
180 STOP
1190 REM *******************************
1191 REM * 4-COLOR MODE 8 GRAPHICS   *
1192 REM *          SUBROUTINES       *
1193 REM * ======================== *
1194 REM *Y=ROW (0-192),X=COL(0-159)*
1195 REM *PLT=0(DRAWTO),PLT=1(PLOT) *
1196 REM *******************************
1200 SA=PEEK(89)+15:REM START OF SCREE
N MEMORY
1210 IF PLT=0 THEN GOTO 1260
1220 IF Y<96 THEN PLOT X,Y:RETURN
1230 POKE 89,SA
1240 PLOT X,Y-96
1250 GOTO 1300
1260 IF (X<80) AND (Y<96) THEN DRAWTO
X,Y:RETURN
1280 POKE 89,SA
1290 DRAWTO X,Y-96
1300 POKE 89,SA-15
1310 RETURN
```

To use this subroutine, set variable X to the column (0 to 160), set variable Y to the row (0 to 191), and variable PLT to 1 for plotting or 0 for drawing. If you use this subroutine for drawing, make sure that you have already performed a PLOT statement in the same region of the screen.

INSERTING TEXT ON THE GRAPHICS SCREEN

The text window is always available for placing text on the same screen as graphics, but no built-in method exists for overlaying text on the graphics images. It is easy to insert text on a two-color graphics screen (graphics mode 4, 6, or 8). The technique involves using a section of memory reserved for the character set.

A *bit map* of the character set resides in memory; location 756 contains the starting address of the character set as a multiple of 256. Each character is defined in eight-byte segments. Once located in the bit map, that character's binary representation can be transferred, byte by byte, to predefined coordinates on the graphics screen. The following program illustrates this technique:

```
10 DIM TXT$(64)
20 GRAPHICS 8
30 INPUT X,Y,TXT$
50 GOSUB 2000
60 GOTO 30
1995 REM TEXT CONVERSION SUBROUTINE
2000 SA=PEEK(89)*256+PEEK(88):REM TOP
OF SCREEN RAM
2010 MODE=PEEK(87):REM DETERMINE GRAPH
ICS MODE
2020 IF MODE=8 THEN COLS=40:ROWS=192
2030 IF MODE=6 THEN COLS=20:ROWS=96
2040 IF MODE=4 THEN COLS=10:ROWS=24
2050 IF Y>ROWS OR X>COLS THEN RETURN
2060 START=SA+Y*COLS+X:REM START ADDRE
SS FOR DISPLAY
2070 FOR E1=1 TO LEN(TXT$)
2080 GOSUB 2200
2090 CHARSET=PEEK(756)*256:REM READ CH
ARACTER SET VECTOR
2100 CHARSET=CHARSET+E3*8
2110 FOR E2=7 TO 0 STEP -1
2120 POKE START+E2*COLS,PEEK(CHARSET+E
2)
2130 NEXT E2
2140 X=X+1:IF X>=COLS THEN START=START
+COLS*8:X=0:REM SCROLL TO NEXT LINE
2150 START=START+1
2160 NEXT E1
2170 RETURN
2195 REM ATASCII CONVERSION ROUTINE
2200 E3=ASC(TXT$(E1,E1))
2210 IF (E3<32) OR (E3>127 AND E3<160)
  THEN E3=E3+64:RETURN
2220 IF E3>31 AND E3<96 THEN E3=E3-32
2230 RETURN
```

Variables X and Y should be set to the column and row where the text will start displaying. TXT$ can be dimensioned to some other length.

Lines 2000 to 2060 determine the graphics mode in effect, set the screen width for text, and calculate the starting memory address for text insertion. The subroutine at lines 2200 to 2230 converts the character code of each letter in TXT$ to an *offset;* that is, the number of bytes from the beginning of the character set table to the character's actual binary definition.

Lines 2100 through 2130 transfer the character's eight-byte, bit-mapped definition to the appropriate area of the screen. Line 2140 scrolls the text to the next line if the next character will not fit on the same line.

The string variable TXT$ holds the string to display, and variables X and Y store the column and row coordinates for the first letter to display. The column coordinate can range from 0 to the number of columns available in the current mode. In mode 4, the screen will fit ten characters across; in mode 6, 20 characters fit across (similar to mode 2), and in mode 8, 40 characters will fit on each row. The row number can range from 0 to the maximum number of rows available in the current graphics mode. Therefore, you can place graphics much more flexibly on the vertical axis.

This subroutine is fairly slow because of the PEEK and POKE statements used, but it is possible to speed up the transfer of data from the character set table to the graphics screen by writing an assembly language program to convert the character data.

With this subroutine it is possible to display upper- and lower-case text and graphics characters. Inverse video characters will display unpredictably.

FILLING THE SCREEN WITH SOLID COLORS

Along with the standard BASIC statements for graphics, a special command to the operating system, called the XIO statement, will fill the screen boundary with a solid color. The XIO statement requires some preparation before use, however. The following BASIC statements set up the screen and draw a shape:

```
10 GRAPHICS 7
20 COLOR 1
30 PLOT 70,40
40 SETCOLOR 2,0,0
50 DRAWTO 35,0
60 DRAWTO 34,0
70 POSITION 0,40
80 POKE 765,1
90 XIO 18,#6,0,0,"S:"
```

Lines 80 and 90 pertain to the actual use of the XIO statement. The POKE statement on line 80 uses the same number as a number used for color register selection in the COLOR statement. Use Table 8-3 to select values to use with the POKE statement. The fill color will respond to SETCOLOR statements as normal point or line graphics on the screen. The XIO statement on line 90 will always have the same format; use it exactly as shown in the example program.

Using the XIO Fill Command

The XIO fill command is designed to work with four-sided figures. However, if you run the example above you will see what appears to be a triangle. Notice the DRAWTO statement from coordinates (35, 0) to (34, 0). This command will act in a predictable fashion only if you follow these steps:

1. Use the PLOT statement to plot a point at the lower right-hand corner of the figure.
2. Use the DRAWTO statement to draw a line to the upper right-hand corner.
3. Draw a line to the upper left-hand corner.
4. Use the POSITION statement to move the cursor to the lower right-hand corner.
5. Use the POKE statement to place a number, equal to the COLOR statement used for plotting, at memory location 765.
6. Perform XIO #6,0,0, "S".

These statements can be executed in the order specified, or you can reverse the order of steps 1 through 4. XIO works unpredictably if the first five steps are not performed in the proper sequence. XIO has other limitations. First, if any illuminated graphics pixels exist between the left and right sides of the figure to be filled, XIO will stop filling the figure at that point. To understand this, enter the following statement along with the example program at the beginning of this section:

```
15 PLOT 25,25
```

The fill command works from left to right only. If the figure defined started at the lower right-hand corner, the fill command will start at the top of the figure. If it started at the upper right-hand corner, the fill operation will begin at the bottom of the figure. This command is fast but very dumb. However, you can use this command creatively to generate attractive graphics very quickly.

GRAPHICS APPLICATIONS

The programs in Figures 8-2, 8-3, and 8-4 serve as examples to use in programming graphics with BASIC. Figure 8-2 illustrates how graphics mode 0 can still be used to communicate graphics quite effectively. Figure 8-3 is a data entry program which is usable in full-screen graphics mode 1 or 2. Compare this program to the String Input subroutine in Chapter 4, written for graphics mode 0 (Figure 4-37). In Figure 8-4, a regression analysis program written for another computer has several graphics statements added to it in order to maximize its usefulness on the ATARI computer. Not only does this program output the numerical data needed, it adds another dimension to the answer by graphing it in two colors.

As your knowledge of graphics grows, you will find yourself able to create more sophisticated graphics displays. Chapter 9 will acquaint you with some of the advanced graphics capabilities unique to the ATARI computer.

```
 10 REM BAR CHART PROGRAM
 11 REM
 12 REM
 15 REM DATA TO BE USED FOR DISPLAY
 16 REM EACH PAIR IS MONTH, THEN SALES
 17 REM
 20 DATA JAN,800,FEB,820,MAR
 21 DATA 765,APR,779,MAY,610
 22 DATA JUN,650,JUL,780,AUG
 23 DATA 800,SEP,825,OCT,840
 24 DATA NOV,870,DEC,910
 25 REM
 26 REM
 30 GRAPHICS 0:SETCOLOR 2,12,12
 35 SETCOLOR 1,0,0
 40 P=12:REM NUMBER OF MONTHS
 50 LINES=20:COLMS=30
 55 REM
 75 REM
 80 DIM MONTH$(P*3),X$(3),SALES(P)
 87 REM
 88 REM READ IN THE SALES DATA
 89 REM
 90 FOR I=1 TO P
100 READ X$:REM READ MONTH NAME
110 MONTH$(LEN(MONTH$)+1)=X$
120 READ NUM
130 SALES(I)=NUM
138 REM
139 REM FIND HIGHEST, LOWEST SALES
140 IF SALES(I)>=HI THEN HI=SALES(I)
150 IF SALES(I)<=LO OR LO=0 THEN LO=SA
LES(I)
160 NEXT I
167 REM
168 REM FIND PLOTTING SCALE
170 MID=(HI+LO)/2:REM EXPECTED MEAN
180 SCALE=INT(HI-LO)/LINES
190 SPACE=INT(COLMS/P):REM SPACING
191 REM
200 POKE 752,1:PRINT "1983 SALES (000'
S)"
211 REM NOW PLOT THE DATA
220 FOR I=1 TO P
230 GOSUB 1000
240 NEXT I
250 FOR I=1 TO P
260 POSITION 31,I+3
270 M=(I-1)*3+1
280 PRINT MONTH$(M,M+2);" ";SALES(I);
```

(continued)

FIGURE 8-2. Bar chart

```
300 NEXT I
310 GOTO 310
1000 REM PLOT SUBROUTINE
1010 X=I*SPACE
1020 Y=((HI-(MID+SALES(I))/2))/SCALE
1025 COLOR ASC(" "):REM PLOT CHAR.
1030 PLOT X,Y
1040 DRAWTO X,LINES
1050 FOR J=1 TO 3
1060 POSITION X,LINES+J
1070 M=(I-1)*3+J
1080 PRINT MONTH$(M,M);
1090 NEXT J
1100 RETURN
```

FIGURE 8-2. Bar chart (continued)

```
10 LENGTH=7:LINE=9:COL=10
15 GRAPHICS 1
20 POSITION 0,LINE:PRINT #6;"ENTER"
30 GOSUB 1200
40 STOP
1200 REM ****************************
1210 REM * GRAPHICS MODE 1 OR 2 DATA*
1220 REM *         ENTRY MODULE     *
1230 REM * ------------------------ *
1240 REM * LENGTH=MAX ENTRY LENGTH  *
1250 REM * LINE=LINE TO ENTER ON    *
1260 REM * COL=COLUMN TO ENTER ON   *
1270 REM ****************************
1280 DIM D$(LENGTH)
1290 IF KBOPEN=0 THEN OPEN #1,4,0,"K:"
:KBOPEN=1
1300 POSITION COL,LINE
1310 FOR I=1 TO LENGTH
1320 ? #6;"_";
1330 NEXT I
1340 POSITION COL,LINE
1350 REM NOW GET DATA FROM THE KEYBOAR
D
1360 GET #1,X
1370 IF X>=32 AND X<=95 AND LEN(D$)<LE
NGTH THEN D$(LEN(D$)+1)=CHR$(X):? #6;C
HR$(X);:GOTO 1360
1380 IF X<>126 THEN 1460:REM BYPASS IF
 NOT BACKSPACE
1390 IF LEN(D$)<1 THEN 1460:REM REJECT
```

(continued)

FIGURE 8-3. Data entry

```
      BACKSPACE IF NO DATA LEFT
1400  IF LEN(D$)=1 THEN D$=""
1410  IF LEN(D$)>1 THEN D$=D$(1,LEN(D$)
-1)
1420  POSITION COL+LEN(D$),LINE
1430  PRINT #6;"_";
1440  POSITION COL+LEN(D$),LINE
1460  IF X=155 THEN RETURN
1470  GOTO 1360
```

FIGURE 8-3. Data entry (continued)

```
0  REM LINEAR REGRESSION WITH PLOTTING
1  REM ADAPTED FROM SOME COMMON BASIC P
ROGRAMS, ATARI ED.
2  REM GRAPHICS SUBROUTINES ADDED AS FOL
LOWS:
3  REM LINE 800 SETS SCREEN PARAMETERS
4  REM LINE 900 SETS SCALING, LINE 1000
   PERFORMS PLOTTING
5  GRAPHICS 0
10 PRINT "LINEAR REGRESSION"
20 PRINT
30 PRINT "NUMBER OF KNOWN POINTS";
40 INPUT N:DIM XY(N,2)
50 GOSUB 700:REM INITIALIZE DATA
60 GOSUB 800:REM SET SCALING
99 REM - LOOP TO ENTER COORDINATES OF
POINTS
100 FOR I=1 TO N
110 PRINT "X,Y OF POINT ";I;
120 INPUT X,Y:XY(I,1)=X:XY(I,2)=Y
125 GOSUB 850:REM FIND DATA BOUNDS
129 REM - ACCUMULATE INTERMEDIATE SUMS
130 J=J+X
140 K=K+Y
150 L=L+X^2
160 M=M+Y^2
170 R2=R2+X*Y
180 NEXT I
189 REM - COMPUTE CURVE COEFFICIENT
190 B=(N*R2-K*J)/(N*L-J^2)
200 A=(K-B*J)/N
220 PRINT "F(X) = ";A;" + (";B;" * X)"
229 REM - COMPUTE REGRESSION ANALYSIS
230 J=B*(R2-J*K/N)
```

(continued)

FIGURE 8-4. Regression analysis with plotting

```
235 GOSUB 900
240 M=M-K^2/N
250 K=M-J
260 PRINT
270 R2=J/M
280 PRINT "COEFFICIENT OF DETERMINATIO
N (R^2):"
282 PRINT R2
283 PRINT
290 PRINT "COEFFICIENT OF CORRELATION:
"
291 PRINT SQR(R2)
292 PRINT
300 PRINT "STANDARD ERROR OF ESTIMATE:
"
301 PRINT SQR(K/(N-2))
310 PRINT
340 PRINT "PRESS ANY KEY TO SEE GRAPH"

350 OPEN #1,4,0,"K:"
360 GET #1,X9
370 GOSUB 1000
380 GOTO 380
699 REM ------------------INITIALIZE AR
RAY------------------
700 FOR I=1 TO N:XY(I,1)=0:XY(I,2)=0:N
EXT I
710 YMAX=0
720 XMAX=0
750 RETURN
799 REM ------------------SET SCREEN PA
RAMETERS------------------
800 ROWS=79
810 COLMS=159
819 REM 80X160 SCREEN FOR GRAPHICS MOD
E 7
820 RETURN
849 REM ------------------TEST BOUNDAR
Y X AND Y VALUES----------
850 IF XY(I,1)>XMAX THEN XMAX=XY(I,1)
860 IF XY(I,2)>YMAX THEN YMAX=XY(I,2)
890 RETURN
899 REM ------------------SET SCALING F
ACTORS FOR PLOTTING--------
900 YSCALE=YMAX/ROWS
910 XSCALE=XMAX/COLMS:REM SPACING
920 RETURN
999 REM ------------------PLOTTING SUBROUT
INE------------------
1000 GRAPHICS 7
```

(continued)

FIGURE 8-4. Regression analysis with plotting (continued)

```
1010 SETCOLOR 0,12,2:REM X/Y AXIS COLO
R
1019 REM DRAW THE X AND Y AXES
1020 PLOT 0,0:DRAWTO 0,ROWS
1030 DRAWTO COLMS,ROWS
1040 COLOR 2:REM ORANGE POINTS
1050 FOR I=2 TO N
1060 PLOT INT(XY(I,1)/XSCALE),ROWS-INT
(XY(I,2)/YSCALE):NEXT I
1069 REM NOW PLOT THE TREND LINE
1070 COLOR 3
1080 PLOT 0,ROWS-(A/YSCALE):REM PLOT Y
 INTERCEPT
1090 FOR I=1 TO N
1100 Y=A+XY(I,1)*B:DRAWTO XY(I,1)/XSCA
LE,ROWS-(Y/YSCALE)
1110 NEXT I
1120 POSITION 0,0:PRINT "ACTUAL DATA=Y
ELLOW; TREND LINE=BLUE"
1130 PRINT "REGRESSION EQUATION:":PRIN
T "F(X)=";B;"X + ";A
1140 RETURN
```

FIGURE 8-4. Regression analysis with plotting (continued)

9
ADVANCED
GRAPHICS

The previous chapter focused on ATARI computer graphics features available in BASIC. The material in this chapter is more difficult, however, because BASIC is not equipped to handle the more advanced graphics capabilities built into the computer's hardware. The ATARI computer is a highly capable graphics machine, but bear in mind that you can face a great deal of frustration trying to understand and exploit these features. Throughout this chapter you will find programs which will help you become more familiar with otherwise difficult material. Some of the programs are written for easy adaptation to subroutines that you can use in your own programs.

This chapter will explore the following topics:

· Animating graphics displays with *character set animation*
· *Display lists*, which allow you to set up custom graphics displays
· *Player-missile graphics*, fast-moving graphics objects for games and other applications.

These are only a portion of the possibilities open to you as you become a more accomplished ATARI computer user.

CHARACTER SET ANIMATION

The character set is a *bit map;* that is, a set of binary representations of each character the computer displays. The standard character set resides in ROM, starting at address 57344 (E000 hexadecimal). Address 756 (2F6 hexadecimal) is the *Character Address Base Register,* abbreviated CHBAS, which is a pointer, or a *vector* to the character set bit map. Normally, CHBAS points to address 57344 (E000 hexadecimal), but by placing a new address in CHBAS, a new character set of

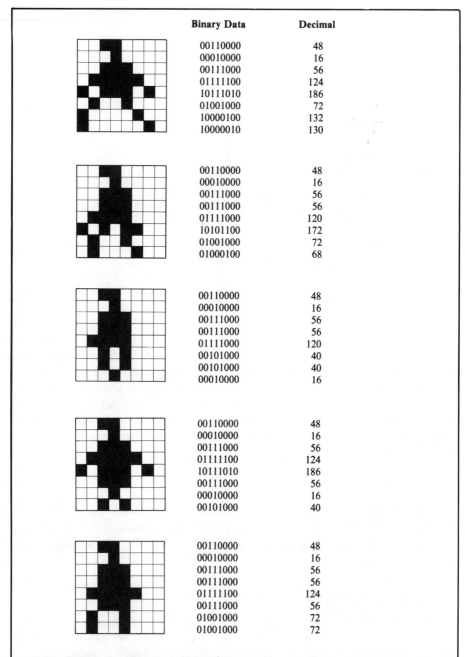

	Binary Data	Decimal
	00110000	48
	00010000	16
	00111000	56
	01111100	124
	10111010	186
	01001000	72
	10000100	132
	10000010	130
	00110000	48
	00010000	16
	00111000	56
	00111000	56
	01111000	120
	10101100	172
	01001000	72
	01000100	68
	00110000	48
	00010000	16
	00111000	56
	00111000	56
	01111000	120
	00101000	40
	00101000	40
	00010000	16
	00110000	48
	00010000	16
	00111000	56
	01111100	124
	10111010	186
	00111000	56
	00010000	16
	00101000	40
	00110000	48
	00010000	16
	00111000	56
	00111000	56
	01111100	124
	00111000	56
	01001000	72
	01001000	72

NOTE: Each character requires eight television scan lines. One memory byte defines which picture elements to illuminate on each scan line.

FIGURE 9-1. Character bit maps

your own design can take the place of standard characters. You can replace the
character set with a font that you like better, or you can invent characters in order to
create your own graphics. Consider the "characters" in Figure 9-1. The five "characters" form a crude, five-step animation sequence.

You can define this animation sequence as characters, place the character definitions in memory with POKE statements, reset the character address base register to
point to the animation characters, and then perform the animation. The following
sample program illustrates simple character set animation:

```
1 REM CHARACTER SET ANIMATION DEMO
5 DIM CHRBASE(5)
10 DATA 48,16,56,124,186,72,132,130
20 DATA 48,16,56,56,120,172,72,68
30 DATA 48,16,56,56,120,40,40,16
40 DATA 48,16,56,124,186,56,16,40
50 DATA 48,16,56,56,124,56,72,72
51 REM -----------CHARACTER SET DEFIN
ED------------
60 GRAPHICS 0
70 SETCOLOR 2,12,8:REM SET GREEN BACKG
ROUND
80 SETCOLOR 1,0,0:REM SET BLACK CHARAC
TERS
90 FOR H=1 TO 5
100 CHRBASE(H)=(PEEK(742)-H*4)*256:REM
 SET CHARACTER BASE ADDRESSES
110 FOR I=CHRBASE(H) TO CHRBASE(H)+7
120 READ X
130 POKE I,X:REM MOVE THE CHARACTER SE
T DATA TO MEMORY
140 NEXT I
150 NEXT H
160 POSITION 0,0
170 LIST :REM PUT TEXT ON THE SCREEN
180 FOR I=1 TO 5
190 POKE 756,INT(CHRBASE(I)/256)
200 IF I=2 THEN GOSUB 9000
210 FOR DLAY=1 TO 15:NEXT DLAY
220 NEXT I
230 GOTO 180
8999 REM ---------MARCHING SOUND SUBR
OUTINE---------
9000 FOR Q=0 TO 3
9010 SOUND Q,255,0,4
9020 NEXT Q
9030 FOR Q=0 TO 3
9040 SOUND Q,0,0,0
9050 NEXT Q
9060 RETURN
```

The DATA statements on lines 10 through 50 define the POKE values for five
characters.

Character Offset

When you design a character set, keep in mind the difference between the ATASCII value for a character and where in the character set table that character's definition lies. In the previous example, the space character definition was replaced in five different character sets; each new character defined would display, rather than a space. By using one POKE statement to cycle between character sets, it is possible to change whole character sets instantly.

Designing your own character set will involve more than creating the bit map it will use. Table 9-1 shows the actual offsets of ATASCII characters from the beginning of the character set table.

Locating the Character Set in Memory

Before placing the new character set anywhere free memory exists, the character set or sets will each have to begin on a 1024-byte boundary when using BASIC graphics mode 0, or on a 512-byte boundary when using BASIC graphics mode 1 or 2. In the previous program example, address 742 contains the high end of user-available memory. In most cases you should be able to set a graphics mode 0 character set table address by subtracting 4 from the current contents of this address. In this case, address 742 provides the *page,* or 256-byte address region, where the table can begin. Subtracting 2 from the contents of address 742 will yield the page where a BASIC graphics mode 1 or mode 2 character set can begin.

USING DISPLAY LISTS

The graphics display on the ATARI computer is controlled by a special microprocessor called *ANTIC.* This chip has its own instruction set, similar in principle to the 6502 microprocessor. The instruction set consists of display instructions, and

TABLE 9-1. Character Definition Offsets*

ATASCII Value	Actual Offset**
0-31	64-95
32-95	0-64
96-127	No change
128-159	192-223
160-223	128-191
224-255	No change

*Add eight times the offset shown to 57344 for the decimal starting location.

**Multiply this offset by 8 to locate the character definition.

by combining a set of display codes you can write a program, called a *display list,* which controls graphics output in ways which are not possible using BASIC.

Actually, the operating system creates display lists whenever a BASIC program executes a GRAPHICS statement. ANTIC executes each instruction in the display list. Based on each instruction, the contents of screen memory are interpreted as text or graphics data. ANTIC then sends video control information to another processor (the CTIA chip). Therefore, ANTIC is a legitimate microprocessor. It has a program counter (called the *instruction register*), a data memory register (called the *memory scan counter*), and several control registers, each of which controls a particular aspect of video output.

ANTIC can switch graphics modes from one display instruction to the next. In other words, it is possible to set up a display with five lines of graphics mode 0 text at the top of the screen, 60 lines of high-resolution graphics under that, and expanded text on the rest of the screen (graphics mode 1 or 2 text, for example). Therefore, you can mix graphics modes in horizontal sections down the screen.

The Display Processing Cycle

The following is a greatly simplified outline of the steps ANTIC performs when executing display list instructions:

1. Fetch the display list instruction and load it into the instruction register.
2. The instruction indicates which graphics mode to use; ANTIC interprets the contents of memory as graphics data or character display data.
3. If the instruction indicates character display data, ANTIC reads a byte of screen memory, looks up the character set bit map, and transfers the bit-mapped character image to the display.
4. If the instruction indicates graphics display data, ANTIC transfers the data directly to the display.
5. Increment the display list counter, which points to the next display list instruction.
6. Increment the memory scan counter by the number of bytes transferred from screen memory to the display.
7. Repeat these steps from the beginning.

ANTIC and Video Output

ANTIC continually reexecutes the display list, fetching instructions, processing the contents of screen memory, outputting video control signals to CTIA (the television signal output controller chip), and jumping back to the beginning of the display list. The television receiver, meanwhile, scans the surface of the screen horizontally with an electron beam, from left to right, as shown in Figure 9-2. When the beam reaches the bottom of the screen, it jumps back to the top line.

Without going into the more complicated aspects of television broadcast theory, each horizontal line on the screen is a *scan line.* The ATARI computer outputs a video signal of 262 scan lines. At the end of every scan line, the television's electron beam turns off and resets to the left-hand side of the next scan line. After the last scan line, the electron beam returns to the upper left-hand corner of the screen, during a latent period called the *vertical blanking interval*. During this interval, the electron beam is shut off until the receiver is ready to scan the screen again.

ANTIC can control each scan line on the television receiver; however, not all 262 lines are visible. Because of a broadcast compensation factor called *overscan*, the actual number of visible scan lines on a television receiver is closer to 200 than 260. In the interest of compatibility with hundreds of different brands of televisions, Atari set a conservative standard of 192 scan lines for its graphics displays under BASIC. Depending on the graphics mode selected by a display list instruction, ANTIC will output from 1 to 16 scan lines of video information for each horizontal line the mode uses.

THE DISPLAY LIST INSTRUCTION SET

The four classes of display list instructions include the following:

- Graphics display
- Character display
- Display blank lines
- Jumps.

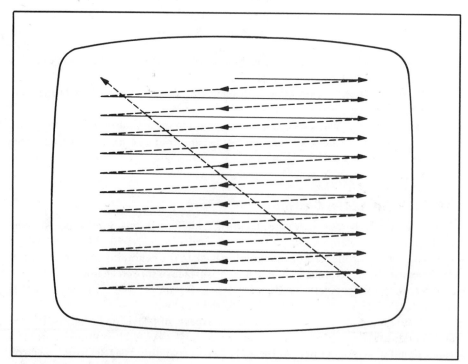

FIGURE 9-2. Television scan lines

In these classes of instructions, the following options are possible:

· Load memory scan counter
· Scroll display
· Call interrupt.

Display List Structure

Every display list should have a structure to it. First, the display list has to compensate for overscan; the blank scan line instructions are designed for this purpose. Second, display lists have to load the memory scan counter with the starting address of memory which contains the actual graphics or text data to display. Third, the display list will contain the actual display instructions, specifying which graphics mode or modes to use. Lastly, a jump instruction directs ANTIC's execution back to the start of the display list. In some cases, the jump instructions are necessary to continue display lists or display memory across address boundaries. This will be discussed in detail shortly.

Blank Scan Line Instructions

Although ANTIC has eight blank scan line instructions (as shown in Table 9-2), the only one that is used frequently is the instruction to send eight blank scan lines (code 112, or 70 hexadecimal) to the screen. This instruction is used at the beginning of the display list.

Load Memory Scan Counter Instruction

The load memory scan counter instruction is not a separate instruction, but rather an option that is available with all display mode instructions. By adding 64 (40 hexadecimal) to an instruction, you effectively set two instructions. First, ANTIC loads the memory scan counter with the address contained in the two bytes immediately following the current instruction. Second, the display mode instruction executes. This option, sometimes called the LMS option, can be added to any display mode instruction.

Jump Instructions

ANTIC uses two types of jump instructions. The first is a simple unconditional jump that reloads the display list counter and continues executing the display list at the new address. The second jump instruction should always be used at the end of a display list. This second jump instruction waits for the start of the vertical blanking interval, a 1400-microsecond pause that the television receiver performs after scanning the last scan line on the screen. During this time, the electron beam used to scan the picture tube returns to the upper left-hand corner of the screen. If ANTIC simply jumps back to the first display list instruction without waiting for the vertical blanking interval, the computer will lose synchronization with the television set, resulting in poor picture quality.

TABLE 9-2. Display List Instructions

	Instruction Code		BASIC Graphics Mode	Horizontal Pixels	Bytes Per Line	Scan Lines Used	Bits Per Pixel	Data/Color Select Mask
	Decimal	Hex						
Output Blank Scan Lines	0	00	-	-	-	1	-	
	16	10	-	-	-	2	-	
	32	20	-	-	-	3	-	
	48	30	-	-	-	4	-	
	64	40	-	-	-	5	-	
	80	50	-	-	-	6	-	
	96	60	-	-	-	7	-	
	112	70	-	-	-	8	-	
Character Modes	2	02	0	40	40	8	8	DDDDDDDD *
	3	03	-	40	40	10	8	
	4	04	-	40	40	8	8	CC CC CC CC †
	5	05	-	40	40	16	8	
	6	06	1	20	20	8	8	CC DDDDDD *†
	7	07	2	20	20	16	8	
Graphics Modes	8	08	3	40	10	8	2	CC †
	9	09	4	80	10	4	1	C C = 0 — Background C = 1 — Register 0
	10	0A	5	80	20	4	2	CC † See codes 6, 7, 8
	11	0B	6	160	20	2	1	See code 9
	12	0C	-	160	20	1	1	
	13	0D	7	160	40	1	2	CC † See codes 6, 7, 8
	14	0E	-	160	40	8	2	
	15	0F	8	320	40	16	1	D *

* D = 0 — Register 2
D = 1 — Register 1

† CC = 00 — Register 0   CC = 10 — Register 2
CC = 01 — Register 1   CC = 11 — Register 3

ANTIC Display Instructions vs. BASIC Graphics Modes

As mentioned earlier, ANTIC does not limit you to one graphics mode per screen. Also, some ANTIC display modes are not available in BASIC. The first three columns of Table 9-2 show ANTIC display instruction codes and their BASIC graphics mode equivalents. Notice that ANTIC modes 3, 4, 5, 12, and 14 are not directly usable with GRAPHICS statements, nor is there a direct correspondence between the display list instruction and its equivalent BASIC graphics mode number. Before going any further, a sample display list might prove helpful as an illustration. Figure 9-3 shows a display list for a screen set up in full-screen BASIC graphics mode 2.

Notice the first three bytes: 112, 112, 112. Look up this instruction code in Table 9-2; this is the display instruction to output eight blank scan lines in the background color. These three instructions take up 24 scan lines at the top of the screen. You should normally place these three instructions at the start of any display list, because they account for television overscan. Although you can omit these three instructions, you might find it impossible to see the top edge of the graphics display as a result.

The next instruction is three bytes long. The first byte, 71 (47 hexadecimal), contains a display instruction with 64 (40 hexadecimal) added to it. This instruction sets up one line of ANTIC mode 7 (BASIC graphics mode 2) text, and also loads the memory scan counter with the two bytes that follow the instruction. Any display mode instruction byte with 64 added to it will signify to ANTIC that the next two bytes after the instruction will be an address to load into the memory scan counter. Therefore, the instruction indicates that ANTIC should read display memory from address 20539 (5038 hexadecimal) — low-order byte first, as usual — unless otherwise directed by another display mode instruction with the load memory scan option.

Byte	Instruction (Decimal Equivalent)	
0	112	These instructions
1	112	set up 24 blank
2	112	scan lines
3	71	BASIC mode 2 instruction with LMS bits set
4	59	(3B) Address where screen memory
5	80	(50) starts (503B hexadecimal)
6	7	
7	7	
8	7	
9	7	
10	7	
11	7	
12	7	
13	7	
14	7	
15	7	
16	7	
17	65	Jump and wait for vertical blank
18	0	(00) Address to jump back to for
19	79	(4F) reexecuting display list

NOTE: These ANTIC instructions set up the equivalent of BASIC graphics mode 2.

FIGURE 9-3. Sample display list program

The next 11 instructions in the display list set the remaining lines of BASIC graphics mode 2 text. After the last ANTIC mode 7 instruction, instruction code 65 precedes yet another two-byte address. This is a jump instruction, followed by the address ANTIC should jump to for its next display list instruction.

This display list is quite simple. Custom display lists are often difficult to create manually, mostly because so many bureaucratic rules apply to their construction and use.

Creating Custom Display Lists

Suppose you wanted to cut a display into horizontal segments, as follows:

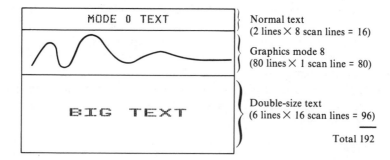

First, you should plan a display screen with 192 scan lines *in addition to* the 24 required blank lines at the top of the display. Looking again at Table 9-2, the column headed "Scan Lines Used" shows how to calculate a proper screen size. The display above will hold exactly 192 scan lines. Make sure you set up the screen properly, because ANTIC will display as many lines as you specify. However, displaying too many lines will often cause an unsightly vertical roll on the video screen.

Display List Placement

Several rules apply to the exact placement of the display list in memory. First, the display list itself cannot cross a 1K address boundary because the display list counter is not a full 16-bit register. Therefore, a portion of a display list that nears a 1K boundary might look like this:

Display List Contents (Decimal)		RAM Address
14		1020
61	Jump one byte past	1021
1 (01)	address 1024	1022
64 (40)		1023
[no instruction]		1024
14		1025

The memory scan counter is not a 16-bit register either. Therefore, a display list will have to contain the LMS option someplace *after* the display list begins in order to reload the memory scan counter before crossing a 4K screen memory boundary. Actually, the memory scan counter has limitations similar to the display list counter. If a display list were constructed with enough display mode lines to cause the memory scan counter to cross a 4K boundary (perhaps in ANTIC mode 15 — BASIC graphics mode 8), the instructions would appear as follows:

Instruction (Decimal)	Instruction Register	Memory Scan Counter	
15	ANTIC mode 15 instruction	16304	Increases by 40 bytes per scan line ANTIC mode 15
79	with LMS mask on	16344	
40	These two bytes	16344	
64	reload the memory	16344	
15	scan counter	16424	Jump instructions do not increment the memory scan counter
.			
.			New scan counter address loaded with the LMS instruction
.			

Other difficulties emerge: where in memory is a good place to put the display list? It is possible to replace the display list set up in memory by the operating system; one excellent area for display lists is page 6 (addresses 1536 to 1791, or 600 to 6FF hexadecimal). ATARI BASIC normally leaves this area untouched.

It is not good practice to overlay existing display lists with new ones unless you have very little memory to experiment with. There should be ample room for a display list on page 6. Once the display list is placed into memory with POKE statements (or using the display list loader program shown in Figure 9-4), the 16-bit address at memory locations 560 and 561 (230 and 231 hexadecimal) must have the new display list starting address placed in it. Next, the DMA control register (SDMCTL) has to be turned off momentarily while the new display list start address is placed at locations 560 and 561 (230 and 231 hexadecimal). Do this by performing a POKE 559,0. Once the new address is in place and the DMA control register is switched back on, the new display list takes effect. This process is shown on lines 150 through 190 of the listing in Figure 9-4.

The Display List Loader Subroutine

Suppose you wanted to set up several different ANTIC modes on one screen. The calculations and planning involved might take hours. The program in Figure 9-4 eliminates virtually all of the tedious details of display list creation; all you have to do is set up a list of DATA statements in the program and identify the starting address you want for the display list. Make sure you have used a GRAPHICS statement to set up the screen mode that takes up the most memory of all the modes you decide to use for the custom screen.

```
1 REM DISPLAY LIST EXAMPLE PROGRAM WIT
H LOADER ROUTINE
10 DIM TOPSCRN(5):REM 'DIM' THIS VARIA
BLE TO NO. OF SEGMENTS + 1
20 GRAPHICS 8:REM SET ASIDE MAXIMUM ME
MORY
30 SETCOLOR 2,0,0
40 DATA 2,3
50 DATA 6,1
60 DATA 7,1
70 DATA 15,144
80 DATA -1,0
87 REM ----THE FIRST FOUR DATA STATEME
NTS
88 REM ----ARE USED BY THE DISPLAY LIS
T
89 REM ----LOADER SUBROUTINE TO SET UP
...
90 REM ----3 LINES OF BASIC MODE 0,
100 REM ---1 LINE  OF BASIC MODE 1,
110 REM ---1 LINE  OF BASIC MODE 2
120 REM ---AND 144 LINES OF BASIC MODE
 8
130 REM ---THE LAST DATA STATEMENT
131 REM ---TERMINATES THE LIST...
140 LST=1536:REM USE THE FREE RAM AREA
, PERFECT FOR DISPLAY LISTS
150 GOSUB 1700:REM SET UP THE DISPLAY
LIST
160 POKE 559,0:REM DISABLE DMA
170 POKE 560,0:REM PLACE NEW DISPLAY L
IST ADDRESS
180 POKE 561,6
190 POKE 559,34:REM RE-ENABLE DMA
200 X=0:GOSUB 430:REM SET SEGMENT 0
210 POKE 87,0:REM MIMIC MODE 0
220 POKE 752,1:REM INHIBIT CURSOR
230 POSITION 15,0
240 PRINT #6;"AN EXAMPLE"
250 POSITION 12,1
260 PRINT #6;"OF WHAT YOU CAN DO"
270 X=1:GOSUB 430:REM SET SEGMENT 1
280 POKE 87,1:REM MIMIC BASIC GRAPHICS
 MODE 1
290 POSITION 0,0
300 PRINT #6;" MIXING SCREEN MODES"
310 X=2:GOSUB 430:REM SET SEGMENT 2
320 POKE 87,2:REM MIMIC BASIC GRAPHICS
 MODE 2
```

(continued)

FIGURE 9-4. Display List Loader program

```
330 POSITION 1,0
340 PRINT #6;"USING DISPLAY LISTS"
350 X=3:GOSUB 430:REM SET LAST SEGMENT
360 POKE 87,8:REM RESET TO GRAPHICS MO
DE 8
370 COLOR 1
380 PLOT 0,0
390 DRAWTO 319,143
400 PLOT 319,0
410 DRAWTO 0,143
420 STOP
430 POKE 88,TOPSCRN(X)-(INT(TOPSCRN(X)
/256)*256)
450 POKE 89,INT(TOPSCRN(X)/256):RETURN
1690 REM ************************
1691 REM * DISPLAY LIST LOADER *
1692 REM * ==================== *
1693 REM * SET LST TO THE START*
1694 REM * ADDRESS OF YOUR OWN *
1695 REM * DISPLAY LIST. THIS  *
1696 REM * ROUTINE CHECKS FOR  *
1697 REM * 1K BOUNDARY ERRORS. *
1698 REM ************************
1700 SEGMENT=1
1710 LOC=LST
1720 TOPSCRN(0)=PEEK(88)+PEEK(89)*256:
REM 'TOP' OF SCREEN' ADDRESS
1730 BOUND=INT((LST/1024+1)*1024):REM
DEFINE NEXT 1K BOUNDARY
1740 BOUND2=INT(TOPSCRN(0)/4096+1)*409
6:REM DEFINE NEXT 4K BOUNDARY
1750 FOR X=LOC TO LOC+2
1760 POKE X,112:REM PLACE THE 'BLANK 8
 LINES' INSTRUCTION AT THE START
1770 LOC=LOC+1
1780 NEXT X
1790 TOPSCRN(SEGMENT)=TOPSCRN(SEGMENT-
1):REM SET ADDRESS FOR THIS SEGMENT
1800 READ MODE,REPEAT
1810 IF MODE<0 THEN OP=65:ADDR=LST:GOS
UB 2030:RETURN
1820 INCR=40:REM SET BYTE INCREMENT FO
R EACH MODE LINE
1830 IF MODE>=6 AND MODE<=12 THEN INCR
=20
1840 IF MODE=8 OR MODE=9 THEN INCR=10
1850 FOR X=1 TO REPEAT
1860 IF LOC<>BOUND-3 THEN 1900:REM CHE
CK FOR 1K BOUNDARY
```

(continued)

FIGURE 9-4. Display List Loader program (continued)

```
1870 OP=1:ADDR=BOUND:GOSUB 2030:REM IN
SERT A JUMP INSTRUCTION
1880 LOC=LOC+1:BOUND=BOUND+1023
1890 GOTO 1900
1900 POKE LOC,MODE:REM POKE THE MODE B
YTE
1910 REM FIRST MODE LINE MUST HAVE THE
 LMS BYTE SET
1920 IF (SEGMENT<>1 OR X<>1) AND (BOUN
D2-TOPSCRN(SEGMENT)>=INCR) THEN 1980
1930 REM SET THE LMS BYTE
1940 OP=MODE+64
1950 ADDR=TOPSCRN(SEGMENT)
1960 IF BOUND2-TOPSCRN(SEGMENT)<INCR T
HEN BOUND2=BOUND2+4096:ADDR=ADDR+INCR
1970 GOSUB 2030
1980 LOC=LOC+1:REM INCREMENT DISPLAY L
IST BYTE POINTER
1990 TOPSCRN(SEGMENT)=TOPSCRN(SEGMENT)
+INCR
2000 NEXT X
2010 SEGMENT=SEGMENT+1
2020 GOTO 1790:REM READ THE NEXT SEGME
NT
2030 POKE LOC,OP:REM STORE JUMP CODE
2040 LOC=LOC+1
2050 POKE LOC,ADDR-(INT(ADDR/256)*256)
2060 LOC=LOC+1
2070 POKE LOC,INT(ADDR/256)
2080 RETURN
```

FIGURE 9-4. Display List Loader program (continued)

The DATA statement format consists of the ANTIC display mode (not BASIC graphics mode) number to select, followed by the number of display lines to set up. Therefore, on lines 40 through 80, three lines of BASIC graphics mode 0 text are specified, one line of BASIC graphics modes 0 and 2, and 144 lines of BASIC graphics mode 8. These display lines add up to 192 scan lines, just the right number for the graphics display. At line 140, the variable LST is set to address 1536 (600 hexadecimal), and addresses 560 and 561 (230 and 231 hexadecimal) contain the low-order and high-order bytes of this address.

Lines 200, 270, 310, and 350 set the variable X to a segment of the screen; that is, segment 0 is the first screen segment defined in a DATA statement. Therefore, by setting X and performing a GOSUB 430, the program resolves the screen addressing errors that would otherwise occur. Try running the example program. Alternatively, you can just use lines 430 to 450 and 1700 to 2080 of the program as subroutines in your own programs.

DISPLAY LIST INTERRUPTS

The interrupt feature is a highly advanced and somewhat exotic feature of ANTIC display lists. At the end of each display mode line, ANTIC fetches the next display instruction. If the display list interrupt *mask* — a predetermined overlay of bits on a byte — is set, ANTIC will turn control over to a special routine which can be as long as 18 machine cycles for the 6502 microprocessor. You can't accomplish much in 18 cycles, but there is often enough time to change a color register value, or reset some register before returning from the interrupt to display list execution. The steps involved are shown below.

Before executing a display list routine with interrupts, do these steps:

1. Load the interrupt routine into some safe area of memory (the 255-byte area starting at address 1536 (600 hexadecimal) is ideal).
2. Modify certain bytes of the display list to execute display list interrupts.
3. Enable display list interrupts with the statement POKE 54286,192.
4. Use the POKE statement to change addresses 512 and 513 (200 and 201 hexadecimal) to the address of the first assembly language instruction to execute in the display list interrupt routine. (Remember that the display list interrupt itself is the mask on the display list instruction; the display list interrupt routine is not executed by ANTIC, but rather by the 6502 microprocessor.)

The interrupt routine itself should do these steps:

1. Save all registers to be used by pushing them onto the 6502 stack.
2. Perform the interrupt routine. Keep it short, and make sure your total routine does not exceed 18 cycles. Interrupt routines longer than 18 cycles will cause ANTIC to broadcast bad video data.
3. Restore the registers you saved by pulling them off the stack and replacing them in their appropriate registers.
4. Perform an assembly language RTI (return from interrupt) instruction to resume display list processing.

Every time the interrupt service routine executes, these steps are required. Otherwise, critical 6502 register values will be destroyed (and possibly your program as well).

Example of a Display List Interrupt

The following example will be especially useful if you have no previous exposure to assembly language programming. Suppose you wanted to have the top half of a graphics mode 0 screen appear as it normally does, but instead of turning the text on the entire screen upside down (as you can do with a POKE 755,3), you wish to turn the *lower* half of the screen upside down.

A display list interrupt mask placed on the display mode instruction halfway down the screen will allow display list processing to stop long enough to set the vertical reflect bit at address 54273 (C141 hexadecimal) to 4. This value does not change until the vertical blanking interval starts. Once ANTIC jumps to the top of the display list again, the vertical reflect bit is automatically reset.

Here is the assembly language listing, placed at the start of memory page 6:

```
0000           10     *=    $600
0600 48        20     PHA             ;SAVE ACCUMULATOR ON STACK
0601 A904      30     LDA   #4
0603 8D01D4    40     STA   $D401     ;SET VERTICAL REFLECT BIT
0606 68        50     PLA             ;RESTORE REGISTER'S PREVIOUS VALUE
0607 40        60     RTI             ;GO BACK TO DISPLAY LIST PROCESSING
```

The following program is the BASIC program used to change the display list. By changing the display instruction for the 12th line of the display, the top and bottom halves of the display have opposite orientations. Try this program; the DATA statements contain the display list interrupt routine:

```
5 GRAPHICS 0
10 DLIST=PEEK(560)+PEEK(561)*256:REM F
IND THE DISPLAY LIST START ADDRESS
20 POKE DLIST+16,130:REM REPLACE LINE
4 OF THE DISPLAY WITH DLI INSTR.
30 FOR I=1536 TO 1543:REM POKE THE DLI
 SERVICE ROUTINE STARTING AT $600
35 DATA 72,169,4,141,1,212,104,64
40 READ X
50 POKE I,X
60 NEXT I
65 POKE 512,0
66 POKE 513,6:REM POKE THE DLI VECTOR
ADDRESS
70 POKE 54286,192:REM ALLOW DLI EXECUT
ION
80 FOR I=0 TO 23
90 POSITION 0,I:? "RIGHTSIDE UP";
100 NEXT I
```

For a detailed look at addresses you can change with display list interrupts, consult the *ATARI Personal Computer System Hardware Manual,* available from Atari, Inc. It is beyond the scope of this chapter to explore all of the possibilities available to you with this interrupt capability. If your interest lies in this area, you can at least see the general structure of the display list interrupt routine in order to apply it effectively.

PLAYER-MISSILE GRAPHICS

It is hard to take a term like "player-missile graphics" and treat it fairly, because it connotes arcade games and other capabilities generally useless for practical applications. Players and missiles are special graphics objects designed for rapid movement on the graphics screen. There are up to four player objects available, each with a corresponding missile. Some simple examples of players are shown in Figure 9-5.

Each player object has a limit on its height, or *vertical definition,* and its width, or *horizontal definition.* Each player object may have a maximum height of 256 vertical lines, which are limited to a width of eight bits. A player can extend from the top to the bottom of the screen. Missiles are movable graphics objects, similar to players but with only two bits of horizontal definition.

Player objects can indeed be used for games, but they can just as easily be used as stationary graphics objects. For instance, a data entry program could use a player object as a cursor, or all four players could be used as borders on the screen. There are three main reasons for using player-missile graphics: independence, rapid movement, and availability of more colors.

Player-missile graphics are totally independent of other ATARI computer graphics. The graphics modes normally available on the ATARI computer are called *playfield* graphics. PRINT, PLOT, DRAWTO, and other BASIC keywords perform playfield graphics. Player-missile graphics, on the other hand, are fully-defined shapes such as those shown in Figure 9-5. Think of the player-missile graphics capability as an overlay on the screen. This overlay has boundaries which exceed the size of the playfield graphics borders and have no relation to the current graphics mode. In addition, player-missile graphics images can appear to be in front of or behind the playfield graphics on the screen, thus allowing you to write programs with the illusion of three dimensions.

Players can move on the screen rapidly, without adversely affecting computing speed. Consider the first player illustration (Figure 9-5), and how you would define it using standard BASIC PLOT and DRAWTO statements. Moving this object around on the screen involves erasing the object from its previous location, calculat-

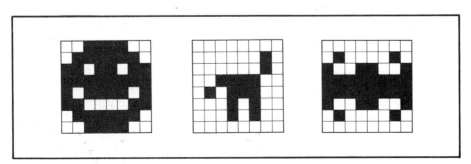

FIGURE 9-5. Sample player bit maps

ing the new screen coordinates for it, and then redrawing the object at the new location. This takes up an enormous amount of computing power, because the 6502 microprocessor is doing most of the work. Player-missile graphics use a technique called *direct memory access,* or DMA, through the ANTIC chip. DMA frees the 6502 microprocessor for other tasks; therefore, less 6502 time is used to move these graphics objects around. Player-missile graphics bypass the 6502 microprocessor, whereas playfield graphics manipulation has to go through the operating system and, therefore, the 6502 microprocessor.

Player-missile graphics add more colors to the graphics display. Each player object has its own color register, and these color registers are independent of those used for playfield graphics. No matter what the playfield graphics mode is, there will always be four extra color registers available for player objects. With player-missile graphics, BASIC graphics mode 0 can have five colors on the screen. In other playfield graphics modes, as many as nine colors can display on the screen at one time.

It is difficult at first to understand player-missile graphics because BASIC only has provisions in the language for playfield graphics. The organization and use of player-missile graphics are quite different and much more involved because they must be used at the machine level. This makes your programs harder to write. However, this section contains subroutines that perform most of the functions necessary to use player-missile graphics with BASIC.

Player-Missile Graphics Memory Organization

If you want to use player-missile graphics in your program, you need to set up a table containing the definition of each player object. The best place for this table is at the high end of RAM, where it will be least likely to interfere with other memory which is already allocated. There is a restriction on where you can locate the table, however. Player-missile graphics memory can be located on any 1024- or 2048-byte boundary in memory, depending on the vertical resolution of the player.

Defining the Player

Each player is eight bits wide. You have to create a bit map of the object drawn. Each part of the grid you filled in will have a binary value of 1, and each unfilled square in the grid will have a value of 0. Therefore, the player's bit-mapped image is a series of one-byte numbers which will go into the player-missile graphics table. The program in Figure 9-6 will help you design a player image. Plug a joystick into port 1 and run the program. Notice that the borders on either side of the screen confine you to a horizontal definition of eight picture cells. When you have finished designing the player, press the RETURN key and the player image will display at close to its actual size. If you want to make more changes to the player image, press the space bar. When the flashing cursor reappears, you can once again use the joystick to alter the player image. By pressing RETURN after looking at the actual-size player image, you will see the player bit map defined on the screen, along with another look at the player you created.

```
5 REM CREATE PLAYER/MISSILE IMAGE
10 DIM CURSOR(2),PLAYER(23,7)
20 GRAPHICS 3
30 SETCOLOR 2,0,0:REM BLACK TEXT WINDO
W
40 PRINT "PLUG JOYSTICK IN PORT 1;PRES
S TRIGGER"
50 GOSUB 610:PRINT
60 PRINT "USE TRIGGER TO DRAW OR ERASE
 PLAYER."
70 PRINT "PRESS <RETURN> WHEN FINISHED
 DRAWING."
80 GOSUB 670:REM SET UP THE SCREEN
90 IF PEEK(764)=12 THEN GOTO 290:REM E
XIT IF <RET> WAS HIT
100 GOSUB 770:REM READ THE JOYSTICK
110 IF (UP AND (CURSOR(2)<=0)) OR (DOW
N AND (CURSOR(2)>=23)) THEN GOTO 90
120 IF (LEF AND (CURSOR(1)<=0)) OR (RI
GT AND (CURSOR(1)>=7)) THEN GOTO 90
130 COLOR 1
140 IF PLAYER(CURSOR(2),CURSOR(1))=0 T
HEN COLOR 0
150 PLOT CURSOR(1)+16,CURSOR(2):REM RE
-POSITION CURSOR
160 CURSOR(2)=CURSOR(2)-UP
170 CURSOR(2)=CURSOR(2)+DOWN
180 CURSOR(1)=CURSOR(1)-LEF
190 CURSOR(1)=CURSOR(1)+RIGT
200 COLOR 2
210 PLOT CURSOR(1)+16,CURSOR(2)
220 X1=STRIG(0):REM IF TRIGGER PRESSED
, TURN PLAYER BIT ON OR OFF
230 IF X1=1 THEN 90
240 PLAYER(CURSOR(2),CURSOR(1))=1-SGN(
PLAYER(CURSOR(2),CURSOR(1)))
250 COLOR 3
260 IF PLAYER(CURSOR(2),CURSOR(1))=0 T
HEN COLOR 0
270 PLOT CURSOR(1)+16,CURSOR(2)
280 GOTO 90
290 GRAPHICS 7:REM RE-DISPLAY THE PLAY
ER IN HIGHER RESOLUTION
300 POKE 764,0:REM CLEAR THE KEYBOARD
310 X2=2:X3=0
320 X1=76:Y1=20
330 GOSUB 910:REM DISPLAY THE PLAYER
350 PRINT "<RETURN> TO END;<SPACE> TO
GO BACK TO PLAYER"
360 IF PEEK(764)=12 THEN GOTO 440:REM
```

(continued)

FIGURE 9-6. Player-Missile Image program

```
                 IF <RET> HIT, DISPLAY PLAYER VALUES
             370 IF PEEK(764)<>33 THEN 360:REM IF N
             OT <SPACE>, KEEP LOOKING FOR KEYPRESS
             380 GRAPHICS 3+16
             390 GOSUB 740:REM RESET THE SCREEN
             400 X1=16:Y1=0
             410 X2=1:X3=0
             420 GOSUB 910
             430 GOTO 90
             440 GRAPHICS 0:REM DISPLAY PLAYER BIT
             MAP AND PLAYER IMAGE
             450 FOR Y=0 TO 23
             460 POSITION 0,Y
             470 PRINT "BYTE ";Y;
             480 X1=0
             490 FOR X=0 TO 7
             500 X2=PLAYER(Y,7-X)
             510 IF X2=0 THEN 530
             520 X1=X1+INT((X2*2)^X+0.01):REM ADD E
             ACH BIT IN ORDER OF SIGNIFICANCE
             530 NEXT X
             540 POSITION 12,Y:PRINT X1;
             550 NEXT Y
             560 X1=24:Y1=0
             570 X2=ASC(" "):X3=ASC(" ")
             580 POKE 752,1
             590 GOSUB 910
             600 GOTO 590
             610 REM ----------------WAIT FOR TRIGG
             ER/EMIT BEEP-------
             620 IF STRIG(0)=1 THEN 620
             630 SOUND 0,50,10,4
             640 FOR DLAY=1 TO 10:NEXT DLAY
             650 SOUND 0,0,0,0
             660 RETURN
             669 REM -------REM INITIALIZE VARIABLE
             S AND SET SCREEN--
             670 CURSOR(1)=0
             680 CURSOR(2)=0
             690 FOR R=0 TO 23
             700 FOR C=0 TO 7
             710 PLAYER(R,C)=0
             720 NEXT C
             730 NEXT R
             740 COLOR 3
             750 PLOT 15,0:DRAWTO 15,23:PLOT 24,0:D
             RAWTO 24,23
             760 GRAPHICS 3+48:RETURN
             769 REM --------ROUTINE TO READ JOYSTI
             CK SETTING--------
```

(continued)

FIGURE 9-6. Player-Missile Image program (continued)

```
770 REM READ JOYSTICK ROUTINE
780 RDNG=STICK(0)
790 DOWN=0
800 UP=0
810 LEF=0
820 RIGT=0
830 IF RDNG=15 THEN RETURN
840 IF RDNG=14 THEN UP=1
850 IF RDNG=7 THEN RIGT=1
860 IF RDNG=13 THEN DOWN=1
870 IF RDNG=11 THEN LEF=1
880 GOSUB 630:REM BEEP THE SPEAKER
890 RETURN
900 REM ----------------DISPLAY THE PL
AYER ----------------
910 FOR Y=0 TO 23
920 FOR X=0 TO 7
930 COLOR X2
940 IF PLAYER(Y,X)=0 THEN COLOR X3
950 PLOT X+X1,Y+Y1
960 NEXT X
970 NEXT Y
980 RETURN
```

FIGURE 9-6. Player-Missile Image program (continued)

Now that you have the player object in a coded form, you can repeat the process for as many as four player objects.

Player Vertical Definition

Player objects can be defined in 128 bytes or 256 bytes. A player object defined in 128 bytes is projected on the display as shown in Figure 9-7. Each byte of this player object takes up two television scan lines. Players defined in 256 bytes will only use one scan line for each byte of the player object, as shown in Figure 9-8.

Note that the player objects differ in their projected sizes on the display. Therefore, players defined in 256 bytes have twice the vertical resolution of 128-byte player objects, and appear less "blocky" on the screen. You should decide whether you need this extra resolution. Because all players must be defined with the same length, this decision can save you a lot of memory. Player objects defined in 128 bytes are called *double-resolution* players, and players defined in 256 bytes are called *single-resolution* players.

The Player-Missile Graphics Table

The player-missile graphics table must start at an address evenly divisible by 1024 for double-resolution players, or 2048 for single-resolution players. The BASIC immediate-mode statement ?PEEK(106)*256 will display the last usable memory address on your computer. In order to properly locate the table in memory, the nearest 1024- or 2048-byte boundary address must be found.

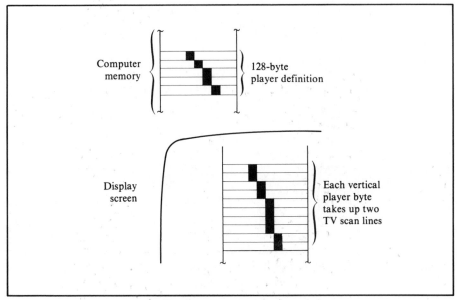

FIGURE 9-7. Displaying double-resolution players

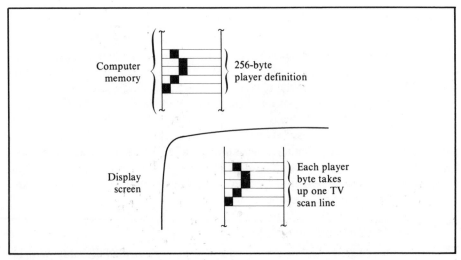

FIGURE 9-8. Displaying single-resolution players

Laying Out the Table

The player-missile graphics table layout is shown in Figure 9-9. The table is fixed in length. No matter how few players you define, the table will always be 1024 bytes or 2048 bytes long in order to fit all four players and missiles. The first section of the table is vacant; this area of the table is available for other uses, such as storing alternate player object definitions or display lists. After this vacant area are five other areas where the missiles and players are defined.

The missile definition area will hold four missile objects, each two bits wide. As with players, missiles can also be defined with double or single resolution.

The next four areas are all of equal size, and each area holds one player object. Figure 9-9 shows the *offset* from the beginning of the player-missile graphics table for each player and missile. You will use these offsets to move the objects on the screen.

The next step is to reset address 106 (6A hexadecimal) with the address of the player-missile graphics table. This step is necessary because the operating system will use all available memory; the highest available addresses are always used to set up the playfield graphics memory area. This conflict of memory use will adversely affect playfield graphics, player-missile graphics, or both. At worst, your computer will lock up.

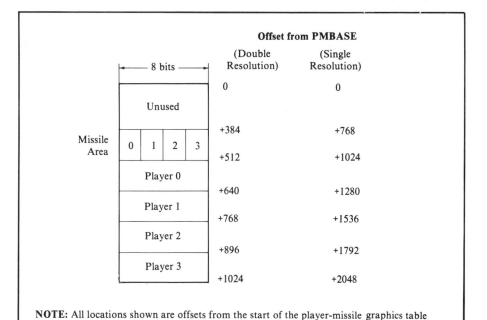

NOTE: All locations shown are offsets from the start of the player-missile graphics table base address (PMBASE).

FIGURE 9-9. Player-missile graphics table layout

Calculating the Start Address

The ATARI computer will not resolve memory conflicts automatically; you will have to do that yourself. Although you already know that the player-missile graphics table has to reside on a 1K or 2K address boundary, the playfield display has restrictions as well. Locating the player-missile graphics table at the highest part of memory will cause addressing problems for playfield graphics. For example, some areas of the display may not be usable, or PLOT statements will not place graphics points at the expected row and column.

If playfield graphics screen memory is allocated normally, you can locate the player-missile graphics table just before it without any memory conflicts. However, if a program changes graphics modes, it is possible to start yet another conflict which would eradicate the player-missile graphics table entirely. This problem would occur if a program switched from GRAPHICS 0 to GRAPHICS 7, for instance. In this case, the table would be erased entirely. The sensible thing to do is to look at the GRAPHICS statements in your program; find the statement that allocates the most RAM and plan the location of the player-missile graphics table accordingly. To calculate the player-missile graphics starting address, perform the following steps:

1. Use the PEEK function to determine the contents of address 560.
2. Use the PEEK function to determine the contents of address 561 and multiply the result by 256.
3. Add the results of steps 1 and 2.
4. Divide the result of step 3 by 1024 if using double-resolution graphics, or by 2048 if using single-resolution graphics.
5. Truncate the remainder, subtract 1, and multiply it by 1024 (double-resolution) or 2048 (single-resolution).

The result of step 5 is the starting address for the player-missile graphics table. In a BASIC program,

```
1000   REM SINGLE = 1 MEANS SINGLE RESOLUTION
1010   PMBASE = PEEK(560) + PEEK(561) * 256
1020   IF SINGLE THEN DIVISOR = 2048
1030   IF (NOT SINGLE) THEN DIVISOR = 1024
1040   PMBASE = INT(PMBASE/ DIVISOR - 1) * DIVISOR
```

Protecting The Player-Missile Graphics Table

Once you determine the ending address of the player-missile graphics table, use a POKE statement to put this two-byte value in locations 14 and 15, with the low-order byte first, as always. The operating system interprets the address contained at locations 14 and 15 as an absolute lower limit for playfield graphics memory allocation. Therefore, setting this address is critical to protecting the player-missile graphics table from destruction whenever a new GRAPHICS statement executes.

Placing Players and Missiles in the Table

Now that memory has been safely set aside for the player-missile graphics table, player and missile bit maps can go into it. The first step is to clear the areas of the table that will actually hold data. Area 1 of the player-missile graphics table is unused. There is no need to clear it, nor is there any need to clear areas of the table which will not contain active bit maps.

Controlling the Player-Missile Graphics Display

There are several *control registers* which, as the name implies, control the actual player-missile graphics display:

- Player-Missile base register
- DMA and graphics control registers
- Width registers
- Color registers
- Horizontal position registers
- Priority control register.

Some of these registers need to be set only once, when setting up player-missile graphics, but others will require constant resetting, depending on how your program will manipulate players and missiles. Atari technical manuals abbreviate the names of these registers. The abbreviations are listed in the section headings which follow.

The Player-Missile Base Register (PMBASE)

Memory locations 54279 and 54280 (D407 and D408 hexadecimal) will contain the starting address of the player-missile graphics table. Since the address has to be on a 1K or 2K boundary, location 54279 must always be 0. Only the page number (high-order byte of the address) is significant.

The Graphics Control Register (GRACTL)

The graphics control register enables direct memory access (DMA) for player-missile graphics, along with the DMA control register explained below. GRACTL is located at address 53277 (D01D hexadecimal), and you can select to enable player DMA only (with a POKE 53277,2), missile DMA only (POKE 53277,1), or combined player-missile DMA (POKE 53277,3).

The DMA Control Register (DMACTL)

Setting the DMA control register will switch player-missile graphics on or off. If the GRACTL register is not set to enable player-missile DMA, you will only see playfield graphics. DMACTL and GRACTL must both be set in order to display players and missiles. DMA acts as a parasite on the 6502 microprocessor, in that it steals machine cycles from the 6502. If you want to stop displaying player-missile

TABLE 9-3. Player-Missile DMA Control Register Values

Value to POKE	Setting Which Results
4	Enable Missile DMA only
8	Enable Player DMA only
12	Enable Player-Missile DMA
Add 16	Single-line resolution (double-line resolution = default)

graphics objects, reset the DMACTL register. This will give the microprocessor some of its speed back.

Use the POKE statement to put a value from those shown in Table 9-3 in address 559 (22F hexadecimal) in order to set the DMACTL register.

Player Width Registers (SIZEP0 – SIZEP3)

Four eight-bit registers, at addresses 53256 through 53259 (D008 through D00B hexadecimal), control the horizontal size of the four players. By changing values at these addresses, you can double or quadruple the width of player objects (but not their height). If player size will not change in your program, the players are left at normal size.

Address 53256 controls the first player's width, address 53257 controls the second player's width, and so on. When writing programs to move the player objects horizontally, the width register setting will affect that player's horizontal position register setting. (See the "Player Horizontal Position Registers" section later in this chapter.) To set a player to double width, set its width register to 1; for quadruple width, set the register to 3. A value of 0 or 2 will set the player to its normal width. As an example, the statement to set the third player to double width would be POKE 53258,1.

Missile Width Register (SIZEM)

One register, at address 53260 (D00C hexadecimal), controls the size of all missiles. The same settings as shown above for the player width registers apply to the missile width register: 0 or 2 for normal width, 1 for double, and 3 for quadruple width.

Player-Missile Color Registers (COLPM0 – COLPM3)

The four player-missile color registers are each one byte long, starting at address 704 (2C0 hexadecimal) for the first player and ending at 707 (2C3 hexadecimal) for the fourth player. Both the player and its associated missile are set to the same color. Table 9-4 shows the values to place in these registers with the POKE statement in order to set the color and luminance combination you want.

TABLE 9-4. Playfield and Player-Missile Color Register Values

	Color Value*	
	Decimal	Hex
Grey	0	0
Gold	16	10
Orange	32	20
Red	48	30
Pink	64	40
Violet	80	50
Purple	96	60
Blue	112	70
Blue	128	80
Light Blue	144	90
Turquoise	160	A0
Blue-Green	176	B0
Green	192	C0
Yellow-Green	208	D0
Orange-Green	224	E0
Light Orange	240	F0

*Add an even number, 2 to 14, to set luminance; 0 = no luminance, 14 = maximum luminance.

Player Horizontal Position Registers (HPOSP0 – HPOSP3)

The player horizontal position registers are used to relocate player objects on the horizontal axis. By simply changing register contents with POKE statements, you can move the player object to the horizontal position you specify. Depending on the width register setting for the player object, you can position a player at the left side of the screen, then set a new horizontal position value which causes the object to immediately reappear elsewhere on the screen. The minimum value of each position register is 0, and the maximum value is 227. Depending on the player size specified in DMACTL, these register settings will range between 40 as the leftmost visible position and 190 as the rightmost position.

These registers are *write-only* registers; that is, you will not be able to use PEEK to determine the location of a player. Therefore, your program will have to maintain variables which contain, among other things, the current horizontal position of player and missile objects on the screen. Later you will see an example of the horizontal position registers in use. Player 0's horizontal position register resides at address 53248 (D000 hexadecimal); player 1 at 53249; player 2 at 53250, and player 3 at 53251.

Missile Horizontal Position Registers (HPOSM0 – HPOSM3)

Starting at address 53252 (D004 hexadecimal), four missile position registers receive values used to reposition missiles on the horizontal axis.

PLAYER-MISSILE GRAPHICS EXAMPLES

This section will present various tricks you can do with player-missile graphics. These programs all use the subroutines introduced earlier in this chapter to set up the player-missile graphics table in memory, initialize and load it, and control the movement of the objects. However, in the previous section, the problem of moving players and missiles up and down was never covered. We will now address this problem.

Moving Players and Missiles Vertically

Player and missile objects move vertically by moving their bit maps higher in memory (to place them lower on the screen), or lower in memory (to place them higher on the screen). This process is very slow in BASIC. Using an assembly language subroutine to perform the movement is much faster. The assembly language program below will move player or missile objects' bit maps byte by byte.

```
0000          10              *=$0600        ;BEGIN ROUTINE HERE
00CB          20 LOCATION     =$00CB         ;PLAYER LOCATION
00CD          30 LENGTH       =$00CD         ;LENGTH OF PLAYER
0600 68       40 MOVEUP       PLA            ;PULL ARGUMENT OFF STACK
0601 A001     50              LDY #$01       ;INITIALIZE INDEX
0603 B1CB     60 UPMORE       LDA (LOCATION),Y
0605 88       70              DEY            ;TRANSFER ONE BYTE UP
0606 91CB     80              STA (LOCATION),Y
0608 C4CD     90              CPY LENGTH     ;FINISHED MOVING PLAYER?
060A C8       0100            INY            ;ADD 2 TO REGISTER
060B C8       0110            INY
060C 90F5     0120            BCC UPMORE     ;KEEP MOVING IF NOT DONE
060E C6CB     0130            DEC LOCATION
0610 60       0140            RTS            ;OTHERWISE RETURN
0611 68       0150 MOVEDOWN   PLA            ;ALSO PULL HERE
0612 A4CD     0160            LDY LENGTH
0614 B1CB     0170 DOWNMORE   LDA (LOCATION),Y
0616 C8       0180            INY            ;MOVE A BYTE DOWN
0617 91CB     0190            STA (LOCATION),Y
0619 88       0200            DEY
061A 88       0210            DEY            ;DECREMENT THE INDEX
061B 10F7     0220            BPL DOWNMORE   ;CONTINUE IF MORE LEFT
061D E6CB     0230            INC LOCATION
061F 60       0240            RTS
```

You can incorporate this subroutine into a BASIC program easily enough by running the following program:

```
4000 REM *******************************
4001 REM * P/M GRAPHICS MOVE ROUTINE*
4002 REM *===========================*
4003 REM * RUN THIS PROGRAM TO LOAD *
4004 REM * THE MOVE ROUTINE INTO RAM*
4005 REM * STARTING AT ADDR 1536.    *
4006 REM *******************************
4010 DATA 104,160,1,177,203,136,145
4020 DATA 203,196,205,200,200,144,245
4030 DATA 198,203,96,104,164,205,177
4040 DATA 203,200,145,203,136,136
```

```
4050 DATA 16,247,230,203,96
4060 FOR I=1536 TO 1567
4070 READ J
4080 POKE I,J
4090 NEXT I
```

All ATARI computers have a reserved area of RAM (locations 1536 through 1791) which will safely store subroutines such as this. Once loaded, the subroutine will remain there until you either turn off the computer or decide to re-use the area for something else. The player-missile graphics examples that follow assume that the assembly language subroutine listed above is already loaded into memory before you run them.

Simple Player Movement

In the example shown below, only one player will be used, and the movement will be on the horizontal axis. The DATA statement at line 30 defines the player object. Once its area is cleared, the player image moves into RAM. The player-missile base register and the graphics and DMA control registers are activated for double-resolution players at standard width. The player's color — blue in this case — is set by placing the composite color and luminance in player 0's color register with a POKE statement on line 130. The player object moves from left to right, by increasing the value of player 0's horizontal position register (lines 190 to 210). Make the following changes to this program. First, experiment with the player's width setting. Then, alter the FOR-NEXT loop to allow movement from right to left. You can also experiment with different color register values. Move on to the next section after trying some variations.

```
10 GRAPHICS 0
20 SETCOLOR 2,0,0
25 REM PLAYER IMAGE DEFINED IN DATA ST
ATEMENTS BELOW
30 DATA 24,60,255,36,66
40 Y=64:REM VERTICAL SETTING FOR PLAYE
R
50 A=PEEK(106)-8:REM FIND END OF MEMOR
Y
60 POKE 54279,A:REM POKE START ADDRESS
 TO PMBASE
70 START=256*A+512:REM START ADDRESS F
OR PLAYER 0 IMAGE
80 POKE 559,46:REM SET DMACTL
90 POKE 53277,3:REM SET GRACTL
100 FOR I=START TO START+127
110 POKE I,0:REM CLEAR PLAYER 0 AREA
120 NEXT I
130 POKE 704,136:REM SET PLAYER 0 COLO
R REGISTER
140 POKE 53248,0:REM SET PLAYER HORIZ.
 POSITION TO 0
```

```
150 FOR I=START+Y TO START+4+Y
160 READ X:REM PUT PLAYER IMAGE IN MEM
ORY
170 POKE I,X
180 NEXT I
190 FOR POS=0 TO 228
200 POKE 53248,POS:REM MOVE PLAYER 0 1
 COLOR CYCLE TO THE RIGHT
210 NEXT POS
220 GOTO 190
```

Vertical and Horizontal Player Movement

The example program in Figure 9-10 shows more elaborate movement than the previous example. The exception here is that the machine language subroutine for vertical player movement is used. Notice also that each FOR-NEXT loop moves the player object a bit differently in order to give some illusion of three dimensions.

Increased Player Resolution

The limitations of player images prevent players from being very useful for some applications. The example shown in Figure 9-11 uses a player with 32 bits of resolution, as defined in Figure 9-12.

As you can see when running the program, BASIC moves the flying saucer across the screen in a jerky manner. This is caused by both the slowness of the language and the concatentation of the four player images.

Using the Priority Registers

A relatively easy example of setting priority between playfield and player-missile graphics can be seen in Figure 9-13. The priority register can have several settings:

1 gives all players priority over playfield.
2 gives players 0 and 1 priority over all playfield registers, plus players 2 and 3.
4 gives playfield priority over players.
8 gives playfield color registers 0 and 1 priority over all players and playfield registers 2 and 3.

```
10 GRAPHICS 1+16
20 SETCOLOR 0,0,12
30 SETCOLOR 2,0,0
40 DATA 153,189,255,189,153
50 GOSUB 360:REM DISPLAY A STAR FIELD
FIRST
```

(continued)

FIGURE 9-10. Player movement

```
60 Y=1
70 A=PEEK(106)-8
80 POKE 106,A
90 POKE 54279,A:REM POKE PMBASE ADDRES
S
100 START=256*A
110 POKE 559,62:REM SINGLE-LINE RESOLU
TION PLAYER DMA
120 POKE 53277,3:REM ENABLE PLAYER DMA
130 POKE 53256,0
140 FOR I=START+1024 TO START+1280
150 POKE I,0:REM CLEAR THE P/M GRAPHIC
S AREA
160 NEXT I
170 PSTART=START+1024+Y
180 POKE 204,INT(PSTART/256):REM POKE
HIGH-ORDER PART OF PLAYER ADDRESS
190 POKE 203,PSTART-(PEEK(204)*256)-1:
REM POKE LOW-ORDER PLAYER ADDRESS
200 POKE 205,5:REM PLAYER LENGTH
210 RESTORE
220 FOR I=PSTART TO PSTART+4
230 READ A
240 POKE I,A
250 NEXT I
260 FOR I=50 TO 120:GOSUB 320:NEXT I
270 POKE 53256,1:REM DOUBLE SIZE
280 FOR I=118 TO 167 STEP 2:GOSUB 320:
GOSUB 320:NEXT I
290 POKE 53256,3:REM QUAD SIZE
300 FOR I=166 TO 250 STEP 2:GOSUB 320:
NEXT I
310 GOTO 130
320 A=USR(1553):POKE 53248,I:COLR=COLR
+1
330 IF COLR>255 THEN COLR=0
340 POKE 704,COLR
350 RETURN
360 FOR M=1 TO 22
370 X=RND(0)*20
380 Y=RND(1)*24
390 POSITION INT(X),INT(Y):? #6;".":RE
M PLOT RANDOM 'STAR' POINTS
400 X=RND(0)*20
410 Y=RND(1)*24
420 POSITION INT(X),INT(Y):PRINT #6;".
"
430 NEXT M
440 RETURN
```

FIGURE 9-10. Player movement (continued)

```
1 REM PLAYER-MISSILE 32-BIT RESOLUTION
2 REM -------------PLAYER/MISSILE BIT MASKS-------------
3 SETCOLOR 2,0,0
10 DATA 0,0,0,0,3,15,119,254,255,63,31,7,4,14,14
20 DATA 1,2,2,31,240,255,255,255,239,254,255,255,240,15,0
30 DATA 128,64,64,248,15,255,255,255,247,127,255,255,15,
         240,0
40 Y=80
45 DATA 0,0,0,0,192,240,236,127,255,252,248,224,32,112,
50 A=PEEK(106)-8:REM FIND END OF MEMORY
60 POKE 54279,A:REM POKE START ADDRESS TO PMBASE
70 START=256*A:REM START ADDRESS FOR PLAYER/MISSILE
          GRAPHICS TABLE
80 POKE 559,46:REM SET DMACTL
90 POKE 53277,3:REM SET GRACTL
100 FOR I=START+512 TO START+1024
110 POKE I,0
120 NEXT I
130 FOR I=704 TO 708
140 POKE I,188
150 NEXT I:REM SET PLAYERS TO AQUA
160 FOR H=0 TO 3
170 POKE 53248+H,X+H*8:REM SET HORIZONTAL POSITIONS
180 POKE 53256+H,1:REM SET PLAYER SIZE
190 FOR I=START+512+Y+(128*H) TO START+526+Y+(128*H)
200 READ X
210 POKE I,X
220 NEXT I
225 NEXT H
230 FOR D=0 TO 228 STEP 4
240 FOR P=0 TO 3
250 POS=D+16*P
260 IF POS<228 THEN POKE 53248+P,POS
270 NEXT P
280 NEXT D
290 GOTO 230
```

FIGURE 9-11. Player with 32 bits of resolution

In the example presented, the player object appears to be in front of the yellow portion of the screen as it heads toward the middle of the picture. Before returning to the left edge of the screen, the priority register is reset to give the yellow playfield priority over the player, thus giving the impression that the player is going behind the yellow playfield.

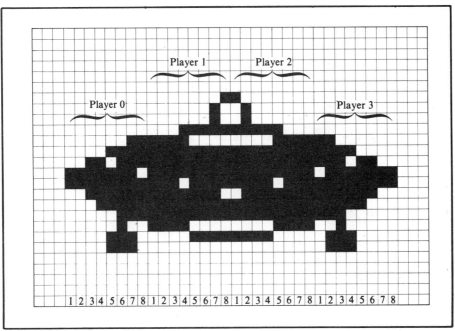

FIGURE 9-12. Combining players

```
5 COLOR 3
10 GRAPHICS 7+16
20 DATA 60,126,219,255,189,195,126,60
30 SETCOLOR 2,0,0
40 PLOT 125,95:REM CREATE A PLAYFIELD
OBJECT
50 DRAWTO 80,0
60 DRAWTO 79,0
70 POSITION 45,95
80 POKE 765,1:REM ORANGE TRIANGLE
85 XIO 18,#6,0,0,"S:"
90 A=PEEK(106)-24:REM FIND END OF MEMO
RY
100 POKE 54279,A:REM POKE START ADDRES
S TO PMBASE
110 START=256*A:REM START ADDRESS FOR
PLAYER/MISSILE GRAPHICS TABLE
120 POKE 559,46:REM SET DMACTL
130 POKE 53277,3:REM SET GRACTL
140 FOR J=START+512 TO START+1024
                                  (continued)
```

FIGURE 9-13. Setting playfield and player-missile graphics priority

```
150 POKE J,0:REM CLEAR PLAYER/MISSILE
AREA
160 NEXT J
170 FOR I=START+580 TO START+587
180 READ X
190 POKE I,X:REM PUT THE PLAYER IN THE
 TABLE
200 NEXT I
230 POKE 623,1:REM GIVE PRIORITY TO PL
AYERS
240 POKE 704,86:REM PURPLE PLAYER
250 FOR K=60 TO 180
260 POKE 53248,K
270 NEXT K
280 POKE 623,4:REM GIVE PLAYFIELD PRIO
RITY
290 FOR J=180 TO 60 STEP -1
300 POKE 53248,J
310 NEXT J
320 GOTO 230
```

FIGURE 9-13. Setting playfield and player-missile graphics priority (continued)

10
SOUND

The ATARI computer can generate sounds and music in two distinctly different ways. It can activate its own built-in speaker, and it can drive the television speaker.

THE BUILT-IN SPEAKER

The ATARI computer clicks its built-in speaker every time you press a key. It also sounds the speaker to cue program recorder operation. The speaker is controlled by memory location 53279. Storing a 0 there sends a pulse to the speaker. Pulsing the speaker several times in rapid succession generates a tone. The faster the pulsing, the higher the tone. The following program demonstrates this:

```
10 PRINT "TONE VALUE (1=HI, 10=LO)"
20 INPUT T
29 REM Loop establishes duration
30 FOR J=1 TO 15
40 POKE 53279,0:REM Speaker
49 REM Delay loop affects tone
50 FOR K=1 TO T
60 NEXT K
70 NEXT J
80 GOTO 10
```

BASIC doesn't execute fast enough to create any high notes on the built-in speaker, but it can be useful on some occasions. For example, you could modify the Display Error Message subroutine (Figure 4-17) so that it sounds the speaker in addition to displaying an error message.

TELEVISION SPEAKER SOUND

The ATARI computer can make a wide variety of sound effects and music come out of the television speaker. Such sounds can be simple or complex: they can have one, two, three, or four voices. Each voice can vary in pitch by more than three octaves. It can vary from a pure tone to a highly distorted one. Each voice has its own loudness level, independent of the television volume setting.

The SOUND Statement

In BASIC, SOUND statements control the TV speaker. Turn up the volume control on your television and try this example:

```
SOUND 0,121,10,8
```

You should hear the note middle C. The numbers tell the computer to generate a pure, undistorted middle C of moderate loudness. Every SOUND statement must have four numbers (Figure 10-1). The first number determines which voice will be used. The second number sets the pitch. The third number regulates distortion. The fourth number controls the loudness. You can use a numeric variable or expression in place of any number.

The sound continues until you turn it off. To do that, set the pitch, distortion, and loudness to 0, like this:

```
SOUND 0,0,0,0
```

Voice

The ATARI computer has four independent voices. This means it can make as many as four different sounds simultaneously. The different voices blend together in the television speaker, like voices in a chorus. The first number in the SOUND statement determines which voice the SOUND statement will affect. Voices are numbered 0 through 3. You must use a separate SOUND statement to control each voice. This sequence of immediate mode statements generates a C chord:

```
SOUND 0,121,10,8

READY
SOUND 1,96,10,8

READY
SOUND 2,81,10,8

READY
SOUND 3,60,10,8

READY
```

A simple FOR-NEXT loop will turn off all sound:

```
FOR J=0 TO 3:SOUND J,0,0,0:NEXT J
```

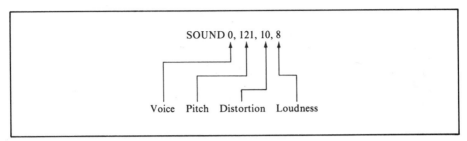

FIGURE 10-1. SOUND statement parameters

Pitch

The second number in a SOUND statement sets the pitch. It can be between 0 and 255. The ATARI computer can produce all notes — sharps, flats, and naturals — from one octave below middle C to two octaves above it (Figure 10-2). It can produce a good many other tones as well. For example, there are six intermediate values between middle C and the tone one-half step below it, B. Such tones do not correspond exactly to any of the notes on the chromatic scale, so they will be of no use for programming music. You can use them for sound effects, however. Run the following program:

```
10 FOR J=-255 TO 255
20 SOUND 0,ABS(J),10,8
30 PRINT "PITCH VALUE: ";ABS(J)
40 FOR K=1 TO 50:NEXT K
50 NEXT J
60 SOUND 0,0,0,0
```

The program above shows off the ATARI computer's complete tonal range. As you listen, notice that the low notes seem to last longer than the high notes. You can see that the program holds each tone for the same length of time (line 30). But the tone produced by a pitch value of 255 is very nearly the same as that produced by pitch values of 254, 253, and even 252. These low tones run together, sounding like one sustained note. In contrast, there is a marked difference betweeen pitch values 11 and 10. Each change in pitch value is definitely discernible. The program glides smoothly through the low tones but ends up hopping choppily through the high tones.

Distortion

The ATARI computer produces both pure and distorted tones. The third number in a SOUND statement regulates distortion. It can be any value between 0 and 15. Distortion values of 10 and 14 generate pure tones. Other even-numbered distortion values (0, 2, 4, 6, 8, 10, and 12) introduce different amounts of noise into the pure tone. The amount of noise depends on both the distortion value and the pitch value.

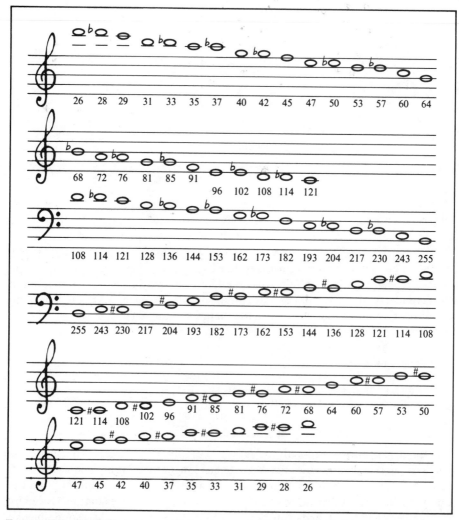

FIGURE 10-2. SOUND statement pitch values and the chromatic scale

Some combinations of distortion and pitch combine to produce an undistorted secondary tone with harmonic overtones. The secondary tone is different in pitch from the pure tone. The following statement produces a pure C#:

```
SOUND 0,230,10,8
```

Change the distortion value to 12, as follows:

```
SOUND 0,230,12,8
```

A much lower secondary tone results. In fact, this secondary tone is lower than the pure tone you get with an undistorted pitch of 255:

```
SOUND 0,255,10,8
```

Unfortunately, a secondary tone does not have a reliable pitch of its own. This program demonstrates:

```
9 REM Start secondary tone
10 SOUND 0,230,12,8
20 FOR K=1 TO 50:NEXT K
29 REM Turn off sound
30 SOUND 0,0,0,0
39 REM Wait random time
40 FOR K=1 TO 50*RND(0):NEXT K
49 REM Repeat; use BREAK to end
50 GOTO 10
```

In the program above, the variable pause that occurs while the sound is off (line 40) randomly changes the pitch of the secondary tone (line 10).

Some combinations of pitch and distortion blank each other out. The result is silence. Try this statement, for example:

```
SOUND 0,123,6,0
```

Generally speaking, odd-numbered distortion values (1, 3, 5, and so on) silence the specified voice. But if the voice is off, a SOUND statement with an odd-numbered distortion value causes a single click, then silence. Turning the voice off then causes another click. Here is a program that demonstrates how odd-numbered distortion values work:

```
10 FOR J=1 TO 20
20 SOUND 0,0,1,8
30 SOUND 0,0,0,0
40 FOR K=1 TO 100:NEXT K
50 NEXT J
```

Table 10-1 summarizes sound characteristics for each distortion factor. The following program will help you explore them in more detail:

```
10 FOR P=0 TO 255
20 FOR D=0 TO 15
30 PRINT "PITCH=";P,"DIST=";D
40 SOUND 0,P,D,10
50 FOR K=1 TO 40:NEXT K
60 NEXT D
70 NEXT P
```

Loudness

The fourth number in a SOUND statement controls the loudness of the specified voice. It lets the program determine the audio level. It also allows the program to mix a multiple-voice sound, with each voice at a different loudness level. You can control the overall volume with the television volume control; if you turn it all the way down, you will hear no sound.

The loudness value can be between 0 (silent) and 15 (loudest). Loudness change is

TABLE 10-1. SOUND Statement Distortion Characteristics

Distortion Value*	Silences**	Secondary Tones †	Comments
14	None	None	Pure tone
12	Many	Many	High tones less distorted
10	None	None	Pure tone
8	None	None	Static (low tones) to white noise (high tones)
6	Few	Few	No change below pitch 200
4	Few	Few	Static (low tones) to throbbing (high tones)
2	Few	Few	Same sounds as 6
0	Few	None	Blend of 4 and 8

  * Any odd-numbered distortion value generates a single click when it turns on a voice. Turning off the voice may generate another click.

** Some combinations of distortion and pitch values generate silence.

  † Some combinations of distortion and pitch values generate a tone with harmonic overtones.

linear: 8 produces a sound half as loud as 15, the value 12 is halfway between 8 and 15 in loudness, and so on. This program demonstrates the loudness range:

```
10 FOR J=-15 TO 15
20 SOUND 0,121,10,ABS(J)
30 NEXT J
40 SOUND 0,0,0,0
```

Pitch affects apparent loudness. For a combination of reasons, the highest-pitched sounds seem quieter. Listen to the output of this program:

```
10 FOR J=-50 TO 50
20 SOUND 0,ABS(J),10,8
30 FOR K=1 TO 50:NEXT K
40 NEXT J
50 SOUND 0,0,0,0
```

Statements that Turn Off Sound

As you have seen, a SOUND statement with 0 volume will turn off a single voice. Some ATARI BASIC statements automatically turn off all four voices. When the computer executes an END statement, it shuts off all four voices as it ends the program. END also works in immediate mode. The RUN statement also turns off all sound. A sound you start in immediate mode will not continue when you run a programmed mode program, unless the program recreates it. Other statements that turn off all sound include CLOAD, CSAVE, DOS, and NEW. Pressing the SYSTEM RESET key turns off all sound voices, but pressing the BREAK key does not.

Duration

A characteristic of sound that is just as important as any other is its duration. The SOUND statement has no duration parameter. There is no way the SOUND statement alone can determine how long a sound remains on. It remains on until the computer executes a statement that turns it off. Clearly this will not happen as long as the computer is busy executing other statements.

One way to control sound duration is to interweave sound statements with other program statements. A constantly changing sound results. The following program generates random tones while it outputs a number:

```
10 DIM N$(40)
20 PRINT CHR$(125):REM Clr screen
29 REM Restart in case of error
30 TRAP 20
40 PRINT "ENTER A NUMBER"
50 INPUT N
70 N$=STR$(N)
80 FOR J=1 TO LEN(N$)
90 SOUND 0,64*RND(0)+16,10,10
100 PRINT N$(J,J);
110 SOUND 1,32*RND(0)+8,10,10
120 NEXT J
130 SOUND 0,0,0,0:SOUND 1,0,0,0
140 GOTO 20
```

Suppose you want a sound to last a specific length of time, then turn off. Your program must turn the sound on, pause the right amount of time, then turn the sound off. You can use SOUND statements to turn the sound on and off, but how do you make the program pause? The easiest way is with a FOR-NEXT loop. Several example programs have used this technique. Here is another:

```
10 SOUND 0,47,10,10
20 FOR K=1 TO 100:NEXT K
30 SOUND 0,64,10,10
40 FOR K=1 TO 100:NEXT K
50 GOTO 10
```

Experiments show that in ATARI BASIC, empty FOR-NEXT loops iterate about 445 times per second. Therefore, a loop that goes from 1 to 100, like the one on line 40 above, causes a pause of just under one-quarter second. However, this timing data is not guaranteed. Your ATARI computer may be slightly different. You can conduct your own experiment to determine the speed of empty FOR-NEXT loops on your computer. You will need a clock or watch with a second hand. Type in this program:

```
10 FOR J=1 TO 35000:NEXT J
```

Now type the command RUN. As you press the RETURN key to start the program, note the position of the second hand. After 30 seconds have elapsed, press the BREAK key. Type this immediate mode statement to calculate the number of empty

FOR-NEXT loop iterations your computer executes every second:
```
?INT(J/30)
```

Sample Sound Effects

The ATARI computer can create many realistic sound effects. All it takes is the
right combination of voices, pitch, distortion, volume, and timing. Finding the right
combination for a particular sound can be difficult. There are no formulas that
apply; you will have to experiment. Experience will reduce the number of experiments it takes to come up with a particular sound. As you learn how to create
different sounds, it will become easier to come up with new ones. Sometimes in the
pursuit of one effect you will discover a sound that would be perfect for another
effect. Make notes of such discoveries; they will expedite future experiments. To get
started, try the programs in Figure 10-3. Experiment with them and see if you can
improve them.

```
10 ? "DURATION";:INPUT D
99 REM === THINK ===
100 FOR J=1 TO D*10
110 SOUND 0,RND(0)*80+50,10,3
120 NEXT J
200 END


99 REM === BALL ===
100 FOR J=25 TO 1 STEP -1
110 FOR K=1 TO 5
120 SOUND 0,125,14,6
130 NEXT K
140 SOUND 0,0,0,0
150 FOR K=1 TO J*5:NEXT K
160 NEXT J
200 END


99 REM === DRAIN ===
100 V=64
110 FOR J=1 TO 30
120 SOUND 0,V-J,10,10
130 SOUND 1,F+J,10;10
140 FOR K=1 TO 30-J:NEXT K
150 SOUND 0,0,0,0
160 SOUND 1,0,0,0
170 FOR K=1 TO 10:NEXT K
180 NEXT J
200 END
```

(continued)

FIGURE 10-3. Sample sound effects program listings

```
99 REM === FILL ===
100 FOR J=140 TO 90 STEP -1
110 SOUND 0,J,10,10
120 FOR K=1 TO 20:NEXT K
130 SOUND 0,0,0,0
140 FOR K=1 TO 10:NEXT K
150 NEXT J
200 END


99 REM === FALLING OBJECT ===
100 FOR J=30 TO 200 STEP 3
110 SOUND 0,J,10,J/25
120 FOR K=1 TO J/10:NEXT K
130 NEXT J
140 SOUND 0,20,0,14
150 SOUND 1,255,10,15
160 FOR K=1 TO 100:NEXT K
200 END


99 REM === EXPLOSION ===
100 FOR J=-10 TO 10
110 SOUND 0,200,4,10-ABS(J)
120 SOUND 1,255,4,10-ABS(J)
130 SOUND 2,225,4,10-ABS(J)
140 SOUND 3,150,4,10-ABS(J)
160 FOR K=1 TO 200:NEXT K
170 NEXT J
200 END


10 PRINT "HOW MANY SHOTS";
20 INPUT D
99 REM === GUNSHOTS ===
100 FOR J=1 TO D
110 SOUND 0,5,0,15
120 FOR K=1 TO 28:NEXT K
130 SOUND 0,0,0,0
140 FOR K=1 TO RND(0)*200:NEXT K
150 NEXT J
200 END


10 PRINT "DURATION";:INPUT D
99 REM === JACKHAMMER ===
```

(continued)

FIGURE 10-3. Sample sound effects program listings (continued)

```
100 FOR J=1 TO D
110 SOUND 0,130+RND(0)*2,2,15
120 FOR K=1 TO 440+RND(0)*100:NEXT K
130 FOR K=1 TO 440+RND(0)*100:NEXT K
140 NEXT J
200 END


10 PRINT "DURATION";:INPUT D
99 REM === SIREN ===
100 FOR J=1 TO D
110 FOR K=-160 TO 160 STEP 2
120 SOUND 0,ABS(K)+95,10,8
130 FOR L=1 TO 10:NEXT L
140 NEXT K
150 NEXT J
200 END


10 PRINT "DURATION";:INPUT D
99 REM === HI-LO SIREN ===
100 FOR J=1 TO D
110 SOUND 0,47,10,8
120 FOR L=1 TO 100:NEXT L
130 SOUND 0,64,10,8
140 FOR L=1 TO 100:NEXT L
150 NEXT J
200 END


10 PRINT "DURATION";:INPUT D
99 REM === HORN ===
100 SOUND 0,121,10,8
110 SOUND 1,128,10,8
120 SOUND 2,8,2,2
130 FOR J=1 TO D*70:NEXT J
200 END


10 PRINT "DURATION";:INPUT D
99 REM === BUZZER ===
100 SOUND 0,42,2,15
110 FOR J=1 TO D*200:NEXT J
200 END


10 PRINT "DURATION";:INPUT D
99 REM === PHONE ===
100 FOR J=1 TO D
110 SOUND 0,86,10,5
```

(continued)

FIGURE 10-3. Sample sound effects program listings (continued)

```
120 SOUND 1,88,10,5
130 SOUND 2,40,2,4
140 FOR K=1 TO 500:NEXT K
150 FOR K=0 TO 3:SOUND K,0,0,0:NEXT K
160 IF J=D THEN GOTO 180
170 FOR K=1 TO 750:NEXT K
180 NEXT J
200 END


10 PRINT "DURATION";:INPUT D
99 REM === BIRDS ===
100 FOR J=1 TO D*5
110 FOR K=3 TO 10
120 SOUND 0,K,10,8
130 NEXT K:NEXT J
200 END


10 PRINT "DURATION";:INPUT D
99 REM === SEA ===
100 FOR L=1 TO D
110 FOR J=0 TO 45
120 SOUND 0,J,8,4
130 FOR K=1 TO 20+RND(0)*10:NEXT K
140 NEXT J
150 FOR J=45 TO 0 STEP -1
160 SOUND 0,J,8,4
170 FOR K=1 TO 50+RND(0)*30:NEXT K
180 NEXT J:FOR K=1 TO 300+RND(0)*300:N
EXT K
190 NEXT L
200 END


99 REM === TAKEOFF ===
100 FOR L=1 TO D
110 FOR J=0 TO 45
120 SOUND 0,J,8,J/3
140 NEXT J
150 FOR J=45 TO 0 STEP -1
160 SOUND 0,J,8,J/6+6
170 FOR K=1 TO 70+J*3:NEXT K
180 NEXT J
190 NEXT L
200 END
```

FIGURE 10-3. Sample sound effects program listings (continued)

11
COMPENDIUM OF BASIC STATEMENTS AND FUNCTIONS

This chapter describes the syntax for all ATARI BASIC statements and functions. Statements are described first, listed in alphabetical order. Then functions are described, also in alphabetical order. Included in the section on statements are descriptions of two single-keystroke commands, BREAK and SYSTEM RESET. These two differ from the rest of the BASIC statements, but are included here because they affect program execution as much as any statement.

This chapter serves as a reference for all statements and functions. The examples in this chapter show you some of the ways you can correctly use each BASIC statement. They by no means exhaust all possibilities. For more examples, many in working programs, refer to earlier chapters.

IMMEDIATE AND PROGRAMMED MODES

All statements can be executed in immediate or programmed mode. In some cases only one mode is practical.

BASIC VERSIONS

The features and attributes of all statements and functions described in this chapter are those of standard ATARI BASIC (also known as Sheperdson BASIC). Other versions of BASIC, such as Microsoft BASIC and BASIC A+, are not specifically covered.

NOMENCLATURE AND FORMAT CONVENTIONS

A standard scheme is used for presenting the general form of each statement and function. Listed below are the punctuation, capitalization, and other mechanical conventions used.

{ }	Braces indicate a choice of items. One of the enclosed items must be present. Braces do not appear in actual statements.
[ ]	Anything enclosed by brackets is optional. Brackets do not appear in actual statements.
. . .	Ellipses mean that the preceding item can be repeated. Ellipses do not appear in actual statements.
Line numbers	A beginning line number is implied for all programmed mode statements.
Other punctuation	All other punctuation marks — commas, semicolons, quotation marks, and parentheses — must appear as shown.
UPPER-CASE	Upper-case words and letters must appear exactly as shown.
italics	Italicized items are used generically, not literally. They show where a certain type of item is required. Definitions of the generic terms describe the type of item required. Wherever an italicized item appears, you must substitute an exact wording or value, according to the generic term definitions listed below and in the statement descriptions.

Generic Term Definitions

The following italicized abbreviations are used generically in statement and function definitions. Any italicized terms not listed here are peculiar to the statement in which they appear. They are defined in the text that describes that statement.

chan	Channel number for input or output; a numeric expression (*numexpr*) where no functions are allowed, and which must evaluate exactly to 1, 2, 3, 4, 5, 6, or 7. Do not use fractional values.
col	Display screen column number; a numeric expression which has a minimum value of 0 and a maximum value of 39 in graphics modes 0 and 3, 19 in modes 1 and 2, 79 in modes 4 and 5, 159 in modes 6 and 7, and 319 in mode 8. Non-integer values are rounded to the nearest integer.
const	Any numeric or string constant. Quotation marks are treated as part of a string constant's value, not as delimiters.
dev	A string constant or variable that specifies an input or output device. Meaningful values are "C:", "E:", "K:", "P:", "R[n]:", "S:", and "D[n]:*filename* [.*ext*]".
D[*n*]	A disk drive number which must be D, D1, D2, D3, or D4.
expr	Any numeric, relational, or Boolean constant, variable, function, or expression; any valid combination thereof.
ext	Any disk file name extension, one, two, or three characters long. Valid characters are letters A through Z and digits 0 through 9.

filename	Any disk file name, one to eight characters long. Valid characters are letters A through Z and digits 0 through 9. The first character must be a letter.
indev	A string constant or variable that specifies an input device. Meaningful values are "C:", "E:", "K:", "R[n]:", "S:", and "D[n]:*filename* [.*ext*]".
linexpr	A numeric expression that evaluates to an existing BASIC program line number. Non-integer values are rounded to the nearest integer.
memadr	A numeric expression, variable, or constant that evaluates to any memory address. Memory addresses may range from 0 to 65535.
numexpr	Any numeric constant, variable, function, or any valid combination thereof.
numvar	Any numeric variable name (not including arrays).
outdev	A string constant or variable that specifies an output device. Meaningful values are "C:", "E:", "P:", "R[n]:", "S:", and "D[n]:*filename*[.*ext*]".
row	Low-resolution graphics row number; a numeric expression which has a minimum value of 0 and a maximum value of 23 in graphics modes 0, 1, and 3; of 11 in mode 2; of 47 in modes 4 and 5; of 95 in modes 6 and 7; and of 191 in mode 8.
strvar	Any string variable name, not including substrings.
string	Any string constant, variable, substring, or function that returns a string value.
var	Any numeric or string variable name, not including substrings or arrays.

Abbreviating Keywords

ATARI BASIC lets you abbreviate many keywords in order to save typing effort. For example, you can type SE. and ATARI BASIC will automatically extend it to SETCOLOR.

In this chapter, abbreviations that are permitted are listed at the beginning of the discussion of each statement. You can use the abbreviated keyword wherever the fully spelled-out keyword is allowed.

STATEMENTS

This section describes all the ATARI BASIC statements. The descriptions include the general format of each statement, as well as one or more examples of the statement in use.

BREAK (BREAK)

Halts program execution and returns the computer to immediate mode.

Format: BREAK
Example: BREAK

Pressing the BREAK key interrupts every BASIC statement, although there is sometimes a brief wait while the computer finishes an input or output operation. Occasionally, the BREAK key will not interrupt the LPRINT statement. In this case, only the SYSTEM RESET key will interrupt the output.

When the interrupt occurs, the computer switches to immediate mode and graphics mode 0, displaying the message **STOPPED AT LINE** *line,* where *line* is replaced by the line number at which the program halted. You can continue program execution with the CONT statement. Execution will resume at the start of the next program line higher than *line.* If you type any other statement before CONT, the programmed mode program will not resume.

In immediate mode, the BREAK key cancels the current logical line. The computer skips to the start of the next logical line.

The BREAK key never turns off any sound voices nor closes any open input/output channels.

BYE (B.)

Switches from BASIC to memo pad mode.

Format: BYE
Examples: BYE
              B.

Does not affect memory used to store the BASIC program or variables. After executing BYE, you can return to BASIC by pressing the SYSTEM RESET key. Any BASIC program lines that were present are still there. The variable name table is unchanged. If before leaving BASIC you booted the disk operating system, the RS-232 serial device handler, or both, they are still booted when you return to BASIC.

CLOAD (CLOA.)

Operates the program recorder in playback mode, transferring a previously recorded program from a cassette to the computer memory.

Format: CLOAD
Examples: CLOAD
              CLOA.

First, the CLOAD statement opens channel 7 for input from the program recorder. If channel 7 is already open to another device, an error occurs. When the error occurs, the channel is closed automatically and you can use CLOAD successfully.

When the computer executes a CLOAD statement, it sounds its speaker once. This signals you to put the right tape in the program recorder, use the FAST FORWARD and REWIND levers to position the tape to the correct spot, then depress the PLAY lever. Finally, press any key on the keyboard (except BREAK). If the volume on the television set is turned up, you will hear several seconds of silence followed by one or more short bursts of sound from the television speaker. These sounds indicate that the program is loading. The sound bursts cease when the loading finishes.

The CLOAD statement can only load a tokenized BASIC program. Therefore, it works with programs recorded by the CSAVE or SAVE statements. It does not work with programs recorded by the LIST statement, which records BASIC text in ATASCII code.

During the loading process, the CLOAD statement also replaces the resident variable name table with the one for the incoming program.

CLOAD Invokes NEW

Using the CLOAD statement automatically invokes the NEW statement. Even before the computer sounds its speaker, it clears all program lines and variables out of memory. If you press the BREAK key when you hear the prompting tone, the CLOAD operation halts, but any program that was in memory will be gone. None of the new program will be present.

When the CLOAD operation ceases (successful or not, or complete or not), the computer shuts off all sound voices and closes all input/output channels except channel 0. Note that it closes channel 6, which many of the graphics statements use.

Halting CLOAD

You can halt the CLOAD operation at any time by pressing the SYSTEM RESET key. The BREAK key also works, except during the first 20 seconds after the CLOAD operation starts, while the program recorder reads past the leader tone that prefixes every program.

CLOSE (CL.)

Unassigns an input/output channel.

> *Format:*   CLOSE #*chan*
> *Examples:*   CLOSE #1
>   CL. #UNITA

You must close a channel that is open for input, output, or both before you can reassign it to a different device with an OPEN statement. Closing a channel that is not open has no effect. No error occurs.

If channel *chan* is open for output to the program recorder or to a disk file, there may be a partial data record in the computer memory, waiting to be output. Normally, the computer only outputs whole records to these two devices. Closing the channel forces output of any partial record, followed by an end-of-file record.

The END statement closes all open channels except channel 0, which BASIC uses for standard communication with the keyboard and display screen.

CLR

Assigns 0 to all numeric variables. Undimensions numeric array variables and string variables. Resets the pointer to the beginning of the list of DATA statement values.

> *Format:*   CLR
> *Example:*   CLR

CLR does not remove variables from the variable name table (VNT); only the

NEW statement does that. Thus, CLR does not make room for new and different variable names in a program that has run afoul of the 128-name limit imposed by the VNT.

The CLR statement does cancel the length attributes of string variables and numeric arrays. Therefore, after executing a CLR statement, you can redimension numeric arrays and string variables as available memory permits.

COLOR (C.)

Determines which color register the next PLOT or DRAWTO statement will use. In graphics modes 0, 1, and 2, also determines which character the next PLOT or DRAWTO statement will display.

Format: COLOR *numexpr*

Examples: COLOR 1
             C. ASC("Z")
             COLOR C1+ADJ/3

The value of *numexpr* specifies which color register will be used by the PLOT or DRAWTO statement. The value must be between 0 and 65535. Non-integer values are rounded to the nearest integer.

There are five color registers, numbered 0 through 4. Table 11-1 correlates values of *numexpr* with color register numbers in each graphics mode. It shows, for example, that a COLOR 2 statement in graphics modes 3, 5, and 7 selects color register 1.

Assigning Colors

Each color register specifies the hue and luminance of a color. The SETCOLOR statement assigns specific hue and luminance attributes to a color register. The color

TABLE 11-1. Color Register Numbering and Availability

SETCOLOR Register Number	COLOR *numexpr* Value in Graphics Modes*		
	3, 5, 7	4, 6	8**
0	1	1	-
1	2	-	1
2	3	-	0
3	-	-	-
4	0	0	-

* In modes 0, 1, and 2, *numexpr* determines the character that will display; see Tables 11-3 and 11-4.

** In mode 8, COLOR chooses luminance only. Color register 2 always controls hue.

TABLE 11-2. Color Register Default Values
            (SETCOLOR register numbers)

Color Register Number	Hue	Luminance	Color
0	2	8	Orange
1	12	10	Green
2	9	4	Dark blue
3	4	6	Red
4	0	0	Black

registers default to the values shown in Table 11-2 whenever you turn on the computer, press the SYSTEM RESET key, or execute a DOS or GRAPHICS statement.

COLOR in Graphics Mode 0

In graphics mode 0, display elements are characters, not points. In this mode, the COLOR statement determines the actual character that the PLOT and DRAWTO statements will display. Table 11-3 lists values of *numexpr* and the character each one produces in graphics mode 0. The value of *numexpr* can be between 0 and 65535, but values above 255 are converted modulo 256 to values between 0 and 255.

COLOR in Graphics Modes 1 and 2

Graphics modes 1 and 2 are similiar to mode 0, but there are two character sets. Each character set has 64 elements. The standard character set contains the usual upper-case letters, numbers, and punctuation. An alternate character set contains special graphics characters and lower-case letters. The standard character set is automatically selected every time you turn on the computer, press the SYSTEM RESET key, or use the GRAPHICS statement. The statement POKE 756,226 selects the alternate character set. The statement POKE 756,224 reselects the standard character set.

Table 11-4 lists the values of *numexpr* which produce each of the 64 characters in both character sets of graphics modes 1 and 2. Notice that each character can be produced by any one of four values. Each of the values produces the same character, but selects a different color register. The value of *numexpr* can be between 0 and 65535, but values above 255 are converted modulo 256 to values between 0 and 255.

COLOR in Graphics Modes 3 through 7

In graphics modes 3 through 7, the value of *numexpr* specifies which color register will determine the hue and luminance that subsequent PLOT and DRAWTO statements will use. Table 11-1 shows which color registers are available in each mode. The value of *numexpr* can be between 0 and 65535; values above 3 are converted modulo 4 to a number between 0 and 3.

TABLE 11-3. COLOR and Graphics Mode 0
(Characters displayed by values of *numexpr*)

Value Norm/Inv.	Character	Value Norm/Inv.	Character	Value Norm/Inv.	Character	Value Norm/Inv.	Character	Value Norm/Inv.	Character	Value Norm/Inv.	Character
0/128	♥	23/151	⊤	46/174	.	69/197	E	92/220	\	115/243	s
1/129	├	24/152	⊥	47/175	/	70/198	F	93/221	]	116/244	t
2/130	│	25/153	▌	48/176	0	71/199	G	94/222	^	117/245	u
3/131	┘	26/154	└	49/177	1	72/200	H	95/223	_	118/246	v
4/132	┤	27/---	E	50/178	2	73/201	I	96/224	♦	119/247	w
5/133	┐	28/156	↑	51/179	3	74/202	J	97/225	a	120/248	x
6/134	/	29/157	↓	52/180	4	75/203	K	98/226	b	121/249	y
7/135	\	30/158	←	53/181	5	76/204	L	99/227	c	122/250	z
8/136	◤	31/159	→	54/182	6	77/205	M	100/228	d	123/251	♠
9/137	▪	32/160		55/183	7	78/206	N	101/229	e	124/252	|
10/138	◣	33/161	!	56/184	8	79/207	O	102/230	f	125/---	clr scrn
11/139	▪	34/162	"	57/185	9	80/208	P	103/231	g	126/254	◀
12/140	▪	35/163	#	58/186	:	81/209	Q	104/232	h	127/255	▶
13/141	▬	36/164	$	59/187	;	82/210	R	105/233	i	---/155	EOL
14/142	─	37/165	%	60/188	<	83/211	S	106/234	j	---/253	◪
15/143	▪	38/166	&	61/189	=	84/212	T	107/235	k		
16/144	♣	39/167	'	62/190	>	85/213	U	108/236	l		
17/145	┌	40/168	(	63/191	?	86/214	V	109/237	m		
18/146	─	41/169	)	64/192	@	87/215	W	110/238	n		
19/147	┼	42/170	※	65/193	A	88/216	X	111/239	o		
20/148	●	43/171	+	66/194	B	89/217	Y	112/240	p		
21/149	▬	44/172	,	67/195	C	90/218	Z	113/241	q		
22/150	│	45/173	-	68/196	D	91/219	[	114/242	r		

COLOR in Graphics Mode 8

In graphics mode 8, color register 2 determines the hue of all points, all lines, and the background. The COLOR statement does not even indirectly control the hue of points and lines, only their luminance. The value of *numexpr* specifies which color register will determine the luminance (see Table 11-1). The value of *numexpr* can be between 0 and 65535; values above 0 are converted modulo 4 to a number between 0 and 3.

TABLE 11-4. COLOR and Graphics Modes 1 and 2
(Characters and color registers selected by values of COLOR *numexpr*)

Value for Color Register				Character*		Value for Color Register				Character*	
0	1	2	3	Std.	Alt.	0	1	2	3	Std.	Alt.
32**	0	160	128	☐	♥	64	96	192	224	@	◆
33	1	161	129	!	⊢	65	97	193	225	A	a
34	2	162	130	"	▮	66	98	194	226	B	b
35	3	163	131	#	⌐	67	99	195	227	C	c
36	4	164	132	$	⊣	68	100	196	228	D	d
37	5	165	133	%	⌐	69	101	197	229	E	e
38	6	166	134	&	╱	70	102	198	230	F	f
39	7	167	135	'	╲	71	103	199	231	G	g
40	8	168	136	(	◤	72	104	200	232	H	h
41	9	169	137	)	▪	73	105	201	233	I	i
42	10	170	138	✳	◣	74	106	202	234	J	j
43	11	171	139	+	▪	75	107	203	235	K	k
44	12	172	140	,	▪	76	108	204	236	L	l
45	13	173	141	...	▬	77	109	205	237	M	m
46	14	174	142	.	▬	78	110	206	238	N	n
47	15	175	143	/	▪	79	111	207	239	O	o
48	16	176	144	0	♣	80	112	208	240	P	p
49	17	177	145	1	⌐	81	113	209	241	Q	q
50	18	178	146	2	─	82	114	210	242	R	r
51	19	179	147	3	+	83	115	211	243	S	s
52	20	180	148	4	●	84	116	212	244	T	t
53	21	181	149	5	▬	85	117	213	245	U	u
54	22	182	150	6	┃	86	118	214	246	V	v
55	23	183	151	7	┳	87	119	215	247	W	w
56	24	184	152	8	┻	88	120	216	248	X	x
57	25	185	153	9	▮	89	121	217	249	Y	y
58	26	186	154	:	┗	90	122	218	250	Z	z
59	27	187	None†	;	␛	91	123	219	251	[	♠
60	28	188	156	<	↑	92	124	220	252	\	┃
61	29	189	157	=	↓	93	None†	221	253	]	◥
62	30	190	158	>	←	94	126	222	254	^	◀
63	31	191	159	?	→	95	127	223	255	...	▶

NOTE:

 * For standard characters, POKE 756,224. For alternate characters, POKE 756,226.

 ** 155 selects the same character and color register as value 32.

 † No value selects this color register/character combination.

COM

Reserves space in memory for numeric arrays and string variables.

Format: COM $\left\{ \begin{array}{l} strvar\ (numexpr) \\ numvar(numexpr\ [,numexpr]) \end{array} \right\} \left[, \left\{ \begin{array}{l} strvar\ (numexpr) \\ numvar(numexpr\ [,numexpr]) \end{array} \right\} ... \right]$

Examples: COM A$(24), ARRAY1(25), ARRAY2(5,5)
            COM NAME$(30), ADDR1$(30), ADDR2$(30), ADDR3$(30)

This statement is exactly the same as the DIM statement.

CONT (CON.)

Resumes execution of the next instruction after a program halt.

Format: CONT
Example: CONT

A program can be halted by executing a STOP or END statement, or by pressing the BREAK key. Use the CONT statement to continue a halted program.

Program execution resumes with the first statement on the program line immediately following the line where the halt occurred. Thus, if the halt occurs before the end of a multiple-statement line, CONT will not finish off the line. Instead, execution will resume at the beginning of the next line.

CONT and the BREAK Key

If you press the BREAK key during a statement that takes some time to finish (INPUT or LIST, for example), that statement will be interrupted and the program will halt. A subsequent CONT statement restarts program execution at the first statement on the *next* program line. The interrupted statement is not resumed.

It is possible to block execution of even the first statement on a program line. If you happen to press the BREAK key just after the computer advances to the start of a new program line, but before it starts executing the first statement on that line, program execution will halt before that first statement is executed. A subsequent CONT statement advances to the next program line and resumes execution there, bypassing the whole program line on which the halt occurred.

CONT With No Halted Program

You may issue the CONT statement even if there is no halted program (that is, there is no program running). The computer acts as though the program halted after the first statement of the first program line. So the CONT statement starts program execution at the beginning of the second program line.

CONT After Errors

Errors can also halt program execution. You can often continue the program with a CONT statement, but the computer never executes the statement which caused the error, nor any statements that follow it on the same program line. So be careful when you use the CONT statement after an error. Continuing programs after an error is risky. The statement which is never executed may be vital. Skipping it because it caused an error will cause problems later in the program. If you correct a program error, resume execution with and immediate mode GOTO instruction.

CONT After SYSTEM RESET

You may attempt to continue program execution with the CONT statement after pressing the SYSTEM RESET key. Execution will resume at the start of the program line immediately following the one where the reset occurred. Chances are slim that the program will work properly after a reset.

CONT in Programmed Mode

Ordinarily, you will only use the CONT statement in immediate mode. While it is perfectly legal in programmed mode, it does nothing except take up extra memory and slow the program down.

CSAVE (CS.)

Operates the program recorder in record mode, transferring a program from the computer memory to a cassette.

Format: CSAVE

Examples: CSAVE
                       CS.

The CSAVE statement uses channel 7 for output to the program recorder. If channel 7 is already open to another device, an error occurs, the channel is closed automatically, and you can use CSAVE successfully.

When CSAVE executes, it sounds the computer speaker twice. This signals you to put the right tape in the program recorder and use the FAST FORWARD and REWIND levers to position the tape to the correct spot. Then depress the RECORD and PLAY levers on the program recorder. Finally, press any key on the keyboard (except BREAK). The computer turns off all active sound voices at this time. If the volume on the television set is turned up, you will hear 20 seconds of a continuous high-pitched tone. This will be followed by one or more short bursts of sound from the television speaker. The sound bursts cease when the recording finishes.

The CSAVE statement records program lines in a tokenized format, not in ATASCII code. It also records the program's variable name table. Only the CLOAD statement can read a program recorded by CSAVE. You cannot use the ENTER or LOAD statements to read a CSAVE recording.

Halting CSAVE

To halt the CSAVE operation, press either the BREAK key or the SYSTEM RESET key. The program recording will be incomplete. CLOAD cannot load an incompletely saved program.

DATA (D.)

Creates a list of values to be assigned to variables by READ statements.

Format: DATA *const* [*,const* ...]

Examples: DATA Sunday, Monday, Tuesday,
              Wednesday, Thursday, Friday, Saturday
              D. 100, -89, 1.414E-2
              DATA 2+2
              D. ARTICHOKE,,BROCCOLI,"SPINACH",

The DATA statement specifies numeric values, string values, or both. The values are assigned to numeric or string variables by one or more READ statements. A comma signals the end of one constant and the start of another. DATA statements may appear anywhere in a program. They need not be executed to be accessed by a READ statement. No other statements may follow DATA statements on a program line.

DATA Statement String Constants

Since commas separate constants, string constants cannot include them. All other characters, including quotation marks and blank spaces, are considered part of a string constant value. In fact, a string constant can consist of nothing but blank spaces, or even of nothing at all. One comma immediately following another in a DATA statement indicates a string constant with no value and a length of 0. The same is true of a comma at the end of a DATA statement.

DATA Statement Numeric Constants

Numeric constants can be expressed in standard arithmetic notation or scientific notation. Unlike string constants, they cannot be null; an error results when a READ statement tries to assign a null constant to a numeric variable.

Arithmetic expressions are not evaluated. Instead, they are treated as string values. For example, the expression 2+2 is considered a three-character string constant, not a numeric constant with a value of 4.

DATA in Immediate Mode

No error occurs if you enter a DATA statement in immediate mode, but the elements will not be accessible to a READ statement.

DEG (DE.)

Tells BASIC to expect arguments in degrees rather than radians, for subsequent trigonometric functions.

Format: DEG

Examples: DEG
              DE.

After executing the DEG statement, BASIC treats the arguments of trigonometric functions as degrees. To switch back to radians, use the RAD statement, turn the computer off and back on again, or press the SYSTEM RESET key. BASIC also reverts to radians after a NEW or RUN statement.

DIM (DI.)

Reserves space in memory for numeric arrays and string variables.

Format: $\text{DIM} \begin{Bmatrix} strvar\ (numexpr) \\ numvar\ (numexpr\ [,numexpr]) \end{Bmatrix} \left[, \begin{Bmatrix} strvar\ (numexpr) \\ numvar\ (numexpr[,numexpr]) \end{Bmatrix} ... \right]$

Examples: DIM A$(24), ARRAY1(25), ARRAY2(5,5)
            DIM NAME$(30), ADDR1$(30), ADDR2$(30), ADDR3$(30)

Numeric arrays and strings must be dimensioned before they can be used in any other way. ATARI BASIC allows numeric arrays of one or two dimensions and simple string variables with a length of one character or more.

Arrays

When an array is dimensioned, space is set aside in memory for each of its elements. The value of each *numexpr* is rounded to the nearest integer to determine the maximum size of the corresponding array dimension — in other words, the maximum value of that array subscript. When a program references an array, the value of each subscript must be no less than 0 and no more than the maximum established for that subscript by the DIM statement.

Strings

DIM statements declare the maximum lengths of string variables. In each case the maximum length is the value of *numexpr*, rounded to the nearest integer. The actual length of a string variable can vary between 0 and this declared maximum.

Size Restrictions

The absolute maximum size of any one string variable is 32,767 characters. Array and string lengths are also limited by the amount of memory available at the time the DIM statement is executed. Once dimensioned, array and string sizes can only be changed after executing a CLR statement, which undimensions all arrays and strings. An error occurs if a second DIM statement is executed in programmed mode for a given array or string variable, even if the dimension or length is unchanged.

DOS (DO.)

Activates the disk operating system utilities menu.

Format: DOS
Examples: DOS
             DO.

TABLE 11-5. DOS Statement Utilities Menus

Disk Operating System	
Version 1.0	**Version 2.0S**
A. Disk Directory	A. Disk Directory
B. Run Cartridge	B. Run Cartridge
C. Copy File	C. Copy File
D. Delete File(s)	D. Delete File(s)
E. Rename File	E. Rename File
F. Lock File	F. Lock File
G. Unlock File	G. Unlock File
H. Write DOS File	H. Write DOS Files
I. Format Disk	I. Format Disk
J. Duplicate Disk	J. Duplicate Disk
K. Binary Save	K. Binary Save
L. Binary Load	L. Binary Load
M. Run at Address	M. Run at Address
N. Define Device	N. Create MEM.SAV
O. Duplicate File	O. Duplicate File

This statement causes the disk operating system menu of 15 utility functions to appear on the display screen. If the disk operating system is not present, the DOS statement puts the computer in memo pad mode (see the BYE statement).

When BASIC encounters a DOS statement, it clears the display screen, resets the color registers to their default values (see Table 11-2), shuts off all sound voices, and closes all input/output channels except channel 0. Note that it closes channel 6, which many of the graphics statements use.

There are two versions of the disk operating system in use, version 1.0 and version 2.0S. The menus for the two versions differ. Table 11-5 itemizes both versions. See Chapter 7 for specific information on each menu item.

Disk Operating System Version 1.0

When you use the DOS statement with version 1.0 of the disk operating system, the utilities menu appears immediately on the display screen. You may choose any one of the utilities, or return to BASIC. Chapter 7 has complete instructions for each utility.

To return to BASIC, press the SYSTEM RESET key, or choose menu selection B. If there was a BASIC program in memory before you executed the DOS statement, it will still be there *unless* you used the DUPLICATE DISK or DUPLICATE FILE menu selections. If you did, your program will be gone when you return to BASIC.

Disk Operating System Version 2.0S

The utilities menu does not appear immediately when you use the DOS statement with version 2.0S of the disk operating system. First the computer must load file

DUP.SYS into memory from Drive 1. This process takes about ten seconds. If file DUP.SYS is not on the diskette in Drive 1, the computer simply returns to BASIC.

Before it loads file DUP.SYS, the computer checks to see if file MEM.SAV exists on Drive 1. If so, the computer uses it to preserve the memory area which file DUP.SYS will use. This area of memory contains the first part of any BASIC program that happens to be in memory. It is also where the RS-232 device handler resides when it is present. This save operation takes another 20 seconds.

After performing all these housekeeping chores, the computer displays the disk utilities menu. You may choose any item, or return to BASIC. Chapter 7 has complete instructions for each utility.

To return to BASIC, press the SYSTEM RESET key, or choose menu selection B. If the RS-232 serial device handler, a program, or both were present before you executed the DOS statement, they will still be there only if the computer can copy them back from file MEM.SAV. The recopy operation takes about seven seconds. If you allow the computer to use the program area of memory during the COPY FILE or DUPLICATE FILE menu selections, or if you used the DUPLICATE DISK menu selection at all, file MEM.SAV cannot restore the RS-232 serial device handler or your program.

If the RS-232 serial device handler is present before using the DOS statement but is not restored from the MEM.SAV file for any reason, and you use menu option B to return to BASIC, any subsequent use of the SYSTEM RESET key causes a system crash recoverable only by switching the computer power off and back on. This will not happen if you return to BASIC with the SYSTEM RESET key.

The DOS Statement in Programmed Mode

The DOS statement is used mainly in immediate mode. You can use it in programmed mode, but it halts your BASIC program. There is no way to continue a program from the point where the DOS statement halted it.

DRAWTO (DR.)

Draws a straight line between the point last displayed and a specified end point.

Format: DRAWTO *col,row*

Examples: DRAWTO 10,15
DR. COL1,ROW1
DR. BASECOL+COLOFFSET,BASEROW+ROWOFFSET

This statement draws a line from the point last displayed by a PLOT or DRAWTO statement to the column and row specified by the values of *col* and *row*, rounded to the nearest integer. The line drawn will be straight or as close to straight as possible. The *staircasing* phenomenon causes a diagonal line to zigzag as it approximates a straight line.

The ATARI computer uses memory location 90 to keep track of the row where the DRAWTO statement will start the next line, and memory locations 91 and 92 for the starting column. The DRAWTO and PLOT statements update these memory locations, but none of the other BASIC statements do. Thus, statements like GET, PUT, and POSITION have no effect on the starting point of the line that the DRAWTO statement constructs.

The most recently executed COLOR statement determines which color register will choose the line color. The DRAWTO statement uses the background color register if no COLOR statement has been executed since you turned on the computer.

DRAWTO in Graphics Modes 0, 1, and 2

The DRAWTO statement is primarily used in graphics modes 3 through 8, but it also works in graphics modes 0, 1, and 2, which display characters rather than points. In these modes, DRAWTO constructs a line of characters starting with the character last displayed and ending at the position specified by *col* and *row*. The line will be straight, subject to the staircasing effect. The last COLOR statement executed determines which character will compose the line, and in modes 1 and 2, which color register will choose the line color (see Tables 11-3 and 11-4). If no COLOR statement has been executed since you turned on the computer, COLOR 0 is used.

END

Causes a program to halt.

> *Format:*   END
> *Example:*   END

In programmed mode, this statement ends the program execution, sets the display screen to graphics mode 0, turns off all sound voices, and closes all input/output channels except channel 0. A program does not have to end with an END statement. When the computer runs out of BASIC statements, it ends the program automatically, just as if it had encountered an END statement.

ENTER (E.)

Transfers a previously recorded BASIC program from cassette or disk to the computer memory.

> *Format:*   ENTER *indev*
> *Examples:*   ENTER "C:"
>   E. PGM$
>   E. "D2:BUDGET.BAS"

The ENTER statement transfers BASIC text from physical device *indev* to its memory. In this way it is like the CLOAD and LOAD statements, but there are some important differences.

The ENTER statement does not erase existing program lines from the computer memory before it transfers new lines into memory. It adds the new lines to any lines already there. If a line to be added has the same line number as a line already in memory, the line in memory is erased and the new line replaces it.

When the ENTER statement finds a new variable name in the incoming program lines, it adds it to the existing variable name table (VNT) in memory. It does not remove any names from the VNT.

The ENTER statement can only transfer BASIC text that is in ATASCII code, so it works only with programs recorded by the LIST statement. It does not work with programs recorded by the SAVE or CSAVE statements, which record programs in a tokenized format.

The ENTER statement uses input channel 7 to receive program lines from the program recorder and disk drive. It works fine even if channel 7 is already open. However, it does close the channel when it finishes, blocking any prior claimant's further use. The ENTER statement also turns off all sound voices.

ENTER with the Program Recorder

The statement ENTER "C:" operates the program recorder in playback mode, transferring a program from cassette to the computer memory. First, the computer sounds its speaker once. This signals you to put the right tape in the program recorder and use the FAST FORWARD and REWIND levers to position the tape to the correct spot. Then depress the PLAY lever on the program recorder. Finally, press any key on the keyboard (except BREAK). If the volume on the television set is turned up, you will hear several seconds of silence followed by one or more short bursts of sound from the television speaker. These sounds mean the program transfer is taking place. The sound bursts cease when the transfer finishes.

ENTER with the Disk Drive

In order to use the ENTER statement with a disk file name, the disk operating system must be in memory as a result of a successful boot when you turned on the computer (see page 27). If the disk operating system is absent, an error results. If it is present but no file exists as specified, an error results. If everything is set up correctly, the computer transfers the BASIC text from diskette to its memory.

Halting ENTER

You can interrupt the ENTER statement by pressing the SYSTEM RESET key. Any program lines added to the computer memory before you press SYSTEM RESET will remain in memory.

Pressing the BREAK key during an ENTER operation will not stop the operation. It will interrupt the operation, but only momentarily. This usually means some pieces of the program being transferred never make it into memory.

Erasing Unused Variables from the VNT

The ENTER statement makes no changes to the existing program or VNT, except to add to them. This suggests a method for eliminating unused variables from a program's VNT. Figure 11-1 elaborates.

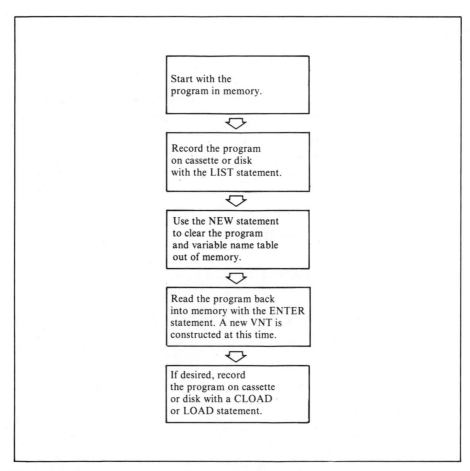

FIGURE 11-1. Clearing out the variable name table

FOR (F.)

Starts a loop that repeats a set of program lines until an automatically incremented variable attains a certain value.

> *Format:*   FOR *numvar* = *startexpr* TO *endexpr* [STEP *stepexpr*]
>
> *Examples:*   FOR COUNT = 1 TO 100
>   F. COUNTDOWN = 100 TO 1 STEP -1
>   F. INTERIM = START TO FINISH STEP INCREMENT

When FOR is first executed, *numvar* is assigned the value of *startexpr*. The statements following FOR are executed until a NEXT statement is reached. *numvar* is then incremented by the value of *stepexpr* (or by 1 if the STEP clause is not present). After that, the new value of *numvar* is compared to the value of *endexpr*.

The sense of the comparison depends on the sign of *stepexpr*. If the sign is positive and the new value of *numvar* is less than or equal to *endexpr,* execution loops back to the statement just after the FOR. The same thing happens if the sign of *stepexpr* is negative and the new value of *numvar* is greater than or equal to *endexpr.* On the other hand, if *numvar* is greater than *endexpr (stepexpr* positive) or less than *endexpr (stepexpr* negative), execution continues with the instruction that follows the NEXT statement. Because the comparison occurs *after* incrementing *numvar,* the statements between FOR and NEXT are always executed at least once.

Nesting FOR-NEXT Loops

FOR-NEXT loops may be nested. Each nested loop must have a unique index variable name (*numvar*). Each nested loop must be wholly contained within the next outer loop; at most, the loops can end at the same point. Since ATARI BASIC allows 128 different variables, you can have at most 128 levels of FOR-NEXT nesting.

Loop Expressions Evaluated Once

The loop's start, end, and increment values are determined from *startexpr, endexpr,* and *stepexpr* only once, on the first execution of the FOR statement. If you change these values inside the loop it will have no effect on the loop itself.

Terminating the Loop Early

You can change the value of *numvar* within the loop. This lets you terminate a FOR-NEXT loop early. Somewhere inside the loop, set *numvar* to the end value (*endexpr*), and on the next pass the loop will terminate itself.

FOR in Immediate Mode

FOR may be used in immediate mode. The entire loop must be entered on one line. If NEXT is not present, the loop will execute once.

Use Caution with FOR-NEXT Loops

Do not start the loop outside a subroutine and terminate it inside the subroutine. Do not branch into the middle of a FOR-NEXT loop; the loop must start with a FOR statement. Avoid branching out of FOR-NEXT loops. This takes up memory by leaving an unresolved entry on the run-time stack.

GET (GE.)

This statement retrieves a single numeric value from a previously opened input/ output channel.

Format: GET #*chan, numvar*
Examples: GET #1, NMBR
          GET #CH, X

Channel *chan* must be open for input. The GET statement assigns a one-byte numeric value between 0 and 255 to *numvar*. The value assigned depends on the device interrogated.

GET with the Keyboard

From the keyboard (device K:), the GET statement assigns to *numvar* the decimal value of the ATASCII code for the next key or combination of keys pressed. Appendix D lists the code produced by each keystroke. Program execution pauses until a key is pressed.

The BREAK key does not produce an ATASCII code; pressing it halts the GET operation. Pressing CTRL-3 in response to a GET statement causes an error. CTRL-1 halts the screen display, as usual. The ⅄ , CAPS/LOWR, SHIFT, and CTRL keys themselves do not produce ATASCII codes of any kind, although they do change the codes which other keys produce. The four yellow special function keys do not produce ATASCII codes.

GET with the Program Recorder

The ATARI computer transfers data from the program recorder in blocks of 128 one-byte values. After opening the program recorder for input, the first GET statement causes the computer to read a block into the cassette buffer area of its memory, assign the first value to *numvar,* and stop the tape. Each subsequent GET statement takes the next sequential value from the cassette buffer in memory. When the entire buffer has been used, the computer starts the tape and reads another block.

Any attempt to get data past the end of a file results in an error. Closing the input channel stops the tape. You can close the input channel with a CLOSE or END statement.

GET with the Disk Drive

The GET statement will read data from a disk file that has been opened for input. The GET statement reads the one-byte values that were recorded by a PUT statement. It can also read the multiple-byte values recorded by a PRINT statement, one byte at a time. Each value it reads is the ATASCII code of the character recorded by the PRINT statement.

The computer reads data from the disk drive in one-sector blocks, not one value at a time. It reads the first block of values into the disk buffer area of its memory when a data file is first opened for reading. A subsequent GET statement takes the first value from the buffer in memory and assigns it to *numvar.* When the entire buffer has been used, the computer fills the buffer from the next sector of the disk file. The ATARI 810 Disk Drive has 125 one-byte values per sector.

The POINT statement causes the computer to read in a new block from the disk file if it specifies a location that is outside the sector currently in memory.

GET with the Display Screen

When used with the display screen (device S: or E:), the GET statement retrieves the code of the character or graphics point displayed at the current cursor position. This code observes the same rules as the one specified by the COLOR statement. In graphics mode 0, the code specifies which character is displayed (see Table 11-3). In graphics modes 1 and 2, the code specifies which color register is in use and which character is displayed (see Table 11-4). In graphics modes 3 through 8, the value retrieved indicates which color register is in use at the particular cursor position (see Table 11-1).

Each time GET reads a value from the display screen, it moves right to the next cursor position. It does this by updating memory location 84 with the row number of the next cursor position, and memory locations 85 and 86 with the next column number. The next statement that stores or retrieves data from the display screen occurs in the new cursor position. However, none of this applies to the DRAWTO or XIO statements, which maintain a separate cursor position in memory locations 90, 91, and 92.

If you use the GET statement on the last column of a given row on the display screen, the cursor advances to the first column of the next line. If you try to access the display screen without first repositioning the cursor after a GET statement at the last column of the last row, an error results.

Executing a PRINT statement after a GET statement may change the code of the character or graphics point just retrieved, spoiling the display. To circumvent this, use the POSITION statement to move the cursor back one space. Then use the PUT statement to rewrite the code just retrieved.

GET with RS-232 Serial Devices

There must be an open input channel to the proper RS-232 serial port of the ATARI 850 Interface Module, and this will be possible only if the RS-232 handler is in memory as a result of a successful boot when you turned the computer on (see page 14). In addition, the serial port must be conditioned for concurrent input and output with an XIO 40 statement. Finally, the translation mode may need to be set with an XIO 38 statement. All this must happen before executing a GET statement on the channel in question.

With this protocol out of the way, a value comes through the serial port to the ATARI 850 Interface Module. It translates the value to an ATASCII code if the translation mode in effect requires it. Appendix D contains a table of ASCII and ATASCII codes. The ATARI 850 Interface Module passes the values on to the computer, one at a time.

GOSUB (GOS.)

Causes the program to branch to the indicated line. When a RETURN statement is subsequently executed, the program branches back to the statement immediately following the GOSUB statement.

Format: GOSUB *linexpr*
Examples: GOSUB 100
              GOS. PYMTCALC
              GOS. BASEAGE+ELAPSED

The GOSUB statement calls a subroutine. ATARI BASIC starts executing the subroutine at line number *linexpr*. This entry point need not necessarily be the subroutine line with the smallest line number.

If *linexpr* does not evaluate to an existing line number, an error results.

Subroutine Termination

Each time the computer executes a GOSUB statement, it saves the return location on the run-time stack. The return location specifies the BASIC statement that follows the GOSUB statement which called the subroutine, even if it is on the same program line as the GOSUB statement. At the end of the subroutine, the RETURN statement clears the run-time stack entry as it branches back to the point where the subroutine was called.

Branching out of a subroutine, for instance with a GOTO statement, will not clear the stack. This takes up memory by leaving an unresolved entry on the run-time stack. A program that does this repeatedly will eventually exhaust available memory, and an error will result. But you can branch out of a subroutine with a GOTO, IF-THEN, or similar statement if you first execute a POP statement to clear the last return location from the run-time stack.

A program rarely runs out of memory because of run-time stack problems, but it can happen. There is always some finite number of GOSUB statements that can occur without a RETURN or POP statement occurring. Subroutines share the run-time stack with FOR-NEXT loops, so the permissible level of subroutine nesting depends on the concurrent level of FOR-NEXT loop nesting.

Subroutine Location

A GOSUB statement may occur anywhere in a program. A subroutine, on the other hand, must begin at the start of a program line.

GOTO (G.)

Unconditionally causes program execution to branch to the line indicated.

Format: GOTO *linexpr*
Examples: GOTO 1120
              G. TABLE+OFFSET

Program execution continues immediately with the first instruction at line number *linexpr*. An error occurs if no such line number exists in the program.

GRAPHICS (GR.)

Sets one of the graphics modes; optionally clears the display screen.

TABLE 11-6. GRAPHICS Statement Options

BASIC Graphics Mode	Suppress Text Window	Suppress Screen Clear	Suppress Both
0	-	32	-
1	17	33	49
2	18	34	50
3	19	35	51
4	20	36	52
5	21	37	53
6	22	38	54
7	23	39	55
8	24	40	56

Format: GRAPHICS *numexpr*

Examples: GRAPHICS 5
              GRAPHICS 20
              GR. 32+MODE

The GRAPHICS statement resets the screen display to the graphics mode specified by the value of *numexpr,* rounded to the nearest integer. This statement normally clears the display screen, too. To suppress this, add 32 to the graphics mode number. Table 11-6 shows the appropriate values for each graphics mode.

When the computer executes a GRAPHICS statement, it reserves the amount of memory required by the specified graphics mode, enables the text cursor (sets memory location 752 to 0), and sets the color registers to their default values (see Table 11-2).

Graphics Modes

ATARI BASIC supports several different graphics modes. Mode 0 is the text mode that you see when you turn on the computer. Modes 1 through 8 are graphics modes that can either be full-screen or can have a four-line text window across the bottom of the screen. The area inside the text window is graphics mode 0. Table 11-7 summarizes the characteristics of the different modes.

The Text Window

Modes 1 through 8 include a four-line text window at the bottom of the screen. Mode 0 text output to channel 0 appears in the text window. The display screen ignores anything that PLOT, DRAWTO, PUT, XIO, or PRINT statements attempt to display in the text window via channel 6.

You can suppress the text window at the time the GRAPHICS statement is executed by adding 16 to the value of *numexpr* (see Table 11-6). This will give you the equivalent of four additional mode 0 lines of space of at the bottom of the display screen.

When the text window is absent, there is no place for output that would normally go to it. Such output includes the question mark printed by an INPUT statement, the ouput of a PRINT statement with no explicit channel number or with channel 0, and the message that appears at any program break, whether caused by an error, a STOP statement, or the BREAK key. If any text output occurs in graphics modes 1 through 8 when no text window is present, the entire display screen reverts to graphics mode 0. The screen is cleared and the text output appears at the top of the screen.

Channels 0 and 6 for Output

The GRAPHICS statement opens channel 6 for output to the display screen (device S:). Once you execute a GRAPHICS statement, you cannot use channel 6 unless you first execute a CLOSE #6 statement. After such a CLOSE statement, you will not be able to use the DRAWTO, PLOT, or LOCATE statements until you reopen the display screen with a GRAPHICS statement (or an OPEN statement).

At the same time the GRAPHICS statement opens channel 6 for output to the display screen graphics area, it opens channel 0 for output to the screen editor (device E:) in the text area. In graphics mode 0, this area coincides with the channel 6 area, taking up the entire screen. In modes 1 through 8 when the graphics window is present, the two areas are clearly separated. In modes 1 through 8 when the graphics window is absent, using channel 0 returns the whole screen to mode 0.

TABLE 11-7. Graphics Modes Summary

Mode No.	Rows		Columns	Color Registers	Memory Required (Bytes)	Mode Type
	Full Screen	With Window				
0	24	-	40	1*, 2†, 4#	993	Text
1	24	20	20	0, 1, 2, 3, 4†#	513	Character Graphics
2	12	10	20	0, 1, 2, 3, 4†#	261	Character Graphics
3	24	20	40	0, 1, 2, 4†#	273	Graphics
4	48	40	80	0, 4†#	537	Graphics
5	48	40	80	0, 1, 2, 4†#	1017	Graphics
6	96	80	160	0, 4†#	2025	Graphics
7	96	80	160	0, 1, 2, 4†#	3945	Graphics
8	192	160	320	1*, 2†, 4#	7900	Graphics

* Character luminance only; hue same as background.

† Background hue and luminance.

Border hue and luminance.

Mode 0

Graphics mode 0 is a pure text mode. Its 24 lines can have as many as 40 characters each. Standard margins exclude the first two columns on the left edge of the screen.

Mode 0 characters always display in the same color as the background, although you can set the luminance of each separately (see Table 11-7).

Mode 0 Margins

You can use the POKE statement to reset the left and right margins. They must be between 0 and 39. Memory location 82 has the left margin, 83 the right. The margins do not stop your program from operating on the entire display screen. They only affect where PRINT statement output will appear.

Mode 0 Cursor

The cursor shows where the next character will be displayed. You can change the location of the cursor with the POSITION statement. You can also make the cursor invisible and play other tricks with it by changing the value of locations 752 and 755 (see Appendix G).

Mode 0 Character Set

Mode 0 can display 128 different characters. Each character can be normal or inverse. The standard character set uses the one-byte ATASCII encoding scheme (see Table 11-3.). You can define your your own character set, as described in Chapter 9.

Mode 0 Logical Lines

The ATARI computer organizes text on the mode 0 display screen into *logical lines*. Logical lines can be 1 to 120 characters long, a maximum of three screen display lines. An end-of-line (EOL) character signals the end of a logical line.

When the cursor reaches the bottom of the screen, the logical line at the top of the screen scrolls off the top, making room for more text at the bottom.

Modes 1 and 2

Modes 1 and 2 are character graphics modes. Each display element comes from a 64-item character set. Mode 2 characters are twice as tall as mode 1 characters, although both are the same width, as shown in Table 11-7. Both modes have characters twice as wide as those in mode 0.

ATARI BASIC has two character sets for modes 1 and 2. The standard character set contains the usual upper-case letters, numbers, and punctuation. An alternate character set contains special graphics characters and lower-case letters. The standard character set is automatically selected every time you turn on the computer, press the SYSTEM RESET key, or use the GRAPHICS statement. The statement POKE 756,226 selects the alternate character set. The statement POKE 756,224 reselects the standard character set. Table 11-4 identifies the characters in both character sets. You can also define your own character sets.

Characters in modes 1 and 2 can appear in any of the colors specified by four color registers. A fifth color register specifies the background color. Part of the same code that determines which character will appear also determines which color register will be used (see Table 11-4). The SETCOLOR statement determines which color the color register produces.

If you print a string that is too long for one line, the extra characters wrap around to the start of the next line. Modes 1 and 2 screens do not scroll, however. If you try to display something below the bottom edge of the screen, an error results.

Modes 3 Through 8

Modes 3 through 8 display points, lines, and solid areas. The point size, number of points per line, number of lines on the display screen, and number of color registers used vary from one of these modes to the next. See Table 11-7 for details.

The cursor is never visible, but can be moved under program control. The POSITION statement changes the cursor position in memory locations 84 (row) and 85 and 86 (column). These locations store the next cursor position, not its present position, and are used by most statements. Memory locations 90 (row) and 91 and 92 (column) store the current cursor position that the DRAWTO, PLOT, and XIO statements use.

The DRAWTO, PLOT, and XIO statements are the most common in modes 3 through 8. You can also use the PUT statement, and even the PRINT # statement if you wish.

IF-THEN

Conditionally causes the program to execute the indicated instruction or instructions.

Formats: IF *expr* THEN *statement* [*:statement* ...]
IF *expr* THEN *linexpr*

Examples: IF NAME$ ="LESTER ROADHOG MORAN" THEN RETURN
IF ZIP > 90000 AND NAME$(1,1) <= "B" THEN PRINT #2;NAME$
IF RESPONSE$ = "Y" THEN PRINT "HOW MANY"; :INPUT QTY
IF A = B THEN 1735
IF COST(N1,N2) THEN 25300+COST(N1,N2)/1E4

In the first format above, if the expression (*expr*) specifies a true condition, BASIC executes the *statements* that follow the keyword THEN on the same program line. If the specified condition is false, control passes to the first statement on the next program line and BASIC does not execute any of the *statements* following the keyword THEN.

In the second format above (the conditional branch format), the program branches to line number *linexpr* if the condition is true. Otherwise, execution continues with the first statement on the program line that follows the IF-THEN statement.

Types of Expressions

The most common types of expressions (*expr*) used with the IF-THEN statement are relational and Boolean expressions, since both evaluate to true or false. The expression may also be a numeric expression. If its value is not 0, the condition is considered true. If its value is 0, the condition is considered false and execution continues at the first statement on the next higher program line. The expression cannot have a string value, although it can compare strings.

Relational expressions which compare for less than (<), greater than (>), or not equal (<>) can use a STR$ function only on one side of the inequality sign. The same limitation applies to the CHR$ function.

String Comparisons

When *expr* is a comparison of strings, the ATASCII codes (listed in Appendix D) for the characters involved determine the relative values of the strings. Strings are compared character by character until a mismatch occurs. Then the string with the higher ATASCII code in the mismatch position is considered greater. If no mismatch occurs, the longer string is greater.

Statement Restrictions

If either a GOTO or REM statement is one of the many statements following the keyword THEN, it must be the last statement on the line. Any statements that follow it on the same program line can never be executed.

Additional IF-THEN statements may appear following the keyword THEN as long as they are completely contained on the original IF-THEN line. However, a Boolean expression is easier to read than nested IF-THEN statements. For example, the following two statements are equivalent, but the second is easier to read.

10 IF A$ = "X" THEN IF B = 2 THEN IF C> D THEN 50
10 IF A$ = "X" AND B = 2 AND C> D THEN 50

INPUT (I.)

Accepts character entry from the keyboard or other input device, evaluates it, and assigns the value or values entered to the variable or variables specified.

Format: INPUT [#chan {:}] var [,var ...]

Examples: INPUT RESPONSES
              I. #4, RECORD$
              I. #2, A, B, C

The INPUT statement gets a line of data from an input device. The input line consists of zero or more ATASCII characters followed by an ATASCII end-of-line (EOL) character. On the keyboard, the RETURN key produces an EOL character to end the input line. No matter what the input device is, the EOL character is required to end the input line.

The computer interprets the input line as a string value, one or more numeric values, or some combination of these. The way it interprets the input line depends on the number and type of variables (*var*), but is entirely unaffected by which input device is used.

When the *chan* option is absent, input comes from the keyboard via the editor (device E:). When the *chan* option is present, the specified channel must be open for input. The OPEN statement specifies the input device.

Multiple-Variable Input

Generally speaking, when a single INPUT statement calls for more than one value, numeric or string, you can put each one on a separate input line by ending each value with the EOL character (the RETURN key). In fact, you must terminate strings this way. But you can also terminate a numeric value with a comma, and enter the next value, whether string or numeric, on the same input line. Commas are treated as part of string values, so they do not work as string value terminators.

Numeric Input

When BASIC encounters a numeric variable, it translates the input line — up to the next comma — into a numeric value. Numeric input follows the rules for numeric constants, detailed in Chapter 3. It consists of an optional sign (+ or -) followed by one or more digits (0 through 9), with one optional decimal point. Blank spaces may prefix or suffix the number, but may not separate the digits, signs, and decimal points from each other.

Also allowed is a suffix for expressing the exponent part of a number in scientific notation. The suffix comprises three parts: the capital letter E, an optional sign, and a one- or two-digit number. The exponent must have a value generally between -99 and -1, or between 1 and 97. A value of 0 is not allowed, nor are fractional exponents. There can be no decimal point in the exponent. The exponent value cannot cause the numeric value as a whole to exceed its allowable range (see below). Blank spaces cannot separate the exponent from the mantissa.

Numeric input must be larger (less negative) than $-1E+98$ and smaller than $1E+98$, Values closer to 0 than $\pm 9.99999999E-98$ are rounded to 0.

If there are no characters before the next comma or EOL character, an error results. This happens on the keyboard if you simply press RETURN. An error also occurs if non-numeric characters occur, or if numeric characters occur in the wrong places. Example include too many decimal points, the sign in the wrong place, or a scientific notation exponent too large or too small.

String Input

Each string value must be on a separate input line. Only an EOL character (the RETURN key) terminates string entry; commas are treated as part of the string value.

The string value is the sequence of ATASCII characters exactly as they occur in the input line, with no conversion or translation. If no characters come in before an EOL character (the RETURN key), the string value is null, its length 0. On the other hand, the number of characters that come in can exceed the dimensioned length of the string variable to which they are assigned. If this happens, the INPUT statement ignores the excess characters until the next EOL character (RETURN key).

INPUT from the Editor or Keyboard

If the INPUT statement uses the editor (device E:), BASIC displays a question mark at the current cursor position on the graphics mode 0 screen as a cue to begin entry. However, if *chan* is present, no question mark appears. With devices other than the editor, no question mark appears on the display screen; this includes the keyboard itself (device K:). If it takes more than one input line to enter all the values for an INPUT statement, a new question mark appears (subject to the rules just stated) at the beginning of each new line as a cue to continue entries.

The keyboard (device E: or K:) works the same way in the context of an INPUT statement as it normally does. The cursor movement keys perform their usual editing functions, the CLEAR key (SHIFT- <) clears the entire display screen, the BREAK key halts the INPUT statement, the RETURN key terminates the entry line, and so on. Chapter 2 explains these features in detail. Do not use the cursor control keys (←, →, ↑, ↓, etc.) to move the cursor out of the logical input line and back in. This may cause the question mark to become part of the input response.

When the input device is the keyboard (device E: or K:), each keystroke adds another ATASCII character code to the input line. The keyboard can produce all 256 codes. Appendix D shows which keys and combinations of keys produce which codes.

INPUT from Other Devices

The rules for the INPUT statement are the same regardless of the input device. From devices other than the keyboard (device E: or K:), the EOL character performs the function of the RETURN key. Commas can separate numeric values requested by a single INPUT statement.

INPUT from the Disk Drive and Program Recorder

The computer transfers data from the disk drive and program recorder to its memory in blocks of characters. On the ATARI 810 Disk Drive, there are 125 characters per block. The program recorder has 128 characters per block.

One block might contain part of a string value, one string value, one numeric value, or several values separated by EOL characters or commas. BASIC assigns values to INPUT statement variables from the block in memory on a first-come, first-served basis. If it needs more characters, it gets another block from the disk drive or program recorder.

Any attempt to get data past the end of a disk or cassette file results in an error.

INPUT with RS-232 Serial Devices

There must be an open input channel to the proper RS-232 serial port of the ATARI 850 Interface Module, and this will be possible only if the RS-232 handler is in memory as a result of a successful boot when you turned on the computer (see page 14). In addition, the serial port must be conditioned for concurrent input and output with an XIO 40 statement. Other XIO statements may be required to condition the serial port. For example, the translation mode (for converting incoming ASCII characters to ATASCII) may need to be set with an XIO 38 statement. All this must happen before executing an INPUT statement on the channel in question.

With this protocol out of the way, input line characters come through the serial port to the ATARI 850 Interface Module. It translates them to ATASCII characters according to the translation mode in effect. Two of the translation modes will change an incoming ASCII carriage return character to the ATASCII EOL character required to end an input line. Appendix D has ASCII and ATASCII code tables.

The ATARI 850 Interface Module passes on the translated characters to the computer, one at a time. It interprets them as a string or numeric value in the manner described above.

LET = (= or LE. =)

The assignment statement, LET =, or simply =, assigns a value to a specified variable.

Format: [LET] *var* = *expr*

Examples: LET A = B
           LE. A$ = "Foreign Correspondent"
           COURSE(1,N) = COURSE(1,N-1) + SIN(X/Y)
           DECISION = RIGHT OR WRONG
           REORDER = ONHAND < = MINIMUM

Variable *var* is assigned the value computed by evaluating *expr*. The variable can be a simple numeric or string variable, a numeric array element, or a substring (subscripted string variable). The variable must be the same type as the expression. An exception allows BASIC to assign the value of a Boolean or relational expression to a numeric variable. Such expressions have a value of 1 if true, 0 if false. Relational expressions that compare simply for less than (<), greater than (>), or not equal (< >) can use a STR$ function only on one side of the inequality. The CHR$ function is similarly restricted.

When you use substring notation to assign characters to a string, only the specified substring is affected. Other parts of the string variable retain their previous values. Parts that had no previous values have random values.

LIST (L.)

Displays all or part of the program currently in memory. Can also transmit all or part of the program currently in memory to a specified output device.

Formats: LIST [*linexpr*$_1$ [,*linexpr*$_2$]]
             LIST *outdev* [,*linexpr*$_1$ [,*linexpr*$_2$]]
Examples: LIST
             L.160
             L. "P:",100,200
             L. "D:DOGBREED.BAS"

The first format above lists program lines to the display screen via the editor (device E:), in graphics mode 0. Characters may list differently than they display in other graphics modes when the program is run. The second format lists program lines to a specific output device, *outdev,* which can be the display screen (device S:, or via the editor, E:), in addition to the printer (device P:), one of the RS-232 serial ports (device R[*n*]:), a disk file (device D[*n*]:*filename* [.*ext*]), or the program recorder (device C:).

Any portion of the program may be listed using either format. If you specify two line numbers and both exist, the program will list starting at *linexpr*$_1$ and continuing through *linexpr*$_2$. The line numbers specified in a LIST statement do not have to exist in the program. If the starting line number (*linexpr*$_1$) does not exist, the listing starts at the next higher line number. If the ending line number (*linexpr*$_2$) does not exist, the listing ends at the next lower line number. If you specify only one line number (*linexpr*$_1$), just that line will be listed, if it exists. If you specify no line numbers, the entire program is listed.

Form of Output

The LIST statement automatically extends any keywords that you abbreviated as you typed them in. It also adds extra spaces around variables and keywords to make the listing more readable.

Program lines are limited to three screen lines each, but these limits are calculated before LIST expands the abbreviations and adds the extra spaces. You can therefore extend the apparent length of a program line past the normal limit by abbreviating extensively and leaving out unneeded spaces when you type it in. However, such a line will be too long to edit.

The LIST statement sends out BASIC text in ATASCII code, no matter which destination device is used. The ENTER statement can read it back from the program recorder or disk drive. The CSAVE and SAVE statements cannot read a LIST statement's recording. The LIST statement does not record the variable name table (VNT). See Figure 11-1 for a way to use the LIST and ENTER statements to reset the VNT.

Input/Output Channels and Sound Voices

The LIST statement transmits to all devices on channel 7, except the display screen, for which it uses channel 0. It works fine even if channel 7 is already open. However, it does close channel 7 when it finishes, disabling any prior use. The LIST statement also closes all sound voices.

LIST with the Program Recorder

The statement LIST "C:" operates the program recorder in record mode, transferring a program from the computer memory to a cassette. First, it sounds the computer speaker twice. This signals you to put the right tape in the program recorder and use the FAST FORWARD and REWIND levers to position the tape to the correct spot. Then depress the RECORD and PLAY levers on the program recorder. Finally, press any key on the keyboard (except BREAK). If the volume on the television set is turned up, you will hear 20 seconds of a continuous high-pitched tone. This will be followed by one or more short bursts of sound from the television speaker. These sounds mean the program transfer is taking place. The sound bursts cease when the recording finishes.

LIST with the Disk Drive

In order to use the LIST statement with a disk file name, the disk operating system must be in memory as a result of a successful boot when you turned on the computer (see page 27). If the disk operating system is absent, an error results. If it is present but no file exists as specified, an error results. If everything is set up correctly, the computer transfers the BASIC text from its memory to diskette.

LIST with the Printer

To print a listing of the program in memory on the ATARI printer, use the statement LIST "P:". The printer must be turned on. The ATARI 825 Printer must also be switched online, and the ATARI 850 Interface Module it connects through must be on as well. Printer character sets differ from the graphics mode 0 character set, so some characters will look different on a printed listing.

The ATARI 825 Printer translates several ATASCII codes as control characters. Strange things can happen when you list a program than contains control characters directly inside question marks. The printer performs the control code functions, ruining the listing. This will not happen if the codes are specified using the CHR$ function.

LIST with the RS-232 Serial Ports

To use the LIST statement with one of the RS-232 serial ports, the RS-232 serial device handler must be in memory as a result of a successful boot when you turned on the computer (see page 14). If the device handler is absent, an error results. The device may require conditioning with XIO statements before executing the LIST statement. If everything checks out, the computer transfers the BASIC text from its memory to the serial port. It does not check to see if the serial device received the listing, or even if there is a serial device.

Halting LIST

Once LIST starts executing, you can interrupt it by pressing either the BREAK key or the SYSTEM RESET key. Output ceases. Output to a cassette file will be incomplete, but you will be able to read the recorded part with an ENTER statement.

When you interrupt a listing to a disk file, chances are very good that the file will simply not exist. But if you use the BREAK key, or the SYSTEM RESET key near the end of the listing, the computer may finish off the file before it halts the LIST operation. And if the timing is wrong, pressing the SYSTEM RESET key will kill the listing, abort the file, and lock up the system. Your only recourse then is to turn the computer off and back on again.

LOAD (LO.)

Transfers a previously recorded BASIC program from an input device to the computer memory.

> *Format:*   LOAD *indev*
>
> *Examples:*   LOAD "C:"
>   LO. "D:PROGRAM1"
>   LO. PRG$

The LOAD statement transfers a BASIC program from physical device *indev* to memory. During the loading process, the LOAD statement also replaces the resident variable name table with the one for the incoming program.

The LOAD statement can only load a tokenized BASIC program recorded by the SAVE statement. It cannot load programs recorded by the CSAVE statement, which uses different timing, or by the LIST statement, which records BASIC text in ATASCII code.

The LOAD statement uses input channel 7 for transfer from the program recorder and disk drive. It works even if channel 7 is already open.

LOAD Invokes NEW

Using the LOAD statement automatically invokes the NEW statement. It clears all previous program lines and variables out of memory.

When the LOAD operation ceases (successful or not, or complete or not), BASIC shuts off all sound voices and closes all input/output channels except channel 0. Note especially that it closes channel 6, which many of the graphics statements use.

LOAD with the Program Recorder

The statement LOAD "C:" operates the program recorder in playback mode, transferring a program from cassette to the computer memory. First, the computer sounds its speaker once. This signals you to put the right tape in the program recorder and use the FAST FORWARD and REWIND levers to position the tape to the correct spot. Then depress the PLAY lever on the program recorder. Finally, press any key on the keyboard (except BREAK). If the volume on the television set is turned up, you will hear several seconds of silence followed by one or more short bursts of sound from the television speaker. These sounds mean the program transfer is taking place. The sound bursts cease when the transfer finishes.

LOAD with the Disk Drive

In order to use the LOAD statement with a disk file name, the disk operating system must be in memory as a result of a successful boot when you turned on the computer (see page 27). If the disk operating system is absent, an error results. If it is present but no file exists as specified, an error results. If everything is set up correctly, the computer transfers the BASIC text from diskette to its memory.

Halting LOAD

Once LOAD starts executing, you can interrupt it by pressing the SYSTEM RESET key. There will be no program lines in the computer memory unless the load operation had a chance to finish. Pressing the SYSTEM RESET key while loading a disk file program may lock up the system. Your only recourse then is to turn the computer off and back on again.

Pressing the BREAK key during a LOAD operation will rarely stop the operation. It will interrupt the operation, but only momentarily. Some pieces of the program being transferred may never make it into memory.

LOCATE (LOC.)

Retrieves the code of the character or graphics point displayed at a specified screen display location.

> *Format:*   LOCATE *col, row, numvar*
>
> *Examples:*   LOCATE 5, 10, PIXEL
> LOC. COL, ROW, SCRNVAL
> LOC. PEEK(86)*256+PEEK(85), PEEK(84), ANSR

The LOCATE statement retrieves the code of the character or graphics point displayed at the column and row specified by the values of *col* and *row*. It assigns the code value to *numvar*.

The code is a one-byte numeric value between 0 and 255. It observes the same rules as the code specified by the COLOR statement. In graphics mode 0, the code specifies which character is displayed (see Table 11-3). In graphics modes 1 and 2, the code specifies which color register is in use and which character is displayed (see Table 11-4). In graphics modes 3 through 8, the value retrieved indicates which color register is in use at the particular cursor position (see Table 11-1).

LOCATE Uses Channel 6

In order for the LOCATE statement to work, channel 6 must be open for input to the display screen. The GRAPHICS statement does this.

Cursor Update

Each time LOCATE reads a value from the display screen, it moves right to the next cursor position. It does this by updating memory location 84 with the row number of the next cursor position, and memory locations 85 and 86 with the next column number. The next statement which stores or retrieves data from the display screen occurs in the new cursor position. However, none of this applies to the DRAWTO or XIO statements, which maintain a separate cursor position in memory locations 90, 91, and 92.

If you use the LOCATE statement on the last column of a given row on the display screen, the cursor advances to the first column of the next line. If you access the display screen without first repositioning the cursor after a LOCATE statement at the last column of the last row, an error results.

PRINT After LOCATE

Executing a PRINT statement after a LOCATE statement may change the code of the character or graphics point just retrieved, spoiling the display. To circumvent this, use the POSITION statement to move the cursor back one space. Then use the PUT statement to rewrite the code just retrieved.

LPRINT (LP.)

Outputs characters to the system printer.

Format: LPRINT [*expr*] [{`;`} ...[*expr*]] ...

Examples: LPRINT "Customer "; CUST
LP. R$;" Score:", INT(POSBL/RIGHT*100)

This statement is like the PRINT statement, except that output goes to a printer attached directly to the serial bus, like the ATARI 820 or 822 Printers, or to a printer attached to the parallel port of the ATARI 850 Interface Module, like the ATARI 825 Printer. The printer must be turned on. The ATARI 850 Interface Module must be on also, if the printer is attached to it. If the printer is not ready to print, the computer waits briefly, then an error occurs.

There are a number of acceptable variations on the LPRINT statement. LPRINT by itself outputs an EOL character. When LPRINT is followed by one or more expressions, the values of those expressions are printed. The way the values appear depends on their nature and on the use of semicolons or commas between values.

Printing Numeric Values

Numeric values within certain limits are printed using standard arithmetic notation. Scientific notation is used for values closer to 0 than ±0.01 and for any values with more than ten digits in front of the decimal point. Negative values are preceded by a minus sign; positive values are not preceded by anything.

Printing String Values

By printing certain string values on some printers, you can activate different type fonts and other special features. Chapter 6 has more information.

Commas and Semicolons

LPRINT statement expressions must be separated by either a comma or a semicolon. Commas and semicolons control the spacing between printed values. A semicolon causes the next value to print immediately after the value just printed; the two are concatenated with no intervening spaces. A comma causes the next value to print at the next column stop, several spaces over from the last value.

Column stops are ten characters apart, at columns 1, 11, 21, and so on. If any character is printed in either of the two spaces just ahead of a column stop (for example, in column 19 or 20), that column stop is inactivated.

LPRINT and the ATARI 825 Printer

The LPRINT statement has some quirks when used with the ATARI 825 Printer. If an LPRINT statement prints more than 40 characters, output from the next LPRINT statement always starts a new line on an ATARI 825 Printer. A comma or semicolon at the end of the LPRINT statement has no effect. But if an LPRINT statement prints 40 characters or less and ends with a semicolon, or 38 characters or less and ends with a comma, output from the next LPRINT statement starts on the same line, at column 41. In either case, output from the next LPRINT statement will start a new line. LPRINT output to the ATARI 825 Printer is normal if no semicolon or comma ends the statement.

Input/Output Channels and Sound Voices

The LPRINT statement uses channel 7 for output to the printer. If channel 7 is already open to another device, an error occurs, which closes the channel. You can then use LPRINT successfully.

The LPRINT statement shuts off all sound voices.

NEW

Deletes the current program and all variables from memory.

Format: NEW
Example: NEW

This statement also shuts off all sound voices; closes all input/output channels except channel 0, which remains open to the editor (device E:); and sets trigonometric functions to radians.

NEXT (N.)

Terminates the loop started by a FOR statement.

Format: NEXT *numvar*
Examples: NEXT COUNT
              N. J

When BASIC executes a NEXT statement, it increments the loop index variable *numvar* by an amount specified in the corresponding FOR statement. The program then either continues with the statement following NEXT or loops back to the corresponding FOR, depending on the parameters set in the FOR statement. (See the discussion of FOR earlier in this chapter.)

If *numvar* does not match the loop variable of the most recently executed FOR statement, an error occurs.

NEXT in Immediate Mode

A NEXT statement will terminate an immediate mode FOR-NEXT loop only if it follows the FOR statement on the same immediate mode program line.

When BASIC encounters a NEXT statement at the beginning of an immediate mode line, it looks for the most recent programmed mode FOR-NEXT loop that matches and is still active. If it finds one, it continues the loop at the FOR statement. If not, an error occurs.

NOTE (NO.)

Determines the current location of the file pointer for the specified disk file.

Format: NOTE #*chan, sectvar, bytevar*

Examples: NOTE #5, SCTR, BYTE
         NO. #FILE2, S, B

This statement checks the current location of the pointer for the disk file open to channel *chan*. It assigns the absolute sector number to numeric variable *sectvar*, and the byte number within the sector to numeric variable *bytevar*. These variables cannot be array elements. Channel *chan* can be open to a disk file for any operation.

NOTE is not available in version 1.0 of the disk operating system.

ON-GOSUB

Provides conditional subroutine calls to one of several subroutines in a program, depending on the current value of an expression.

Format: ON *numexpr* GOSUB *linexpr* [,*linexpr* ...]

Examples: ON X GOSUB 100, 200, 300
         ON SI GOSUB B+L*100,12000,12050,100

The program branches to the first line number (*linexpr*) if the integer value of *numexpr* is 1, the second if it is 2, and so on. The next RETURN statement encountered sends the program back to the statement that follows the ON-GOSUB statement.

The expression must have a value in the range 0 through 255 or an error occurs. If the expression evaluates to 0 or to a value greater than the number of line numbers listed, program execution continues with the next statement following the ON-GOSUB.

ON-GOTO

Causes a conditional branch to one of several lines in a program, depending on the current value of an expression.

Format: ON *numexpr* GOTO *linexpr* [,*linexpr* ...]

Examples: ON RESPONSE GOTO 1000, 2000, 3000, 4000, 5000
             ON RND(0)*10 GOTO 100+SPEED*10, 2000, 3000, 3000, 3000

The program branches to the first line number (linexpr) if the integer value of *numexpr* is 1, the second if it is 2, and so on.

The expression must have a value in the range 0 through 255 or an error occurs. If the expression evaluates to 0 or to a value greater than the number of line numbers listed, program execution continues with the next statement following the ON-GOTO.

OPEN (O.)

Assigns an input/output channel number to a specific device, including a disk file.

Format: OPEN #*chan, taskexpr, auxexpr, dev*

Examples: OPEN #1, 4, 0, "C:"
             O. #5, ACT, 0, "D:SCORE.DAT"
             O. #2, 8, 0, "P:"

Before BASIC can access an external device for input or output, it must open a channel (*chan*) to it. If the channel is already open to another device, an error occurs.

The value of the first expression (*taskexpr*) specifies the kind of activity (for example, input or output) that will be going on; Table 11-8 elaborates. In most cases, the second expression (*auxexpr*) is unused, as Table 11-9 shows. The following sections explain the details for each device.

The final parameter in the OPEN statement, *dev,* selects the device that the input/output channel will be associated with. The *dev* parameter can be a string constant or a string variable. Table 11-10 lists the standard device names.

OPEN with the Program Recorder

The program recorder can be open for input or output, but not for both input and output simultaneously.

Opening for input operates the program recorder in playback mode. The computer sounds its speaker once. This signals you to put the right tape in the program recorder and use the FAST FORWARD and REWIND levers to position the tape to the correct spot. Then depress the PLAY lever on the program recorder. Finally, press any key on the keyboard (except BREAK). The program recorder takes about 20 seconds to read past the leader which starts every cassette file. Before it reaches the end of the leader, the computer must input the first data value with a GET or INPUT statement. After that, the tape stops, unless the program recorder receives more instructions to keep it going.

TABLE 11-8. OPEN Parameter Number 1 (*taskexpr*)

Device	Task Number	Task Description			
Program recorder (C:)	4 8	Read Write			
Disk file (D[n]:*filename* [.*ext*])	4 6 8 9 12	Read Read disk directory Write — new file Write — append Read and write — update			
Screen editor (E:)	8 12 13	Screen output Keyboard input & screen output Screen input & output			
Keyboard (K:)	4	Read			
Printer (P:)	8	Write			
RS-232 serial port (R[n]:)	5 8 9 13	Concurrent read Block write Concurrent write Concurrent read and write			
		Clear Screen	Text Window†	Read	Write
Screen display (S:)	8 12 24 28	Yes Yes Yes Yes	No No Yes Yes	No Yes No Yes	Yes Yes Yes Yes
	40 44 56 60	No* No* No* No*	No No Yes Yes	No Yes No Yes	Yes Yes Yes Yes

* Screen always cleared in graphics mode 0.
† No separate text window in graphics mode 0.

Opening for output operates the program recorder in record mode. The computer sounds its speaker twice. This signals you to put the right tape in the program recorder and use the FAST FORWARD and REWIND levers to position the tape to the correct spot. Then depress the RECORD and PLAY levers on the program recorder. Finally, press any key on the keyboard (except BREAK). If the volume on the television set is turned up, you will hear a continuous high-pitched marker tone being written as the cassette file leader. Within about 30 seconds of the time the OPEN statement is executed, the program must output 128 data bytes or close the output channel. Otherwise, garbage will be recorded on the file and an error will occur when the file is read back.

TABLE 11-9. OPEN Parameter Number 2 (*auxexpr*)

Device	Function Description	Value
Program recorder (C:)	Normal inter-record gaps Short inter-record gaps	0 128
Disk drive (D[n]:*filename* [.*ext*])	Ignored	0
Screen editor (E:)	Ignored	0
Keyboard (K:)	Ignored	0
Printer (P:)	Normal characters Sideways characters (ATARI 820)	0 83
RS-232 serial port (R[n]:)	Ignored	0
Screen display (S:)	BASIC graphics mode 0 BASIC graphics mode 1 BASIC graphics mode 2 BASIC graphics mode 3 BASIC graphics mode 4 BASIC graphics mode 5 BASIC graphics mode 6 BASIC graphics mode 7 BASIC graphics mode 8	0 1 2 3 4 5 6 7 8

TABLE 11-10. OPEN External Devices (*dev*)

Device	Name
Program recorder	C:
Disk file	D[n]:*filename* [.*ext*]
Screen editor	E:
Keyboard	K:
Printer	P:
RS-232 serial port	R[n]:
Display screen	S:

OPEN with a Disk File

In order to use the OPEN statement with a disk file name, the disk operating system must be in memory as a result of a successful boot when you turned on the computer (see page 27). If the disk operating system is absent, an error results.

A disk file can be opened for data input, directory input, and for output in several different modes. The value of *taskexpr* determines the mode, as Table 11-8 shows. Normally, a maximum of three files can be open at one time. Chapter 7 explains a way to increase this limit to seven files with version 2.0S of the disk operating system.

A file name is required when opening the disk for directory input, but it need not actually exist. The specified file name must exist when the task is input, update, or append, or else an error occurs. If the task is simple output and the file does not exist, it is created. If the task is simple output and the file exists, it is erased and a new one created. If a newly created file is not closed properly, the sectors allocated for it may remain allocated but unusable until the disk is reformatted.

OPEN with the Printer

The printer can only be opened for output. It must be turned on when the OPEN statement is executed. If there is an ONLINE/LOCAL switch on the printer, it must be in the "online" position as well. If the printer connects through the ATARI 850 Interface Module, it must be on also. If any of these conditions are not met, an error occurs.

OPEN with the RS-232 Serial Ports

To use the OPEN statement with one of the serial devices, the RS-232 serial device handler must be in memory as a result of a successful boot when you turned on the computer (see page 14). If the device handler is absent, an error results. But the computer reports no error if the device attached to the specified port is off, there is no device attached, or the ATARI 850 Interface Module itself is off.

In addition to being opened, the serial device may require conditioning with XIO statements. A given port can only be open on one channel at a time.

OPEN with the Display Screen

The OPEN statement links channel *chan* with the display screen when *dev* is S:. The value of *auxexpr* specifies the graphics mode. The value of *taskexpr* determines whether to clear the screen, whether a text window will be present, and whether the screen is open for output only, or both input and output (see Table 11-8).

Each time the display screen is opened, the text cursor is reset, the color registers are set to their default colors (see Table 11-2), and tab stops are set at columns 7, 15, 23,..., 103, 111, and 119. In graphics mode 0 the screen is always cleared. Also, the cursor is visible unless you turn it off with a POKE 755,0 statement.

The different graphics modes require different amounts of memory. The OPEN statement reserves memory for screen data and the display list in the highest part of available memory.

OPEN with the Screen Editor

The screen editor is an input/output device that uses the keyboard for input and the graphics mode 0 display screen for output. Each time the screen editor is opened, the graphics mode is set to 0, the display screen is cleared, the text cursor is reset, the color registers are set to their default colors (see Table 11-2), and tab stops are set at columns 7, 15, 23,. . ., 103, 111, and 119.

The value of *taskexpr* determines whether the screen editor is opened for input, output, or both. It can also enable a special input mode which causes INPUT statements to use the display screen as the input device. When this happens, the logical line where the cursor is located provides the value for the current INPUT statement variable. The value ends at the next EOL character on the screen; the RETURN key is ignored.

OPEN with the Keyboard

The keyboard (device K:) can be opened only for input.

PEEK

Listed in the Functions section at the end of this chapter.

PLOT (PL.)

Displays a point at the specified location on the display screen.

> *Format:*   PLOT *col, row*
> *Examples:*   PLOT 5,15
>   PL. COL, ROW

This statement plots a single dot of color on the screen at the column and row specified by the values of *col* and *row*. The maximum row and column values vary with the graphics mode (see Table 11-7). The most recently executed COLOR statement determines which color register will choose the point color. The PLOT statement uses the background color register if no COLOR statement has been executed since you turned on the computer.

The PLOT statement updates memory location 90 with the row number at which it plots, and memory locations 91 and 92 with the column number. A subsequent DRAWTO statement will use this as the starting point of the line it constructs.

PLOT in Graphics Modes 0, 1, and 2

The PLOT statement is primarily used in graphics modes 3 through 8, but it also works in graphics modes 0, 1, and 2. In these modes, PLOT places a character, rather than a dot, on the screen. The last COLOR statement executed determines which character will display, and in modes 1 and 2, which color register will choose the character color (see Tables 11-3 and 11-4). If no COLOR statement has been executed since you turned on the computer, COLOR 0 is used.

POINT (P.)

Changes a disk file's pointer to a specified location.

> *Format:*   POINT #*chan, sectvar, bytevar*

Examples: POINT #5, SCTR, BYTE
P. #FILE2, S, B

This statement moves the file pointer to the sector number specified by the value of numeric variable *sectvar,* and to the byte within the sector as specified by numeric variable *bytevar.* If *sectvar* is outside the limits of the file, an error will occur. The value of *bytevar* must be between 0 and 125. Channel *chan* must be open to a disk file for input, update, or append (see OPEN).

This statement is not available in version 1.0 of the disk operating system.

POKE (POK.)

Stores a byte of data in a specified memory location.

Format: POKE *memadr, bytexpr*

Example   POKE 756,226

A value between 0 and 255, provided by *bytexpr,* is written into memory at location *memadr.* If the memory location specified exceeds the maximum location in memory (for example, 16383 if you have 16K of memory), or accesses a read-only memory location, POKE has no effect.

Use caution with POKE. Some memory locations contain information essential to the computer's uninterrupted operation. Change random memory locations and you can destroy your program or lock up your system.

POP

Causes BASIC to forget the return location for the most recently executed FOR, GOSUB, or ON-GOSUB statement.

Format: POP

Example: POP

The FOR, GOSUB, and ON-GOSUB statements place a return location on the run-time stack. BASIC uses this location when it encounters a NEXT or RETURN statement. The POP statement removes one entry from the top of the run-time stack. No error occurs if the run-time stack is empty.

POP effectively changes the most recently executed GOSUB or ON-GOSUB statement into a GOTO or ON-GOTO statement, after the fact. The next RETURN statement executed will branch to the instruction immediately following the second most recently executed GOSUB or ON-GOSUB.

A POP statement executed inside a FOR-NEXT loop terminates the loop. BASIC behaves as though it never executed the most recent FOR statement.

POSITION (POS.)

Moves the cursor to a specified location on the display screen.

Format: POSITION *col, row*

Example: POSITION 10,3
POS. 5, BASE + N3

All display screen input and output statements except DRAWTO, PLOT, and XIO obtain the next cursor position from memory locations 84 (row) and 85 and 86 (column). The POSITION statement changes the contents of these memory locations. The value of *col* specifies the new column, and the value of *row* specifies the new row. The next GET, PRINT, PUT, INPUT, or LOCATE statement to the display screen occurs at the new cursor position. The cursor does not visibly move when the POSITION statement is executed; it moves when a subsequent statement accesses the display screen.

If the POSITION statement moves the cursor off the edge of the screen, no error occurs until a subsequent statement tries to use the display screen.

PRINT (PR. or ?)

Outputs characters to the display screen or another output device.

Format: $\text{PRINT}\left[\begin{Bmatrix} expr \\ \#chan \end{Bmatrix}\right]\left[\begin{Bmatrix} : \\ , \end{Bmatrix} \cdots \left[expr\right]\right] \cdots$

Examples: PRINT "Beware the Dog"
PR. "REMAINING ENERGY"; RE;
? #6, "X-axis"
? #3; A$,A,B$,B,C$,C

There are a number of acceptable variations on the PRINT statement. PRINT by itself outputs an ATASCII end-of-line (EOL) character. When PRINT is followed by one or more expressions, the values of these expressions go out on channel *chan,* which must be open for output. The way the values appear depends on their nature and on the use of semicolons or commas between values, but does not depend on the output device at all.

Printing Numeric Values

Numeric values within certain limits are printed using standard arithmetic notation. Scientific notation is used for values closer to 0 than ±0.01 and for any values with more than ten digits in front of the decimal point. Negative values are preceded by a minus sign; positive values are not preceded by anything.

Commas and Semicolons

PRINT statement expressions must be separated by either a comma or a semicolon.

Commas and semicolons control the spacing between printed values. A semicolon causes the next value to print immediately after the value just printed; the two are concatenated with no intervening spaces. A comma inserts blank spaces between the end of the value just printed and the next column stop.

Column stops are ten characters apart, at columns 11, 21, 31, and so on, across an entire logical line. If any character is printed in either of the two spaces just ahead of a column stop (for example, in column 19 or 20), that tab stop is temporarily inactivated.

A single PRINT statement can output an entire line or just part of a line. If the list of PRINT statement expressions does not end with a comma or semicolon, the computer outputs an EOL character after the last item on the list, terminating the output line.

A comma or semicolon will suppress the EOL character. If the list ends with a semicolon, the next PRINT statement outputs its first character directly after the last character output by the current PRINT statement, with no intervening spaces. If the list ends with a comma, the next output will be in the first position of the next column field, with blank spaces in between.

PRINT with the Display Screen

PRINT statement output goes to the display screen if the *chan* option is absent, or if it is present and opened for output to device S: or E:. Regardless of the graphics mode, the PRINT statement always outputs characters from the 256-element graphics mode 0 character set (see Table 11-3). In mode 0, the computer displays these characters as is. It translates them to another character set for graphics modes 1 and 2, and to dots of color for graphics modes 3 through 8.

Graphics modes 1 and 2 have two character sets. Roughly speaking, the standard set includes upper-case letters, digits, and punctuation, and the alternate set includes lower-case letters and graphics characters. There are no inverse characters in either set, but each character can appear via any of four color registers. Table 11-4 shows both character sets.

Two things affect the translation of PRINT statement characters for a mode 1 or 2 display screen. First, memory location 756 chooses between standard and alternate characters. POKE 756,226 chooses standard; POKE 756,224 chooses alternate. Second, the ATASCII code of the PRINT statement character chooses the color register and the exact character. To translate, look up the mode 0 character in Table 11-3 and note its ATASCII code. Be sure to differentiate between the codes for normal and inverse characters. Then find the code from Table 11-3 in Table 11-4. The column heading above the code in Table 11-4 gives the color register number that the PRINT statement will use. Read across to the right in Table 11-4 to get the mode 1 and 2 characters, both standard and alternate.

In graphics modes 3 through 8, the ATASCII codes of the PRINT statement characters determine which color registers will choose the dot colors. In modes 3, 5, and 7, the ATASCII code is reduced modulo 4 to a number between 0 and 3. In modes 4, 6, and 8, the ATASCII code is reduced to 0 or 1: even codes are 0 and odd codes are 1. The results of the reductions choose the color register the same way the parameter of a COLOR statement does (see Table 11-1).

PRINT statement output starts at the current cursor location, which is stored in memory locations 84 (row) and 85 and 86 (column). The DRAWTO, GET, INPUT, LOCATE, PLOT, POSITION, PRINT, PUT, and XIO statements all affect the cursor position.

PRINT with the Program Recorder

To use the PRINT statement with the program recorder, channel *chan* must be open for output to the program recorder.

A single PRINT statement might output only part of a record, so the computer stores data headed for the program recorder in its memory until it has 128 bytes. Then the entire block of data goes out. An EOL character forces output of the block, even if it is not full. In this case, the 128th byte contains the length of the block, stored as a hexadecimal number.

If the output channel is open for normal inter-record gaps, the tape can stop and start in between blocks. With short inter-record gaps, the tape keeps moving and your program must keep up with it, or garbage gets recorded.

PRINT with a Disk File

To use the PRINT statement with a disk file, channel *chan* must be open for output, update, or append to the disk file.

In most respects, data is output to a disk file in the same way it is output to the display screen. The computer transfers data to the disk drive in blocks. It stores output from PRINT statements in its memory until it has a full block. An EOL character forces output of the block, even if it is not full. The ATARI 810 Disk Drive has 125 characters per block.

PRINT with the Printer

To use the PRINT statement with the printer, channel *chan* must be open for output to the printer. The printer must be turned on when the PRINT statement is executed. If there is an ONLINE/LOCAL switch on the printer, it must be in the online position as well. If the printer connects through the 850 Interface Module, it must be on also. If any of these conditions are not met, an error occurs.

Character sets on most printers differ from the one in graphics mode 0. None of the ATARI printers can print the graphics characters, for example. The character that does appear depends on the printer. Tables 6-1 and 6-2 summarize the ATARI printer character sets.

PRINT with the RS-232 Serial Ports

To use the PRINT statement with one of the serial devices, channel *chan* must be open for output to the proper RS-232 serial port. This will be possible only if the RS-232 handler is in memory as a result of a successful boot when you turned on the computer (see page 14). In addition, XIO statements may be required to condition the serial port. For example, the translation mode (for converting incoming ASCII characters to ATASCII) may need to be set with an XIO 38 statement. All this must happen before executing a PRINT statement on the channel in question. The computer reports no error if the device attached to the specified port is off, there is no device attached, or the ATARI 850 Interface Module itself is off.

With this protocol out of the way, PRINT statement characters go through the ATARI 850 Interface Module to the serial port. It translates them to ATASCII characters according to the translation mode in effect. Two of the translation modes will change an outgoing ATASCII EOL character to an ASCII carriage return character. Appendix D has ASCII and ATASCII code tables.

PUT (PU.)

Sends a single numeric value to a previously opened output channel.

Format: PUT #*chan, numexpr*

Examples: PUT #1, NMBR
             PU. #CH, X

Channel *chan* must be open for output. The PUT statement outputs the value of *numexpr,* rounded to the nearest integer. If the value is not between 0 and 255, it is output modulo 256 (256 goes out as 0, 257 as 1, 258 as 2, etc.).

PUT with the Program Recorder

To use the PUT statement with the program recorder, channel *chan* must be open for output to the program recorder.

A single PUT statement might output only part of a record, so the computer stores data headed for the program recorder in its memory until it has 128 bytes. Then the entire block of data goes out. An EOL character forces output of the block, even if it is not full. In this case, the 128th byte contains the length of the block, stored as a hexadecimal number.

If the output channel is open for normal inter-record gaps, the tape can stop and start in between blocks. With short interrecord gaps, the tape keeps moving and your program must keep up with it, or garbage gets recorded.

PUT with the Disk Drive

The PUT statement will write data on a disk file that is open for output. The PUT statement outputs one-byte values that can be read by a GET statement. The INPUT statement cannot read the individual values a PUT statement writes.

The computer writes data to the disk drive in one-sector blocks, rather than one value at a time. PUT statements fill the disk buffer area of computer memory, one byte at a time. When the buffer is full, the computer writes the entire contents on the disk file. The CLOSE statement writes out any bytes left in the buffer. On the ATARI 810 Disk Drive, there are 125 values per sector.

The POINT statement can cause the computer to read in a new block from the disk file if it specifies a location that is outside the sector currently in memory.

PUT with the Display Screen

When used with the display screen (devices S: or E:), the PUT statement displays either a character or a graphics point at the current cursor position, depending on the graphics mode. In graphics mode 0, the value of *numexpr* determines which character to display (see Table 11-3). In graphics modes 1 and 2, the value of *numexpr* determines which color register to use and which character to display (see Table 11-4). In graphics modes 3 through 8, the value of *numexpr* determines which color register to use at the particular cursor position (see Table 11-1).

Each time PUT displays a value on the display screen, it moves right to the next cursor position. It does this by updating memory location 84 with the row number of the next cursor position, and memory locations 85 and 86 with the next column number. The next statement that stores or retrieves data from the display screen occurs in the new cursor position. However, this does not affect the DRAWTO or XIO statements, which maintain a separate cursor position in memory locations 90, 91, and 92.

If you use the PUT statement on the last column of a given row on the display screen, the cursor advances to the first column of the next line. If you try to access the display screen without first repositioning the cursor after a PUT statement at the last column of the last row, an error results.

PUT with the Printer

To use the PUT statement with the printer, channel *chan* must be open for output to the printer. The printer must be turned on when the PUT statement is executed. If there is an ONLINE/LOCAL switch on the printer, it must be in the online position as well. If the printer connects through the ATARI 850 Interface Module, it must be on also. If any of these conditions are not met, an error occurs.

PUT with the RS-232 Serial Ports

There must be an open output channel to the proper RS-232 serial port of the Interface Module, and this will be possible only if the RS-232 handler is in memory as a result of a successful boot when you turned on the computer (see page 14). In addition, XIO statements may be required to condition the serial port. For example, the translation mode may need to be set with an XIO 38 statement. All this must happen before executing a PUT statement on the channel in question. The computer reports no error if the device attached to the specified port is off, there is no device attached, or the ATARI 850 Interface Module itself is off.

With this protocol out of the way, PUT statement values go through the ATARI 850 Interface Module to the serial port. It translates them to ATASCII characters according to the translation mode in effect.

RAD

Tells BASIC to expect arguments in radians, rather than degrees, for subsequent trigonometric functions.

Format: RAD
Example: RAD

After executing the RAD statement, BASIC treats the arguments of trigonometric functions as radians. To switch to degrees, use the DEG statement. BASIC defaults to radians when it executes a NEW or RUN statement, or when you press the SYSTEM RESET key or turn the computer off and back on again.

READ (REA.)

Assigns values from DATA statements to variables.

Format:	READ *var* [,*var* ...]
Examples:	READ NAME$, RANK$, SERIALNO
	REA. LEVEL, GRADE, EVAL$

There is a pointer to the DATA list that determines which value to assign to the first variable (*var*) in the READ statement. At the start of the program and after a RESTORE statement, the pointer points to the first DATA statement value. As each READ statement variable gets a value, the pointer moves ahead to the next value.

The variables must match the type of the corresponding DATA statement values. A numeric value assigned to a string variable causes no problem. A string assigned to a numeric variable causes an error.

DATA statements need not be executed for the READ statement to find them. An error occurs if the READ statement cannot find enough DATA statement values.

READ in Immediate Mode

The READ statement may be executed in immediate mode as long as the program in memory contains enough DATA statement values. Otherwise, an error occurs.

REM (R. or .)

Allows you to place explanatory comments, or remarks, in a program.

Format:	REM *comment*
Examples:	REM Error Handling Subroutine
	R. Compute Interest
	. Get user response (Y or N only)

The *comment* is any sequence of characters that will fit on the current program line.

Remark statements are reproduced in program listings, but are otherwise ignored. A REM statement may be on a line of its own or it may be the last statement of a multiple-statement line.

REM cannot occur ahead of any other statements on a multiple-statement line, since BASIC treats all text following the REM statement as a comment, and executes none of it.

RESTORE (RES.)

Resets the pointer to the list of DATA statement values.

Format: RESTORE [*linexpr*]

Examples: RESTORE
RES. 140

The pointer determines which value the next READ statement will start with. When no line number (*linexpr*) is specified, the RESTORE statement moves the pointer to the start of the first DATA statement in the program. When a line number is specified, the pointer moves to the start of the first DATA statement on or after that program line.

RETURN (RET.)

Causes the program to branch to the statement immediately following the most recently executed GOSUB or ON-GOSUB statement.

Format: RETURN

Examples: RETURN
RET.

The RETURN statement gets the return location from the run-time stack. If a POP statement has removed an entry from the stack, the program branches to the statement following the *next* most recent GOSUB or ON-GOSUB statement.

If more RETURN (and POP) than GOSUB statements are executed in a program, an error occurs.

RUN (RU.)

Switches from immediate mode to programmed mode. Optionally loads a program from some input device to the computer memory. Executes the program in memory.

Format: RUN [*indev*]

Examples: RUN
RUN "C:"
RU. P$
RU. "D2:BUDGET.BAS"

Program execution starts at the lowest numbered line in the program. The RUN statement turns off all sound voices and closes all input/output channels, thereby disabling any graphics modes. It sets trigonometric functions to radians.

Program Load Feature

When the *indev* option is present, the RUN statement transfers a BASIC program from physical device *indev* to memory, then runs that program.

The RUN statement can only load a tokenized BASIC program recorded by the SAVE statement. It cannot load programs recorded by the CSAVE statement, which uses different timing, or by the LIST statement, which records BASIC text in ATASCII code.

During the loading process, any program previously in memory is erased. The variable name table for the incoming program replaces the one in memory.

The RUN statement uses input channel 7 for transfer from the program recorder and disk drive. It works even if channel 7 is already open. However, it does close the channel when it finishes.

RUN with the Program Recorder

The statement RUN "C:" operates the program recorder in playback mode, transferring a program from cassette to the computer memory. First, the computer sounds its speaker once. This signals you to put the right tape in the program recorder and use the FAST FORWARD and REWIND levers to position the tape to the correct spot. Then depress the PLAY lever on the program recorder. Finally, press any key on the keyboard (except BREAK). If the volume on the television set is turned up, you will hear several seconds of silence followed by one or more short bursts of sound from the television speaker. These sounds mean the program transfer is taking place. The sound bursts cease when the transfer finishes.

RUN with the Disk Drive

In order to use the RUN statement with a disk file name, the disk operating system must be in memory as a result of a successful boot when you turned on the computer (see page 27). If the disk operating system is absent, an error results. If it is present but no file exists as specified, an error results. If everything is set up correctly, the computer transfers the BASIC text from diskette to its memory and executes it.

Halting RUN

Once program execution begins, you can interrupt it by pressing the SYSTEM RESET key. If the computer was in the middle of loading a program, there will be no program lines in the computer's memory unless the load operation had a chance to finish. Pressing the SYSTEM RESET key while loading a disk file program may lock up the system. Your only recourse then is to turn the computer off and back on again.

Pressing the BREAK key stops the program. It rarely stops a program load. It will interrupt the load, but only momentarily. Some pieces of the program being transferred may never make it into memory.

SAVE (S.)

Transfers a BASIC program from the computer's memory to an output device.

Format: SAVE *outdev*

Examples: SAVE "C:"
S. "D:PROGRAM1"
S. PRGM$

The SAVE statement transfers a BASIC program from memory to output device *outdev.* Normally *outdev* specifies the program recorder (device C:) or a disk file (device D[*n*]:*filename* [*.ext*]). Specifying another output device, such as the printer or display screen, generally results in gibberish showing up on the device. It may make sense to use the SAVE statement with one of the RS-232 serial ports (devices R[*n*]:), depending on what you have attached to the port.

The SAVE statement outputs a tokenized BASIC program that only the LOAD and RUN statements can load. The CLOAD and ENTER statements cannot load a program that the SAVE statement saves. During the recording process, the SAVE statement also saves the variable name table for the outgoing program.

Input/Output Channels and Sound Voices

The SAVE statement uses channel 7 for output. It works even if channel 7 is already open. However, it does close the channel when it finishes. The SAVE statement also shuts off all sound voices.

SAVE with the Program Recorder

The statement SAVE "C:" operates the program recorder in record mode, transferring a program from the computer's memory to a cassette. First, it sounds the computer speaker twice. This signals you to put the right tape in the program recorder and use the FAST FORWARD and REWIND levers to position the tape to the correct spot. Then depress the RECORD and PLAY levers on the program recorder. Finally, press any key on the keyboard (except BREAK). If the volume on the television set is turned up, you will hear 20 seconds of a continuous high-pitched tone. This will be followed by one or more short bursts of sound from the television speaker. These sounds mean the program transfer is taking place. The sound bursts cease when the recording finishes.

SAVE with the Disk Drive

In order to use the SAVE statement with a disk file name, the disk operating system must be in memory as a result of a successful boot when you turned on the computer (see page 27). If the disk operating system is absent, an error results. If everything is copasetic, the computer transfers the BASIC text from its memory to diskette. If the specified file already exists, it is replaced by the program in memory.

SAVE with the RS-232 Serial Ports

To use the SAVE statement with one of the RS-232 serial ports, the RS-232 serial device handler must be in memory as a result of a successful boot when you turned on the computer (see page 14). If the device handler is absent, an error results. The device may require conditioning with XIO statements before executing the SAVE statement. If everything checks out, the computer transfers the BASIC text from its memory to the serial port. It does not check to see if the serial device received the program, or even if there is a serial device.

Halting SAVE

You can halt the SAVE operation at any time by pressing either the BREAK key or the SYSTEM RESET key. The program recording will be incomplete. The LOAD and RUN statements cannot load an incompletely saved program.

SETCOLOR (SE.)

Assigns hue and luminance attributes to one of the color registers.

Format: SETCOLOR *regexpr, huexpr, lumexpr*

Examples: SETCOLOR 2,2,2
               SE. REGNO, HUE, LUM

Numeric expression *regexpr* must have a value between 0 and 4. It determines which color register is affected by the current SETCOLOR statement.

The value of *huexpr* must be between 0 and 15. It specifies one of the 16 hues (colors) listed in Table 11-11.

The value of numeric expression *lumexpr* establishes the luminance (brightness) of the hue. Its value must be an even number between 0 and 14. Odd numbers yield the same luminance as the next lowest even number (e.g., 3 produces the same result as 2).

If the values of any of the expressions are not integers, they are rounded to the nearest integer. The values of *huexpr* and *lumexpr* may actually range up to 65535, though values larger than 15 are converted modulo 16 to values between 0 and 15.

The color registers are set to the default values listed in Table 11-2 whenever you

TABLE 11-11. Hues (Values of *huexpr* for SETCOLOR statement)

Number	Hue Range*
0	Black to white
1	Brown to gold
2	Orange to yellow
3	Terra cotta to pink
4	Mulberry to magenta
5	Violet to lavender
6	Indigo to white
7	Sky blue
8	Royal blue to baby blue
9	Turquoise blue
10	Ultramarine to powder blue
11	Midnight blue to aquamarine
12	Sea green to turquoise green
13	Forest green to Kelly green
14	Olive
15	Khaki to yellow

* Television adjustment affects hue radically, as does luminance value.

TABLE 11-12. Color Register Uses

Graphics Mode	Color Register				
	0	1	2	3	4
0	-	C*	C, Ba	-	Bo
1	C	C	C	C	Ba, Bo
2	C	C	C	C	Ba, Bo
3	P	P	P	-	P, Ba, Bo
4	P	-	-	-	P, Ba, Bo
5	P	P	P	-	P, Ba, Bo
6	P	-	-	-	P, Ba, Bo
7	P	P	P	-	P, Ba, Bo
8	-	P*	P, Ba	-	Bo

NOTE: C = Character   Ba = Background   * Determines luminance only; hue same
       P = Point or Line   Bo = Border   as background.

turn on the computer, press the SYSTEM RESET key, or execute a DOS or GRAPHICS statement.

The Color Registers

ATARI BASIC uses five memory locations to specify colors on the field of the display screen. These locations are called *color registers*.

The COLOR statement chooses which of the color registers many graphics statements will use when they display characters, points, or lines. Thus it works in conjunction with the SETCOLOR statement to determine the hue and luminance of items on the display screen. Table 11-12 summarizes color register use in the various BASIC graphics modes.

There are five color registers, numbered 0 through 4. Table 11-1 correlates the COLOR statement with color registers in each graphics mode. It shows, for example, that a COLOR 2 statement in graphics modes 3, 5, and 7 selects color register 1.

SOUND (SO.)

Turns one sound voice on or off. Also sets the voice's pitch, distortion, and volume.

Format: SOUND *voicexpr, pitchexpr, distexpr, volexpr*

Examples: SOUND 2, 100, 10, 15
             SO. V1, P, D, V2

Each SOUND statement sets the tone produced by one of the ATARI computer's four voices. Numeric expression *voicexpr* determines which voice is affected. Its value must be between 0 and 3.

The value of numeric expression *pitchexpr* sets the pitch. Its values range from 0 (highest note) to 255 (lowest note), as Table 11-13 shows.

The value of numeric expression *distexpr* establishes the distortion of the tone. Its value must be an even number between 0 and 14. A value of 10 or 14 is a pure tone. For *pitchexpr* values between 126 and 255, *distexpr* values 0 and 4 produce about the same sound. If a voice is on, an odd value of *distexpr* turns the voice off.

Numeric expression *volexpr* adjusts the voice's volume setting. The value must be between 0 (no sound) and 15 (full volume). Values can be as high as 65535 without causing an error, but above 15 they turn the voice off.

When pitch, distortion, and volume are all 0, the voice is silenced. A subsequent odd-numbered distortion produces a single click. Alternately executing a SOUND statement that has 0 pitch, distortion, and volume with a SOUND statement that has an odd-numbered distortion produces a stream of clicks.

If the values of any of the expressions are not integers, they are rounded to the nearest integer. The values of *pitchexpr* and *distexpr* may actually range up to 65535, although values larger than 15 are converted modulo 16 to values between 0 and 15.

All four voices are turned off when you press SYSTEM RESET or when BASIC executes any of the following statements: CLOAD, CSAVE, DOS, END, ENTER, LIST (except to the display screen), LOAD, NEW, RUN, SAVE.

STATUS (ST.)

Retrieves the status of the most recent input or output operation on the specified channel.

Format: STATUS #*chan, numvar*

TABLE 11-13. Musical Notes for Pitch Values
(Values of *pitchexpr* in SOUND statement)

Value	Note	Value	Note
29	C	91	F
31	B	96	E
33	A#/Bb	102	D#/Eb
35	A	108	D
37	G#/Ab	114	C#/Db
40	G	121	C
42	F#/Gb	128	B
45	F	136	A#/Bb
47	E	144	A
50	D#/Eb	153	G#/Ab
53	D	162	G
57	C#/Db	173	F#/Bb
60	C	182	F
64	B	193	E
68	A#/Bb	204	D#/Eb
72	A	217	D
76	G#/Ab	230	C#/Db
81	G	243	C
85	F#/Gb		

Examples: STATUS #5, STAT
               ST. #C, S

This statement assigns the status code of the last activity on channel *chan* to variable *numvar*. If the code is higher than 128, an error occurred. Status codes are listed in Appendix B.

If *numvar* is an array element, BASIC reports no error when it executes the STATUS statement. However, subsequent references to the same array result in errors, until the array is redimensioned.

STOP (STO.)

Causes a BASIC program to halt execution.

Format: STOP
Examples: STOP
               STO.

The computer returns to immediate mode (graphics mode 0). The message **STOPPED AT LINE *line*** is displayed, where *line* is the line number at which the STOP was executed. If the STOP statement is executed in immediate mode, the line number information does not appear.

The CONT statement will restart the program at the beginning of the program line that immediately follows the one where the halt occurred. CONT will not restart a multiple-statement immediate mode line.

The STOP statement does not turn off any sound voices or close any open input/output channels.

SYSTEM RESET (SYSTEM RESET)

Halts program execution immediately; returns the computer to immediate mode.

Format: SYSTEM RESET
Example: SYSTEM RESET

Pressing the SYSTEM RESET key stops the computer dead in its tracks, no matter what it is doing. An initialization process occurs. Trigonometric functions use radians, not degrees. Color registers return to their default values (Table 11-2). The display screen comes under control of the screen editor in graphics mode 0. Display screen margins and tab stops are reset. All sound voices are silenced. All input/output channels except channel 0 are closed abruptly; data may be lost.

You may attempt to continue program execution with the CONT statement. Execution will resume at the start of the next program line higher than the one where the reset occurred. The program is not likely to work properly after a reset.

TRAP (T.)

Branches to the line number indicated when a subsequent error occurs in a BASIC program.

Format: TRAP *linexpr*
Examples: TRAP 20000
                T. ERRLINE

This statement sets a flag that causes the program to branch to the line number indicated (*linexpr*) when an error occurs subsequently. This disables the automatic error handling which halts the BASIC program. Instead, the BASIC program must handle the error condition itself. TRAP must be executed *before* an error occurs, or no branch takes place when the error does occur.

Each type of error has a code number. The code of the most recently occurring error is stored in memory location 195. PEEK(195) retrieves the error code. The error codes and their messages are listed in Appendix A.

The expression 256 * PEEK(187) + PEEK(186) reveals the line number on which the error occurred. If the error occurred in immediate mode, the line number is not meaningful.

The occurrence of an error clears the flag set by the TRAP statement. Executing another TRAP statement resets the flag. Executing a TRAP statement where the value of *linexpr* is between 32768 and 65535 turns off the flag.

XIO (X.)

General input/output statement.

Format: XIO *cmd*, #*chan*, *numexpr*$_1$, *numexpr*$_2$, *dev*
Examples: XIO 18,#6,0,0,"S:"
                XIO LOCK, #3, 0, 0, FILE1$

The XIO statement can perform a wide variety of input and output operations. The value of *cmd* specifies the operation. Table 11-14 lists the possibilities.

Channel *chan* needs to be open for input or output, as appropriate, except for the XIO 3 (open) statement. The final parameter, *dev,* selects the input or output device. The remaining parameters provide supplementary information; the exact use depends on the operation. All parameters must always be present, although not all are always used. Tables 11-14 through 11-17 present each XIO operation's requirements for the various parameters. In each case, BASIC rounds numeric values to the nearest integer if necessary.

FUNCTIONS

ATARI BASIC functions are described below in alphabetical order. Nomenclature and abbreviations are described at the beginning of this chapter.

ABS

Returns the absolute value of a number. This is the value of the number without regard to sign.

Format: ABS(*numexpr*)
Example: IF A = ABS(A) THEN PR. "POSITIVE"

TABLE 11-14. XIO Commands

Action	Command	BASIC Equivalent	numexpr$_1$	numexpr$_2$
General:				
Open channel	3	OPEN	Table 11-8	Table 11-9
Read line	5	INPUT	0	0
Get character	7	GET	0	0
Write line	9	PRINT	0	0
Put character	11	PUT	0	0
Close channel	12	CLOSE	0	0
Channel status	13	STATUS	0	0
Screen graphics:				
Draw Line[1]	17	DRAWTO	0	0
Fill Area[2]	18	None	0	0
Disk:[3]				
Rename file[4]	32	DOS Menu	0	0
Delete file[5]	33	DOS Menu	0	0
Lock file[5]	35	DOS Menu	0	0
Unlock file[5]	36	DOS Menu	0	0
Move pointer[5,6]	37	POINT[6]	0	0
Find file pointer[5,6]	38	NOTE[6]	0	0
Format entire disk[5]	254	DOS Menu	0	0
RS-232 serial port:[7]				
Output partial block	32	None	0	0
Control DTR, RTS, XMT	34	None	Table 11-15	0
Baud rate, word size, stop bits, and ready monitoring	36	None	Table 11-16	Table 11-16
Translation mode	38	None	Table 11-17	ATASCII code
Concurrent mode	40	None	0	0

NOTES:

[1] Move cursor to start of line with POSITION statement before XIO 17.

[2] Use POKE 765, numexpr to choose fill color register, and draw vertical boundary lines before XIO 18.

[3] Disk operating system must be in memory.

[4] The dev parameter of XIO 32 specifies file to change.

[5] The dev parameter specifies the file, not the file to which #chan is open.

[6] Not available with version 1.0 of the disk operating system.

[7] The RS-232 serial device handler must be in memory.

TABLE 11-15. XIO 34 (Serial) Parameter *numexpr*$_1$

Add one number from each column to get value of *numexpr*$_1$				Selected values of *numexpr*$_1$			
	DTR	RTS	XMT	DTR	RTS	XMT	Value
No change	0	0	0	Off	Off	0	162
Turn off	128	32	2	Off	Off	1	163
(XMT to 0)				Off	On	0	178
				Off	On	1	179
Turn on	192	48	3	On	Off	0	226
(XMT to 1)				On	Off	1	227
				On	On	0	242
				On	On	1	243

TABLE 11-16. XIO 36 (Serial) Parameters *numexpr*$_1$ and *numexpr*$_2$

numexpr$_1$ (Add one value from each column)						*numexpr*$_2$			
Stop Bits	Value	Word Size	Value	Baud Rate	Value	DSR	CTS	CRX	Value
1	0	8 bits	0	300	0	No	No	No	0
2	128	7 bits	16	45.5	1	No	No	Yes	1
		6 bits	32	50	2	No	Yes	No	2
		5 bits	48	56.875	3	No	Yes	Yes	3
				75	4	Yes	No	No	4
				110	5	Yes	No	Yes	5
				134.5	6	Yes	Yes	No	6
				150	7	Yes	Yes	Yes	7
				300	8				
				600	9				
				1200	10				
				1800	11				
				2400	12				
				4800	13				
				9600	14				
				9600	15				

ADR

Returns the decimal starting address of a string variable or string constant in the computer's memory.

Format: ADR(*string*)

Example: A = USR(ADR(SUBR$))

TABLE 11-17. XIO 38 (Serial) Parameter *numexpr*₁

Add one value from each column			
Line Feed Append Value	Translation ATASCII — ASCII Mode Value	Input Parity Mode Value	Output Parity Mode Value
No 0 Yes* 64	Light 0 Heavy 16 None 32	Ignore 0 Odd† 4 Even† 8 Ignore† 12	No change 0 Odd 1 Even 2 Bit on 3

* Line feed character appended after carriage return (ATASCII EOL).

† Check parity as indicated, then clear parity bit.

It is possible to put a machine language program in a BASIC string variable. The ADR function can determine the starting address of the string variable, which is the same as the starting address of the machine language program in it. This address can be used with the USR function to execute the machine language program.

ASC

Returns the ATASCII code number for a specified character.

Format: ASC(*string*)

Example: IF ASC(RESPONSE$) < 78 THEN 990

If the string is longer than one character, ASC returns the ATASCII code for the first character in the string. If *string* is empty, ASC returns 44. ATASCII codes are listed in Appendix D.

ATN

Returns the arctangent of the argument.

Format: ATN(*numexpr*)

Example: PRINT ATN(T)

Computes the arctangent in radians of *numexpr*, or in degrees if the DEG statement is in effect. The angle returned is in the range $-\pi/2$ through $+\pi/2$.

CHR$

Returns the string value of the specified ATASCII code.

Format: CHR$(*numexpr*)

Example: PRINT CHR$(65))

Returns the character represented by the integer value of *numexpr*, interpreted as an ATASCII code. Appendix D has a table of ATASCII character codes. Meaningful values of *numexpr* lie between 0 and 255. The value can range up to 65535 without error; values 256 and higher are converted modulo 256 to numbers between 0 and 255.

Relational expressions that compare for less than (<), greater than (>), or not equal (<>) can use a CHR$ function only on one side of the inequality sign.

CLOG

Returns the common logarithm of a number.

Format: CLOG(*numexpr*)

Example: A = B*CLOG(A)

Computes the common (base 10) logarithm of *numexpr*. An error occurs if *numexpr* is 0 or negative.

COS

Returns the cosine of an angle.

Format: COS(*numexpr*)

Example: COS(3.1415)

Computes the cosine of *numexpr* radians, or *numexpr* degrees if the DEG statement is in effect.

EXP

Returns *e* raised to a power.

Format: EXP(*numexpr*)

Example: RATE = EXP(SUMPOW)

Computes *e* (the base of natural logarithms, 2.71828179) raised to the power *numexpr*.

FRE

Returns the number of bytes of RAM memory currently available.

Format: FRE(*numexpr*)

Example: ? FRE(0)

The memory available to you is that which is not already taken by the operating system, the disk operating system, the display screen data, the display list, or a BASIC program and its data.

The value of *numexpr* is not used by FRE. An error occurs if it is absent or its value is outside the range ±9.99999999E+98.

INT

Returns the integer portion of a number.

Format: INT(*numexpr*)

Example: A = (INT(A/2)*100+.5)/100

Returns the largest integer less than or equal to the value of *numexpr*.

LEN

Returns the length of a string.

Format: LEN(*string*)

Example: A$(LEN(A$)+1) = B$

Counts the number of characters in *string,* including all spaces and nonprinting characters, from the start of the string to the last character used.

LOG

Returns the natural logarithm of a number.

*Format:*LOG(*numexpr*)

*Example:*A = B*LOG(A)

Computes the natural (base *e*) logarithm of *numexpr.* An error occurs if *numexpr* is 0 or negative.

PADDLE

Returns the current value of the paddle specified.

Format: PADDLE(*numexpr*)

Example: PLOT PADDLE(0)/6, PADDLE(1)/12

The value returned is an integer between 1 and 228 based on the rotation of paddle number *numexpr* (Figure 11-2), or the resistance of a device connected to game controller jack *numexpr.* The paddles are numbered 0 through 7. If the paddle number is less than 0 or greater than 255, an error occurs. If the paddle number is between 8 and 255, PADDLE returns a somewhat unpredictable number.

PEEK

Returns the contents of a memory location.

Format: PEEK(*memadr*)

Example: LMARGN = PEEK(82)

The value returned is the decimal equivalent of the binary value stored at memory location *memadr.* Appendix G lists some useful memory locations.

PTRIG

Determines whether the trigger button of the specified paddle is on or off.

Format: PTRIG(*numexpr*)

Example: IF PTRIG(1) = 0 THEN PRINT "Boom!"

The value returned is 0 if the trigger of paddle number *numexpr* is being pressed, 1 if released. The paddles are numbered 0 through 7. If the paddle number is less

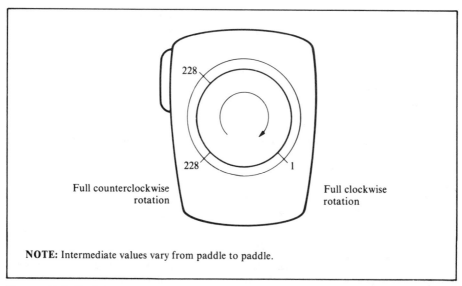

NOTE: Intermediate values vary from paddle to paddle.

FIGURE 11-2. PADDLE values

than 0 or greater than 255, an error occurs. If the paddle number is between 8 and 255, PTRIG returns a somewhat unpredictable number.

RND

Returns a random number.

Format: RND(*numexpr*)

Example: IF RND(0) < 0.3 THEN DAMAGE = ON

Returns a floating point number greater than or equal to 0 and less than 1. The value of *numexpr* has no effect on the value of the random number returned, but it must be present.

SGN

Identifies a number as positive, negative, or zero.

Format: SGN(*numexpr*)

Example: IF SGN(A) = -1 THEN PRINT "NEGATIVE"

The SGN function returns +1 if *numexpr* is positive, -1 if it is negative, and 0 if it is zero.

SIN

Returns the sine of an angle.

Format: SIN(*numexpr*)

Example: SIN (ANG)

Computes the sine of *numexpr* radians, or *numexpr* degrees if the DEG statement is in effect.

SQR

Returns the square root of a positive number.

Format: SQR(*numexpr*)

Example: HYPOT = SQR(LEG1^2 + LEG2^2)

A negative value of *numexpr* causes an error. SQR (*numexpr*) operates faster than (*numexpr*)^(0.5).

STICK

Identifies the current position of a joystick.

Format: STICK(*numexpr*)

Example: IF STICK(0) = 14 THEN ROW = ROW - 1

The value returned is an integer between 0 and 15, based on the position of stick number *numexpr* (Figure 11-3). The joysticks are numbered 0 through 3. If the stick number is less than 0 or greater than 255, an error occurs. If the stick number is between 4 and 255, STICK returns a somewhat unpredictable number.

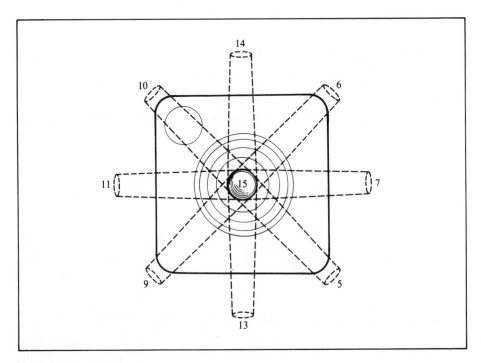

FIGURE 11-3. STICK values

STRIG

Determines whether the trigger button of the specified joystick is on or off.

Format: STRIG(*numexpr*)

Example: IF STRIG(1) = 0 THEN PRINT "Boom!"

The value returned is 0 if the trigger of stick number *numexpr* is being pressed, 1 if released. The sticks are numbered 0 through 3. If the stick number is less than 0 or greater than 255 an error occurs. If the stick number is between 4 and 255, STRIG returns a somewhat unpredictable number.

STR$

Converts a numeric value to a string.

Format   STR$(*numexpr*)

Example: ZIP$ = STR$(ZIP)

The value of *numexpr* is converted to ATASCII string characters. The characters are the same as those that would be printed by a PRINT *numexpr* statement. Therefore, STR$ (2/3) = "0.6666666666" and STR$ (12300000000) = "1.23E + 10." If *numexpr* exceeds the limits for numeric values, an error occurs.

Relational expressions that compare for less than (<), greater than (>), or not equal (< >) can use a STR$ function only on one side of the inequality sign.

USR

Branches to a machine language program, optionally passing values.

Format: USR(*memadr* [,*numexpr* ...])

Example: A = USR(1536,ADR(A$),ADR(B$))

When BASIC encounters a USR function, it pushes its current location within the BASIC program on the hardware stack and calls the machine language program which starts at memory location *memadr*. The machine language routine must already be there. Figure 11-4 illustrates how the USR function uses the hardware stack.

Function Arguments

The value of each USR function argument, *numexpr,* must be between 0 and 65535. BASIC passes the values to the machine language program via the hardware stack. Starting with the last *numexpr* on the list, BASIC evaluates each expression, converts the value to a two-byte hexadecimal integer, and pushes the integer onto the hardware stack (Figure 11-4). After pushing the final value onto the stack, it pushes a one-byte count of the number of arguments. The machine language program must pull all this off the stack (with PLA instructions, for example) before it returns to BASIC. Even if there are no arguments, the machine language program *must* pull the one-byte argument count off the stack.

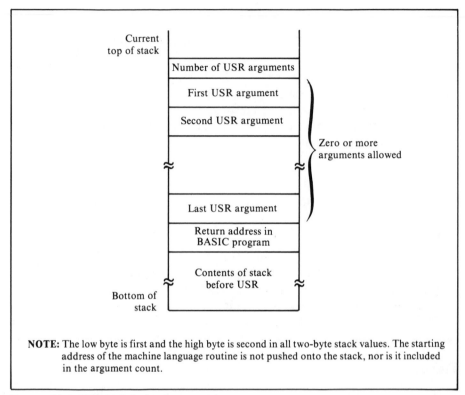

NOTE: The low byte is first and the high byte is second in all two-byte stack values. The starting address of the machine language routine is not pushed onto the stack, nor is it included in the argument count.

FIGURE 11-4. USR and the hardware stack

Function Value

The machine language program can return a two-byte hexadecimal value via memory locations 212 and 213, low byte in 212, high byte in 213. When the machine language program returns, BASIC converts the contents of these locations to a numeric value between 0 and 65535.

Returning to BASIC

The machine language program returns to BASIC by executing an assembly language RTS instruction, which pulls the return location off the hardware stack (Figure 11-4). This fact makes it clear why the machine language program must pull all argument-related data off the stack before returning.

VAL converts a numeric string to a numeric value.

    Format: VAL(*string*)

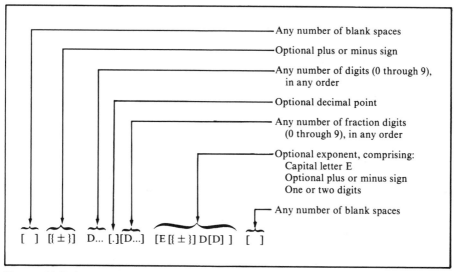

FIGURE 11-5. Acceptable numeric format for VAL

Example: TOT = VAL(A$) + VAL(B$)

Returns the numeric value represented by *string*. If the first character of *string* is not a numeric character, an error occurs. Otherwise, *string* is converted character by character until a non-numeric character is encountered. Figure 11-5 illustrates acceptable numeric format in string values.

If the numeric value of *string* is too large or too small (for example, 1E99), an error occurs.

A
ERROR MESSAGES
AND EXPLANATIONS

The ATARI computer reports errors by number. This appendix explains what those numbers mean. Some of the error titles in this appendix differ slightly from error titles in standard Atari, Inc., manuals. In those cases, the standard title appears in lighter type directly beneath the title used in this appendix.

2 Out of Memory
Memory Insufficient

There is not enough RAM available for the BASIC program or variables, or there are too many levels of FOR-NEXT loop nesting or subroutine nesting.

3 Bad Value
Value Error

A numeric value is too large, too small, or negative when it should be positive.

4 Too Many Variables

A program can have at most 128 different variable names. Variable names once used but now absent may still count toward this limit (see Figure 11-1).

5 String Length Exceeded
String Length Error

A substring specifies a character past the end of the dimensioned string length.

6   DATA List Exhausted
Out of Data Error

A READ statement tried to read past the end of the DATA statement list of values.

7   Number Greater Than 32767

A numeric value is negative or greater than 32767 in a situation where such a value is not allowed.

8   INPUT Statement Type Mismatch
INPUT Statement Error

An INPUT statement encountered a mismatch betweeen variable and value type. Numeric values cannot contain letters, puctuation, graphics characters, and so forth.

9   Array or String Dimension Error

A DIM statement includes a string variable or array that is already dimensioned, or an array larger than 32,767 bytes. Or, the program tried to use an undimensioned string variable or array, or a nonexistent array element.

10   Expression Too Complex
Argument Stack Overflow

An expression has too many levels of parentheses or function nesting.

11   Numeric Overflow
Floating Point Overflow/Underflow Error

The program tried to divide by zero, or in some other way tried to calculate or use a number larger in magnitude than $9.99999999 \times 10^{97}$.

12   Line Not Found

A GOSUB, GOTO, IF-THEN, ON-GOSUB, or ON-GOTO statement tried to branch to a nonexistent line number.

13   NEXT Without FOR
No Matching FOR Statement

No FOR statement was executed for the NEXT statement just executed. Possibly nested FOR-NEXT loops are crossed. A POP statement (which does not follow a GOSUB statement) in the middle of a FOR-NEXT loop effectively disables the most recently executed FOR statement.

14   Line Too Long

The statement is too complex or exceeds one logical line.

15   GOSUB or FOR Line Deleted

A RETURN or NEXT statement can no longer find the line which contained its companion GOSUB or FOR statement.

16   RETURN Without GOSUB
RETURN Error

A RETURN statement was executed before a GOSUB statement.

17   Undecipherable Statement Encountered
Garbage Error

Faulty RAM, a POKE statement, or a machine language subroutine changed a program statement to meaningless, unexecutable garbage.

18   Invalid String Character

The program tried to convert a non-numeric string to a numeric value with the VAL function.

19   Program Too Large
LOAD Program Too Long

The program being loaded will not fit in the available RAM.

20   Bad Channel Number
Device Number Larger

The program tried to use channel 0 or a channel number larger than 7.

21   Not LOAD Format
LOAD File Error

A LOAD statement tried to load a program and found data or a program that was recorded by the CSAVE or ENTER statement.

128   BREAK Abort

You pressed the BREAK key while the computer was in the middle of an input or output operation.

129   Channel Already Open
IOCB Already Open

The program tried to use a channel that was already in use. BASIC graphics statements automatically use channel 6; other statements use channel 7. When this error occurs, the troublesome channel may be automatically closed.

130   Unknown Device
Nonexistent Device

The program tried to use an unknown device. Table 11-10 lists standard device names. Note that the serial ports (device names R:, R1:, R2:, R3:, and R4:) are recognized only if the RS-232 serial device handler is present as the result of a successful boot when you turned on the computer (see Chapter 2).

131   Output Only
IOCB Write Only

A GET or INPUT statement used a channel opened for output only.

132   XIO Syntax Error
Invalid Command

Something is wrong with an XIO command.

133   Channel Not Open
Device or File Not Open

The program tried to use a channel before opening it.

134   Unknown Channel Number
Bad IOCB Number

The program can only use channels 1, 2, 3, 4, 5, 6, and 7.

135   Input Only
IOCB Read Only

A PRINT or PUT statement tried to use a channel that was open for input only.

136   End of File
EOF

The program encountered an end-of-file record or tried to read a disk sector that was not part of the open file.

137   Record Truncated
Truncated Record

The computer encountered a data record longer than 256 bytes and truncated it.

138   Device Does Not Respond
Device Timeout

The specified external device does not respond in a reasonable amount of time. Make sure that all power switches are on, all connecting cables are properly and securely attached, and all ONLINE/LOCAL switches are in the "online" position.

139   Device Malfunctions or Refuses Command
Device NAK

The program recorder or disk drive malfunctioned or cannot perform a command. The ATARI 850 Interface Module cannot perform a command, typically five-bit, six-bit, or seven-bit input at a too-high baud rate, or serial device not ready (readiness checking enabled).

140   Framing Error
Serial Bus

Serial bus data inconsistency. Cassette or diskette may be faulty or defective.

141   Cursor Out of Range

Row and column limits vary with different graphics modes (see Table 11-7).

142   Data Frame Overrun
Serial Bus Data Frame Overrun

Serial bus data inconsistency. Cassette or diskette may be faulty or defective.

143   Data Frame Checksum
Serial Bus Data Frame Checksum

Serial bus data inconsistency. Bad recording on, or readback from, cassette or diskette. Cassette or diskette may be faulty or defective.

144   Disk Error
Device Done Error

The diskette is physically protected against writing, or the diskette directory is scrambled.

145   Read-After-Write Compare Error, or
Bad Screen Mode Handler

The disk drive detected a difference between what it wrote and what it was supposed to write. Or, there is something wrong with the screen handler.

146   Function Not Implemented

The program tried to output to the keyboard, input from the printer, or some such impossible action.

147   Insufficient RAM for Graphics Mode
Insufficient RAM

Different graphics modes require different amounts of RAM (see Table 11-7).

150   Serial Port Open
Port Already Open

Each serial port can be open to only one channel at a time.

151   Concurrent Mode Error
Concurrent Mode I/O Not Enabled

A serial port must be opened for concurrent mode *before* enabling current mode input/output with the XIO 40 statement (see Tables 11-8 and 11-14).

152   Concurrent Mode Buffer Error
Illegal User-Supplied Buffer

The program specified an inconsistent buffer length and address during the startup of concurrent input/output using the optional program-provided buffer feature.

153   Concurrent Mode Active
Active Concurrent Mode I/O Error

The program tried to conduct input or output on a serial port while another serial port was open and active in concurrent mode.

154   Concurrent Mode Inactive
Concurrent Mode I/O Not Active

The input or output just attempted via a serial port requires concurrent mode.

160   Drive Number Unknown
Drive Number Error

The drive number can only be D:, D1:, D2:, D3:, or D4:.

161   Too Many Files Open

Normally, only three disk files can be open at the same time. Chapter 7 explains a way to extend this limit with DOS 2.0S.

162   Disk Full

There is no room on the diskette; all sectors are in use.

163   Unrecoverable System Error
Unrecoverable System Data I/O Error

During the input or output of data the computer found an error which it cannot determine the cause of nor recover from.

164   File Number Mismatch

A POINT statement moved the file pointer to a sector not part of the open file. Or, a disk file is scrambled; the intra-sector links are disorganized and inconsistent.

165   Bad File Name
File Name Error

A file name started with a lower-case letter, contained illegal characters, or used wild card characters (* and ?) improperly.

166   POINT Data Length Error

A POINT statement tried to move to a nonexistent byte number in a sector.

167   File Locked

Locked disk files cannot be written to or erased, or have their names changed.

168   Unknown XIO Command
Command Invalid

The program tried to use an XIO command that does not exist or is not defined for the specified device.

169   Directory Full

A diskette directory has room for 64 file names. The amount of disk space available (number of sectors free) has no bearing on this.

170   File Not Found

The specified file name is not in the directory of the diskette now in the specified disk drive.

171   POINT Invalid

The program tried to access a disk sector that is not part of the open file.

B
STATUS STATEMENT CODES

This appendix lists the values returned by the STATUS statement, followed by a message telling what the number means. For a more detailed description of the messages, see Appendix A.

Decimal Code	Meaning
1	Operation complete and OK
3	End of file approaching: next read gets last data in file*
128	BREAK abort
129	I/O channel already open (IOCB in use)
130	Unknown device
131	Opened for write only
133	Device or file not open
134	Unknown I/O channel number
135	Opened for read only
136	End of file
137	Record truncated
138	Device does not respond
139	Device malfunctions or refuses command
140	Serial bus input framing error
141	Cursor out of range
142	Serial bus data frame overrun error
143	Serial bus data frame checksum error

*This code differs from the error code in Appendix A.

Decimal Code	Meaning
144	Disk write-protected
145	Bad screen mode/Read-after-write compare error
146	Function not supported by handler
147	Insufficient RAM for screen mode
160	Disk drive number unknown
161	Too many open disk files
162	Disk full
163	Fatal I/O error
164	Disk file number mismatch
165	File name error
166	POINT data length error
167	File locked
168	Unknown XIO command
169	Directory full (64 files)
170	File not found
171	POINT invalid

C
DERIVED
TRIGONOMETRIC
FUNCTIONS

While the following list of derived functions is by no means complete, it does provide some of the most frequently used formulas. Certain values of x will invalidate some functions (for example, if $COS(x) = 0$ then $SEC(x)$ is nonreal), so your program should check for them.

ARCCOS(x) = -ATN(x/SQR(-x * x + 1)) + 1.5707633
    Returns the inverse cosine of x(ABS(x) < 1).

ARCCOT(x) = -ATN(x) + 1.5707633
    Returns the inverse cotangent of x.

ARCCOSH(x) = LOG(x + SQR(x * x - 1))
    Returns the inverse hyperbolic cosine of x(x >= 1).

ARCCOTH(x) = LOG((x + 1)/(x - 1))/2
    Returns the inverse hyperbolic cotangent of x(ABS (x > 1).

ARCCSC(x) = ATN(1/SQR(x * x - 1)) + (SGN(x) - 1) * 1.5707633
    Returns the inverse cosecant of x(ABS (x) > 1).

ARCCSCH(x) = LOG((SGN(x) * SQR(x * x + 1) + 1)/x)
    Returns the inverse hyperbolic cosecant of x(x > 0).

ARCSEC(x) = ATN((SQR(x * x - 1)) + (SGN(x) - 1) * 1.5707633
    Returns the inverse secant of x(ABS(x) >= 1).

ARCSECH(x) = LOG((SQR(-x * x + 1) + 1)/x)
    Returns the inverse hyperbolic secant of x (0 < x <= 1).

ARCSIN(x) = ATN(x/SQR(-x * x + 1))
    Returns the inverse sine of x (ABS(x) < 1).

ARCSINH(x) = LOG(x + SQR($x * x$ + 1))
   Returns the inverse hyperbolic sine of x.

ARCTANH(x) = LOG((1 + x)/(1 - x))/2
   Returns the inverse hyperbolic tangent of x (ABS(x) < 1).

COSH(x) = (EXP(x) + EXP(-x))/2
   Returns the hyperbolic cosine of x.

COT(x) = COS(x)/SIN(x)
   Returns the cotangent of x ($x <> 0$).

COTH(x) = EXP(-x)/(EXP(x) - EXP(-x)) $*$ 2 + 1
   Returns the hyperbolic cotangent of x ($x <> 0$).

CSC(x) = 1/SIN(x)
   Returns the cosecant of x ($x <> 0$).

CSCH(x) = 2/(EXP(x) - EXP(-x))
   Returns the hyperbolic cosecant of x ($x <> 0$).

LOG$_a$(x) = LOG(x)/LOG(a)
   Returns the base a logarithm of x ($a > 0, x > 0$).

LOG$_{10}$(x) = LOG(x)/2.30258509
   Returns the common (base ten) logarithm of x ($x > 0$).

MODa(x) = INT((x/a - INT(x/a)) $*$ a + 0.05) $*$ SGN(x/a)
   Returns x modulo a: the remainder after division of x by a ($a <> 0$).

SEC(x) = 1/COS(x)
   Returns the secant of x ($x <> \pi /2$).

SECH(x) = 2/(EXP(x) + EXP(-x))
   Returns the hyperbolic secant of x.

SINH(x) = (EXP(x) - EXP(-x))/2
   Returns the hyperbolic sine of x.

TAN(x) = SIN(x)/COS(x)
   Returns the tangent of x ($x <> 0$).

TANH(x) = -EXP(-x)/EXP(x) + EXP(-x)) $*$ 2 + 1
   Returns the hyperbolic tangent of x.

D
CODES,
CHARACTERS,
AND KEYSTROKES

Table D-1 lists all 256 characters in the standard ATARI display screen graphics mode 0 character set. It gives the ATASCII code for each character. You can use the code with the CHR$ function to generate the character itself. All these characters can also be produced by a keystroke or combination of keystrokes. Table D-1 also includes that information.

The keystroke(s) shown in Table D-1 always produce the code number indicated. As long as the computer is operating in graphics mode 0, they also generate the character shown. But in other graphics modes, a particular code may produce a different character (see Table 11-4), or even a graphics dot.

A few of the codes generate control characters. When displayed by a PRINT statement, nothing actually appears on the screen. Instead, the cursor moves or some other control process occurs. You can output control characters with a PRINT statement: either use the CHR$ function or type an escape sequence inside quotation marks (see Chapter 4). When you type an escape sequence, a character appears on the screen, but the control process does not occur. The process happens only when the control character is displayed while the program is running. The character you see only represents the control process that will take place. However, if a program displays ATASCII code 27 immediately before the control character, the representative character displays and the control process does not occur. Table D-1 shows the representative characters, marked with footnotes that explain the control processes the characters implement.

Lower-Case Characters

Many of the characters can be typed directly only when the keyboard is in lower-case mode. Such characters are marked in the "Keystrokes to Produce Character" column of Table D-1 with the symbol (LOWR). Pressing the LOWR key once puts the keyboard in lower-case mode. Pressing the CAPS key (SHIFT-LOWR key) puts the keyboard back in upper-case mode.

Inverse Characters

Almost half the characters are inverse characters. To type them directly, the keyboard must be in inverse mode. Such characters are marked in the "Keystrokes to Produce Character" column of Table D-1 with the symbol (⅄). Pressing the ⅄ key once puts the keyboard in inverse mode. Pressing it again puts it in normal mode. Every time this key is pressed, it switches to the opposite mode.

TABLE D-1. Codes, Characters, and Keystrokes

Decimal Code	ATASCII Character	ASCII Character (If Any)	Keystrokes to Produce Character	Decimal Code	ATASCII Character	ASCII Character (If Any)	Keystrokes to Produce Character
0	♥	NULL	CTRL-,	11	■	VT	CTRL-K
1	├	SOH	CTRL-A	12	■	FF	CTRL-L
2	▌	STX	CTRL-B	13	▀	CR	CTRL-M
3	┘	ETX	CTRL-C	14	▬	SO	CTRL-N
4	┤	EOT	CTRL-D	15	■	SI	CTRL-O
5	┐	ENQ	CTRL-E	16	♣	DLE	CTRL-P
6	╱	ACK	CTRL-F	17	┌	DC1	CTRL-Q
7	╲	BEL	CTRL-G	18	▬	DC2	CTRL-R
8	◢	BS	CTRL-H	19	✚	DC3	CTRL-S
9	■	HT	CTRL-I	20	●	DC4	CTRL-T
10	◣	LF	CTRL-J	21	▬	NAK	CTRL-U

TABLE D-1. Codes, Characters, and Keystrokes (continued)

Decimal Code	ATASCII Character	ASCII Character (If Any)	Keystrokes to Produce Character	Decimal Code	ATASCII Character	ASCII Character (If Any)	Keystrokes to Produce Character
22	▮	SYN	CTRL-V	42	✳	*	*
23	┳	ETB	CTRL-W	43	✚	+	+
24	┻	CAN	CTRL-X	44	,	,	,
25	▮	EM	CTRL-Y	45	····	-	-
26	┗	SUB	CTRL-Z	46	·	.	.
27	E [1]	ESC	ESC\ESC	47	/	/	/
28	↑ [2]	FS	ESC\CTRL--	48	0	0	0
29	↓ [3]	GS	ESC\CTRL-=	49	1	1	1
30	← [4]	RS	ESC\CTRL-+	50	2	2	2
31	→ [5]	US	ESC\CTRL-*	51	3	3	3
32	(blank)	Space	SPACE BAR	52	4	4	4
33	!	!	SHIFT-1	53	5	5	5
34	"	"	SHIFT-2	54	6	6	6
35	#	#	SHIFT-3	55	7	7	7
36	$	$	SHIFT-4	56	8	8	8
37	%	%	SHIFT-5	57	9	9	9
38	&	&	SHIFT-6	58	⬦	:	SHIFT-;
39	'	'	SHIFT-7	59	⬦	;	;
40	(	(	SHIFT-9	60	<	<	<
41	)	)	SHIFT-0	61	≡	=	=

TABLE D-1. Codes, Characters, and Keystrokes (continued)

Decimal Code	ATASCII Character	ASCII Character (If Any)	Keystrokes to Produce Character	Decimal Code	ATASCII Character	ASCII Character (If Any)	Keystrokes to Produce Character
62	>	>	>	82	R	R	R
63	?	?	SHIFT-/	83	S	S	S
64	@	@	SHIFT-8	84	T	T	T
65	A	A	A	85	U	U	U
66	B	B	B	86	V	V	V
67	C	C	C	87	W	W	W
68	D	D	D	88	X	X	X
69	E	E	E	89	Y	Y	Y
70	F	F	F	90	Z	Z	Z
71	G	G	G	91	[	[	SHIFT- ;
72	H	H	H	92	\	\	SHIFT- ,
73	I	I	I	93	]	]	SHIFT- +
74	J	J	J	94	^	↑	SHIFT- *
75	K	K	K	95	....	←	SHIFT--
76	L	L	L	96	♦	′	CTRL-.
77	M	M	M	97	a	a	(LOWR) A
78	N	N	N	98	b	b	(LOWR) B
79	O	O	O	99	c	c	(LOWR) C
80	P	P	P	100	d	d	(LOWR) D
81	Q	Q	Q	101	e	e	(LOWR) E

TABLE D-1. Codes, Characters, and Keystrokes (continued)

Decimal Code	ATASCII Character	ASCII Character (If Any)	Keystrokes to Produce Character	Decimal Code	ATASCII Character	ASCII Character (If Any)	Keystrokes to Produce Character
102	f	f	(LOWR) F	122	z	z	(LOWR) Z
103	g	g	(LOWR) G	123	♣	{	CTRL-;
104	h	h	(LOWR) H	124	|	|	SHIFT- =
105	i	i	(LOWR) I	125	[6]	}	ESC\CTRL-< or ESC\SHIFT-<
106	j	j	(LOWR) J	126	[7]	~	ESC\BACK S
107	k	k	(LOWR) K	127	[8]	DEL	ESC\TAB
108	l	l	(LOWR) L	128	♥		(ʌ) CTRL-,
109	m	m	(LOWR) M	129			(ʌ) CTRL-A
110	n	n	(LOWR) N	130			(ʌ) CTRL-B
111	o	o	(LOWR) O	131			(ʌ) CTRL-C
112	p	p	(LOWR) P	132			(ʌ) CTRL-D
113	q	q	(LOWR) Q	133			(ʌ) CTRL-E
114	r	r	(LOWR) R	134			(ʌ) CTRL-F
115	s	s	(LOWR) S	135			(ʌ) CTRL-G
116	t	t	(LOWR) T	136			(ʌ) CTRL-H
117	u	u	(LOWR) U	137			(ʌ) CTRL-I
118	v	v	(LOWR) V	138			(ʌ) CTRL-J
119	w	w	(LOWR) W	139			(ʌ) CTRL-K
120	x	x	(LOWR) X	140			(ʌ) CTRL-L
121	y	y	(LOWR) Y	141			(ʌ) CTRL-M

TABLE D-1. Codes, Characters, and Keystrokes (continued)

Decimal Code	ATASCII Character	ASCII Character (If Any)	Keystrokes to Produce Character	Decimal Code	ATASCII Character	ASCII Character (If Any)	Keystrokes to Produce Character
142			(⅄) CTRL-N	162			(⅄) SHIFT-2
143			(⅄) CTRL-O	163			(⅄) SHIFT-3
144			(⅄) CTRL-P	164			(⅄) SHIFT-4
145			(⅄) CTRL-Q	165			(⅄) SHIFT-5
146			(⅄) CTRL-R	166			(⅄) SHIFT-6
147			(⅄) CTRL-S	167			(⅄) SHIFT-7
148			(⅄) CTRL-T	168			(⅄) SHIFT-9
149			(⅄) CTRL-U	169			(⅄) SHIFT-0
150			(⅄) CTRL-V	170			(⅄) *
151			(⅄) CTRL-W	171			(⅄) +
152			(⅄) CTRL-X	172			(⅄) ,
153			(⅄) CTRL-Y	173			(⅄) -
154			(⅄) CTRL-Z	174			(⅄) .
155	EOL[9]		(⅄) RETURN	175			(⅄) /
156	[10]		ESC\SHIFT-BACK S	176			(⅄) 0
157	[11]		ESC\SHIFT->	177			(⅄) 1
158	[12]		ESC\CTRL-TAB	178			(⅄) 2
159	[13]		ESC\SHIFT-TAB	179			(⅄) 3
160			(⅄) SPACE BAR	180			(⅄) 4
161			(⅄) SHIFT-1	181			(⅄) 5

TABLE D-1. Codes, Characters, and Keystrokes (continued)

Decimal Code	ATASCII Character	ASCII Character (If Any)	Keystrokes to Produce Character	Decimal Code	ATASCII Character	ASCII Character (If Any)	Keystrokes to Produce Character
182	6		(⋏) 6	202	J		(⋏) J
183	7		(⋏) 7	203	K		(⋏) K
184	8		(⋏) 8	204	L		(⋏) L
185	9		(⋏) 9	205	M		(⋏) M
186	:		(⋏) SHIFT-;	206	N		(⋏) N
187	;		(⋏) ;	207	O		(⋏) O
188	<		(⋏) <	208	P		(⋏) P
189	=		(⋏) =	209	Q		(⋏) Q
190	>		(⋏) >	210	R		(⋏) R
191	?		(⋏) SHIFT-/	211	S		(⋏) S
192	@		(⋏) SHIFT-8	212	T		(⋏) T
193	A		(⋏) A	213	U		(⋏) U
194	B		(⋏) B	214	V		(⋏) V
195	C		(⋏) C	215	W		(⋏) W
196	D		(⋏) D	216	X		(⋏) X
197	E		(⋏) E	217	Y		(⋏) Y
198	F		(⋏) F	218	Z		(⋏) Z
199	G		(⋏) G	219	[		(⋏) SHIFT-,
200	H		(⋏) H	220	\		(⋏) SHIFT-+
201	I		(⋏) I	221	]		(⋏) SHIFT-.

TABLE D-1. Codes, Characters, and Keystrokes (continued)

Decimal Code	ATASCII Character	ASCII Character (If Any)	Keystrokes to Produce Character	Decimal Code	ATASCII Character	ASCII Character (If Any)	Keystrokes to Produce Character
222	∧		(⋏) SHIFT-*	239	o		(⋏) (LOWR) O
223			(⋏) SHIFT--	240	p		(⋏) (LOWR) P
224	♦		(⋏) CTRL-.	241	q		(⋏) (LOWR) Q
225	a		(⋏) (LOWR) A	242	r		(⋏) (LOWR) R
226	b		(⋏) (LOWR) B	243	s		(⋏) (LOWR) S
227	c		(⋏) (LOWR) C	244	t		(⋏) (LOWR) T
228	d		(⋏) (LOWR) D	245	u		(⋏) (LOWR) U
229	e		(⋏) (LOWR) E	246	v		(⋏) (LOWR) V
230	f		(⋏) (LOWR) F	247	w		(⋏) (LOWR) W
231	g		(⋏) (LOWR) G	248	x		(⋏) (LOWR) X
232	h		(⋏) (LOWR) H	249	y		(⋏) (LOWR) Y
233	i		(⋏) (LOWR) I	250	z		(⋏) (LOWR) Z
234	j		(⋏) (LOWR) J	251	♣		(⋏) CTRL-;
235	k		(⋏) (LOWR) K	252	|		(⋏) SHIFT-=
236	l		(⋏) (LOWR) L	253	[14]		ESC\CTRL-2
237	m		(⋏) (LOWR) M	254	[15]		(⋏) ESC\ CTRL-BACK S
238	n		(⋏) (LOWR) N	255	[16]		(⋏) ESC\CTRL->

Notes

[1]The character **E** represents a control character. In most cases, this control character does nothing; CHR$(27) is generally a nondisplaying character. However, if the next character displayed is a control character (ATASCII codes 27, 28, 29, 30, 31, 125, 126, 127, 156, 157, 158, 159, 253, 254, or 255), the control process does not take place. Instead, the representative character itself appears.

TABLE D-1. Codes, Characters, and Keystrokes (continued)

Notes (continued):

[2]The character ⬆ represents the control character which moves the cursor up one row. If the character displayed just before this was ATASCII code 27, the character ⬆ displays; the cursor does not move.

[3]The character ⬇ represents the control character which moves the cursor down one row. If the character displayed just before this was ATASCII code 27, the character ⬇ displays; the cursor does not move.

[4]The character ⬅ represents the control character which moves the cursor one column left. If the character displayed just before this was ATASCII code 27, the character ⬅ displays; the cursor does not move.

[5]The character ➡ represents the control character which moves the cursor one column right. If the character displayed just before this was ATASCII code 27, the character ➡ displays; the cursor does not move.

[6]The character ◥ represents the control character which clears the screen and moves the cursor to the home position. If the character displayed just before this was ATASCII code 27, the character ◥ displays; the screen is not cleared.

[7]The character ◀ represents the control character which moves the cursor one column left and replaces the character there with a blank space. If the character displayed just before this was ATASCII code 27, the character ◀ displays; the cursor does not move.

[8]The character ▶ represents the control character which advances the cursor to the next tab stop. If the character displayed just before this was ATASCII code 27, the character ▶ displays; the cursor does not move.

[9]The ATASCII end-of-line character.

[10]The character ⬆ represents the control character which deletes the line on which the cursor is located. If the character displayed just before this was ATASCII code 27, the character ⬆ displays; the deletion does not occur.

[11]The character ⬇ represents the control character which inserts a line above the one on which the cursor is located. If the character displayed just before this was ATASCII code 27, the character ⬇ displays; the insertion does not occur.

[12]The character ◀ represents the control character which clears the tab stop (if any) at the current cursor position. If the character displayed just before this was ATASCII code 27, the character ◀ displays; no tab stop is affected.

[13]The character ▶ represents the control character which sets a tab stop at the current cursor position. If the character displayed just before this was ATASCII code 27, the character ▶ displays; no tab stop is set.

[14]The character ◥ represents the control character which beeps the built-in speaker; nothing is displayed. If the character displayed just before this was ATASCII code 27, the character ◥ displays; the speaker remains silent.

[15]The character ◀ represents the control character which deletes the character to the right of the cursor, shifting the remainder of the logical line one space to the left. If the character displayed just before this was ATASCII code 27, the character ◀ displays; no deletion occurs.

[16]The character ▶ represents the control character which inserts a blank space to the right of the cursor, shifting the remainder of the logical line one space to the right. If the character displayed just before this was ATASCII code 27, the character ▶ displays; no insertion occurs.

E
ATARI BASIC KEYWORDS AND ABBREVIATIONS

Keyword	Abbrev.	Keyword	Abbrev.	Keyword	Abbrev.
ABS		GOTO	G.	PUT	PU.
ADR		GRAPHICS	GR.	RAD	
AND		IF		READ	REA.
ASC		INPUT	I.	REM	R. or .
ATN		INT		RESTORE	RES.
BYE	B.	LEN		RETURN	RET.
CLOAD	CLOA.	LET	LE.	RND	
CHR$		LIST	L.	RUN	RU.
CLOG		LOAD	LO.	SAVE	S.
CLOSE	CL.	LOCATE	LOC.	SETCOLOR	SE.
CLR		LOG		SGN	
COLOR	C.	LPRINT	LP.	SIN	
COM		NEW		SOUND	SO.
CONT	CON.	NEXT	N.	SQR	
COS		NOT		STATUS	ST.
CSAVE	CS.	NOTE	NO.	STEP	
DATA	D.	ON		STICK	
DEG	DE.	OPEN	O.	STRIG	
DIM	DI.	OR		STOP	STO.
DOS	DO.	PADDLE		STR$	
DRAWTO	DR.	PEEK		THEN	
END		PLOT	PL.	TO	
ENTER	E.	POINT	P.	TRAP	T.
EXP		POKE	POK.	USR	
FOR	F.	POP		VAL	
FRE		POSITION	POS.	XIO	X.
GET	GE.	PRINT	PR. or ?		
GOSUB	GOS.	PTRIG			

F
MEMORY USAGE

The ATARI computer memory is divided into three general categories: random access memory (RAM), read-only memory (ROM), and input/output locations (I/O). Figure F-1 shows how memory is generally allocated on an ATARI computer. The other figures and tables in this appendix amplify this figure.

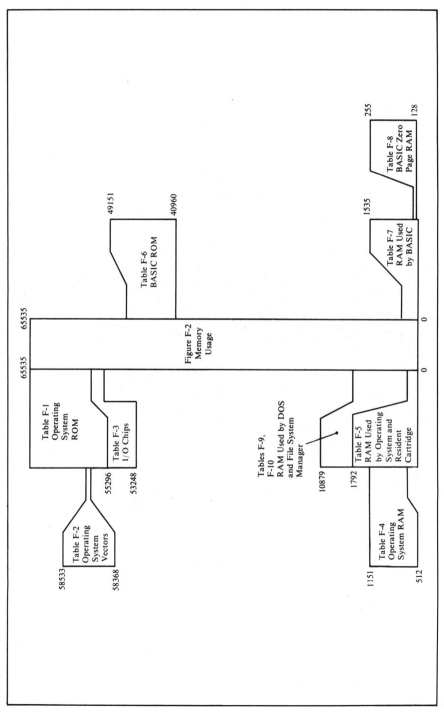

FIGURE F-1. ATARI 400/800 computer memory map

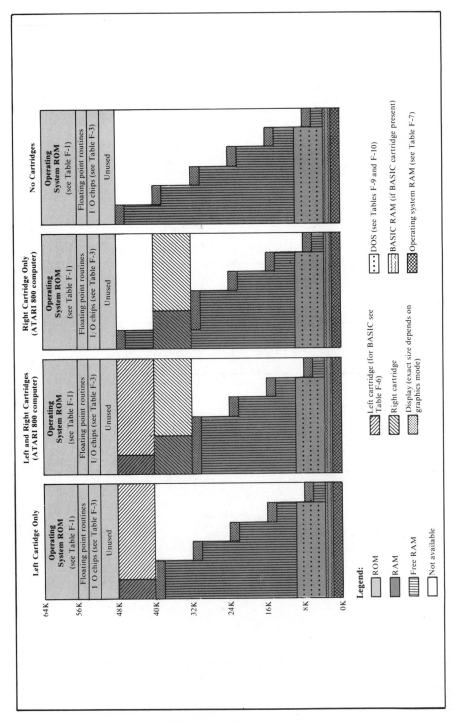

FIGURE F-2. Memory usage

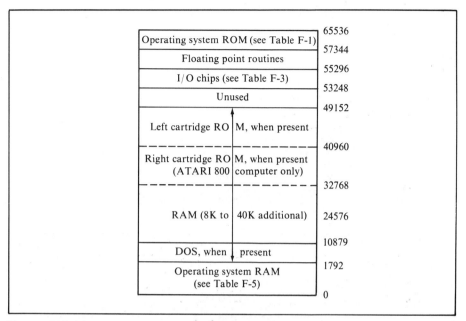

FIGURE F-3. Memory locations without BASIC resident

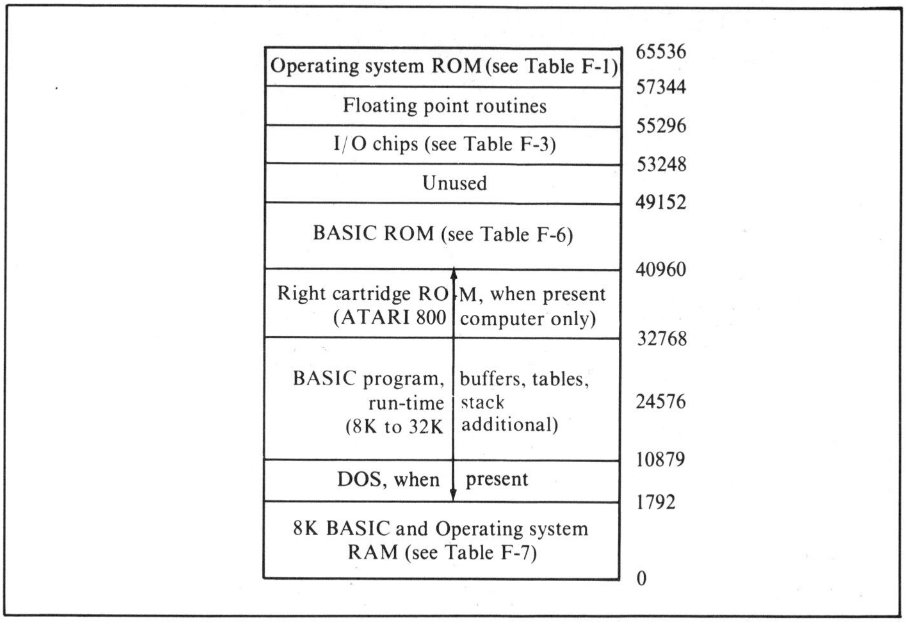

FIGURE F-4. Memory locations with standard ATARI BASIC resident

TABLE F-1. Operating System ROM
(Memory Locations 55296-65535)

Location	Usage
55296-57393	Floating point routines
57344-58367	Character set
58368-58533	Vectors (see Table F-2)
58534-59092	CIO
59093-59715	Interrupt handler
59716-60905	SIO
60906-61047	Disk handler
61048-61248	Printer handler
61249-61666	Cassette handler
61667-62435	Monitor
62436-65535	Display and keyboard handler

TABLE F-2. Operating System Vectors
(Memory Locations 58368-58533)

Location	Type of Memory	Usage
58368-58383	ROM	Editor
58384-58399	ROM	Screen
58400-58415	ROM	Keyboard
58416-58431	ROM	Printer
58432-58447	ROM	Cassette
58448-58495	ROM	Jump vectors
58496-58533	ROM	Initial RAM vectors

TABLE F-3. I/O Chips (Memory Locations 53248-55295)

Location	Type of Memory	Usage
53248-53503	I/O	CTIA or GTIA
53504-53759	I/O	Unused
54760-54015	I/O	POKEY
54016-54271	I/O	PIA
54272-54783	I/O	ANTIC
54784-55295	I/O	Unused

TABLE F-4. Operating System RAM (Memory Locations 512-1151)

Location	Usage
512-553	Interrupt vectors
554-623	Miscellaneous
624-647	Game controllers
648-655	Miscellaneous
656-703	Screen RAM (depends on graphics mode)
704-711	Colors
712-735	Spare
736-767	Miscellaneous
768-779	DCB
780-793	Miscellaneous
794-831	Handler address tables
832-847	I/O Channel 0 (IOCB0)
848-863	I/O Channel 1 (IOCB1)
864-879	I/O Channel 2 (IOCB2)
880-895	I/O Channel 3 (IOCB3)
896-911	I/O Channel 4 (IOCB4)
912-927	I/O Channel 5 (IOCB5)
928-943	I/O Channel 6 (IOCB6)
944-959	I/O Channel 7 (IOCB7)
960-999	Printer buffer
1000-1020	Spare
1021-1151	Cassette buffer

TABLE F-5. RAM Used by Operating System, Resident Cartridge, or Free RAM (Memory Locations 0-2047)

Location	Usage
0-127	Operating system zero page RAM
128-255	User zero page RAM
256-511	Stack
512-1151	Operating System RAM (see Table F-4)
1152-1791	User RAM
1792-2047	User Boot Area

TABLE F-6. BASIC* ROM (Memory Locations 40960-49151)

Location	Usage
40960-41036	Cold start
41037-41055	Warm start
41056-42081	Syntax
42082-42158	Search
42159-42508	Statement name table
42509-43134	Syntax tables
43135-43358	Memory manager
43359-43519	Execute CONT
43520-43631	Statement table
43632-43743	Operator table
43744-44094	Execute expression
44095-44163	Operator precedence
44164-45001	Execute operator
45002-45320	Execute function
45321-47127	Execute statement
47128-47381	CONT subroutines
47382-47542	Errors
47543-47732	Graphics
47733-48548	I/O routines
48549-49151	Floating point

* Applies to standard ATARI BASIC only.

TABLE F-7. RAM Used by BASIC* (Memory Locations 0-255F)

Location	Usage
0-127	Operating system zero page RAM
128-255	BASIC zero page RAM (see Table F-8)
256-511	Stack
512-1151	Operating system RAM
1152-1405	Syntax stack
1406-1535	Input line buffer
1536-1791	Free RAM
1792-End of free RAM	BASIC program:
	Syntax buffer or argument stack**
	Name table**
	Value table**
	Tokenized program**
	Array-strings area**
	Run-time stack**

* Applies to standard ATARI BASIC only.
** The actual memory locations depend on program and variable usage.

TABLE F-8. BASIC Zero Page RAM (Memory Locations 128-255)

Location	Usage
128-145	Program pointers
146-202	Misc. BASIC RAM
203-209	Unused
210-255	Floating point work area

TABLE F-9. RAM Used by DOS Version 1.0 and
File Management System (FMS)

Location	Usage
1792-4863	File management system RAM
4864-9855	Disk operating system (DOS) RAM
9856-10879	Disk I/O buffers

TABLE F-10. RAM Used by DOS Version 2.0S and
File Management System (FMS)

Location	Usage
1792-4863	File management system RAM
4864-9855	Disk operating system (DOS) RAM
9856-10879	Drive 1-4 buffers and sector buffers 1-2
10880-LOMEM	Disk operating system (DOS) Utility programs (Sector buffers 3-7)

G
USEFUL PEEK AND POKE LOCATIONS

Many memory locations are dedicated to certain specific uses. This appendix lists the locations that are of interest to BASIC programmers. Locations not listed are of little interest or are most easily accessed via standard BASIC statements. The PEEK function lets you read the contents of memory locations, and the POKE statement lets you change the contents.

In BASIC, all memory locations and their contents are expressed in terms of decimal numbers. Memory locations are addressed by number, from 0 to 65535. Each memory location contains a numeric value between 0 and 255. It takes two consecutive memory locations to store values greater than 255. In this case, the total value equals the value of the first location, plus 256 times the value of the second. For example, PEEK(85) + 256 * PEEK(86) is the current column position of the cursor. Conversely, the statements POKE 85, COL - INT(COL/256) * 256 and POKE 86, INT(COL/256) * 256 change the cursor column to the value of variable COL.

Some memory locations are known by name as well as numeric location. Such names are listed in parentheses after the memory location title.

Memory Configuration

14,15   Display Screen Lower Limit (APPMHI)

These locations contain the highest location available for program lines and variables. Memory above that is used for the screen display.

88,89   Screen Memory Address (SAVMSC)

These addresses contain the lowest address of the screen memory. The value at that address is displayed at the upper left-hand corner of the screen.

106   Top of RAM Address (Most Significant Byte) (RAMTOP)

This location contains a value 16 times the number of 4K RAM blocks present. PEEK (740)/4 gives the number of 1K blocks present.

741,742   Free Memory High Address (MEMTOP)

At any time, PEEK(741) + 256 * PEEK(742) - 1 is the highest memory location in the free memory area. The value changes when power is turned on, SYSTEM RESET occurs, or a channel is opened to the display.

743,744   Free Memory Low Address (MEMLO)

This location contains the address of the first location in the free memory region. The value changes when power is turned on or SYSTEM RESET occurs.

Display Screen

77   Attract Mode On/ Off (ATRACT)

Setting this location to 0 disables attract mode on the display screen. This happens automatically whenever a key on the keyboard is pressed. Setting this location to 254 enables attract mode. This happens automatically after nine minutes without a key being pressed.

82   Left Margin of Text Area (LMARGN)

Specifies the column of the graphics mode 0 left margin. PEEK (82) will be between 0 and 39, 0 being the left edge of the screen. The default is 2.

83   Right Margin of Text Area (RMARGN)

Specifies the column of the graphics mode 0 right margin. PEEK (83) will be between 0 and 39, 39 being the right edge of the screen. The default is 39.

84   Current Row Cursor Position (ROWCRS)

Specifies the row where the next read or write to the main screen will occur. PEEK (84) will be at least 0; its highest value depends on the graphics mode (see Table 11-7).

85,86   Current Column Cursor Position (COLCRS)

Specifies the column where the next read or write to the main screen will occur. PEEK (85) will be at least 0; its highest value depends on the graphics mode (see Table 11-7). Location 86 will always be 0 in graphics modes 0 through 7.

87   Display Mode (DINDEX)

This location contains the current screen mode.

90   Starting Graphics Cursor Row (OLDROW)

This location determines the starting row for the DRAWTO and XIO 18 (graphics FILL) statements.

93   Cursor Character Save/Restore (OLDCHR)
This location contains the character that is underneath the visible text cursor. The value is used to restore the hidden character when the cursor moves.

91,92   Starting Graphics Cursor Column (OLDCOL)
This location determines the starting column for the DRAWTO and XIO 18 (graphics FILL) statements.

94,95   Cursor Memory Address (OLDADR)
This location contains the memory address of the current visible text cursor. The value is used in conjunction with OLDCHR (location 93) to restore the original character hidden by the cursor when the cursor moves.

96   Ending Graphics Cursor Row (NEWROW)
This location determines the ending row for the DRAWTO and XIO 18 (graphics FILL) statements.

97,98   Ending Graphics Cursor Column (NEWCOL)
This location determines the ending column for the DRAWTO and XIO 18 (graphics FILL) statements.

201   Display Screen Tab Interval (PTABW)
Specifies the number of columns between each tab stop. The first tab will be at column number PEEK (201). The default is 10.

656   Text Cursor Row Position (TXTROW)
Specifies the row where the next read or write to the split-screen text window will occur. PEEK (656) will be between 0 and 3, 0 being the top of the split-screen text window.

657,658   Text Cursor Column Position (TXTCOL)
Specifies the column position where the next read or write to the split-screen text window will occur. PEEK (657) will be between 0 and 39, 0 being the first column of the split-screen text window. Location 658 is always 0 unless you change it.

675-680   Display Screen Tab Stop Map (TABMAP)
The tab stops are retained in a 15-byte (120-bit) map. Each bit corresponds to a column on a logical line. If the bit is on, a tab stop is set in that column (see Figure G-1). Whenever you open the display screen (device S: or E:), each byte of this map is assigned the value 1, thereby providing default tab stops at columns 7, 15, 23, and so on.

752   Cursor Inhibit (CRSINH)
When this location has a value of 0, the display screen cursor will be visible. When the value is nonzero, the cursor will be invisible. Cursor visibility does not change until the next time the cursor moves.

755   Character and Cursor Control (CHACT)
This location normally has a value of 2. Other values can make the cursor opaque or invisible and can make all characters display upside-down. Table G-1 lists the other values and characteristics.

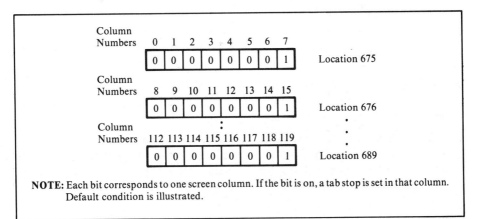

FIGURE G-1. Tab stop bit map

TABLE G-1. Cursor and Character Control (Values of PEEK(755))

Decimal Value	Cursor				Characters	
	Transparent	Opaque	Present	Absent	Normal	Inverted
0	X			X	X	
1		X		X	X	
2	X		X		X	
3		X	X		X	
4	X			X		X
5		X		X		X
6	X		X			X
7		X	X			X

756 Character Address Base (CHBAS)

This variable determines which character set will be used in screen modes 1 and 2. A value of 224 provides the capital letters and number set; a value of 226 provides the lower-case letters and graphics character set.

765 Fill Data (FILDAT)

This location contains the data value for the region to be filled by an XIO 18 command.

766 Display Control Characters (DSPFLG)

When this location is 0, the ATASCII codes 27-31, 123-127, 187-191, and 251-255 perform their normal display screen control functions (see Table 4-1). When this location is nonzero, these ATASCII codes generate characters on the display screen (see Table 4-1).

659 Split-Screen Text Window Screen Mode (TINDEX)

This location contains the current split-screen mode.

660,661   Split-Screen Memory Address (TXTMSC)

These locations contain the lowest address of the split-screen memory. The value of that address is displayed at the upper-left hand corner of the split-screen text window.

665-667   Split-Screen Cursor Data

These locations contain the split-screen equivalents of OLDCHR (location 93) and OLDADR (locations 94 and 95).

763   Last ATASCII Character or Plot Point (ATACHR)

This location contains the ATASCII code for the character most recently written or read, or the value of the graphics point last displayed. The value at this location is used to determine the line color when a DRAW or XIO 18 (FILL) is performed.

54273   Character Control Register (CHACTL)

Same as location 755 (CHACT).

Display Lists

512,513   Display List Interrupt Vector (VDSLST)

These locations store the address of the instructions that will be executed in the event of a display list interrupt.

559   DMA Control Register (SDMCTL)

This location enables or disables direct memory access. The default value is 22, which enables DMA for fetching display list instructions and for retrieving normal playfield display data. A value of 0 disables DMA. Table 9-3 lists values which relate to player-missile DMA.

560,561   Display List Address (SDLST)

This location stores the address of the active display list.

54286   Non-maskable Interrupt Enable (NMIEN)

This location enables or disables the display list interrupt and the vertical blank interrupt. A value of 0 disables the display list, 128 disables the vertical blank and enables the display list, and 192 enables both.

Player-Missile Graphics

623   Player/Playfield Priorities (GPRIOR)

This location determines what color will display when players overlap playfield objects. A value of 1 gives all players priority over the playfield. A value of 2 gives players 0 and 1 priority over all playfield registers, and priority over players 2 and 3 as well. A value of 4 gives the playfield priority over players. A value of 8 gives playfield color registers 0 and 1 priority over all players and priority over playfield registers 2 and 3.

704-707   Player-Missile Color Registers (COLPM0-COLPM3)

Each of these locations determines the color of a player and its associated missile. Table 9-4 lists the values which produce the available colors.

53248-53251   Player Horizontal Position Registers (HPOSP0-HPOSP3)

Each of these locations determines the horizontal position of one player. Values range between 0 (the left edge of the screen) and 277 (the right edge of the screen).

53256-53259   Player Width Registers (SIZEP0-SIZEP3)

Each location changes the magnification factor used to display one player. A value of 0 or 2 displays a player at normal width, 1 displays twice normal width, and 3 displays quadruple width.

53260   Missile Width Register (SIZEM)

This location controls the magnification of all four missiles. A value of 0 or 2 displays missiles at normal width, 1 displays twice normal width, and 3 displays quadruple width.

53277   Graphics Control Register (GRACTL)

Along with location 559 (DMACTL), this location controls DMA for player-missile graphics. A value of 2 enables player DMA only, a value of 1 enables missile DMA only, and a value of 3 enables both

54279,54280   Player-Missile Base Register (PMBASE)

These locations contain the starting address of the player-missile definition table.

Cassette Buffer

61   Cassette Buffer Pointer (BPTR)

This location contains a pointer to the next location to be used in the cassette buffer. The value may be anything from 0 to the value in BLIM (location 650). If BPTR = BLIM, then the buffer is full if writing or empty if reading.

63   Cassette End-of-File Flag (FEOF)

This location is used by the cassette handler to indicate whether an end-of-file has been detected. If the value of this location is 0, an end-of-file has not yet been detected; if the value is not 0, it has been detected.

64   Beep Count (FREQ)

This location contains the number of beeps requested by the cassette handler.

649   Cassette Read/Write Mode Flag (WMODE)

This location specifies whether the current cassette operation is read (value = 0) or write (value = 128).

650   Cassette Buffer Size (BLIM)

This location contains the number of active data bytes in the cassette buffer. BLIM will have a value from 0 to 128.

1021-1151   Cassette Buffer (CASBUF)

These locations are a buffer used by the cassette handler to read data from and write data to the program recorder.

Keyboard

17   BREAK Key Flag (BRKKEY)

A 0 in this location indicates that the BREAK key has been pressed.

694   Inverse Video Keystrokes (INVFLG)

When this location is 0, keystrokes generate ATASCII codes for normal video characters. If the value is nonzero, keystrokes generate ATASCII codes for inverse video characters.

702   Shift/Control Lock Flag (SHFLOK)

Meaningful values for this location are 0 (normal mode — no locks in effect), 64 (caps lock), and 128 (control lock).

764   Keyboard Character (CH)

This location reports the value of the most recently pressed key, or the value 255, which indicates no key has been pressed.

767   Start/Stop Display Screen (SSFLAG)

When this location is 0, screen output is not stopped. If the value is 255, output to the screen is stopped. The value is complemented by pressing CTRL-1.

53279   CONSOLE Switch Port (CONSOL)

This location has two uses. PEEK (53279) tells whether a special function key is pressed. To ensure an accurate reading, do a POKE 53279,8 before doing a PEEK(53279). Table G-2 lists the values that result from various combinations of special function keys.

POKE 53279,0 extends the cone of the built-in speaker. POKE 53279,8 retracts it. Alternate the two statements repeatedly to produce a series of clicks from the speaker. The operating system effectively does an automatic POKE 53279,8 every 1/60 second.

Sound Control

65   Input/Output Noise Control (SOUNDR)

This location is normally nonzero. In that case, noise is audible over the television audio circuit during disk or cassette read and write operations. If this location is 0, the noise is inhibited.

Printer

29   Printer Buffer Pointer (PBPNT)

This location specifies the current position in the computer's printer buffer. The value ranges from 0 to PBUFSZ (location 30).

TABLE G-2. Special Function Key Detection (Values of PEEK (53279))

Decimal Value	Function Key(s) Being Pressed
0	OPTION, SELECT, and START
1	OPTION and SELECT
2	OPTION and START
3	OPTION
4	SELECT and START
5	SELECT
6	START
7	None

30   Printer Buffer Size (PBUFSZ)

This location specifies the size of the computer's printer buffer. The value is 40 for normal mode or 29 for sideways mode.

960-999   Printer Buffer (PRNBUF)

The printer handler collects output from LPRINT statements to the printer in the computer's printer buffer, sending it out when an EOL occurs, or when the buffer is full.

Free Area

1536-1663   Conditionally Available

These locations are normally free for machine language programs, display lists, and so forth. However, whenever the INPUT statement retrieves more than 128 characters, it uses these locations to hold the characters in excess of 128.

1664-1791   Unconditionally Available

These locations are always free for machine language programs, display lists, and so forth.

BASIC Program Control

186,187   Stop Line Number (STOPLN)

These locations report the line number in which a BASIC program halts because of a STOP or TRAP statement, an error, or use of the BREAK key.

195   Error Number (ERRSAV)

If an error occurs, its number is placed in this location. Appendix A translates error numbers to messages.

212,213   USR Function Value (FR0)

A machine language program or subroutine can use these locations to send a numeric value to the BASIC program which called it.

251 Radians or Degrees (RADFLG or DEGFLG)

If the value of this location is 0, trigonometric functions calculate in terms of radians, if 6, in terms of degrees.

TABLE G-3. Interrupt Status/Enable Bits

Bit	Interrupt
0	Timer 1
1	Timer 2
2	Timer 4
3	Serial output (byte) transmission finished
4	Serial output data needed
5	Serial input data ready
6	Other key
7	BREAK key

564 and 565   Light Pen Position (LPENH and LPENV)

Location 564 reports the horizontal position of a light pen. Location 565 reports the vertical position. These are not the same as the actual screen row and column numbers. There are 228 horizontal positions (each is called *color clock*). The leftmost horizontal position is 67. Each time you move the light pen one position to the right, the value in location 564 increases by 1. After the value reaches 255, it resets to 0 and resumes counting by 1 from there. The rightmost horizontal position is 7. There are 96 vertical positions, numbered from 16 at the top of the screen to 111 at the bottom.

Interrupt Control

53744   IRQ Interrupt Status/Enable (IRQST/IRQEN)

This location reports interrupt status via PEEK, or enables interrupts via POKE. Each bit corresponds to a different interrupt (see Table G-3). With PEEK, a 0 bit means the corresponding interrupt is present and a 1 bit means it is not present. With POKE, a 0 bit disables the corresponding interrupt and a 1 bit enables it.

H
CONVERSION TABLES

This appendix contains the following conversion tables:

- Hexadecimal-Binary Numbers
- Hexadecimal-Decimal Integers

Use Table H-1 to convert between hexadecimal numbers in the range 0-0F and binary numbers in the range 0000-1111.

Convert larger binary numbers to hexadecimal numbers by converting four binary digits at a time, working from right to left. If there are fewer than four binary digits in the leftmost group, add leading zeros. Here is an example:

$$100101_2 = \underbrace{0010}_{2}\underbrace{0101}_{5}$$
$$25_{16}$$

Convert hexadecimal numbers larger than 0F to binary one digit at a time. Here is an example:

$$37_{16}$$
$$3 \qquad 7$$
$$\overline{0110} \quad \overline{0111}$$
$$01100111_2$$

TABLE H-1. Hexadecimal-Binary Conversion

Hexadecimal	Binary	Hexadecimal	Binary
00	0000	08	1000
01	0001	09	1001
02	0010	0A	1010
03	0011	0B	1011
04	0100	0C	1100
05	0101	0D	1101
06	0110	0E	1110
07	0111	0F	1111

TABLE H-2. Hexadecimal-Decimal Integer Conversion

The table below provides for direct conversions between hexa-decimal integers in the range 0–FFF and decimal integers in the range 0–4095. For conversion of larger integers, the table values may be added to the following figures:

Hexadecimal	Decimal	Hexadecimal	Decimal
01 000	4 096	20 000	131 072
02 000	8 192	30 000	196 608
03 000	12 288	40 000	262 144
04 000	16 384	50 000	327 680
05 000	20 480	60 000	393 216
06 000	24 576	70 000	458 752
07 000	28 672	80 000	524 288
08 000	32 768	90 000	589 824
09 000	36 864	A0 000	655 360
0A 000	40 960	B0 000	720 896
0B 000	45 056	C0 000	786 432
0C 000	49 152	D0 000	851 968
0D 000	53 248	E0 000	917 504
0E 000	57 344	F0 000	983 040
0F 000	61 440	100 000	1 048 576
10 000	65 536	200 000	2 097 152
11 000	69 632	300 000	3 145 728
12 000	73 728	400 000	4 194 304
13 000	77 824	500 000	5 242 880
14 000	81 920	600 000	6 291 456
15 000	86 016	700 000	7 340 032
16 000	90 112	800 000	8 388 608
17 000	94 208	900 000	9 437 184
18 000	98 304	A00 000	10 485 760
19 000	102 400	B00 000	11 534 336
1A 000	106 496	C00 000	12 582 912
1B 000	110 592	D00 000	13 631 488
1C 000	114 688	E00 000	14 680 064
1D 000	118 784	F00 000	15 728 640
1E 000	122 880	1 000 000	16 777 216
1F 000	126 976	2 000 000	33 554 432

Hexadecimal fractions may be converted to decimal fractions as follows:

1. Express the hexadecimal fraction as an integer times 16^{-n}, where n is the number of significant hexadecimal places to the right of the hexadecimal point.

$$0.\,CA9BF3_{16} = CA9\,BF3_{16} \times 16^{-6}$$

2. Find the decimal equivalent of the hexadecimal integer

$$CA9\,BF3_{16} = 13\,278\,195_{10}$$

3. Multiply the decimal equivalent by 16^{-n}

$$\begin{array}{r} 13\,278\,195 \\ \times\ 596\,046\,448 \times 10^{-16} \\ \hline 0.791\,442\,096_{10} \end{array}$$

Decimal fractions may be converted to hexadecimal fractions by successively multiplying the decimal fraction by 16_{10}. After each multiplication, the integer portion is removed to form a hexadecimal fraction by building to the right of the hexadecimal point. However, since decimal arithmetic is used in this conversion, the integer portion of each product must be converted to hexadecimal numbers.

Example: Convert 0.895_{10} to its hexadecimal equivalent

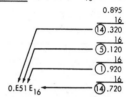

	0	1	2	3	4	5	6	7	8	9	A	B	C	D	E	F
00	0000	0001	0002	0003	0004	0005	0006	0007	0008	0009	0010	0011	0012	0013	0014	0015
01	0016	0017	0018	0019	0020	0021	0022	0023	0024	0025	0026	0027	0028	0029	0030	0031
02	0032	0033	0034	0035	0036	0037	0038	0039	0040	0041	0042	0043	0044	0045	0046	0047
03	0048	0049	0050	0051	0052	0053	0054	0055	0056	0057	0058	0059	0060	0061	0062	0063
04	0064	0065	0066	0067	0068	0069	0070	0071	0072	0073	0074	0075	0076	0077	0078	0079
05	0080	0081	0082	0083	0084	0085	0086	0087	0088	0089	0090	0091	0092	0093	0094	0095
06	0096	0097	0098	0099	0100	0101	0102	0103	0104	0105	0106	0107	0108	0109	0110	0111
07	0112	0113	0114	0115	0116	0117	0118	0119	0120	0121	0122	0123	0124	0125	0126	0127
08	0128	0129	0130	0131	0132	0133	0134	0135	0136	0137	0138	0139	0140	0141	0142	0143
09	0144	0145	0146	0147	0148	0149	0150	0151	0152	0153	0154	0155	0156	0157	0158	0159
0A	0160	0161	0162	0163	0164	0165	0166	0167	0168	0169	0170	0171	0172	0173	0174	0175
0B	0176	0177	0178	0179	0180	0181	0182	0183	0184	0185	0186	0187	0188	0189	0190	0191
0C	0192	0193	0194	0195	0196	0197	0198	0199	0200	0201	0202	0203	0204	0205	0206	0207
0D	0208	0209	0210	0211	0212	0213	0214	0215	0216	0217	0218	0219	0220	0221	0222	0223
0E	0224	0225	0226	0227	0228	0229	0230	0231	0232	0233	0234	0235	0236	0237	0238	0239
0F	0240	0241	0242	0243	0244	0245	0246	0247	0248	0249	0250	0251	0252	0253	0254	0255

TABLE H-2. Hexadecimal-Decimal Integer Conversion (continued)

	0	1	2	3	4	5	6	7	8	9	A	B	C	D	E	F
10	0256	0257	0258	0259	0260	0261	0262	0263	0264	0265	0266	0267	0268	0269	0270	0271
11	0272	0273	0274	0275	0276	0277	0278	0279	0280	0281	0282	0283	0284	0285	0286	0287
12	0288	0289	0290	0291	0292	0293	0294	0295	0296	0297	0298	0299	0300	0301	0302	0303
13	0304	0305	0306	0307	0308	0309	0310	0311	0312	0313	0314	0315	0316	0317	0318	0319
14	0320	0321	0322	0323	0324	0325	0326	0327	0328	0329	0330	0331	0332	0333	0334	0335
15	0336	0337	0338	0339	0340	0341	0342	0343	0344	0345	0346	0347	0348	0349	0350	0351
16	0352	0353	0354	0355	0356	0357	0358	0359	0360	0361	0362	0363	0364	0365	0366	0367
17	0368	0369	0370	0371	0372	0373	0374	0375	0376	0377	0378	0379	0380	0381	0382	0383
18	0384	0385	0386	0387	0388	0389	0390	0391	0392	0393	0394	0395	0396	0397	0398	0399
19	0400	0401	0402	0403	0404	0405	0406	0407	0408	0409	0410	0411	0412	0413	0414	0415
1A	0416	0417	0418	0419	0420	0421	0422	0423	0424	0425	0426	0427	0428	0429	0430	0431
1B	0432	0433	0434	0435	0436	0437	0438	0439	0440	0441	0442	0443	0444	0445	0446	0447
1C	0448	0449	0450	0451	0452	0453	0454	0455	0456	0457	0458	0459	0460	0461	0462	0463
1D	0464	0465	0466	0467	0468	0469	0470	0471	0472	0473	0474	0475	0476	0477	0478	0479
1E	0480	0481	0482	0483	0484	0485	0486	0487	0488	0489	0490	0491	0492	0493	0494	0495
1F	0496	0497	0498	0499	0500	0501	0502	0503	0504	0505	0506	0507	0508	0509	0510	0511
20	0512	0513	0514	0515	0516	0517	0518	0519	0520	0521	0522	0523	0524	0525	0526	0527
21	0528	0529	0530	0531	0532	0533	0534	0535	0536	0537	0538	0539	0540	0541	0542	0543
22	0544	0545	0546	0547	0548	0549	0550	0551	0552	0553	0554	0555	0556	0557	0558	0559
23	0560	0561	0562	0563	0564	0565	0566	0567	0568	0569	0570	0571	0572	0573	0574	0575
24	0576	0577	0578	0579	0580	0581	0582	0583	0584	0585	0586	0587	0588	0589	0590	0591
25	0592	0593	0594	0595	0596	0597	0598	0599	0600	0601	0602	0603	0604	0605	0606	0607
26	0608	0609	0610	0611	0612	0613	0614	0615	0616	0617	0618	0619	0620	0621	0622	0623
27	0624	0625	0626	0627	0628	0629	0630	0631	0632	0633	0634	0635	0636	0637	0638	0639
28	0640	0641	0642	0643	0644	0645	0646	0647	0648	0649	0650	0651	0652	0653	0654	0655
29	0656	0657	0658	0659	0660	0661	0662	0663	0664	0665	0666	0667	0668	0669	0670	0671
2A	0672	0673	0674	0675	0676	0677	0678	0679	0680	0681	0682	0683	0684	0685	0686	0687
2B	0688	0689	0690	0691	0692	0693	0694	0695	0696	0697	0698	0699	0700	0701	0702	0703
2C	0704	0705	0706	0707	0708	0709	0710	0711	0712	0713	0714	0715	0716	0717	0718	0719
2D	0720	0721	0722	0723	0724	0725	0726	0727	0728	0729	0730	0731	0732	0733	0734	0735
2E	0736	0737	0738	0739	0740	0741	0742	0743	0744	0745	0746	0747	0748	0749	0750	0751
2F	0752	0753	0754	0755	0756	0757	0758	0759	0760	0761	0762	0763	0764	0765	0766	0767
30	0768	0769	0770	0771	0772	0773	0774	0775	0776	0777	0778	0779	0780	0781	0782	0783
31	0784	0785	0786	0787	0788	0789	0790	0791	0792	0793	0794	0795	0796	0797	0798	0799
32	0800	0801	0802	0803	0804	0805	0806	0807	0808	0809	0810	0811	0812	0813	0814	0815
33	0816	0817	0818	0819	0820	0821	0822	0823	0824	0825	0826	0827	0828	0829	0830	0831
34	0832	0833	0834	0835	0836	0837	0838	0839	0840	0841	0842	0843	0844	0845	0846	0847
35	0848	0849	0850	0851	0852	0853	0854	0855	0856	0857	0858	0859	0860	0861	0862	0863
36	0864	0865	0866	0867	0868	0869	0870	0871	0872	0873	0874	0875	0876	0877	0878	0879
37	0880	0881	0882	0883	0884	0885	0886	0887	0888	0889	0890	0891	0892	0893	0894	0895
38	0896	0897	0898	0899	0900	0901	0902	0903	0904	0905	0906	0907	0908	0909	0910	0911
39	0912	0913	0914	0915	0916	0917	0918	0919	0920	0921	0922	0923	0924	0925	0926	0927
3A	0928	0929	0930	0931	0932	0933	0934	0935	0936	0937	0938	0939	0940	0941	0942	0943
3B	0944	0945	0946	0947	0948	0949	0950	0951	0952	0953	0954	0955	0956	0957	0958	0959
3C	0960	0961	0962	0963	0964	0965	0966	0967	0968	0969	0970	0971	0972	0973	0974	0975
3D	0976	0977	0978	0979	0980	0981	0982	0983	0984	0985	0986	0987	0988	0989	0990	0991
3E	0992	0993	0994	0995	0996	0997	0998	0999	1000	1001	1002	1003	1004	1005	1006	1007
3F	1008	1009	1010	1011	1012	1013	1014	1015	1016	1017	1018	1019	1020	1021	1022	1023

TABLE H-2. Hexadecimal-Decimal Integer Conversion (continued)

	0	1	2	3	4	5	6	7	8	9	A	B	C	D	E	F
40	1024	1025	1026	1027	1028	1029	1030	1031	1032	1033	1034	1035	1036	1037	1038	1039
41	1040	1041	1042	1043	1044	1045	1046	1047	1048	1049	1050	1051	1052	1053	1054	1055
42	1056	1057	1058	1059	1060	1061	1062	1063	1064	1065	1066	1067	1068	1069	1070	1071
43	1072	1073	1074	1075	1076	1077	1078	1079	1080	1081	1082	1083	1084	1085	1086	1087
44	1088	1089	1090	1091	1092	1093	1094	1095	1096	1097	1098	1099	1100	1101	1102	1103
45	1104	1105	1106	1107	1108	1109	1110	1111	1112	1113	1114	1115	1116	1117	1118	1119
46	1120	1121	1122	1123	1124	1125	1126	1127	1128	1129	1130	1131	1132	1133	1134	1135
47	1136	1137	1138	1139	1140	1141	1142	1143	1144	1145	1146	1147	1148	1149	1150	1151
48	1152	1153	1154	1155	1156	1157	1158	1159	1160	1161	1162	1163	1164	1165	1166	1167
49	1168	1169	1170	1171	1172	1173	1174	1175	1176	1177	1178	1179	1180	1181	1182	1183
4A	1184	1185	1186	1187	1188	1189	1190	1191	1192	1193	1194	1195	1196	1197	1198	1199
4B	1200	1201	1202	1203	1204	1205	1206	1207	1208	1209	1210	1211	1212	1213	1214	1215
4C	1216	1217	1218	1219	1220	1221	1222	1223	1224	1225	1226	1227	1228	1229	1230	1231
4D	1232	1233	1234	1235	1236	1237	1238	1239	1240	1241	1242	1243	1244	1245	1246	1247
4E	1248	1249	1250	1251	1252	1253	1254	1255	1256	1257	1258	1259	1260	1261	1262	1263
4F	1264	1265	1266	1267	1268	1269	1270	1271	1272	1273	1274	1275	1276	1277	1278	1279
50	1280	1281	1282	1283	1284	1285	1286	1287	1288	1289	1290	1291	1292	1293	1294	1295
51	1296	1297	1298	1299	1300	1301	1302	1303	1304	1305	1306	1307	1308	1309	1310	1311
52	1312	1313	1314	1315	1316	1317	1318	1319	1320	1321	1322	1323	1324	1325	1326	1327
53	1328	1329	1330	1331	1332	1333	1334	1335	1336	1337	1338	1339	1340	1341	1342	1343
54	1344	1345	1346	1347	1348	1349	1350	1351	1352	1353	1354	1355	1356	1357	1358	1359
55	1360	1361	1362	1363	1364	1365	1366	1367	1368	1369	1370	1371	1372	1373	1374	1375
56	1376	1377	1378	1379	1380	1381	1382	1383	1384	1385	1386	1387	1388	1389	1390	1391
57	1392	1393	1394	1395	1396	1397	1398	1399	1400	1401	1402	1403	1404	1405	1406	1407
58	1408	1409	1410	1411	1412	1413	1414	1415	1416	1417	1418	1419	1420	1421	1422	1423
59	1424	1425	1426	1427	1428	1429	1430	1431	1432	1433	1434	1435	1436	1437	1438	1439
5A	1440	1441	1442	1443	1444	1445	1446	1447	1448	1449	1450	1451	1452	1453	1454	1455
5B	1456	1457	1458	1459	1460	1461	1462	1463	1464	1465	1466	1467	1468	1469	1470	1471
5C	1472	1473	1474	1475	1476	1477	1478	1479	1480	1481	1482	1483	1484	1485	1486	1487
5D	1488	1489	1490	1491	1492	1493	1494	1495	1496	1497	1498	1499	1500	1501	1502	1503
5E	1504	1505	1506	1507	1508	1509	1510	1511	1512	1513	1514	1515	1516	1517	1518	1519
5F	1520	1521	1522	1523	1524	1525	1526	1527	1528	1529	1530	1531	1532	1533	1534	1535
60	1536	1537	1538	1539	1540	1541	1542	1543	1544	1545	1546	1547	1548	1549	1550	1551
61	1552	1553	1554	1555	1556	1557	1558	1559	1560	1561	1562	1563	1564	1565	1566	1567
62	1568	1569	1570	1571	1572	1573	1574	1575	1576	1577	1578	1579	1580	1581	1582	1583
63	1584	1585	1586	1587	1588	1589	1590	1591	1592	1593	1594	1595	1596	1597	1598	1599
64	1600	1601	1602	1603	1604	1605	1606	1607	1608	1609	1610	1611	1612	1613	1614	1615
65	1616	1617	1618	1619	1620	1621	1622	1623	1624	1625	1626	1627	1628	1629	1630	1631
66	1632	1633	1634	1635	1636	1637	1638	1639	1640	1641	1642	1643	1644	1645	1646	1647
67	1648	1649	1650	1651	1652	1653	1654	1655	1656	1657	1658	1659	1660	1661	1662	1663
68	1664	1665	1666	1667	1668	1669	1670	1671	1672	1673	1674	1675	1676	1677	1678	1679
69	1680	1681	1682	1683	1684	1685	1686	1687	1688	1689	1690	1691	1692	1693	1694	1695
6A	1696	1697	1698	1699	1700	1701	1702	1703	1704	1705	1706	1707	1708	1709	1710	1711
6B	1712	1713	1714	1715	1716	1717	1718	1719	1720	1721	1722	1723	1724	1725	1726	1727
6C	1728	1729	1730	1731	1732	1733	1734	1735	1736	1737	1738	1739	1740	1741	1742	1743
6D	1744	1745	1746	1747	1748	1749	1750	1751	1752	1753	1754	1755	1756	1757	1758	1759
6E	1760	1761	1762	1763	1764	1765	1766	1767	1768	1769	1770	1771	1772	1773	1774	1775
6F	1776	1777	1778	1779	1780	1781	1782	1783	1784	1785	1786	1787	1788	1789	1790	1791

TABLE H-2. Hexadecimal-Decimal Integer Conversion (continued)

	0	1	2	3	4	5	6	7	8	9	A	B	C	D	E	F
70	1792	1793	1794	1795	1796	1797	1798	1799	1800	1801	1802	1803	1804	1805	1806	1807
71	1808	1809	1810	1811	1812	1813	1814	1815	1816	1817	1818	1819	1820	1821	1822	1823
72	1824	1825	1826	1827	1828	1829	1830	1831	1832	1833	1834	1835	1836	1837	1838	1839
73	1840	1841	1842	1843	1844	1845	1846	1847	1848	1849	1850	1851	1852	1853	1854	1855
74	1856	1857	1858	1859	1860	1861	1862	1863	1864	1865	1866	1867	1868	1869	1870	1871
75	1872	1873	1874	1875	1876	1877	1878	1879	1880	1881	1882	1883	1884	1885	1886	1887
76	1888	1889	1890	1891	1892	1893	1894	1895	1896	1897	1898	1899	1900	1901	1902	1903
77	1904	1905	1906	1907	1908	1909	1910	1911	1912	1913	1914	1915	1916	1917	1918	1919
78	1920	1921	1922	1923	1924	1925	1926	1927	1928	1929	1930	1931	1932	1933	1934	1935
79	1936	1937	1938	1939	1940	1941	1942	1943	1944	1945	1946	1947	1948	1949	1950	1951
7A	1952	1953	1954	1955	1956	1957	1958	1959	1960	1961	1962	1963	1964	1965	1966	1967
7B	1968	1969	1970	1971	1972	1973	1974	1975	1976	1977	1978	1979	1980	1981	1982	1983
7C	1984	1985	1986	1987	1988	1989	1990	1991	1992	1993	1994	1995	1996	1997	1998	1999
7D	2000	2001	2002	2003	2004	2005	2006	2007	2008	2009	2010	2011	2012	2013	2014	2015
7E	2016	2017	2018	2019	2020	2021	2022	2023	2024	2025	2026	2027	2028	2029	2030	2031
7F	2032	2033	2034	2035	2036	2037	2038	2039	2040	2041	2042	2043	2044	2045	2046	2047
80	2048	2049	2050	2051	2052	2053	2054	2055	2056	2057	2058	2059	2060	2061	2062	2063
81	2064	2065	2066	2067	2068	2069	2070	2071	2072	2073	2074	2075	2076	2077	2078	2079
82	2080	2081	2082	2083	2084	2085	2086	2087	2088	2089	2090	2091	2092	2093	2094	2095
83	2096	2097	2098	2099	2100	2101	2102	2103	2104	2105	2106	2107	2108	2109	2110	2111
84	2112	2113	2114	2115	2116	2117	2118	2119	2120	2121	2122	2123	2124	2125	2126	2127
85	2128	2129	2130	2131	2132	2133	2134	2135	2136	2137	2138	2139	2140	2141	2142	2143
86	2144	2145	2146	2147	2148	2149	2150	2151	2152	2153	2154	2155	2156	2157	2158	2159
87	2160	2161	2162	2163	2164	2165	2166	2167	2168	2169	2170	2171	2172	2173	2174	2175
88	2176	2177	2178	2179	2180	2181	2182	2183	2184	2185	2186	2187	2188	2189	2190	2191
89	2192	2193	2194	2195	2196	2197	2198	2199	2200	2201	2202	2203	2204	2205	2206	2207
8A	2208	2209	2210	2211	2212	2213	2214	2215	2216	2217	2218	2219	2220	2221	2222	2223
8B	2224	2225	2226	2227	2228	2229	2230	2231	2232	2233	2234	2235	2236	2237	2238	2239
8C	2240	2241	2242	2243	2244	2245	2246	2247	2248	2249	2250	2251	2252	2253	2254	2255
8D	2256	2257	2258	2259	2260	2261	2262	2263	2264	2265	2266	2267	2268	2269	2270	2271
8E	2272	2273	2274	2275	2276	2277	2278	2279	2280	2281	2282	2283	2284	2285	2286	2287
8F	2288	2289	2290	2291	2292	2293	2294	2295	2296	2297	2298	2299	2300	2301	2302	2303
90	2304	2305	2306	2307	2308	2309	2310	2311	2312	2313	2314	2315	2316	2317	2318	2319
91	2320	2321	2322	2323	2324	2325	2326	2327	2328	2329	2330	2331	2332	2333	2334	2335
92	2336	2337	2338	2339	2340	2341	2342	2343	2344	2345	2346	2347	2348	2349	2350	2351
93	2352	2353	2354	2355	2356	2357	2358	2359	2360	2361	2362	2363	2364	2365	2366	2367
94	2368	2369	2370	2371	2372	2373	2374	2375	2376	2377	2378	2379	2380	2381	2382	2383
95	2384	2385	2386	2387	2388	2389	2390	2391	2392	2393	2394	2395	2396	2397	2398	2399
96	2400	2401	2402	2403	2404	2405	2406	2407	2408	2409	2410	2411	2412	2413	2414	2415
97	2416	2417	2418	2419	2420	2421	2422	2423	2424	2425	2426	2427	2428	2429	2430	2431
98	2432	2433	2434	2435	2436	2437	2438	2439	2440	2441	2442	2443	2444	2445	2446	2447
99	2448	2449	2450	2451	2452	2453	2454	2455	2456	2457	2458	2459	2460	2461	2462	2463
9A	2464	2465	2466	2467	2468	2469	2470	2471	2472	2473	2474	2475	2476	2477	2478	2479
9B	2480	2481	2482	2483	2484	2485	2486	2487	2488	2489	2490	2491	2492	2493	2494	2495
9C	2496	2497	2498	2499	2500	2501	2502	2503	2504	2505	2506	2507	2508	2509	2510	2511
9D	2512	2513	2514	2515	2516	2517	2518	2519	2520	2521	2522	2523	2524	2525	2526	2527
9E	2528	2529	2530	2531	2532	2533	2534	2535	2536	2537	2538	2539	2540	2541	2542	2543
9F	2544	2545	2546	2547	2548	2549	2550	2551	2552	2553	2554	2555	2556	2557	2558	2559

TABLE H-2. Hexadecimal-Decimal Integer Conversion (continued)

	0	1	2	3	4	5	6	7	8	9	A	B	C	D	E	F
A0	2560	2561	2562	2563	2564	2565	2566	2567	2568	2569	2570	2571	2572	2573	2574	2575
A1	2576	2577	2578	2579	2580	2581	2582	2583	2584	2585	2586	2587	2588	2589	2590	2591
A2	2592	2593	2594	2595	2596	2597	2598	2599	2600	2601	2602	2603	2604	2605	2606	2607
A3	2608	2609	2610	2611	2612	2613	2614	2615	2616	2617	2618	2619	2620	2621	2622	2623
A4	2624	2625	2626	2627	2628	2629	2630	2631	2632	2633	2634	2635	2636	2637	2638	2639
A5	2640	2641	2642	2643	2644	2645	2646	2647	2648	2649	2650	2651	2652	2653	2654	2655
A6	2656	2657	2658	2659	2660	2661	2662	2663	2664	2665	2666	2667	2668	2669	2670	2671
A7	2672	2673	2674	2675	2676	2677	2678	2679	2680	2681	2682	2683	2684	2685	2686	2687
A8	2688	2689	2690	2691	2692	2693	2694	2695	2696	2697	2698	2699	2700	2701	2702	2703
A9	2704	2705	2706	2707	2708	2709	2710	2711	2712	2713	2714	2715	2716	2717	2718	2719
AA	2720	2721	2722	2723	2724	2725	2726	2727	2728	2729	2730	2731	2732	2733	2734	2735
AB	2736	2737	2738	2739	2740	2741	2742	2743	2744	2745	2746	2747	2748	2749	2750	2751
AC	2752	2753	2754	2755	2756	2757	2758	2759	2760	2761	2762	2763	2764	2765	2766	2767
AD	2768	2769	2770	2771	2772	2773	2774	2775	2776	2777	2778	2779	2780	2781	2782	2783
AE	2784	2785	2786	2787	2788	2789	2790	2791	2792	2793	2794	2795	2796	2797	2798	2799
AF	2800	2801	2802	2803	2804	2805	2806	2807	2808	2809	2810	2811	2812	2813	2814	2815
B0	2816	2817	2818	2819	2820	2821	2822	2823	2824	2825	2826	2827	2828	2829	2830	2831
B1	2832	2833	2834	2835	2836	2837	2838	2839	2840	2841	2842	2843	2844	2845	2846	2847
B2	2848	2849	2850	2851	2852	2853	2854	2855	2856	2857	2858	2859	2860	2861	2862	2863
B3	2864	2865	2866	2867	2868	2869	2870	2871	2872	2873	2874	2875	2876	2877	2878	2879
B4	2880	2881	2882	2883	2884	2885	2886	2887	2888	2889	2890	2891	2892	2893	2894	2895
B5	2896	2897	2898	2899	2900	2901	2902	2903	2904	2905	2906	2907	2908	2909	2910	2911
B6	2912	2913	2914	2915	2916	2917	2918	2919	2920	2921	2922	2923	2924	2925	2926	2927
B7	2928	2929	2930	2931	2932	2933	2934	2935	2936	2937	2938	2939	2940	2941	2942	2943
B8	2944	2945	2946	2947	2948	2949	2950	2951	2952	2953	2954	2955	2956	2957	2958	2959
B9	2960	2961	2962	2963	2964	2965	2966	2967	2968	2969	2970	2971	2972	2973	2974	2975
BA	2976	2977	2978	2979	2980	2981	2982	2983	2984	2985	2986	2987	2988	2989	2990	2991
BB	2992	2993	2994	2995	2996	2997	2998	2999	3000	3001	3002	3003	3004	3005	3006	3007
BC	3008	3009	3010	3011	3012	3013	3014	3015	3016	3017	3018	3019	3020	3021	3022	3023
BD	3024	3025	3026	3027	3028	3029	3030	3031	3032	3033	3034	3035	3036	3037	3038	3039
BE	3040	3041	3042	3043	3044	3045	3046	3047	3048	3049	3050	3051	3052	3053	3054	3055
BF	3056	3057	3058	3059	3060	3061	3062	3063	3064	3065	3066	3067	3068	3069	3070	3071
C0	3072	3073	3074	3075	3076	3077	3078	3079	3080	3081	3082	3083	3084	3085	3086	3087
C1	3088	3089	3090	3091	3092	3093	3094	3095	3096	3097	3098	3099	3100	3101	3102	3103
C2	3104	3105	3106	3107	3108	3109	3110	3111	3112	3113	3114	3115	3116	3117	3118	3119
C3	3120	3121	3122	3123	3124	3125	3126	3127	3128	3129	3130	3131	3132	3133	3134	3135
C4	3136	3137	3138	3139	3140	3141	3142	3143	3144	3145	3146	3147	3148	3149	3150	3151
C5	3152	3153	3154	3155	3156	3157	3158	3159	3160	3161	3162	3163	3164	3165	3166	3167
C6	3168	3169	3170	3171	3172	3173	3174	3175	3176	3177	3178	3179	3180	3181	3182	3183
C7	3184	3185	3186	3187	3188	3189	3190	3191	3192	3193	3194	3195	3196	3197	3198	3199
C8	3200	3201	3202	3203	3204	3205	3206	3207	3208	3209	3210	3211	3212	3213	3214	3215
C9	3216	3217	3218	3219	3220	3221	3222	3223	3224	3225	3226	3227	3228	3229	3230	2231
CA	3232	3233	3234	3235	3236	3237	3238	3239	3240	3241	3242	3243	3244	3245	3246	3247
CB	3248	3249	3250	3251	3252	3253	3254	3255	3256	3257	3258	3259	3260	3261	3262	3263
CC	3264	3265	3266	3267	3268	3269	3270	3271	3272	3273	3274	3275	3276	3277	3278	3279
CD	3280	3281	3282	3283	3284	3285	3286	3287	3288	3289	3290	3291	3292	3293	3294	3295
CE	3296	3297	3298	3299	3300	3301	3302	3303	3304	3305	3306	3307	3308	3309	3310	3311
CF	3312	3313	3314	3315	3316	3317	3318	3319	3320	3321	3322	3323	3324	3325	3326	3327

TABLE H-2. Hexadecimal-Decimal Integer Conversion (continued)

	0	1	2	3	4	5	6	7	8	9	A	B	C	D	E	F
D0	3328	3329	3330	3331	3332	3333	3334	3335	3336	3337	3338	3339	3340	3341	3342	3343
D1	3344	3345	3346	3347	3348	3349	3350	3351	3352	3353	3354	3355	3356	3357	3358	3359
D2	3360	3361	3362	3363	3364	3365	3366	3367	3368	3369	3370	3371	3372	3373	3374	3375
D3	3376	3377	3378	3379	3380	3381	3382	3383	3384	3385	3386	3387	3388	3389	3390	3391
D4	3392	3393	3394	3395	3396	3397	3398	3399	3400	3401	3402	3403	3404	3405	3406	3407
D5	3408	3409	3410	3411	3412	3413	3414	3415	3416	3417	3418	3419	3420	3421	3422	3423
D6	3424	3425	3426	3427	3428	3429	3430	3431	3432	3433	3434	3435	3436	3437	3438	3439
D7	3440	3441	3442	3443	3444	3445	3446	3447	3448	3449	3450	3451	3452	3453	3454	3455
D8	3456	3457	3458	3459	3460	3461	3462	3463	3464	3465	3466	3467	3468	3469	3470	3471
D9	3472	3473	3474	3475	3476	3477	3478	3479	3480	3481	3482	3483	3484	3485	3486	3487
DA	3488	3489	3490	3491	3492	3493	3494	3495	3496	3497	3498	3499	3500	3501	3502	3503
DB	3504	3505	3506	3507	3508	3509	3510	3511	3512	3513	3514	3515	3516	3517	3518	3519
DC	3520	3521	3522	3523	3524	3525	3526	3527	3528	3529	3530	3531	3532	3533	3534	3535
DD	3536	3537	3538	3539	3540	3541	3542	3543	3544	3545	3546	3547	3548	3549	3550	3551
DE	3552	3553	3554	3555	3556	3557	3558	3559	3560	3561	3562	3563	3564	3565	3566	3567
DF	3568	3569	3570	3571	3572	3573	3574	3575	3576	3577	3578	3579	3580	3581	3582	3583
E0	3584	3585	3586	3587	3588	3589	3590	3591	3592	3593	3594	3595	3596	3597	3598	3599
E1	3600	3601	3602	3603	3604	3605	3606	3607	3608	3609	3610	3611	3612	3613	3614	3615
E2	3616	3617	3618	3619	3620	3621	3622	3623	3624	3625	3626	3627	3628	3629	3630	3631
E3	3632	3633	3634	3635	3636	3637	3638	3639	3640	3641	3642	3643	3644	3645	3646	3647
E4	3648	3649	3650	3651	3652	3653	3654	3655	3656	3657	3658	3659	3660	3661	3662	3663
E5	3664	3665	3666	3667	3668	3669	3670	3671	3672	3673	3674	3675	3676	3677	3678	3679
E6	3680	3681	3682	3683	3684	3685	3686	3687	3688	3689	3690	3691	3692	3693	3694	3695
E7	3696	3697	3698	3699	3700	3701	3702	3703	3704	3705	3706	3707	3708	3709	3710	3711
E8	3712	3713	3714	3715	3716	3717	3718	3719	3720	3721	3722	3723	3724	3725	3726	3727
E9	3728	3729	3730	3731	3732	3733	3734	3735	3736	3737	3738	3739	3740	3741	3742	3743
EA	3744	3745	3746	3747	3748	3749	3750	3751	3752	3753	3754	3755	3756	3757	3758	3759
EB	3760	3761	3762	3763	3764	3765	3766	3767	3768	3769	3770	3771	3772	3773	3774	3775
EC	3776	3777	3778	3779	3780	3781	3782	3783	3784	3785	3786	3787	3788	3789	3790	3791
ED	3792	3793	3794	3795	3796	3797	3798	3799	3800	3801	3802	3803	3804	3805	3806	3807
EE	3808	3809	3810	3811	3812	3813	3814	3815	3816	3817	3818	3819	3820	3821	3822	3823
EF	3824	3825	3826	3827	3828	3829	3830	3831	3832	3833	3834	3835	3836	3837	3838	3839
F0	3840	3841	3842	3843	3844	3845	3846	3847	3848	3849	3850	3851	3852	3853	3854	3855
F1	3856	3857	3858	3859	3860	3861	3862	3863	3864	3865	3866	3867	3868	3869	3870	3871
F2	3872	3873	3874	3875	3876	3877	3878	3879	3880	3881	3882	3883	3884	3885	3886	3887
F3	3888	3889	3890	3891	3892	3893	3894	3895	3896	3897	3898	3899	3900	3901	3902	3903
F4	3904	3905	3906	3907	3908	3909	3910	3911	3912	3913	3914	3915	3916	3917	3918	3919
F5	3920	3921	3922	3923	3924	3925	3926	3927	3928	3929	3930	3931	3932	3933	3934	3935
F6	3936	3937	3938	3939	3940	3941	3942	3943	3944	3945	3946	3947	3948	3949	3950	3951
F7	3952	3953	3954	3955	3956	3957	3958	3959	3960	3961	3962	3963	3964	3965	3966	3967
F8	3968	3969	3970	3971	3972	3973	3974	3975	3976	3977	3978	3979	3980	3981	3982	3983
F9	3984	3985	3986	3987	3988	3989	3990	3991	3992	3993	3994	3995	3996	3997	3998	3999
FA	4000	4001	4002	4003	4004	4005	4006	4007	4008	4009	4010	4011	4012	4013	4014	4015
FB	4016	4017	4018	4019	4020	4021	4022	4023	4024	4025	4026	4027	4028	4029	4030	4031
FC	4032	4033	4034	4035	4036	4037	4038	4039	4040	4041	4042	4043	4044	4045	4046	4047
FD	4048	4049	4050	4051	4052	4053	4054	4055	4056	4057	4058	4059	4060	4061	4062	4063
FE	4064	4065	4066	4067	4068	4069	4070	4071	4072	4073	4074	4075	4076	4077	4078	4079
FF	4080	4081	4082	4083	4084	4085	4086	4087	4088	4089	4090	4091	4092	4093	4094	4095

I
BIBLIOGRAPHY

BASIC

Albrecht, Finkel, and LeBaron. *What to Do After You Hit Return.* Rochelle Park, N.J.: Hayden Book Company.

Coan, James S. *Advanced BASIC.* Rochelle Park, N.J.: Hayden Book Company.

Coan, James S. *Basic BASIC.* Rochelle Park, N.J.: Hayden Book Company.

Dwyer, T., and Critchfield, Margot. *BASIC and the Personal Computer.* Reading, Mass.: Addison-Wesley, 1980.

Neirson, John M. *The Little Book of BASIC Style.* Reading, Mass.: Addison-Wesley, 1978.

Assembly Language Programming

DeJong, Marvin. *Programming and Interfacing the 6502, With Experiments.* Indianapolis: Howard W. Sams, 1980.

Foster, Caxton C. *Programming a Microcomputer: 6502.* Reading, Mass.: Addison-Wesley, 1978.

Leventhal, Lance A. *6502 Assembly Language Programming.* Berkeley: Osborne/McGraw-Hill, 1979.

Osborne, Adam. *An Introduction to Microcomputers: Volume 1 — Basic Concepts.* 2nd ed. Berkeley: Osborne/McGraw-Hill, 1980.

Scanlon, Leo J. *6502 Software Design.* Indianapolis: Howard W. Sams.

Zaks, Rodnay. *6502 Applications Book.* Berkeley: Sybex, 1979.

Periodicals

Atari Connection. 1265 Borregas Avenue, P.O. Box 427, Sunnyvale, California 94086.

BYTE. 70 Main Street, Peterborough, New Hampshire 03458.

Compute! P.O. Box 5406, Greensboro, North Carolina 27403.

Creative Computing. 39 East Hamover Avenue, Morris Plains, New Jersey 07950.

Desktop Computing. 80 Pine Street, Peterborough, New Hampshire 03458.

Micro. P.O. Box 6502, Chelmsford, Massachusetts 01824.

Microcomputing. 80 Pine Street, Peterborough, New Hampshire 03458.

Personal Computing. P.O. Box 13916, Philadelphia, Pennsylvania 19101.

Popular Computing. 70 Main Street, Peterborough, New Hampshire 03458.

Purser's Magazine. P.O. Box 466, El Dorado, California 95623.

Recreational Computing. 1263 El Camino Real, Menlo Park, California 94025.

Atari Publications

The following publications are available from Atari, Inc., 1265 Borregas Avenue, P.O. Box 427, Sunnyvale, California 94086.

Albrecht, Bob; Brown, Jerald R.; Finkel, LeRoy. *Atari BASIC.* New York, Chichester, Brisbane, Toronto: John Wiley & Sons, Inc., 1979.

ATARI 810 Disk Drive Operator's Manual.

ATARI 400/800 Disk Utility.

ATARI 400/800 Operating Systems.

ATARI 825 80-Column Printer Operator's Manual.

ATARI 850 Interface Module Operator's Manual.

ATARI Personal Computer System Operating Systems User's Manual and Hardware Manual.

ATARI 400/800 Basic Reference Manual.

ATARI 400/800 Disk Operating Systems Reference Manual.

INDEX